Child Sexual Abuse: Disclosure, Delay, and Denial

Editei

Margaret-Ellen Pipe
National Institute of Child Health and Human Development

Michael E. Lamb
University of Cambridge, United Kingdom

Yael Orbach
National Institute of Child Health and Human Development

Ann-Christin Cederborg
Linkoping University, Sweden

LEA LAWRENCE ERLBAUM ASSOCIATES, PUBLISHERS
2007 Mahwah, New Jersey   London

Senior Acquisitions Editor: Lori Handelman
Editorial Assistant: Anthony Messina
Cover Design: Tomai Maridou
Full-Service Compositor: MidAtlantic Books & Journals, Inc.

This book was typeset in 10.5/12 pt. Goudy Old Style, Italic, Bold, and Bold Italic with Americana.

Lawrence Erlbaum Associates, Inc., Publishers
10 Industrial Avenue
Mahwah, New Jersey 07430
www.erlbaum.com

CIP information for this volume can be obtained by contacting the Library of Congress.

ISBN 978-0-8058-5284-4 — 0-8058-5284-0 (case)
ISBN 978-0-8058-6317-8 — 0-8058-6317-6 (paper)
ISBN 978-1-4106-1589-3 — 1-4106-1589-8 (ebook)

Books published by Lawrence Erlbaum Associates are printed on acid-free paper, and their bindings are chosen for strength and durability.

Printed in the United States of America
10 9 8 7 6 5 4 3 2 1

*Dedicated to the memory of Kathleen Sternberg
who was involved in much of the
research reported in this volume.*

Contents

Foreword

A 5-year-old girl with a sexually transmitted disease was asked in a forensic interview if anyone had hurt or touched her in a bad way. The girl denied that anything had happened.

Based on the belief that young children do not readily disclose and that leading questions are often needed to elicit true disclosures, investigators in the McMartin and Kelley Michaels cases in the United States were not satisfied when the preschoolers denied that they had been sexually violated. Instead of stopping there, the investigators asked one leading question after another until finally the children disclosed child sexual abuse by their teachers.

The 13-year-old incest victim who testified at trial against her father had finally disclosed the sexual abuse following years of silence. Once her father was convicted, he killed himself, but only after sending her a letter blaming her for his crime and suicide.

These cases, taken from our research and consultations, exemplify why understanding disclosure of child sexual abuse is crucial for protecting child victims and for protecting innocent adults. However, as these examples also highlight, disclosure is an emotionally laden, multifaceted topic. For that reason and others, studying disclosure from an objective scientific stance is no easy task. As a result, until recently, there has been a paucity of directly relevant, high-quality research. Quite fortunately, a new wave of scientific studies has emerged to transform our understanding of disclosure.

The present book captures that wave in the first edited volume devoted solely to children's disclosure of child sexual abuse. As such, the book brings together state-of-the art information on what is known, both from scientific and practitioner perspectives, about child sexual abuse disclosure. The authors skillfully integrate research with legal, clinical, and/or policy concerns. To the editors' great credit, the book provides a well-rounded coverage of what can be a highly controversial subject.

Disclosing sexual abuse and evaluating such disclosures are topics fraught with complexity, so much so that controversy is not surprising. Although most professionals agree that many children on their own do not readily disclose sexual violation, agreement quickly ends there. Researchers still hotly debate whether children promptly disclose if simply asked. For example, they debate whether children easily disclose to such open-ended questions as "Has anyone ever done something to you that you didn't like?" And they debate the likelihood that children once they disclose will later take back their accusations, that is, recant. Finally, researchers question if recantation means the allegation was likely false to begin with, or instead is evidence for what Roland Summit called the Child Abuse Accommodation Syndrome.

How to obtain accurate and complete statements from children while limiting false reports is central to controversies surrounding disclosure. Resolving the controversies will require appreciation of developmental, social, cognitive, and emotional influences on children. These influences determine, on the one hand, children's willingness and ability to recount sexual acts they have experienced. On the other hand, the same influences can affect children's ability to resist false suggestions, specifically, that they experienced sexual acts when they have not.

We already know that children's limitations make them susceptible to adult influence. Well researched is the fact that such susceptibility results in some children, under certain circumstances, being vulnerable to false reports. However, the flip side is worthy of equal, if not greater, attention—that some children can be all too easily influenced not to disclose, including when directly asked. Even in laboratory studies involving relatively innocuous acts, parents and other adults can easily silence children such that interviewers' leading questions do not result in disclosure. How much more powerful must adults' commands for secrecy be about such taboo and potentially shameful acts as sexual abuse.

To fully understand the complexity of disclosure, it is necessary to consider the potential consequences to children once they have disclosed. It is beyond debate that these consequences can be dramatic. Some parents, although perhaps revolted by what they just learned, are strongly supportive of their children. But others call their children liars, beat them, blame them, or discount their claims. Some children will be removed from home; others, like the 13-year-old incest victim mentioned earlier, will end up in court.

It is not surprising then that children are often fearful that they or a loved one will suffer if they disclose. The same 13-year-old incest victim didn't disclose for years because of fears that she would lose parental love and care, that her father would go to jail, and that she would be removed from home. Perhaps the 5-year-old girl who never disclosed how she obtained a sexually transmitted disease was protecting a loved one. Our own research revealed that children delay disclosure in part out of concern for others, even more so at times than out of concern for themselves. Such fears affect the ways in which children disclose, or if they ever disclose at all.

What if the disclosures are false? The consequences are no less serious, of course for the falsely accused, but also for children themselves. Children may come to believe they were abuse victims when in fact they were not, or they may have to live with the guilt of sending an innocent person to jail. As much as parents and authorities typically want to protect children from sexual abuse, they also rightly fear the consequences of false reports. Therefore, when suspicions of child sexual abuse arise, adults may hesitate to ask, or they may ask too indirectly; they may communicate to children that such topics are taboo or such claims are not to be believed. Concerns over false reports affect how children are questioned—or are not questioned—about sexual abuse, which in turn affects the likelihood and process of disclosure.

Clearly, the stakes here are high. The stakes add urgency to obtaining an objective, scientific understanding of disclosure. Fortunately, the current book represents a breakthrough in the attempt to shine empirical light on this crucial topic. The editors are world renowned for their research and writings on child forensic interviews. They have assembled a group of international experts on disclosure. That there is still much debate about how best to recognize reluctance and help children disclose, how often leading questions result in false disclosures, and how often children recant, adds an electrifying dynamic to this book. Readers will learn about the latest research advances as well as how to tackle relevant legal, policy, and professional dilemmas. Anyone who cares about child protection or worries about false reports will find this volume invaluable. Thanks to the editors' and authors' creativity and dedication, this book helps us learn how and when to listen to children.

Gail S. Goodman, PhD
Distinguished Professor of Psychology
University of California, Davis

Tina Goodman Brown, PhD
Private Practice

I
INTRODUCTION

1

Seeking Resolution in the Disclosure Wars: An Overview

Margaret-Ellen Pipe
Brooklyn College, CUNY

Yael Orbach
National Institute of Child Health and Human Development

Michael E. Lamb
University of Cambridge, UK

Ann-Christin Cederborg
Linkoping University, Sweden

Every year, investigative and protective service agencies in all the developed countries receive millions of reports that children may have been maltreated (more than 4 million per year in the United States alone). Many more children who are abused never come to the attention of professional services, government agencies, or the criminal justice system. Indeed, in some cases even caregivers remain ignorant of their child's abuse. But just how much of a problem is unreported sexual abuse? How many children remain silent about their abuse, deny it if interviewed, or, if they do disclose, do so belatedly, incompletely, perhaps even recanting their allegations over time?

Answers to these questions have far-reaching implications, both for the legal system and for professionals working with children, particularly in the areas of child protection and forensic interviewing. If children's nondisclosures are taken at face value to indicate that abuse has not occurred, the triggering suspicions should not be further investigated. If a significant number of nondisclosing children have been abused, however, taking the nondisclosures at face value would place these children at risk of further abuse, and other children may also be placed at risk of being abused by the same perpetrators. Furthermore, with respect to the legal system, what should researchers tell the courts about the ways in which children disclose abuse? If a child delays reporting, even denies the abuse when initially interviewed, but later makes an allegation, should the delay or denial cast doubt on the reliability of the allegation? Do some children need to be interviewed about suspected abuse on more than one, perhaps even multiple, occasions, if they are to disclose at all? Despite their importance, answers to these questions have become increasingly controversial over the past decade.

In a paper that has become something of a lightening rod in the debate about abuse disclosure, Summit (1983) attempted more than two decades ago to explain why children might not always report abuse readily. He argued that some children, particularly those abused by a caregiver on whom they were dependent, may keep the abuse secret, make partial and incomplete disclosures, or retract and recant their disclosures. Although Summit initially used the term "Child Sexual Abuse Accommodation Syndrome" (CSAAS) to account for delayed, incomplete, and inconsistent disclosures, he later acknowledged that the 'syndrome' label was inappropriate (Summit, 1992). Summit's account was based on clinical experience and resonated with the experiences of many professionals working with suspected abuse victims. However, although researchers have provided some evidence consistent with it, others have argued that the accuracy and generality of Summit's claims are simply not known because a scientifically rigorous analysis remains to be undertaken (London, Bruck, Ceci, & Schuman, 2005). Thus, while the notion of a syndrome has generally been discarded, the important question remains: Do the patterns of nondisclosure proposed by Summit accurately describe *how* children disclose abuse?

This question is at the heart of "the disclosure wars" that have, to a large extent, replaced the "memory wars" of the previous decade. On the one hand, some professionals in the field argue that the delays, denials, and recantations of disclosures are at the very least not rare or uncommon. Others, in contrast, take an opposing position. Bruck and Ceci (2005), for example, described the belief that children do not disclose their abuse as one of the "major misconceptions" widely held about the disclosure of childhood sexual abuse. These very different views of just how common it is that children do not disclose abuse have been supported by reports in the literature of very discrepant rates of nondisclosure. Reviews by London et al. (2005, and chapter 2) indicate that, across studies, reported rates of nondisclosure have ranged from 4% to 75%. That almost all children interviewed disclose abuse (96% in the study by Bradley & Wood, 1996) appears to support the view that, once suspected, abuse will be disclosed when children are formally interviewed. Yet high rates of *non*disclosure or delayed disclosure (75% in the study by Sorenson & Snow, 1991) are consistent with the view that there are many impediments to disclosure.

The "disclosure wars" differ in important ways from the "memory wars" that divided researchers and practitioners in the 1990s: Whereas the memory wars focused on adults' memories of childhood sexual abuse and on very specific questions relating to possible repression and recovery, the disclosure wars focus on children's developmental abilities and motivational issues that might hinder disclosure. Although memory failure may be a contributing factor, specific and unique memory processes have generally not been invoked to account for children's failure to disclose. Rather, reasons for nondisclosure of abuse during childhood have typically been conceptualized in terms of a lack of understanding, inadequate verbal (reporting) skills, or motives not to divulge the abuse.

We acknowledge from the outset that we will never know the true incidence of childhood sexual abuse or have a precise estimate of the rate of nondisclosure of abuse. There will always be instances of abuse that are not disclosed or even suspected. Sexual abuse is a very private, well-concealed crime typically involving only the victim and perpetrator, with no witnesses. We are reliant on contemporaneous or retrospective verbal disclosure for estimates of its incidence. The child's or adult's verbal disclosure of abuse is typically the primary, indeed often the only, evidence that the abuse occurred; corroborative evidence indicating whether a child has indeed been abused is very much the exception rather than the norm, although of course, corroboration of other aspects of a child's account may be possible.

Thus, we come back to the question: When a suspected victim does not disclose abuse when interviewed, how do we know whether the child has indeed not been abused (a true negative) or is simply unwilling to disclose abuse that has occurred (a false negative)? The corresponding question—when a child *does* disclose abuse, how do we distinguish between true and false positives—has been the focus of an enormous literature on suggestibility and the implantation of false memories. In contrast, the question of whether there is a substantial problem of nondisclosure among abused children is far less well understood. Identifying both the conditions under which nondisclosure is most likely to occur and the barriers to disclosure is surely the first important step in ensuring that children who have been abused will disclose that abuse.

At first glance, the question of whether nondisclosure of abuse is common appears seductively easy to resolve. Why not, for example, take cases in which there is incontrovertible evidence of abuse (such as sexually transmitted disease) and ask how frequently this is encountered in the absence of a verbal disclosure of abuse? But as quickly becomes apparent (and as is amply illustrated in the chapters by London et al. and Lyon), issues of sampling bias and questions regarding the generalizability of findings from highly selected samples of child sexual abuse victims inevitably arise. Moreover, we have to be clear about what we mean by nondisclosure when trying to reconcile very disparate findings. Is nondisclosure the same as denial of abuse when interviewed? Or is nondisclosure more inclusive and not dependent on the child having been formally interviewed? For example, when adults retrospectively report that they were abused during childhood but had not disclosed the abuse to anyone, should we refer to such cases as nondisclosure whether or not they had ever been asked about it? And do delayed disclosures, by definition, include a period during which the child was a "nondiscloser"? Different (often implicit) definitions of just what constitutes nondisclosure have further contributed to the debate.

The chapters collected together in this volume provide the first rigorous examination of the available evidence relating to the patterns of disclosure and nondisclosure of childhood sexual abuse, and the first systematic consideration of the practical and policy implications of the research findings. The contributors provide a critical and comprehensive analysis of the ways in which children disclose abuse and, in turn, the best evidence-based answers to the questions of relevance to child protection workers, clinicians, forensic interviewers, and the courts.

The first two chapters (London et al., chapter 2; Lyon, chapter 3) provide a historical overview of the underlying controversy and closely examine the extant literature on disclosure. They highlight difficulties in conducting the research needed to determine how often children fail to disclose sexual abuse, delay disclosing it, provide incomplete accounts, and/or recant their disclosures. They attribute the difficulties to the fact that evidence concerning patterns of disclosure is typically based either on the analyses of investigative interviews with children suspected of having been abused or on retrospective surveys of adults who report not having disclosed abuse during childhood.

London et al. and Lyon adopt different strategies for distinguishing between true nondisclosures (the children were not abused and do not report abuse) from false nondisclosures (the children were abused but do not report it) and in so doing highlight very different problems that may arise from sampling biases. London et al. cogently argue that because the highest rates of nondisclosure are associated with the weakest evidence that the abuse did, in fact, occur, most nondisclosures are true negatives. Lyon, on the other hand, argues that children may deny being abused even when there is strong evidence that it happened (such as STDs), and that many studies reporting low rates of nondisclosure are tainted by "suspicion" and "substantiation" biases. Undoubtedly, the issues discussed in these two chapters contribute to the very discrepant reported rates of disclosure and nondisclosure.

Despite their different emphases, the chapters by London et al. and Lyon converge on two conclusions. First, at least some children do not disclose abuse even when questioned about it, and second, delayed disclosures of sexual abuse are not uncommon. Research on identifying the conditions under which nondisclosures are most likely to occur, the reasons children delay disclosing abuse, and, importantly, what precipitates the decision to disclose after delaying is addressed in the second section of the book.

Specifically, the authors of the next four chapters examine individual and contextual factors that determine whether, when, and how childhood sexual abuse is disclosed. They demonstrate for the first time that the way in which children are interviewed has an important impact on disclosure patterns. Detailed description and analysis of this has been a striking omission in all previous studies of disclosure during childhood. These four chapters are, therefore, unique in that each provides detailed information about how reluctant or nondisclosing children were interviewed. In all four studies forensic interviewers followed the National Institute of Child Health and Human Development (NICHD) investigative interview protocol (Orbach et al., 2000), which emphasizes open-ended recall and limited interviewer input. Hershkowitz, Horowitz, and Lamb (chapter 4) examine a data set comprising information about more than 25,000 suspected victims of physical and sexual abuse in Israel during a five year time period. Unlike convenience samples or samples drawn from specific agency files, therefore, the sample was not subject to the usual selection biases. Contrary to concerns that heavy reliance on open-ended interview strategies may lead to elevated rates of nondisclosure, the disclosure rates reported by Hershkowitz et al. are well within the range expected. In a much smaller and more selective U.S. sample, Pipe, Lamb, Orbach, Stewart, Sternberg, and Esplin (chapter 5) report similarly high rates of disclosure using the NICHD protocol's open-ended approach to interviewing. Because they are able to examine a broad range of information about the children, suspects, and alleged offenses, Pipe et al. are able to elucidate the associations between nondisclosure and these variables as well as the ways in which they are qualified by interactions, in particular with age. They report, for example, that nondisclosure of abuse is likely to be multiply determined and that the correlates of nondisclosure are different at different ages. Discrepant rates of nondisclosure in the studies reviewed by London et al. may thus depend, at least in part, on variations in the groups sampled.

Hershkowitz, Orbach, Lamb, Sternberg, Pipe, and Horowitz (chapter 6) and Orbach, Shiloach, and Lamb (chapter 7) place individual investigative interviews under the microscope, examining the dynamics of interviews conducted with children who do disclose, disclose reluctantly, or do not disclose at all. Specifically, they examine in detail the types of prompts used by interviewers, and the children's responses to these, as well as the interviewers' supportive and nonsupportive comments. Hershkowitz et al. find that, compared to children who do disclose abuse, children who do not disclose abuse (despite good reason to believe that they have been abused) appear reluctant early in the presubstantive phase of the interview, before any focus on the suspected abuse. Importantly, Hershkowitz et al. point to the influence of such reluctance on the interviewers' behavior with respect to both the type of prompts used and the provision of supportive comments, and this may have significant implications for further research on how best to modify the ways in which nondisclosing children should be interviewed. Orbach et al. similarly find that children who are reluctant to disclose appear reluctant already, in the presubstantive phases of the interview, and that when they do disclose they remain relatively uninformative. These findings again underscore the need to consider how children who are reluctant early in the interview should be treated. Hershkowitz et al. raise the possibility that it may sometimes be necessary to delay discussing possible abuse until the child is more forthcoming, even if it means interviewing reluctant witnesses on more than one occasion, for example.

Bottoms, Quas, and Davis (chapter 8) then review the literature and report new data on the importance of interviewer approaches and characteristics. In accord with clinical intuition, they show that interviewers who are warm and supportive elicit more and more accurate information than those who are cold and not empathetic. Although their review focuses on analogue studies in which children not suspected of having been abused are interviewed about nonabusive events, it is likely that interviewer demeanor is even more important when children are reluctant, fearful, embarrassed or shy. Unfortunately, we know least about strategies for overcoming reluctance in these children, as Saywitz, Esplin, and Romanoff (chapter 12) emphasize when they return to this issue from a clinical perspective, in the third section.

Cederborg, Lamb, and Laurell (chapter 9) next examine the reasons why children delay disclosing abuse, if they disclose at all, and thus remain vulnerable to repeated abuses over time, paying close attention to some of the strategies that perpetrators use to maintain children's silence about the abuse. None of the 12 children abused by a Swedish pedophile who videotaped the abuse disclosed what had happened before the videotapes were discovered. Cederborg et al. show that children may be reluctant to disclose abuse because they are unable to understand what they had experienced or are manipulated into silence by the perpetrator (i.e., threatened or urged to keep a secret). As they note, developmental issues need to be taken into account when considering the reasons children delay disclosure or fail to disclose abuse. Barriers to disclosure may change during childhood, and approaches to dealing with them will need to be developmentally sensitive.

The final two chapters in this section examine adults' recall of childhood sexual abuse. Bottoms, Rudnicki, and Epstein (chapter 10) examine prior disclosure of both sexual and physical abuse, as reported retrospectively by a somewhat diverse (in terms of ethnicity and socioeconomic status) sample of American college students. Respondents indicated not only whether they had experienced different forms of abuse but also whether they had disclosed this previously to another person. In contrast to the other studies in this section, Bottoms et al. failed to find that prior disclosure of either physical or sexual abuse was less likely when the perpetrator was a close family member. Although other researchers have reported similar results (see London et al., chapter 2), this may reflect the relatively small numbers of close family members identified as perpetrator in these samples, and that such variables may well depend on age at the time of the alleged abuse. Bottoms and her colleagues not only confirm that many children may never disclose their abuse as children, leading to what they describe as "huge under-reporting" of child maltreatment but also found that many of the adults who confirmed having been abused did not appear to perceive themselves as victims of abuse. Specifying what abuse is and what it is not arouses controversy, but it is clear that self-labeling may lead to different estimates of disclosure than sampling specific behaviors.

Connolly and Read (chapter 11) adopt a unique approach to understanding barriers to the "timely" disclosure of abuse. They examine a small, nonrepresentative sample of adults who had made a criminal complaint of abuse that was alleged to have taken place in the distant past (historical child sexual abuse). By comparing such cases to "timely complaints" of abuse, they ask whether it is possible to differentiate delayed complaints from those made soon after the abuse occurred. Consistent with the studies of childhood disclosure, they find that delayed complaints are more likely when family members are suspected and when the abuse was more severe. Interestingly, children between the ages of 7 and 11 at the time of the alleged abuse were overrepresented in the cases of delayed complaints. In general, the convergence of these findings with those based on other samples, comprising both children and adults, is striking.

Chapters in the third section turn to the broader implications of nondisclosure. When children do not verbally disclose abuse, yet child-care professionals remain concerned about the child's well-being, what should happen next? This is a thorny issue, as the discussion by Saywitz et al. (chapter 12) highlights. Forensic investigations do not take place in a vacuum but are part of a larger process aimed at child care, well-being, and protection. Is the investigative process, including the formal forensic interview, at odds with, for example, clinical considerations? Can we learn from child clinical psychology how to interview children who are reluctant to disclose? Conversely, could solutions derived from the forensic field be incorporated into therapeutic practices and interventions so that children's mental health needs are met without compromising evidence or undermining their legal cases? Saywitz et al. effectively challenge researchers and clinicians alike to pursue research agendas that overlap to a much greater degree than they have in the past.

Gumpert (chapter 13) also considers the potentially conflicting demands of clinical and legal processes and how they are dealt with in Sweden. Like Saywitz et al., Gumpert argues that it is mutually beneficial for professionals from the two different domains to have some understanding of the other's perspective. Gumpert presents examples from a unique study in which victims of childhood sexual abuse were interviewed in detail about the disclosure process, providing yet another window on when and why children may find it difficult to disclose abuse in a timely manner.

The chapters by Wilson (chapter 14) and Horowitz (chapter 15) continue the international perspective, focusing on the problems that delayed disclosure, incomplete disclosure, and nondisclosure pose for clinicians, social workers, forensic interviewers, prosecutors, policy makers, and legal professionals. Perhaps because of their small populations, both New Zealand and Israel have adopted standardized approaches to forensic interviews, and the chapters by Wilson and Horowitz describe their respective approaches and treatment of nondisclosing children. Both acknowledge that not all nondisclosing children have been abused but also acknowledge that some abused children do not disclose in a single forensic interview. Horowitz examines methods used by children's investigators in Israel to deal with reluctant children in the context of Israeli laws concerning the protection of abused children. In Israel, child-witnesses' interviews are conducted by social workers or psychologists specially trained as youth investigators who are required to use the NICHD protocol (Orbach et al., 2000) when interviewing children. Various additional techniques may be used with reluctant children when there is evidence that abuse occurred, including repeated interviews at the investigators' office or at the reported scene of the alleged crime.

Finally, Lindblad (chapter 16) reflects on the various meanings of the terms disclosure and nondisclosure and the related concepts of delayed disclosure and the disclosure process. His discussion reminds us that apparently straightforward and unambiguous concepts are laden with implicit meanings, and that the terms may be used quite differently in scientific, clinical, and legal contexts. Lindblad counsels against rejecting the term "disclosure" outright, a solution that has been suggested; instead, he argues for a thorough analysis of how the term is used and what it means to different people. If we did not agree with Lindblad's final word, this volume would indeed have had a different title!

REFERENCES

Bradley, A. R., & Wood, J. M. (1996). How do children tell? The disclosure process in child sexual abuse. *Child Abuse & Neglect, 20*(9), 881–91.

Bruck, M., & Ceci, S. (2004). Forensic developmental psychology. *Current Directions in Psychological Science, 13*(6), 229–32.

London, K., Bruck, M., Ceci, S., & Shuman, D. (2005). Disclosure of child sexual abuse: What does the research tell us about the ways that children tell? *Psychology, Public Policy, and Law, 11*, 194–226.

Orbach, Y., Hershkowitz, I., Lamb, M. E., Sternberg, K. J., Esplin, P. W., & Horowitz, D. (2000). Assessing the value of structured protocols for forensic interviews of alleged child abuse victims. *Child Abuse and Neglect, 24*(6), 733–52.

Sorensen, T., & Snow, B. (1991). How children tell: The process of disclosure in child sexual abuse. *Child Welfare, 70*(1), 3–15.

Summit, R. (1983). The child sexual abuse accommodation syndrome. *Child Abuse & Neglect, 7*(2), 177–93.

———. (1992). Abuse of the child sexual abuse accommodation syndrome. *Journal of Child Sexual Abuse, 1*(4), 153–63.

2

Disclosure of Child Sexual Abuse: A Review of the Contemporary Empirical Literature

Kamala London, Maggie Bruck
University of Toledo

Stephen J. Ceci
Cornell University

Daniel W. Shuman
Southern Methodist University

Although it is widely acknowledged that the sexual assault of children is a major societal concern, it is not known how many children in the United States are victims of sexual abuse (Ceci & Friedman, 2000). There are two major reasons for this lack of data. First, current estimates of the incidence of child sexual abuse (CSA) do not reflect the number of unreported cases or the number of cases reported to agencies other than Child Protective Services (e.g., sheriff's offices or professionals such as mental health diversion programs). Second, the diagnosis of CSA is often difficult because definitive medical or physical evidence is lacking or inconclusive in the vast majority of cases (Bays & Chadwick, 1993; Berenson, Heger, & Andrews, 1991), and because there are no unique psychological symptoms specific to sexual abuse (Kendall-Tacket, Williams, & Finkelhor, 1993; see Poole & Lindsay, 1998; J. Wood & Wright, 1995). Given these limitations of medical and psychological evidence, children's statements typically comprise the central evidence for judging the occurrence of CSA. In making these judgments, professionals often must address the thorny issue concerning *how* children disclose abuse.

According to some experts, a major problem with relying on children's statements in forensic investigations is that many sexually abused children remain silent about abuse, they deny that abuse ever occurred, or they produce a series of disclosures of abuse followed by recantations of these disclosures. This hypothesized model of incremental abuse disclosure has been put forth by a number of authors (e.g., Macfarlane & Krebs, 1986; Sgroi, Bunk, & Wabrek, 1988; Summit, 1983). The central tenet of these models is that sexually abused children are reluctant to disclose sexual abuse. When children do reveal abuse, disclosure will be incremental over time, a process that often includes outright denials and recantations of prior disclosures and then reinstatements of the abuse. Although this hypothesized pattern of incremental abuse disclosure has taken on different names, we will refer to it as Child Sexual Abuse Accommodation (CSAA).

The CSAA model has been endorsed by many clinicians and scholars and has been the basis of clinical and forensic judgments. For example, Summit's (1983) paper describing a model of incremental abuse disclosure was rated by professionals as one of the most influential papers in the field of child sexual abuse (Oates & Donnelly, 1997). The central assumptions of the CSAA model are echoed in some contemporary guidelines for assessment and diagnosis of CSA. For example, the National Children's Advocacy Center (Carnes, 2000) states in one of its publications, "Forensic evaluation is a process of extended assessment of a child when that child is too frightened or young to be able to fully disclose their experiences on an initial forensic interview" (p. 14) and "Reluctance is commonplace and difficult to overcome in suspected child sexual abuse cases" (p. 42). In fact, some professionals have gone so far as to treat behaviors such as denials and recantations of abuse as indicators that sexual abuse likely occurred (Fisher, 1995; Kovera & Borgida, 1998; Robin, 1991; Summit, 1992).

Given the widespread appeal and currency of CSAA-type models in the mental health community and their acceptance in the forensic arena, especially when used to rehabilitate the credibility of a child witness, it is important to examine the empirical basis for these theories (Summit, 1983, p. 180; Summit, 1992, p. 156; and see London, Bruck, Ceci, & Shuman, 2005, for extended discussion). In this paper, we critically review the existing empirical data to assess the scientific support for the behavioral components of CSAA-type models—secrecy/silence, denial, and recantation. We draw on two major sources of empirical data on children's disclosure patterns: (1) retrospective accounts from adults who claimed to have been sexually abused as children, and (2) examinations of children undergoing sexual abuse evaluations. Each source contributes some information to our understanding of CSA disclosure patterns although both data sources contain limitations. To foreshadow the results of this review, we conclude that although a substantial proportion of children delay reporting or altogether fail to report incidents of child sexual abuse (the secrecy stage), there is little evidence to suggest that denials, recanta-tions, and redisclosures are typical when abused children are directly asked about abuse during forensic interviews.

PATTERNS OF SEXUAL ABUSE DISCLOSURE AMONG ADULTS IN RETROSPECTIVE SURVEYS

Disclosure Rates

We conducted a review of the literature to locate studies that yielded statistics on the proportion of adults with reported childhood histories of abuse who dis-closed their abuse during childhood (London, et al., 2005). We selected stud-ies that were published since 1990 in order to control for potential cohort effects that might be present due to the many changes in education, advocacy, increased sensitivity, and legal procedures related to sexual abuse and sexual abuse investigations. Table 2.1 lists 11 retrospective studies that fit these cri-teria. Studies that did not specify the rate of disclosure during childhood are not listed in the table but are cited when relevant for related topics (for exam-ple, predictors of disclosure patterns).

Before beginning this review, it is important to point out that there are several difficulties in interpreting the findings of this literature. The first issue regarding accuracy of the retrospective data lies in accuracy of the abuse re-ports. Specifically, it is possible that some adults in these retrospective studies had been abused but continued to deny abuse (which would work to reduce the overall CSA prevalence rates and inflate the disclosure rates; see Lyon, chapter 3, this volume). Additionally, it is possible that some adults in these retrospective studies had not been abused but claimed to have been (e.g., due to false memories encouraged by suggestive psychological therapeutic prac-tices). Such false allegations would inflate the incidence of CSA and render the data on disclosure nonmeaningful. A second issue surrounding the accu-racy of the retrospective data lies in the accuracy of adults' disclosure reports; that is, whether and when they reported the abuse to others as children. Some adults might have disclosed abuse in childhood, despite their reports to the contrary. In other words, they may in fact have told someone but failed to re-member having done so. A rich cognitive psychology literature demonstrates the myriad retrospective biases, even when the events in question are highly emotional (e.g., Freyd, 1996; Read & Lindsay, 1997; Neisser, 1997; Ross, 1989). In their investigation of flashbulb memories, Schooler and colleagues (Schooler, Ambadar, & Bendiksen, 1997; Schooler, Bendiksen, & Ambadar, 1997) coined the term *forgot-it-all-along-effect* to describe the finding that peo-ple sometimes inaccurately recall to whom, when, and whether they reported an important life event. Adults' denial of CSA reports that were actually made during childhood would not affect prevalence rates of CSA but would lead to an underestimation of disclosure rates. Despite these many confounding

TABLE 2.1
Childhood Disclosures of Sexual Abuse: Retrospective Studies

Study	N =	Sample Source[a]	Definition of CSA	Reports abuse at survey (%)	Childhood disclosure (%)	Report to authorities (%)	Ave. age at time of abuse	Ave. age of sample (yrs)
Arata (1998)	860[b] (f)[c]	College sample	Unwanted contact before 14 yrs	24	31 (at time of abuse)	10	8.5	23
Smith et al. (2000)	3,220 (f)	National probability sample	Rape	9	34 (within 6 months of abuse)	12	10.9	45
Roesler & Wind (1994)	286 (f)	CSA hotline callers	Intra-familial before 16 yrs	100	36	n/a	6	41
Lamb & Edgar-Smith (1994)	48(f) 12 (m)[d]	Newspaper ad	Not specified	100	36 (by age 13)	n/a	8.15	30
Roesler (1994)	168 (f); 20(m)	Abuse center	Genital contact before 16 yrs	100	37	n/a	< 16	41
Tang (2002)	1,151 (f) 887 (m)	Hong Kong Chinese college students	Unwanted sexual experiences before age 18	6	38	n/a	11	21
Finkelhor et al. (1990)	1,481(f) 1,145 (m)	National probability sample	Before 18 yrs	27 (f) 16 (m)	42 within 1 year of abuse	n/a	Median = 9.7	30–39
Somer & Szwarcberg (2001)	41(f)	Israeli abuse center	CSA survivors	100	45 (by age 17)	n/a	7.11	32

(continued)

TABLE 2.1 (*Continued*)

Study	N =	Sample Source[a]	Definition of CSA	Reports abuse at survey (%)	Childhood disclosure (%)	Report to Authorities (%)	Ave. age at time of abuse	Ave. Age of Sample (yrs)
Ussher & Dewberry (1995)	775 (f)	1991 Women's Magazine Survey	Unwanted sexual attention	100	54	18	8.5	38
Fergusson et al. (1996)	1,019 (m&f)	New Zealand longitudinal study	Unwanted experience before 16 yrs	10	87 (by age 18)	n/a	< 16	18
Hanson et al. (1999)	4,008(f)	National probability sample	Nonconsensual penetration assaults before age 18	8.5	n/a	13	< 18	37.5

a. Unless noted, all studies were conducted in the United States.
b. Some studies sampled general populations while others specifically sampled sexually abused. We have provided in this table the percentage of abused participants endorsing abuse. Hence, data on disclosure are based on the percentage of the total samples that endorsed CSA.
c. [c]Female.
d. [d]Male.

15

variables in the interpretation of the existing data, some common themes emerge across studies, as we discuss below.

As shown in table 2.1, the modal childhood disclosure rate (in 6 out of 10 studies) is just over 33%. Three other studies (7, 8, 9) reported slightly higher, but still low, rates of disclosure. These low disclosure rates are consistent with the claims of the CSAA model that nondisclosure of sexual abuse (silence) in childhood is very common. Only 1 of the 11 studies in table 2.1 reported relatively high rates of disclosure. The study was carried out in New Zealand by Fergusson, Lynskey, and Horwood (1996) and involved a longitudinal study on 1,265 children. Sexual abuse was defined broadly in their study, ranging from noncontact activities such as indecent exposure or lewd suggestions (including experiences with same-aged peers) to rape before age 16. At 18 years old, 87% of the abused subsample reported that they had told someone about the abuse. There are several reasons why Fergusson and colleagues obtained higher disclosure rates than other researchers. Fergusson et al. noted the high disclosure rates may partially reflect the young age of the adults in their sample: Possibly some were still denying the abuse, thus producing lower rates of CSA with concomitantly inflated rates of disclosure. Another possibility is that the high disclosure rates could be driven by unknown victim, perpetrator, or abuse variables. For example, the high rates of disclosure could, in part, be an artifact of their abuse definition. Many of their subjects reported noncontact activities such as lewd suggestions, which many of the participants reportedly did not consider as incidents of CSA. This could also explain why many of Fergusson et al.'s (1996) subjects denied abuse history during a three year follow up interview (Fergusson, Horwood, & Woodward, 2000).

In summary, although one study yielded high disclosure rates (Fergusson et al., 1996), the other retrospective studies indicated that just over one-third of adults who suffered CSA appear to reveal the abuse to anyone during childhood. Furthermore, among children who do disclose during childhood, delay of disclosure is common (also see Kellogg & Hoffman, 1995; Kellogg & Huston, 1995). As shown in column 7 of table 2.1, an even smaller minority reported that the abuse was disclosed to authorities during childhood. Given the differences in methodology, definitions of abuse, and sample characteristics, the general consistency of these findings across these studies is noteworthy.

Predictors of Nondisclosure/Disclosure

In addition to providing overall disclosure rates, some studies examined predictors of disclosure rates. That is, what kinds of abuse, victim, and perpetrator characteristics emerge in this literature that might help explain some of the variance in CSA disclosure during childhood? In this section we examine associations of some of these predictors from data within studies and, when possible, across studies.

Some authors have posited that CSA disclosure may be mediated by the nature of the relationship between the victims and perpetrators. Two research groups (Hanson, Resnick, Saunders, Kilpatrick, & Best, 1999; Smith, Letourneau, Saunders, Kilpatrick, Resnick, & Best, 2000) reported that CSA disclosure was more likely when the perpetrator was a stranger rather than a family member. Consistent with these findings, Ussher and Dewberry (1995) reported longer delays to disclosure among intra- versus nonfamilial abuse. In contrast, five research groups found no association between victim–perpetrator relationship and CSA disclosure (Arata, 1998; Kellogg & Hoffman, 1995; Kellogg & Huston, 1995; Lamb & Edgar-Smith, 1994; Roesler, 1994). Taken together, at least when there is an association between disclosure and relationship to perpetrator, close relationships lead to decreased disclosure. It is impossible to know at this point why only some of the studies have found this association, and there are several possible explanations. The association between disclosure and relationship to perpetrator may not be robust. Alternatively, some methodological factors might be suppressing the effect: The samples may not allow adequate detection of the relationship due to sample homogeneity on this variable; or there may be other abuse-related variables that suppress the effect of relationship to perpetrator. The retrospective data are insufficient at this time, then, to conclude whether there is a consistent association between relationship to perpetrator and childhood disclosure of sexual abuse.

Next, we examined the retrospective studies for trends in age at time of abuse and abuse disclosure. Age at time of abuse has not consistently been associated with abuse disclosure. Although Smith et al. (2000) found that younger victims were more likely to delay disclosure than older child victims, other researchers (e.g., Arata, 1998; Kellogg & Hoffman, 1995) failed to find any relationship between age and delay of disclosure. There is one important caveat to this conclusion. When study subjects reported experiencing CSA during adolescence, this was consistently accompanied by high disclosure rates (Everill & Waller, 1995; Kellogg & Hoffman, 1995). For example, Kellogg and Huston found that 85% of their sample of young adults (mean current age = 19.5 years, mean age of abuse = 14 years) had disclosed at some point in the past. Adolescents most commonly disclosed to a peer (Lamb & Edgar-Smith, 1994; Tang, 2002). In contrast, adults reporting that they revealed CSA as school-aged children did so to a parent rather than to a peer (Arata, 1998; Lamb & Edgar-Smith, 1994; Palmer, Brown, Rae-Grant, & Loughlin, 1999; Roesler, 1994; Roesler & Wind, 1994; but see Somer & Szwarcberg, 2001; Smith et al., 2000). These studies, taken together, imply that disclosure rates may vary as a function of age of CSA onset, which in turn is associated with the availability of a same-aged confidante.

No systematic relationships have been reported between demographic variables such as race and ethnicity and childhood disclosure rates (e.g., Arata, 1998; Hanson et al., 1999; Kellogg & Hoffman, 1995; Kellogg & Huston,

1995; Smith et al., 2000). However, most of the retrospective studies have too little variability in their sample's demographic composition to test for differences. (For discussions on how demographic variables—race and gender—might relate to CSA disclosure see Fontes, 1993; Kazarian & Kazarian, 1998; Kenny & McEachern, 2000; Levesque, 1994; Toukmanian & Brouwers, 1998.)

We examined the existing data to assess support for the assumption that disclosure is related to the amount of fear or violence associated with the abuse. According to the assumption, children do not disclose because they fear the perpetrators who physically coerced, harmed, or threatened them. In general, the data do not support the hypothesis that disclosure rates are related to severity of abuse. Although Arata (1998) found lower disclosure rates for contact versus noncontact abuse, she found no relationship between disclosure and method of coercion (e.g., threat, gift, curiosity, appeal to authority, physical force). Most researchers, however, have either found the opposite pattern (i.e., higher disclosure rates are associated with incidents involving life threat and physical injury; Kellogg & Hoffman, 1995; Hanson et al., 1999), or they have found no significant relationship between severity or method of coercion and disclosure (Lamb & Edgar Smith, 1994; Roesler, 1994; Smith et al., 2000).

Another way to examine the relationship between severity/coercion/physical harm and disclosure is to compare the rates among studies in Table 2.1 in terms of the types of abuse that were included in the study. Some experimenters defined CSA broadly (unwanted sexual attention by anyone) and some defined it more narrowly (e.g., forcible penetration). Despite the differences in definitions, disclosure rates reported across studies were very similar, except in Fergusson et al.'s (1996) study.

Next, we searched for studies that examined the relationship between threats that were used to secure the child's silence ("Don't tell or else . . .") and disclosure. We only found a few such studies, but a common problem was that in many cases it is not possible to determine whether the measure of "threat" referred to statements or actions during the commission of the assault to engender physical compliance or to threats used to engender silence (e.g., see Arata, 1998; Hanson et al., 1999; Roesler, 1994; Smith et al., 2000). This failure to provide operational definitions of threats is problematic on methodological grounds (how did the study participant interpret the question?) and on interpretational grounds (how does the consumer of the literature interpret the statistics?). Hence, the extant retrospective data are not informative as to the nature of the association between threats to remain silent and childhood disclosure rates. Future studies are needed that clearly define the term "threaten" to participants and to readers.

Summary

The results of the retrospective studies make two important contributions to our knowledge about the patterns of children's disclosure of abuse. First, when taken at face value, these data reveal that approximately 60–70% of adults do not recall ever disclosing their abuse as children and that only a small minority of subjects (10–18%) recalled that their cases were reported to the authorities. Thus, the retrospective studies provide evidence to support the assumption that many incidents of CSA go unreported and that the silence component in CSAAS models has a strong empirical foundation.

Second, analyses of predictor variables in these retrospective studies provide few insights into the factors associated with disclosure. They do, however, suggest that commonly held assumptions, such as fewer disclosures among more severe cases of CSA or in cases of intrafamilial abuse, lack adequate empirical support. We must await further data to examine these issues more definitively. In general, the reviewed studies were not designed to examine specific predictors of disclosure, and most of the analyses were post hoc in nature. Generally, the retrospective literature is limited in detecting associations between abuse variables and disclosure due to factors such as insufficient sample size, lack of homogeneity of samples, varying definitions of the variables, and a failure to provide clear operational definitions of the variables. Given these limitations, it we conclude that the existing data are inconsistent and these issues remain relatively unexplored.

Finally, it is important to stress constraints on the generalizability of these findings. Although these studies yield data on disclosure rates, they do not provide any data on the two other main components of the CSAA models: the frequency of denials or of recantations of abuse. This is because the surveys in these retrospective studies did not contain items that asked subjects if they were directly asked about abuse during childhood. Thus, in terms of data on denial of abuse, it is not known from the retrospective data if the nondisclosers were asked about and denied abuse or if the nondisclosers were simply not asked. In order to examine trends in abuse denials and recantations, the literature on children's patterns of CSA disclosure must be examined.

PATTERNS OF DISCLOSURE AMONG CHILDREN TREATED OR EVALUATED FOR SEXUAL ABUSE

In this section, we review studies of disclosure patterns of children who were specifically assessed or treated for sexual abuse in terms of delay of disclosure, denial, and recantation. Each section also includes a discussion of the correlates of delay, denial, and recantation. As with the retrospective studies, we excluded studies published prior to 1990 because of possible cohort effects that could be due to the changes in interviewing practices and prevention programs (for children) that have occurred in the decade of the 1990s.

Most of the studies presented in this section involved "chart reviews" of children who were interviewed by CPS, mental health, or medical professionals specializing in the assessment and treatment of sexual abuse. Children presented at these clinics or centers for a variety of reasons that included a prior disclosure to an adult, a suspicion of abuse by an adult or an agency, or the need for a second opinion or more extensive interviewing. Thus, across and within studies, there is often great variability in the methods by which children were interviewed, in the information collected (including differences and sometimes ambiguity in operational definitions of abuse-related terms such as threats), and in the procedures of diagnosing child sexual abuse. Furthermore, in some studies, as will be noted, researchers categorized the children according to the likelihood of abuse (e.g., highly probable, unclear, not abused); in other studies only children who met some prespecified criteria for abuse were included, and in still other studies, the certainty of abuse status was not specified. Of course, as with the adult retrospective reports, the diagnosis of sexual abuse, whether as substantiation or unfounded, almost always comes with some degree of uncertainty. Some children may falsely claim to have been abused after undergoing suggestive, coercive interviewing from a biased investigator or because they were pressured to do so from a parent undergoing a messy divorce; alternatively, some children may falsely deny abuse because of a variety of reasons including pressure from a parent to do so. Substantiation of abuse is a thorny issue, and we return to this issue to discuss its impact on the disclosure data in a subsequent section. As with the retrospective studies, then, the data from the child samples are not without limitations; some common themes do, nonetheless, emerge across studies.

Delay of Disclosure (Silence)

The results of these studies on child samples echo the adult retrospective finding regarding delay of abuse disclosure; namely, when children do disclose, it often takes them a long time to do so. For example, disclosure rates of children whose cases were referred for prosecution were examined by Goodman, Taub, Jones, England et al. (1992) and by Sas and Cunningham (1995). Although 37–42% of the children had disclosed within 48 hours of the abuse, it took between 6 to 12 months for many of the children to disclose abuse. Even higher rates of delayed disclosure were obtained in Elliott and Briere's (1994) study, in which 75% of children did not disclose CSA within the first year following the abuse, and 18% waited more than five years to disclose the abuse. Similarly, Henry (1997) reported an average of two years delay between abuse and disclosure.

Some of the variability in the length of delay in the child studies may reflect the settings in which the data were collected. Shorter periods of delay may show up in surveys of children in criminal trials simply because cases that do not show this pattern are excluded from consideration because of the inherent difficulty in obtaining convictions. Therefore, it may be that cases in the prosecutor's office are unrepresentative of those that never reach the courtroom.

Few of the studies on delay of disclosure examine associations between abuse-related variables and latency to disclosure. There are some data on gender differences, suggesting that males may be more reluctant to disclose than females (e.g., DeVoe & Faller, 1999; Goodman-Brown, Edelstein, Goodman, Jones, & Gordon, 2003; Gries, Goh, & Cavanaugh, 1996; Sas and Cunningham, 1995; Stroud, Martens, & Barker, 2000; but see DiPietro, Runyan, & Fredrickson, 1997; Keary & Fitzpatrick, 1994, who report no gender differences). However, as Goodman-Brown et al. (2003) discuss, gender differences in disclosure rates may be suppressed by other variables associated with gender (e.g., prior disclosure, relationship to perpetrator). For example, males may be more frequently abused by nonfamily members than females. Hence, potential differences in abuse dynamics between boys and girls should be kept in mind when considering any potential gender differences in disclosure patterns. Additionally, there are reasons to suspect that members of certain ethnic groups might face additional and culture-specific barriers to CSA disclosure (see Futa, Hsu, & Hansen, 2001; Rao, DiClemente, & Ponton, 1992; Shaw, Lewis, Loeb, Rosado, & Rodriguez, 2001; Toukmanian & Brouwers, 1998; Wong, 1987). However, to date there is no coherent account of the effects of demographic variables on abuse disclosure in childhood.

Some researchers have examined the association between different abuse characteristics and disclosure. As was the case with the adult studies, the data on "threats" are difficult to interpret because most studies fail to provide operational definition of threats (i.e., Were threats used during abuse or after abuse? Were threats used to obtain compliance or silence?). When clearly defined data on abuse characteristics do exist, they are sparse and not very consistent. For example, Sas and Cunningham (1995) found that children waited longer to disclose abuse when the perpetrator "groomed" them and established a close relationship than if the perpetrator used force. Some researchers have found that children who are victims of familial abuse tend to delay disclosure longer than those experiencing extra familial abuse (DiPietro et al., 1997; Goodman-Brown et al., 2003; Sjöberg & Lindblad, 2002). However, the majority of studies we examined either failed to find such an association or failed to report an association. Note that none of the studies covered in this section address issues concerning denial. These are addressed in the next section.

Rates of Sexual Abuse Disclosure (or Denials) in Interviews With Child Samples

In this section we review 17 papers published since 1990 that contained statistics on the frequency of denial and/or recantations for children who were questioned about abuse. Table 2.2 lists the 17 studies that provided childhood disclosure rates, in ascending order of denials. Additionally, table 2.2 provides data on some of the central characteristics of the studies. When relevant, we cite other studies in this section that did not provide data on the rate of childhood disclosure in their sample but that do throw light on the correlates of disclosure.

The pooled mean of disclosures for the studies listed in table 2.2 is 64% (range 24–96%), or, put another way, the mean of denials is 36%. For reasons discussed below, however, these figures should not be viewed as the best

TABLE 2.2
Disclosure and Recantation Rates From Child Clinic Studies

Study	N	Ages (mean/range)	(%) Disclosing	(%) Recantations	# SSI Citations	Type of interview
Gonzalez et al. (1993)	63	(2:11–12)	24	27	16	Therapy
Sorenson & Snow (1991)	116	Mode = 6–9 (3–17)	25	22	80	Therapy
Lawson & Chaffin (1992)	28	M = 7 (4–	43	n/a	40	Social worker
Carnes et al (2001)	147	M = 6 (2–17)	45	n/a	66	CSA Team
Wood et al. (1996)	55	M = 5.7 (6–11)	49	n/a	6	CSA Team
Bybee & Mowbray (1993)	106	M = 5.6 (2–11)	58	11	8	DPS and therapy records
Cantlon et al. (1996)	1535	Mode = 4 (2–17)	61	n/a	7	CSA Team
Gries et al. (1996)	96	M = 8.3 (3–17)	64	15	9	CSA Clinic
Stroud et al. (2000)	1043	M = 8.4 (2–18)	65	n/a	10	CSA Clinic
Gordon & Jaudes (1996)[a]	141	M = 6.4 (3–14)	74[b]	n/a	6	CSA Team
DiPietro et al. (1997)	179	M = 7.5 (1.4–22)	76[c] (47)	n/a	12	CSA Team
Dubowitz et al. (1992)	132	M = 6 (under 12)	83[c] (59)	n/a	26	CSA Clinic
Elliott & Briere (1994)	399	M = 11.03 (8–15)	85[c] (57)	9	50	Clinician
DeVoe & Faller (1999)	76	M = 6.8 (5–10)	87[c] (62)	n/a	15	Soc. Worker
Keary & Fitzpatrick 1994)	251	Mode = 6–10	91[c] (50)	n/a	24	CSA Team
Bradley & Wood (1996)	234	M = 10 (1–18)	96[c]	4	28	DPS
Faller & Henry (2000)	323	M = 11.7 (3–21)	N/A	6.5	8	DPS/Police

a. We do not report Gordon and Jaudes' (1996) "recantation" rate because the child was not interviewed under the same clinical watch, but rather the first interview was a brief medical screening. Also, the authors include parents' disclosures (i.e., as historian) in the base rate.

b. This rate is the percentage of children from the total sample disclosing during the investigative interview. The authors do not report the percent disclosing during the investigative interview for substantiated cases.

c. Denotes studies based on cases classified as probable abuse cases; the first disclosure rate is that of children classified as substantiated, high probability, etc., and the second disclosure rate is that for all children examined, regardless of classification of abuse likelihood.

estimate of central tendency. We focus on four factors that may account for the enormous between-study variability in order to highlight methodological and design factors that need to be considered in evaluating the generalizability, validity, and reliability of the findings in table 2.2. These factors are age of the child, previous disclosure of abuse, substantiation of abuse, and representative nature of the selected sample. We conclude that when such factors are considered, mean disclosure rates are quite high when children are explicitly asked about sexual abuse.

Developmental Differences. The wide variation in the ages of the children both within and between studies (see table 2.2, column 3) could partially account for differences in the rates of disclosure across studies. In order to examine this hypothesis, age-denial associations were examined within studies. Although no significant relationships between age and denial were found in two studies (Bradley & Wood, 1996; DeVoe & Faller, 1999), the more common finding was that school-aged children were more likely than preschoolers to disclose abuse during formal evaluation. For example, B. Wood, Orsak, Murphy, and Cross (1996) found that older children made more credible disclosures of abuse than younger children (also see Goodman-Brown et al., 2003; Mordock, 1996).[1] Similarly, DiPietro et al. (1997) found that older children were more likely to disclose than younger children and that children generally became more likely to disclose abuse after age four (also see Cantlon, Payne, & Erbaugh, 1996; Gries, Goh, & Cavanaugh, 1996; Keary and Fitzpatrick, 1994; Sas & Cunningham, 1995).

There are several possible explanations for these developmental differences in children's abuse disclosures. They could reflect the single influence or combined influences of linguistic, cognitive, and social/emotional factors. Thus, younger children may not have the same linguistic skills to convey their abuse experience; or, younger children may not understand the "meaning" of abusive acts and thus fail to make explicit disclosures. In support of these positions, it has been found that younger children are more likely to make accidental disclosures whereas older children are more likely to make purposeful disclosures (Campis, Hebden-Curtis, & DeMaso, 1993; Fontanella, Harrington, & Zuravin 2000; Nagel, Putnam, Noll, & Trickett, 1997). That is, younger children are more likely to make spontaneous statements about abuse that are not consistent with the topic of conversation or of the ongoing activity (e.g., stating, while watching TV, "Uncle Bob hurt my bottom"). In contrast, older children are more likely to report the abuse to an adult when asked.

---

[1] B. Wood et al. (1996) defined a credible disclosure as one that "was adequate for use as evidence in a future legal and/or child protection proceedings" (p. 84). The *not credible* category included cases "where the child did not disclose, denied sexual abuse, refused to cooperate, provided insufficient in detail or was not believable" (p. 84). The authors did not cite the number of children falling into each of the not credible subcategories.

Although the conclusions are consistent across studies, it is important to point out that the ages of the "younger" and "older" children are not the same across studies. Thus, in one study the "younger group" might be of the same age as the "older group" in another study. Therefore, it is not clear at what age children become more likely to disclose abuse.

A second possible explanation for developmental differences in rates of denial is that there may be higher rates of true denials among younger than older children. This hypothesis is based on several interrelated findings. Younger children may be more likely than older children to be brought for assessment due to caregivers' concerns about behaviors (rather than an abuse disclosure) that often are ambiguous and do not necessarily reflect CSA (see Campis et al., 1992; Fontanella et al., 2000; Levy, Markovic, Kalinowski, Ahart, & Torres, 1995; Nagel et al., 1997). Thus, in any sample there may be a greater proportion of younger nonabused children than of older nonabused children, and the higher denial rates by younger children would then reflect a higher rate of denials that are true negatives. For example, Keary and Fitzpatrick (1994) were less likely to categorize younger children as sexually abused compared to older children; in addition, the younger children were less likely to disclose abuse. Unfortunately, these researchers did not present data on age differences in denial rates among children who were classified as "founded" by the assessment team.

Although most of the data indicate that younger children may be less likely to disclose than older children, upon closer investigation, there may also be patterns specific to adolescents. At least among cases that reach authorities, children are most apt to reveal the abuse to their primary caregiver (Berliner & Conte, 1990; Campis et al., 1992; Faller & Henry, 2000; Fontanella et al., 2000; Gray, 1993; Henry, 1997; Sas & Cunningham, 1993). However, adolescents may have a greater appreciation of the consequences of disclosing intrafamilial abuse and thus withhold information. It is also possible that they may not readily disclose extrafamilial abuse to family members or to investigators because they feel it is their own business or they have already disclosed to peers, as noted in the retrospective studies reviewed in the first part of this paper. Hence, the rate of CSA disclosure to parents and authorities may resemble an inverted U-pattern, with an increase in disclosure as one moves from preschoolers to school-aged children, followed by an apparent decrease as one moves into adolescence. There are, however, few data on disclosure patterns in adolescence, and we must await these before drawing any definite conclusions.

Prior Disclosure of Abuse Predicts Disclosure During Formal Assessment. The studies included in table 2.2 focus on children's reports during forensic interviews and psychotherapy. That is, the children in these studies were specifically brought to a clinic, mental health professional, or law enforcement agency either because they had previously made a claim of abuse or because there was a suspicion of abuse that required further investigation. Thus, most of the children in each study had been questioned by someone (e.g., teacher, parent) about abuse prior to the formal interviews or therapy sessions. This factor is important because, as shown in table 2.3, the most significant predictor of disclosure in the formal interview is whether the child had disclosed before (e.g., to a parent, a teacher, a CPS worker). For example, Keary and Fitzpatrick (1994) reported that of the 123 children who had made a prior disclosure, 86% disclosed again during the formal interview; in contrast only 14% of the 128 children with no prior disclosures disclosed at interview.[2] Similar patterns of results were found by Gries et al., (1996), DiPietro et al. (1997), and DeVoe and Faller (1999).

This pattern of consistency of disclosure is most common in older children. Among children who had disclosed prior to formal assessment, younger children were less likely than older children to disclose again during formal assessment (Keary & Fitzpatrick, 1994; also see Ghetti, Goodman, Eisen, Qin, & Davis, 2002).

In sum, several studies suggest that once children have made an abuse disclosure, they are likely to maintain their allegations during formal assessments. This finding suggests that if children have already told a professional or a caretaker about an abusive event, then they are more likely to disclose in a formal investigation. Discrepant cases (where a child discloses before the formal interview but denies at the time of the formal interview) represent a minority and appear to occur most commonly among very young children.

Abuse Substantiation. The third and perhaps most important methodological factor that accounts for variation in disclosure patterns across studies concerns the validity of the diagnosis of child sexual abuse. In conducting studies of CSA disclosure patterns, it is of utmost importance to ensure that the group under study had in fact experienced childhood sexual abuse; otherwise, counts of frequency of delay to disclosure, denials, recantations, and restatements are uninterpretable. That is, children may deny because they in fact never were abused; children may take a long time to disclose because it is only with repeated suggestive interviewing that they will make disclosures which are false; and children may recant in order to correct their prior false disclosures.

In order to address problems of substantiation of abuse, some researchers have classified children in their sample in terms of the likelihood of abuse. Children meeting one or more of the following criteria (depending on the

---

[2] When children have made a prior allegation but do not repeat it during a formal investigation, this should not be categorized as a recantation because it is possible that the child's first allegation was incorrect or misinterpreted and the report during the formal investigation is accurate. In this paper, recantations are defined as those that are made to the same assessment team who heard the disclosure.

TABLE 2.3
Rates of Prior Disclosure and Disclosure during Formal Interviews

Disclosure During Assessment	Prior Disclosure (%)	
Study	Yes	No
Devoe & Faller (1999)	74	25
DiPietro et al. (1997)	77	7
Keary & Fitzpatrick (1994)	86	14
Gries et al. (1996)	93	40

study) are classified as abused: perpetrator convictions, plea bargains or confessions, medical evidence, other physical evidence, and children's statements. Although the use of such criteria is a good start, it should be noted that there are problems with each of these criteria. First, the accused may be persuaded to accept a plea bargain due to the stress, financial burden, and uncertain outcome of facing trial. There are some accused who have been falsely convicted despite the absence of direct evidence to prove child abuse, and on appeal their convictions have been overturned (Ceci & Bruck, 1995). Although this may not be common, it does happen. Next, medical evidence is not always an accurate indicator of abuse. In the statistically rare case where genital or anal abnormalities are found, similar abnormalities can sometimes be found among nonabused children (Berenson et al., 1991). Finally, in terms of the studies that are included in this report, the children's statements at the time of formal interview are used as indicators of abuse. But this is a circular exercise whereby children who make spontaneous disclosures with much elaboration, for example, are categorized in the "high certainty" group. Then the analysis of the disclosure patterns of the high certainty group indicates that the children disclosed spontaneously and/or with much elaboration (or did not deny).

Notwithstanding these problems with the use of certainty criteria, there must be some reliable bases to categorize the children in studies of disclosure of CSA, lest the disclosure rates obtained merely reflect the overall responses of children (abused and nonabused alike) who are assessed for sexual abuse. Keeping these reservations in mind, we now review those studies that have examined disclosure patterns as a function of the certainty of abuse diagnosis. We will argue that with a few exceptions, high rates of disclosure rates are obtained in studies where the abuse status of the child is well defined, and low disclosure rates are associated with samples where the diagnoses of abuse are either unknown or questionable.

Referring to table 2.2, the eight studies with the highest disclosure rates (96% to 76%) contain the statements of children with high certainty diagnoses of abuse (sometimes these cases are labeled "substantiated," and, in general, the researchers or clinicians considered it highly likely that the children had been abused). The rates of disclosure are greatly lowered in these same studies when the data from the unsubstantiated or unclear cases are averaged with the high-certainty cases (see data in parentheses in column 4). Thus, although only 62% of DeVoe and Faller's (1999) sample of 5- to 10-year-olds disclosed abuse, when only substantiated cases are included, the disclosure rate rises to 87%. The overall rate of disclosure in the Keary and Fitzpatrick study (1994) is 50%; however, when only the substantiated cases are included, the rate is 95%. DiPietro et al. (1997) classified each of the children in their sample who were assessed because of suspicions of CSA as unfounded, possible, probable, or definitive abuse. Rates of disclosure during the first visit increased as a function of abuse certainty with 7%, 8%, 59%, and 76%, of cases classified as unfounded, possible, probable, or definitive abuse, respectively, disclosing abuse. The overall disclosure rate in Dubowitz, Black, and Harrington (1992) was 58%; however, among their cases rated by an interdisciplinary team as holding low to possible likelihood, the disclosure rate was only 19%, compared to disclosure rates of 83% for the moderate to high likelihood cases and 75% of cases with abnormal medical findings seen as indicative of abuse (e.g., abnormal anal or genital findings). Elliott and Briere (1994) examined the case records of 399 8- to 15-year-olds who were seen at a child sexual assault assessment center. Overall, 57% of the 399 cases disclosed abuse, with 20 of these children later recanting. When only children who were in the "abused" category were included in the calculation, the rate of disclosure increased to 84%. It is interesting to compare the profiles of these children to the 20% of the sample who were categorized as "unclear". The latter sample all made noncredible disclosures or noncredible denials of abuse. These children classified as unclear were more likely to be referred by a mandated reporter because of a suspicion of abuse, more likely to be male, and more likely to exhibit more sexual acting out behavior.

Returning to table 2.2, studies that include cases without providing information on their diagnostic certainty (in ascending order Gordon & Jaudes, 1996; Stroud et al., 2000; Gries et al., 1996) yield disclosure rates (61%–74%) that are lower than those of the studies just discussed. In these studies, there is no other evidence to confirm the abuse status of these children, and hence the disclosure rates of corroborated abuse cases are not ascertainable from the data.

Table 2.2 shows that the lowest rates of disclosure are provided by Sorenson and Snow (1991) and Gonzalez, Waterman, Kelly, McCord, and Oliveri (1993). Based on our analysis of the cases included in these studies, we conclude that these low rates reflect the unreliable diagnoses of sexual abuse in these two studies. Because the Sorenson and Snow study is most frequently cited as supporting the notion that sexually abused children deny and recant (see table 2.2 column 6), it is important to carefully review this study and the characteristics of the sample.

Sorenson and Snow (1991) selected 116 cases of "confirmed" CSA from a larger sample of 633 children who were involved in child sexual abuse allegations from 1985 to 1989. Sorenson and Snow reported that 72% of children denied abuse when first questioned by either a parent or an investigative interviewer; 78% moved into a "tentative disclosure" stage with partial, vague, or vacillating disclosures of sexual abuse. Eventually, 96% of children made an active disclosure that involved detailed, coherent, first-person descriptions of the abuse.

Although Sorenson and Snow's data often are cited as supporting the notion that children commonly deny and recant abuse allegations, there is serious reason to suspect that their findings are an artifact of their therapeutic practices. Sorenson and Snow's declared beliefs and practices that took place in the late 1980's parallel those that we now know run a high risk of producing erroneous, suggestive reports from children (see London et al., 2005, for further discussion of Sorenson & Snow's data). Perhaps the major concern about this study is the fact that Sorenson and Snow assessed and treated a significant number of children for ritualistic childhood abuse which involved allegations of repetitive, bizarre, sexual, physical, and psychological abuse of children that includes supernatural and/or religious activities (Snow & Sorenson, 1990). It appears that a number of such children were subjects in Sorenson & Snow's 1991 study (see London et al., 2005 for further discussion). The problem with the inclusion of these types of cases into studies of disclosure patterns is that there is no evidence to support the once poplar belief that ritualistic sexual abuse is common and further that the large proportion of reported cases of ritualistic abuse can be accounted for by the practices of a small minority of clinicians (see Bottoms, Shaver & Goodman, 1996; Goodman, Qin, Bottoms, & Shaver, 1995; Lanning, 1991; Nathan & Snedekor, 1995). Because Sorenson and Snow diagnosed so many "ritually abused" children in their practice, this, by inference, leads to the possibility that these children's allegations were a product of the practices and beliefs of these clinicians.

Given the nature of the "validated" cases in the Sorenson and Snow sample, as well as their use of apparently biased and suggestive interviewing/therapeutic techniques, the results of the study are uninterpretable. The patterns of disclosure may merely be characteristic of children who come to make false allegations as a result of suggestion. This would explain why these children originally denied having been abused (because they were telling the truth), why they eventually disclosed (because they were pressured into making allegations), and why they recanted (they wanted to restate the truth).

The Gonzalez et al. (1993) study suffers from many of the same problems. These authors examined the disclosure and recantation patterns of 63 children in therapy for sexual and ritualistic abuse in daycare. Gonzalez et al.'s source of data was the therapists' retrospective accounts of the reports made by their patients. They found that within the first 4 weeks of therapy, 76% of the children had made vague disclosures ("bad things had happened"); by 8 weeks,

45% of the children had disclosed highly specific terrorizing acts (killing of adults, children, and animals); and by 20 weeks, 43% of the children had reported aspects of ritualistic abuse (organized cults). However, for the same reasons that apply to the Snow and Sorenson article, the findings of this study are scientifically problematic. First, the children in this study were from the Mc-Martin Preschool case and other cases that arose in the community at the same time. The allegations in this case, which involved claims of ritualistic abuse, arose after multiple highly suggestive interviews with evaluators and therapists (see Nathan & Snedekor, 1995). At the time of their study, children had been in therapy on average for over one year. There was no physical or corroborative evidence of abuse and the charges in these cases were eventually all dropped. The interviewing methods used by children's therapists and evaluators have been documented elsewhere (e.g., Garven, Wood, Malpass, & Shaw, 1998), and the scientific evidence now shows that these methods can produce erroneous reports when used in interviews with children.

Finally, the results of the Bybee and Mowbray study (1993) may be open to the same criticism as detailed above. The subjects in this study were all involved in a Michigan daycare case that involved multiple perpetrators. The case eventually resulted in only one conviction, which was overturned on appeal. Compared to the other studies in table 2.2, disclosure rates were quite low; 58% of the 106 children disclosed abuse.

In sum, the three studies with the lowest disclosure rates (Bybee & Mowbray, 1993; Gonzalez et al., 1993; Sorenson & Snow, 1991) suffer some serious methodological difficulties. There is reason to be concerned that the patterns of disclosures made by children in the Gonzalez et al. and Sorenson and Snow studies may represent those of children who make false disclosures as a result of suggestive interviewing practices.

Representativeness of Selected Sample. Some studies reported data on samples specifically selected because the children had not previously disclosed sexual abuse. Such studies that focus on children who had not disclosed abuse during an initial interview do not provide a representative view of the disclosure patterns during forensic interviews; rather these studies merely reveal the disclosure rates of children who have previously denied abuse. Thus the studies with this type of design provide information on the degree to which deniers disclose sexual abuse with repeated interviewing. Three studies in table 2.2 (Carnes, Nelson-Gardell, Wilson, & Orgassa, 2001; B. Wood et al., 1996; and Lawson & Chaffin, 1992) involved such sampling procedures.

The Lawson and Chaffin (1992) study will be used to illustrate the point because this sample included children with medical substantiations of sexual abuse; thus, the degree of abuse certainty is high in this study. From a sample of over 800 children who tested positive for a sexually transmitted disease (STD) at a large pediatric hospital, cases that met the following criteria were selected: the presenting complaint was solely physical, there was no prior dis-

closure or suspicion of abuse, and the child was older than 3 and premenar-
cheal. A sample of 28 girls met these criteria, with a mean age of 7 years. These
28 children and their mothers were called back to the hospital after they tested
positive for an STD. During this interview, the mothers were given the diagnosis for the first time and then were interviewed about sexual abuse. Next,
their daughters were interviewed by a trained social worker. Only 43% of the
girls made an abuse disclosure during this initial interview.[3] This rate, however,
is based upon a very different population than sampled in other studies, in
which children were brought in either because of a suspicion or disclosure of
abuse. Rather, in the Lawson and Chaffin study, children were selected because of their medical history and because there was no prior abuse disclosure
or suspicion of abuse. Because it is not known how many of the 800 children
in the larger sample had already disclosed abuse, this subgroup of 28 children
with no prior disclosure might comprise an unusual sample; that is, they may
represent the small hard core of children who do not disclose abuse when directly asked. If they are a small minority, then these results are not generaliz-
able to the entire population of children with STDs. In addition, it should be
remembered that very few children who have been sexually abused have any
physical symptoms or STDs and thus this sample again is not representative of
the CSA population. There is a second factor that is important to consider. In
this study, when the children were called back to the hospital, their mothers
were first informed of the STD diagnosis of their children. Children whose
mothers accepted the possibility of abuse (the parents were labeled as supportive) were more likely to disclose (63% of this group disclosed) than children whose parents were not supportive and did not believe their child had
been abused (only 17% of these children disclosed). Thus, differences among
studies might reflect the role of parental support, which might be quite low
when parents are first confronted with the fact that their children were abused,
as was the case in the Lawson and Chaffin study (also see Elliott & Briere,
1994).[4]

Two studies reported disclosure rates for children who had undergone
forensic interviews but had not disclosed. B. Wood et al. (1996) examined 55
videotaped interviews of children referred by CPS to a multidisciplinary assessment center. All 55 children had been interviewed previously by CPS or
law enforcement officials but had not disclosed. Hence, the disclosure rate of

---

[3] In a follow up study, Chaffin, Lawson, Selby, and Wherry (1997) located 5 of these 28
subjects. Though not specifically asked about their children's disclosure, four out of five
mothers spontaneously mentioned that the child disclosed CSA subsequent to this initial
evaluation.

[4] Although many mothers do not support their children's disclosures of abuse, many *are*
supportive, especially if the defendant is an estranged husband or partner rather than a current one. In many studies, the support rate is between 50% and 85% (see Lyons, 1999, notes
238–39 for details).

49% in table 2.2 is based on the percentage of children disclosing out of these 55 children who had not previously disclosed. The study does not report on the number of children seen (and disclosing) from the general population of children presenting for CSA concerns. Finally, Carnes et al. (2001) reported that their sample of children undergoing extended CSA assessment because of failure to initially disclose represented approximately 10–15% of the total population presenting for assessment to the clinics in their study. Thus, the results of this study merely indicate the response patterns of children who had previously failed to disclose abuse. Furthermore, although this is not the case for the Lawson and Chaffin study, there are no data on the number of children in both the B. Wood and the Carnes et al. study who met acceptable criteria for diagnosis of sexual abuse. Thus, children who did or did not disclose with extra assessment may or may not have been abused.

Recantations. Eight studies have examined the frequency of recantations of abuse reports (see table 2.2 column 5). All but one of these studies also included information on disclosure rates. For the one exception, Faller and Henry (2000) examined the recantation rates of children who testified at trial about their sexual abuse. Thus, all these children had made prior disclosures that were considered credible by the prosecutors' office.

Before reviewing the findings reported in the studies, it is important to point out that there could be two different interpretations of recantation. The first is that the child is withdrawing a true statement of abuse. The second is that the child is withdrawing a false allegation of abuse. The relevant evidence is not available in most studies to determine the child's underlying motivation for recantation.

The recantation rates of the studies listed in table 2.2 range from 4% to 27%. Our analysis of the variability is very similar to that just carried out with respect to the denial rates; namely, the highest rates of recantation are obtained for studies that have the least certain diagnoses of sexual abuse. The two studies with the highest recantation rates were those of Gonzalez et al. (1993) and Sorenson and Snow (1991) in which the recantation rates were 27% and 22%, respectively. Because of concerns about the actual abuse status of the children in these studies, one might argue that recantation rates reflect the number of children who attempt to discredit their own previous false allegations by setting the record straight.[5] (If this is indeed the case, then the Gonzalez et al. (1993) and Sorenson and Snow (1991) data suggest that these attempts appeared to have failed, however, as most of the children reinstated their earlier accusations.)

---

[5] There were also issues concerning the validity of the sexually abused sample in Bybee and Mowbray (1993) who reported a much lower recantation rate of 11%. Thus, recantation rates do not necessarily have to be high for doubtful cases.

The lowest rates of recantation are obtained for samples that have the most certain diagnoses of sexual abuse [4% (Bradley & Wood, 1996); 6.5% (Faller & Henry, 2000; 9% of cases classified as abused, Elliott & Briere, 1994)]. The slightly higher rate of 15% reported by Gries et al. (1996) is difficult to interpret because there is no information on the number of children who were diagnosed as clear or unclear cases of abuse.

Although our analysis shows that some children recant sexual abuse, the results of this analysis show that recantation is uncommon among high probability sexually abused children. In fact, it shows just the opposite: When considering cases for which there is a high probability of abuse, a small percentage of children in these studies recant.

CONCLUSIONS

We began this paper by describing the widespread belief that sexually abused children do not readily disclose their abuse and that even when they disclose, they commonly recant such disclosures. Given the frequency with which these claims are made in the literature (as well as in proffered expert testimony), we sought to examine their scientific basis. A review of retrospective studies showed that most adults with histories of CSA recall that they never told anyone about the abuse during childhood. This pattern confirms the view that failure to disclose is common among sexually abused children. However, these findings do not address the issue of whether children will deny abuse or recant their disclosures once they have come to the attention of forensic interviewers. In order to examine these issues, it is necessary to study how sexually abused children disclose abuse when asked directly. Because it is difficult if not impossible to obtain accurate information if the first disclosure is made outside a formal setting (e.g., to a parent, friend, or teacher), we have to rely on studies in which children are questioned in formal investigative interviews. We identified 17 studies that contained relevant data and found, when focusing on children with high probabilities of abuse history, most children do disclose abuse within the first or second interview and that only a small minority of children recant their abuse. Even if analyses were broadened to include children with less certain CSA diagnoses, in all but two studies the majority of children disclosed abuse when directly asked, and only a small fraction of them recanted their previous disclosures.

One of the basic problems in interpreting the literature on children's disclosure of sexual abuse involves the issue of the validity of the diagnosis of sexual abuse. As we stated above, in many of the cited studies, classification of abuse was often based in part upon children's disclosures; consequently, the conclusion that abused children do disclose abuse during formal interviews may be circular. However, there is some evidence that when children are classified as abused based on medical evidence or on other nonchild factors (confession, material evidence) that most of these children do disclose abuse. In the Elliot and Briere (1994) study, for example, 118 of the 399 children had positive physical findings: 84% of these children at one point disclosed abuse (although 20, or 17%, of these 118 children later recanted their abuse reports). In Dubowitz et al. (1992), 28 of the 132 children had medical examination findings considered indicative of abuse; 75% of this subsample disclosed abuse. Finally, in the Gordon and Jaudes (1996) study, 78% of the children with medical evidence disclosed abuse. Before leaving this topic, it is important to point out that the disclosure rates for the medical subsamples of these studies were very close to the overall disclosure rates for the entire sample. Nonetheless, it must be noted that medical evidence itself is not always be a reliable benchmark (e.g., genital redness may be due to causes other than abuse), which raises the possibility that an unknown number of children with medical findings considered indicative of abuse actually were not abused.

The chapter by Lyon in this volume explicitly deals with methodological problems of calculating reliable denial and recantation rates. His solution is to select samples of children with confirmed sexual abuse history (children with medical evidence) where there has been no prior suspicion of sexual abuse; according to this argument, disclosure rates will be untainted by "suspicion biases" that tend to inflate disclosure rates. This solution, however, must be considered in terms of the generalizability obtained from such findings and the degree to which they can be applied to real world issues. We argue that the results of studies of disclosure patterns of children with medical histories of sexual abuse where there has been no prior suspicion or disclosure do not bear on the most important issue that faces professionals in the forensic arena. Specifically, if a child is brought for CSA assessment because of concern (and probable prior questioning), how likely will it be that this child provides a credible disclosure or a credible denial? In other words, the behavior of the highly selected samples proposed by Lyon does not pertain to the types of cases that require expert testimony or clinical assessment; namely, what are the disclosure patterns among children who come to the attention of forensic interviewers? We hope that our discussion makes clear some of the very difficult methodological and conceptual problems that are inherent to the study of disclosure patterns of sexually abused children.

In most of the studies cited in this paper, there was little if any detailed information about how the children were interviewed and the degree to which standardized and validated protocols were used. One is unable to glean from the literature whether, for example, disclosure rates might be related to the type of interviewing or whether the individual underwent psychological therapy. In future studies it would be important to compare the disclosure patterns of children interviewed with contemporary standardized interviews (e.g., Sternberg, Lamb, Esplin, Orbach, & Hershkowitz, 2002). If these protocols do in fact optimize the elicitation of reliable statements from children, then the disclosure patterns produced by these instruments would provide the most reliable data to test various hypotheses about the disclosure patterns of sexually abused children and to explore the factors that distinguish disclosers from nondisclosers.

Although there are a number of studies to address issues of patterns of disclosure, several overriding issues remain to be addressed. Specifically, although the data clearly demonstrate that children involved in high probability abuse cases do disclose and do not later recant when interviewed, there do exist a minority of children who fit the behavioral pattern of denials and recantations that is put forth in CSAA models. The outstanding issues thus focus on the characteristics of these children and whether these children fit the psychological profiles of the CSAA model (e.g., factors related to the characteristics of the abuse, the perpetrator, and the victim). In terms of abuse and perpetrator characteristics, further data are needed to examine whether factors such as use of threats or relationship to perpetrator are associated with abuse disclosure. In terms of victim characteristics, there needs to be a greater focus on developmental differences in disclosure patterns. In many of the studies we reviewed, children ranged in age from early preschool to late adolescence. Clearly, it is not very informative to provide group means when age ranges are so great. Studies are needed to examine potential developmental trends in loyalty to family and peers, reactions to fear, need for privacy, choice of confidants, and then to relate these factors to disclosure patterns in children of various ages. Another important area concerns the potential role of threats. In this future research venture, it is crucial to distinguish threats that were used to coerce the child into molestation from threats that were used to secure the child's silence.

The status of the scientific findings of disclosure patterns is of importance not only for diagnostic and assessment purposes but also for issues regarding interviewing of children. As mentioned above, the CSAA model has provided a basis for experts to advocate that when children deny abuse when directly asked, they should be questioned further and even should be questioned suggestively (e.g., Carnes, 2000; Faller & Toth, 1995; Macfarlane & Krebs, 1986). In order for such practices to be empirically grounded, it is important to demonstrate first that children will commonly deny abuse when questioned (thus calling forth the need for special strategies), and second that the use of special strategies will lead to accurate reports of abuse. The findings presented in this paper address the first issue only. The second issue has been addressed by a multitude of researchers in the past decade (e.g., Ceci & Bruck, 1995; Ghetti & Goodman, 2001; Poole & Lindsay, 2002; J. Wood & Garven, 2000). Professionals need to be aware that although suggestive techniques *might* produce true abuse reports from otherwise silent children, these same techniques, especially when used by biased interviewers, entail a risk of producing false allegations (e.g., Bruck, Ceci, & Hembrooke, 2002; Poole & Lamb, 1998). Part of the bias may include the notion that when children deny abuse they must be pursued until they disclose their abuse; however, as we demonstrated in this chapter, the need for suggestive interviewing is probably overestimated because denial of sexual abuse to professionals is not as rampant as previously suspected. At least among the subsample of sexually abused children to undergo forensic evaluation, our analysis indicates that when children who have been abused are questioned in formal settings, they will usually tell, obviating the need for suggestive questioning strategies. We believe that child abuse professionals should be aware of this information and incorporate it into their clinical practice as well as into their expert courtroom testimony. If the field is to be guided by scientifically validated concepts, then it must be predicated on the literature that comes closest to the standards of science.

ACKNOWLEDGMENTS

Portionsof this chapter appear in London, Bruck, Ceci, and Shuman (2005).

REFERENCES

Arata, C. M. (1998). To tell or not to tell: Current functioning of child sexual abuse survivors who disclosed their victimization. *Child Maltreatment, 3*, 63–71.

Bays, J., & Chadwick, D. (1993). Medical diagnosis of the sexually abused child. *Child Abuse & Neglect, 17*, 91–110.

Berenson, A., Heger, A., & Andrews, S. (1991). Appearance of the hymen in newborns, *Pediatrics, 87*, 458–65.

Berliner, L., & Conte, J. R. (1990). The process of victimization: The victims' perspective. *Child Abuse & Neglect, 14*, 29–40.

Bottoms, B. L., Shaver, P. R., Goodman, G. S. (1996). An analysis of ritualistic and religion-related child abuse allegations. *Law & Human Behavior, 20*, 1–34.

Bradley, A. R., & Wood, J. M. (1996). How do children tell? The disclosure process in child sexual abuse. *Child Abuse & Neglect, 20*, 881–91.

Bruck, M., Ceci, S. J., & Hembrooke, H. (2002). The nature of children's true and false narratives. *Developmental Review, 22*, 520–54.

Bybee, D., & Mowbray, C. T. (1993). An analysis of allegations of sexual abuse in a multi-victim day care center case. *Child Abuse & Neglect, 17*, 767–83.

Campis, L. B., Hebden-Curtis, J., & DeMaso, D. R. (1993). Developmental differences in detection and disclosure of sexual abuse. *Journal of the American Academy of Child and Adolescent Psychiatry, 32*, 920–24.

Cantlon, J., Payne, G., & Erbaugh, C. (1996). Outcome-based practice: Disclosure rates of child sexual abuse comparing allegation blind and allegation informed structured interviews. *Child Abuse & Neglect, 20*, 113–1120.

Carnes, C. N. (2000). *Forensic evaluation of children when sexual abuse is suspected*, 2nd ed., National Children's Advocacy Center, Huntsville, AL.

Carnes, C. N., Nelson-Gardell, D., Wilson, C., & Orgassa, U. C. (2001). Extended forensic evaluation when sexual abuse is suspected: A multisite field study. *Child Maltreatment, 6*, 230–42.

Ceci, S. J., & Bruck, M. (1995). *Jeopardy in the courtroom: A scientific analysis of children's testimony*. Washington, D.C.: American Psychological Association.

Ceci, S. J., & Friedman, R. D. (2000). The suggestibility of children: Scientific research and legal implications. *Cornell Law Review, 86*, 34–108.

Chaffin, M., Lawson, L., Selby, A., & Wherry, J. N. (1997). False negatives in sexual abuse interviews: Preliminary investigation of a relationship to dissociation. *Journal of Child Sexual Abuse, 6,* 15–29.

DeVoe, E. R., & Faller, K. C. (1999). The characteristics of disclosure among children who may have been sexually abused. *Child Maltreatment, 4,* 217–27.

DiPietro, E. K., Runyan, D. K., & Fredrickson, D. D (1997). Predictors of disclosure during medical evaluation for suspected sexual abuse. *Journal of Child Sexual Abuse, 6,* 133–42.

Dubowitz, H., Black, M., & Harrington, D. (1992). The diagnosis of child sexual abuse. *American Journal of Diseases of Children, 146,* 668–93.

Elliott, D. M., & Briere, J. (1994). Forensic sexual abuse evaluations of older children: Disclosures and symptomatology. *Behavioral Sciences and the Law, 12,* 261–77.

Everill, J., & Waller, G. (1995). Disclosure of sexual abuse and psychological adjustment in female undergraduates. *Child Abuse & Neglect, 19,* 93–100.

Faller, K. C., & Henry, J. (2000). Child sexual abuse: A case study in community collaboration. *Child Abuse & Neglect, 24,* 1215–25.

Faller, K. C., & Toth, P. (1995). *Forensically defensible interviewing.* American Professional Society on the Abuse of Children.

Fergusson, D. M., Horwood, L. J., & Woodward, L. J. (2000). The stability of child abuse reports: A longitudinal study of the reporting behaviour of young adults. *Psychological Medicine, 30,* 529–44.

Fergusson, D. M., Lynskey, M. T., & Horwood, L. J. (1996). Childhood sexual abuse and psychiatric disorder in young adulthood: I. Prevalence of sexual abuse and factors associated with sexual abuse. *Journal of the American Academy of Child & Adolescent Psychiatry, 35,* 1355–64.

Finkelhor, D., Hotaling, G., Lewis, I.A., & Smith, C. (1990). Sexual abuse in a national survey of adult men and women: Prevalence, characteristics, and risk factors. *Child Abuse & Neglect, 14,* 19–28.

Fisher, C. B. (1995). American Psychological Association's (1992) Ethics Code and the validation of sexual abuse in day care settings. *Psychology, Public Policy, and Law, 1,* 461–78.

Fontanella, C., Harrington, D., & Zuravin, S. J. (2000). Gender differences in the characteristics and outcomes of sexually abused preschoolers. *Journal of Child Sexual Abuse, 9,* 21–40.

Fontes, L. A. (1993). Disclosures of sexual abuse by Puerto Rican children: Oppression and cultural barriers. *Journal of Child Sexual Abuse, 2,* 21–35.

Freyd, J. J. (1996). *Betrayal trauma theory: The logic of forgetting childhood abuse.* Cambridge, MA: Harvard University Press.

Futa, K. T., Hsu, E., & Hansen, D. J. (2001). Child sexual abuse in Asian American families: An examination of cultural factors that influence prevalence, identification, and treatment. *Clinical Psychology: Science and Practice, 8,* 189–209.

Garven, S., Wood, J. M., Malpass, R., & Shaw, J. S. (1998). More than suggestion: Consequences of the interviewing techniques from the McMartin preschool case. *Journal of Applied Psychology, 83,* 347–59.

Ghetti, S., & Goodman, G. S. (2001). Resisting Distortion. *Psychologist, 14,* 592–95.

Ghetti, S., Goodman, G. S., Eisen, M. L., Qin, J., & Davis, S. L. (2002). Consistency in children's reports of sexual and physical abuse. *Child Abuse & Neglect, 26,* 977–95.

Gonzalez, L. S., Waterman, J., Kelly, R., McCord, J., & Oliveri, K. (1993). Children's patterns of disclosures and recantations of sexual and ritualistic abuse allegations in psychotherapy. *Child Abuse & Neglect, 17,* 281–89.

Goodman, G., Qin, J., Bottoms, B., & Shaver, P. (1994). *Characteristics of allegations of ritualistic child abuse.* Final Report to National Center on Child Abuse and Neglect.

Goodman, G. S., Taub, E. P., Jones, D. P., England, P., et al. (1992). Testifying in criminal court: Emotional effects on child sexual assault victims. *Monographs of the Society for Research in Child Development, 57,* v–142.

Goodman-Brown, T. B., Edelstein, R. S., Goodman, G. S., Jones, D. P. H., & Gordon, D. S. (2003). Why children tell: A model of children's disclosure of sexual abuse. *Child Abuse & Neglect, 27,* 525–40.

Gordon, S., & Jaudes, P. K. (1996). Sexual abuse evaluation in the emergency department: Is the history reliable? *Child Abuse & Neglect, 20,* 315–22.

Gray, E. (1993). *Unequal justice: The prosecution of child sexual abuse.* New York: Free Press.

Gries, L. T., Goh, D. S., & Cavanaugh, J. (1996). Factors associated with disclosure during child sexual abuse assessment. *Journal of Child Sexual Abuse, 5,* 1–20.

Hanson, R. F., Resnick, H. S., Saunders, B. E., Kilpatrick, D. G., & Best, C. (1999). Factors related to the reporting of childhood rape. *Child Abuse & Neglect, 23,* 559–69.

Henry, J. (1997). System intervention trauma to child sexual abuse victims following disclosure. *Journal of Interpersonal Violence, 12,* 499–512.

Kazarian, S. S., & Kazarian, L. Z. (1998). Cultural aspects of family violence. In S. S. Kazarian & D. R. Evans (Eds.), *Cultural clinical psychology: Theory, research, and practice* (pp. 316–47). New York: Oxford University Press.

Keary, K., & Fitzpatrick, C. (1994). Children's disclosure of sexual abuse during formal investigation. *Child Abuse & Neglect, 18,* 543–48.

Kellogg, N. D., & Hoffman, T. J. (1995). Unwanted and illegal sexual experiences in childhood and adolescence. *Child Abuse & Neglect, 19,* 1457–468.

Kellogg, N. D., & Huston, R. L. (1995). Unwanted sexual experiences in adolescents: Patterns of Disclosure. *Clinical Pediatrics, 34,* 306–12.

Kendall-Tacket, K. A., Williams, L. M., & Finkelhor, D. (1993). Impact of sexual abuse on children: A review and synthesis of recent empirical studies. *Psychological Bulletin, 113,* 164–80.

Kenny, M. C., & McEachern, A. G. (2000). Racial, ethnic, and cultural factors of childhood sexual abuse: A selected review of the literature. *Clinical Psychology Review, 20,* 905–22.

Kovera, M. B., & Borgida, E. (1998). Expert scientific testimony on child witnesses in the age of Daubert. In S. Ceci & H. Hembrooke (Eds.), *Expert witnesses in child abuse case: What can and should be said in court* (pp. 185–215). Washington, DC: American Psychological Association.

Lamb, S., & Edgar-Smith, S. (1994). Aspects of disclosure: Mediators of outcome of childhood sexual abuse. *Journal of Interpersonal Violence, 9,* 307–26.

Lanning, K. (1991). Ritual Abuse: A law enforcement view or perspective. *Child Abuse & Neglect, 15,* 171–73.

Lawson, L., & Chaffin, M. (1992). False negatives in sexual abuse disclosure interviews: Incidence and influence of caretaker's belief in abuse in cases of accidental abuse discovery by diagnosis of STD. *Journal of Interpersonal Violence, 7,* 532–42.

Levesque, J. R. (1994). Sex differences in the experience of child sexual victimization. *Journal of Family Violence, 9,* 357–69.

Levy, H. B., Markovic, J., Kalinowski, M. N., Ahart, S., & Torres, H. (1995). Child sexual abuse interviews: The use of anatomic dolls and the reliability of information. *Journal of Interpersonal Violence, 10,* 334–53.

London, K., Bruck, M., Ceci, S. J., & Shuman, D. W. (2005). Disclosure of child sexual abuse: What does the research tell us about the ways that children tell? *Psychology, Public Policy, and the Law, 11,* 194–226.

Macfarlane, K., & Krebs, S. (1986). Techniques for interviewing and evidence gathering. In K. Macfarlane & J. Waterman (Eds.), *Sexual abuse of young children* (pp. 67–100). New York: Guilford Press.

Nagel, D. E., Putnam, F. W., Noll, J. G., & Trickett, P. K. (1997). Disclosure patterns of sexual abuse and psychological functioning at a 1-year follow-up. *Child Abuse & Neglect, 21,* 137–47.

Nathan, D., & Snedekor, M. (1995). *Satan's silence: Ritual abuse and the making of a modern American witch hunt.* NY: Basic Books.

Neisser, U. (1997). Jane Doe's Memories: Changing the Past to Serve the Present. *Child Maltreatment, 2,* 126–33.

Oates, R. K., & Donnelly, A. C. (1997). Influential papers in child abuse. *Child Abuse & Neglect, 21,* 319–26.

Palmer, S. E., Brown, R. A., Rae-Grant, N. I., & Loughlin, M. J. (1999). Responding to children's disclosure of familial abuse: What survivors tell us. *Child Welfare, 78,* 259–82.

Poole, D. A., & Lamb, M. E. (1998). *Investigative interviews of children: A guide for helping professionals.* Washington DC: American Psychological Association.

Poole, D. A., & Lindsay, D. S. (1998). Assessing the accuracy of young children's reports: Lessons from the investigation of child sexual abuse. *Applied & Preventative Psychology, 7,* 1–26.

————. (2002). Children's suggestibility in the forensic context. In M. L. Eisen, J. A. Quas, & G. S. Goodman, (Eds). *Memory and suggestibility in the forensic interview. Personality and clinical psychology series* (pp. 355–81). Mahwah, NJ: Lawrence Erlbaum Associates.

Rao, K., DiClemente, R., & Ponton, L. E. (1992). Child sexual abuse of Asians compared with other populations. *Journal of the American Academy of Child and Adolescent Psychiatry, 31,* 880–86.

Read, J. D., & Lindsay, D.S. (Eds.). (1997) *Recollections of trauma: Scientific research and clinical practice.* NY: Plenum.

Robin, M. (1991). Beyond validation interviews: An assessment approach to evaluating sexual abuse allegations. *Child and Youth Services, 17,* 93–113.

Roesler, T. A. (1994). Reactions to disclosure of childhood sexual abuse: The effect on adult symptoms. *The Journal of Nervous and Mental Disease, 182,* 618–24.

Roesler, T. A., & Wind, T. W. (1994). Telling the secret: Adult women describe their disclosures of incest. *Journal of Interpersonal Violence, 9,* 327–38.

Ross, M. (1989). Relation of implicit theories to the construction of personal histories. *Psychological Review, 96,* 341–57.

Sas, L. D., & Cunningham, A. H. (1995). *Tipping the balance to tell the secret: The public discovery of child sexual abuse.* London, Ontario: London Family Court Clinic.

Schooler, J. W., Ambadar, Z., & Bendiksen, M. A. (1997). A cognitive corroborative case. In D. S. Lindsay (Eds.), *Recollections of trauma: Scientific research and clinical practice* (pp. 379–88). New York: Plenum.

Schooler, J. W., Bendiksen, M. A., & Ambadar, Z. (1997). Taking the middle line: Can we accommodate both fabricated and recovered memories of sexual abuse? In M. Conway (Ed.), *Recovered and False Memories* (pp. 251–92). Oxford: Oxford University Press.

Sgroi, S. M., Bunk, B. S., & Wabrek, C. J. (1988). Children's sexual behaviors and their relationship to sexual abuse. In S. M. Sgroi (Ed.), *Vulnerable populations, Vol. 1: Evaluation and treatment of sexually abused children and adult survivors* (pp. 1–24). Lexington, MA, England: Lexington Books.

Shaw, J. A., Lewis, J. E., Loeb, A., Rosado, J., & Rodriguez, R. A. (2001). A comparison of Hispanic and African-American sexually abused girls and their families. *Child Abuse & Neglect, 25,* 163–1379.

Sjöberg, R. L., & Lindblad, F. (2002). Delayed disclosure and disrupted communication during forensic investigation of child sexual abuse: A study of 47 corroborated cases. *Acta Paediatrica, 91,* 1391–96.

Smith, D., Letourneau, E. J., Saunders, B. E., Kilpatrick, D. G., Resnick, H. S., & Best, C. L. (2000). Delay in disclosure of childhood rape: Results from a national survey. *Child Abuse & Neglect, 24,* 273–87.

Somer, E., & Szwarcberg, S. (2001). Variables in delayed disclosure of childhood sexual abuse. *American Journal of Orthopsychiatry, 71,* 332–41.

Sorensen, T., & Snow, B. (1991). How children tell: The process of disclosure of child sexual abuse. *Child Welfare, 70,* 3–15.

Snow, B., & Sorensen, T. (1990). Ritualistic child abuse in a neighborhood setting. *Journal of Interpersonal Violence, 5,* 474–87.

State v. Hadfield, 788 P.2d 506 (Utah 1990).

Stroud, D., Martens, S. L., & Barker, J. (2000). Criminal investigation of child sexual abuse: A comparison of cases referred to the prosecutor to those not referred. *Child Abuse & Neglect, 24,* 689–700.

Summit, R. C. (1983). The child sexual abuse accommodation syndrome. *Child Abuse & Neglect, 7,* 177–93.

———. (1992). Abuse of the Child Sexual Abuse Accommodation Syndrome. *Journal of Child Sexual Abuse, 1,* 153–63.

Tang, C. S. (2002). Childhood experience of sexual abuse among Hong Kong Chinese college students. *Child Abuse & Neglect, 26,* 23–37.

Toukmanian, S. G., & Brouwers, M. C. (1998). Cultural aspects of self-disclosure and psychotherapy. In S. S. Kazarian & D. R. Evans (Eds.), *Cultural clinical psychology: Theory, research, and practice* (pp. 106–26). New York: Oxford University Press.

Ussher, J. M., & Dewberry, C. (1995). The nature and long-term effects of childhood sexual abuse: A survey of women survivors in Britain. *British Journal of Clinical Psychology, 34,* 177–92.

Wood, B., Orsak, C., Murphy, M., & Cross, H.J. (1996). Semistructured child sexual abuse interviews: Interview and child characteristics related to credibility of disclosure. *Child Abuse & Neglect, 20,* 81–92.

Wood, J. M., & Garven, S. (2000). How sexual abuse interviews go astray: Implications for prosecutors, police, and child protection services. *Child Maltreatment: Journal of the American Professional Society on the Abuse of Children, 5,* 109–18.

Wood, J. M., & Wright, L. (1995). Evaluation of children's sexual behaviors and incorporation of base rates in judgments of sexual abuse. *Child Abuse & Neglect, 19,* 1263–73.

3

False Denials: Overcoming Methodological Biases in Abuse Disclosure Research

Thomas D. Lyon
University of Southern California

When Roland Summit published his paper on child sexual abuse accommodation (Summit, 1983), the notion that sexually abused children disclose abuse only reluctantly and ambivalently was thought "so basic that it contributed nothing new to the literature" (Summit, 1992, p. 155). Summit's paper was neither original research nor a systematic review of research, and he emphasized that his conclusions were largely based on his work as a clinical consultant and "endorsements" from professionals, victims, and their families (Summit, 1983, p. 180).

Summit's reliance on clinical observations left him open to the subsequent criticism that scientific support for child sexual abuse accommodation is lacking (Bradley & Wood, 1996; Kovera & Borgida, 1997; Mason, 1995). Although the courts are friendly to expert testimony supporting accommodation (Lyon, 2002), they have also become accepting of expert testimony attacking accommodation's scientific foundation (Bruck, 1999; United States v. Rouse, 2004). Indeed, one federal court, persuaded by a prominent experimental psychologist that accommodation is no longer accepted in the scientific community, held that defense lawyers confronted with expert testimony supporting accommodation have a constitutional duty to consult with experts capable of disputing such claims (Gersten v. Senkowski, 2004).

Summit's emphasis on the clinical basis for accommodation was unfortunate. Subsequent critics have overlooked research cited by Summit demonstrating low rates of childhood disclosure of sexual abuse in surveys of adults (Finkelhor, 1979; Finkelhor, 1980; Gagnon, 1965; Russell, 1983). Moreover, they have overlooked research that Summit himself neglected to cite, including both surveys of adults (Landis, 1956) and child samples (Conte & Berliner, 1981; DeFrancis, 1969; DeJong, Emmet, & Hervada, 1982; Rimsza & Niggemann, 1982) finding delays in disclosure and relations between a close relationship with the perpetrator and both delays and nondisclosure. Subsequently, nationally representative surveys of adults have confirmed that most of those who state they had been abused as children never disclosed during childhood (Anderson, Martin, Mullen, Romans, & Herbison, 1993; Fleming, 1997; Laumann, Gagnon, Michael, & Michaels, 1994).

Contemporary reviews of the literature have acknowledged that child victims usually delay reporting abuse, and most often never tell anyone (London, Bruck, Ceci & Shuman, chapter 2, this volume, 2005; Lyon, 2002; Paine & Hansen, 2002). At first glance, victims' persistent tendency to endure abuse in silence supports the proposition that many abused children will maintain their silence if questioned about abuse. However, the notion that abused children will deny abuse when questioned has been characterized as a "stubborn urban legend among frontline workers" (Bruck, Ceci, & Hembrooke, 1998). The critics' explanation for the low rates of childhood disclosure in adult surveys is simple: Most never disclosed abuse because *they were never asked*. Rather, the "methodologically superior studies" examining disclosure rates among children suspected of being abused demonstrate that when abused children "are directly asked, they do not deny, but tell" (Bruck & Ceci, 2004, p. 230). Indeed, rates of disclosure among children questioned about abuse run as high as 96% (Bradley & Wood, 1996).

The assertion that false denials of abuse are rare has implications for assessing the reliability of children's disclosures. As disclosure rates approach 100%, false denials approach zero, and a child's denial of abuse becomes conclusive evidence that abuse did not occur. Following a denial with a more leading question, or with a follow-up interview, only risks a false allegation. Consider a case in which a child disclosed, but only after persistent questioning. Imagine that a suggestibility expert believes that the kind of questions asked *might* produce a false allegation in nonabused children. In such a scenario, if false denials are common, then a false allegation is at most a possibility; if false denials are nonexistent, a false allegation is certain. Conversely, as false denials become more frequent, denials provide less compelling evidence to discredit children's disclosures. Moreover, researchers should find means of reducing false denials at the same time that they seek to minimize false allegations.

An emphasis on methodological issues in assessing the literature on disclosure is a positive development in the debate over sexual abuse accommodation. Critics of accommodation have emphasized the false positive problem—the possibility that low rates of disclosure are attributable to high percentages of nonabused children in disclosure research. However, one should be equally cognizant of how research on disclosure is likely to understate reluctance and false denials among children who have been abused. Because disclosure is usually the means by which abuse is suspected and substantiated, samples of children suspected of being abused will inflate abused children's apparent willingness to disclose.

In this chapter I describe these methodological problems more fully, expanding on arguments I have made elsewhere (Lyon, 2002). I show how research on children with gonorrhea can reduce the false positive problem as well as biases due to how abuse is suspected and substantiated. Indeed, review of the research on gonorrhea in children reveals that false denials are quite common, and that medical researchers have understood reluctance and denial of abuse by children for nearly a century (Pollack, 1909). I also address methodological problems that remain, including uncertainties over the kinds of questions asked in interviews and the kinds of answers that qualify as disclosure. Finally, I compare my approach to that of London and colleagues (this volume) and show how an exclusive focus on the false positive problem can obscure evidence of significant rates of false denials.

METHODOLOGICAL ISSUES: FALSE POSITIVES, SUSPICION BIAS, AND SUBSTANTIATION BIAS

There are three major methodological issues in interpreting research on children's willingness to disclose. The first is the false positive problem: We are often unsure whether the children in a sample have in fact been abused. External evidence of sexual abuse is rare and rarely conclusive. If a study finds a low rate of disclosure among children suspected of being sexually abused, this may simply mean that the suspicions were untrue. If children who have not really been abused deny abuse at higher rates than children who have been abused, then samples with large numbers of children falsely believed to have been abused will have lower rates of disclosure. In this volume, London and her colleagues emphasize the false positive problem in interpreting research finding low rates of disclosure.

Whereas the false positive problem may depress observed disclosure rates, two other methodological concerns may, in contrast, inflate disclosure rates. These problems can be called *suspicion bias* and *substantiation bias*. Suspicion bias occurs when disclosure is the reason abuse is suspected in the first place. If disclosure increases suspicions of abuse, the percentage of children disclosing abuse in samples suspected of having been sexually abused will be inflated. Substantiation bias occurs when disclosure is a reason why abuse is substantiated by authorities. If disclosure increases the likelihood that abuse will be substantiated, then the percentage of disclosure in substantiated samples of abuse will be inflated. Both suspicion bias and substantiation bias are likely if disclosure is the primary evidence of abuse.

Suspicion bias may operate in at least two ways. If an abused child never discloses abuse, this may decrease the likelihood that anyone will question the child about abuse. If an abused child shows soft signs of abuse (e.g. sexualized behavior), but does not acknowledge abuse to caretakers, this may decrease the likelihood that anyone will have the child formally evaluated. Children who never tell, or who deny abuse when questioned by caretakers, may, as a result, be disproportionately excluded from samples of children evaluated for suspected sexual abuse.

Suspicion bias is evinced by high rates of prior disclosure in disclosure studies. For example, in Bradley and Wood's sample of children substantiated as sexually abused by social services (1996; Bradley, 1995), at least 72% of the children had previously disclosed abuse. In contrast, national surveys of adults reveal that most victims of sexual abuse report having never disclosed as children, and less than 15% of the cases had been brought to the attention of authorities (Fleming, 1997; Hanson, Resnick, Saunders, Kilpatrick, & Best, 1999; Mullen, Martin, Anderson, Romans, & Herbison, 1993). Hence, a representative sample of abused children would find a lower rate of prior disclosure.[1]

Substantiation bias operates in a similar fashion. Surveys of social workers document that disclosure is the primary means by which sexual abuse cases are substantiated (Everson & Boat, 1989; Haskett, Wayland, Hutcheson, & Tavana, 1995). The substantiation process weeds out children who do not disclose, or whose disclosure does not satisfy legal standards of proof. Substantiation bias operates at every step of the legal process so that the less forthcoming and less consistent child witnesses are less likely to be referred for prosecution by the police (Davis, Hoyano, Keenan, Maitland, & Morgan, 1999; Stroud, Martens, and Barker, 2000) and more likely to be rejected for prosecution by prosecutors (Gray, 1993).

One might try to solve the substantiation bias problem by treating as true all cases suspected of being abused. However, this increases the false positive problem because many suspicions are unfounded. On the other hand, one might try to solve the false positive problem by limiting one's analysis to substantiated cases. This is the solution offered by London and colleagues, who find that substantiated cases show much higher rates of disclosure. But this increases the substantiation bias problem because substantiation is usually dependent upon disclosure (Everson & Boat, 1989; Haskett, Wayland, Hutcheson, & Tavana, 1995). For example, London and colleagues note that disclosure rates in DiPietro, Runyan, and Fredrickson (1997) "increased as a

---

[1] One might argue that the retrospective surveys understate the rate of official intervention because some respondents are reporting abuse falsely or have forgotten that intervention occurred (cf. London et al., chapter 2, this volume). However, to the extent that official intervention is less likely if abuse is never disclosed, the surveys likely exaggerate the rate of official intervention because they miss the victims who maintain their silence about abuse even when questioned by surveyors (Fergusson, Horwood, & Woodward, 2000).

function of abuse certainty," suggesting that as the number of true cases increases, disclosure increases. As the authors of the original research emphasize, however, "the medical opinion of certainty of abuse was related to disclosure which would be expected in that a clear history is a major contributor to diagnoses" (DiPietro, et al., 1997, p. 140).

Insofar as substantiation is dependent on disclosure, focusing on substantiated cases doesn't really solve the false positive problem. Children who disclose abuse may not be telling the truth. Adults may have elicited the abuse disclosures through highly suggestive questioning. Further, in the "push and pull" between substantiation bias and the false positive problem, the suspicion bias problem remains no matter how one decides to count cases as true abuse.

INDEPENDENT CORROBORATIVE EVIDENCE OF ABUSE

The reader has probably wondered by now whether a way out of this dilemma is to focus on those cases for which there is corroborative evidence of abuse. If one can be more confident that children classified as abused were in fact abused, the false positive problem is reduced. If corroborative evidence allows one to substantiate abuse without a disclosure, then substantiation bias is reduced as well. Under some circumstances, corroborative evidence can even reduce suspicion bias. Recall that suspicion bias occurs if abuse is initially suspected because of the disclosure of abuse. If corroborative evidence is the *first* indication that a child has been abused, then suspicion bias is less of a concern.

It is important to add, however, that the corroborative evidence must be *independent* of disclosure. If disclosure increases the likelihood that corroborative evidence will be discovered, or if corroborative evidence increases the likelihood that disclosure will occur, then estimates of disclosure in corroborated cases of sexual abuse will be inflated. As an example of corroboration that is highly dependent upon disclosure, consider a criminal conviction of abuse. Prosecutors will rarely go forward without a disclosure by the child, and subsequent inconsistencies or recantations increase the likelihood of dismissals and, most probably, acquittals. Hence, disclosure rates associated with convictions are likely to be inflated (indeed, they are virtually 100%; Faller & Henry, 2000). Confessions are also sometimes cited as corroborative evidence of abuse. However, confessions are not clearly independent of disclosure. Confessions both trigger disclosure and are triggered by disclosure. If the child has disclosed, this can be a tool to elicit confessions, and if the offender has confessed, this can be a tool to elicit disclosures. This positive relation will inflate disclosure rates in cases with confessions.

Medical evidence of abuse is likely to have fewer dependency problems, although one can speculate about how they might occur. The fact that a child exhibits medical signs of sexual abuse may lead interviewers to push harder to elicit a disclosure. If this does, in fact, increase the likelihood of disclosure, then the percentage of disclosures among cases with medical evidence will be inflated. Conversely, the fact that a child has disclosed abuse may make medical examiners look harder for medical signs of abuse, or may lead them to call ambiguous medical conditions supportive of abuse. To the extent that this increases the likelihood that positive medical evidence will be found, the percentage of disclosures among cases with medical evidence will be inflated. On the other hand, suspicion bias and substantiation bias will be minimized to the extent that the medical condition is both reliably diagnosed and diagnosed without knowledge of the child's disclosure. Examining research on disclosure rates among children with medical evidence of abuse is thus likely to reduce but not eliminate substantiation bias and suspicion bias.

In order to reduce the false positive problem, the corroborative evidence must indeed corroborate abuse. London and colleagues are skeptical that criminal convictions are truly corroborative. The dependency of criminal convictions on disclosure makes them suspect insofar as those disclosures might be the product of suggestibility. Some medical findings occasionally considered corroborative of sexual abuse (e.g. erythema; Gordon & Jaudes, 1996) should also be treated with caution because of their frequent appearance among nonabused children (e.g., Emans, Woods, Flagg, & Freeman, 1987).

GONORRHEA AND DISCLOSURE

Among the most convincing corroborative evidence of sexual abuse is the presence of a sexually transmitted disease (STD) in a child too old to have acquired the disease congenitally. Gonorrhea is considered diagnostic of sexual contact in toddlers and older children (American Academy of Pediatrics Committee on Child Abuse & Neglect, 1998). Examining samples of children diagnosed with gonorrhea makes it possible to avoid the false positive problem (since one is confident the children were, in fact, abused) and to minimize substantiation bias (since abuse can be substantiated without disclosure).

To the extent that suspicions of sexual abuse lead to testing for gonorrhea, however, the suspicion bias problem remains. If disclosure leads to suspicions of abuse, and suspicions lead to testing for gonorrhea that would otherwise go undetected, then disclosure rates among children with gonorrhea will be inflated. Samples of children "suspected of being sexually abused" will exhibit suspicion bias. On the other hand, if gonorrhea is detected without prior suspicions of abuse (as often occurs with the discovery of a genital discharge), then suspicion bias is minimized.

Lawson and Chaffin (1992) examined the rate of nondisclosure among children with sexually transmitted diseases, a large proportion of whom suffered from gonorrhea. The authors excluded children who were so young they may have acquired the STD congenitally, thus minimizing the false positive problem. They excluded children too young to provide a verbal disclosure of abuse, and children who were old enough to have conceivably acquired the STD through consensual sex with peers. In order to minimize suspicion bias, they also excluded children for whom the presenting complaint was sexual abuse. Of course, because STDs are strong evidence of sexual abuse, substantiation bias was also minimized. (There may have been some dependence between the STD finding and disclosure to the extent that interviewers, aware of children's diagnosis, pressed harder for a disclosure.) The authors found that 43% (12/28) of the children made allegations of sexual abuse during the initial interview. Among children whose parents were supportive, 63% (10/16) disclosed abuse. Significantly, these rates of disclosure are among the lowest cited by London and colleagues for substantiated cases of sexual abuse.

London and colleagues take issue with the methodological strengths of the Lawson and Chaffin study. First, they argue that Lawson and Chaffin's sample is unrepresentative because sexual abuse was *not* suspected before the STD was diagnosed. But it is children who *are* suspected of being sexually abused who are unrepresentative of abused children in general (since, according to the retrospective surveys of adults, most abuse is never disclosed in childhood). Moreover, because of suspicion bias, children suspected of having been abused are disproportionately likely to have disclosed abuse. Second, London and colleagues assert that the sample is a small group of "hard core" children who have denied abuse when questioned. But Lawson and Chaffin *excluded* children for whom there had been prior suspicions of abuse. Hence, children who had been questioned about abuse (and either disclosed or denied abuse) were not part of the sample.

Third, London and colleagues assert that because only a small percentage of abused children have STDs, children with STDs are not representative of abused children. While this may be true, London et al. do not explain how this should affect disclosure rates, and in particular why it would lead to an underestimation of disclosure. Given their argument that disclosure rates are not related to other aspects of abuse, it is hard to imagine what would make children with STDs unusually reticent. It may be the case that children diagnosed with STDS have been abused relatively recently (Chaffin, Lawson, Selby, & Wherry, 1997), given the latency periods for occurrence of symptoms. However, a relation between recency of abuse and nondisclosure would also be consistent with child sexual abuse accommodation, according to which children may delay disclosure and initially deny abuse when questioned.

Lawson and Chaffin (1992) are not the only researchers to consider disclosure rates among children with sexually transmitted diseases. Research on children with gonorrhea dates back at least 95 years and reports low rates of disclosure as well as anticipates the themes of sexual abuse accommodation. In 1909, Pollack examined 187 children treated for gonorrhea at the Johns Hopkins hospital, and observed that

> in the *vast majority of cases* no clue to the perpetrator of the crime is ever obtained; often because of the youth of the little patient; at times through the unwillingness of the family to betray one of its members; and again, and perhaps oftenest, because the child has been attacked by a stranger or is too intimidated to tell what she knows (p. 144; emphasis added)

In 1931 Beilin reported on gonorrhea in 91 boys and found that a history of abuse could be established in only 44% (40) of the cases, which included either a disclosure by the child or a history of abuse provided by "parents, relatives, or police officers" (p. 76). Beilin commented:

> Unfortunately, it is often difficult to elicit the true source of infection of the young in spite of the most minute and painstaking inquiries, as the origin in many cases is kept secret very skillfully at times by either the patient, the parent or by both. The reasons for this secrecy would seem to be apparent. The children, through intimidation or through fear of punishment, will not reveal what has happened to them...(p.72).

In 1940, Cohn, Steer,and Adler described 177 girls with gonorrhea, and concluded that "[i]nfection as a result of rape may have occurred in about 8 percent of our children," adding that "[o]bviously, this type of history was not obtainable unless careful, persistent questioning was carried on by some one trained in child psychology" (p. 218).

Because the ages of the children in these early studies are not described, some may have been preverbal and thus unable to disclose abuse. However, this cannot be the sole explanation for the low rates of disclosure. Rice, Cohn, Steer, and Adler (1941) reported on 381 children with gonorrhea and noted that only 35% of "infected girls between the age of 6 years and puberty admitted sexual contacts" (p. 1768).

I have identified 21 subsequent studies (from 1965 to 1993) examining gonorrhea in children from which one can calculate upper bounds of abuse disclosure (see table 3.1). Although some studies explicitly refer to disclosures by children, some refer to a "history" of abuse, which could come from a child or an adult, or a "conclusion" that abuse was involved, which may or may not involve disclosure. For example, Ingram and colleagues (1992) accepted as proof of sexual contact a "history of males isolating themselves with the children under unusual circumstances that the family believed resulted in sexual contact" (p. 995). Despite the fact that this approach exaggerates disclosure rates, the average rate of "disclosure" was only 43% (250/579).[2]

Whenever possible I removed children younger than three years of age, who may be too young to disclose abuse. If one excludes the five studies in which it was impossible to separately analyze children three years and older (4, 14, 17, 18, and 21), the rate of "disclosure" across the remaining 16 studies was 42% (185/437).

Consistent with child sexual abuse accommodation, the authors of these reports frequently emphasized the difficulty that interviewers had in eliciting

---

2 Some of the studies included teenagers, who may have acquired gonorrhea through consensual sex with peers (2, 3, 6, 7, 9, 12, 17). In two studies, it was possible to exclude the oldest group of children, thus excluding teenagers (2, 17).

TABLE 3.1
Studies Reporting Rates of Confirmed Sexual Abuse Among Children With Gonorrhea

Study	Notes
1. Fink (1965), 4 children 4–12 years of age, "possibility" of "sexual contacts" was "denied in all cases" (p. 124).	The complete sample consisted of 6 children from 2 to 12 years of age. Both children and their families were questioned.
2. Branch & Paxton (1965), 25 children 5–9 years of age, 25 "history of sexual contact" (p. 351)	The complete sample consisted of 180 children from birth to 14 years. The history was obtained from the parent if the child was "too young" (p. 349).
3. Nazarian (1967), 6 children 3–14 years of age, 2 "admitted sexual contacts" (p. 372)	The complete sample consisted of 9 children from 11 months to 14 years.
4. Burry and Thurn (1971), 28 children under 10 years of age, "history of definite sexual exposure" obtained in 3 cases (p. 691)	An unspecified number of children may have been preverbal. The authors note that sexual activity was "suspected" in 3 cases.
5. Shore & Winkelstein (1971), 10 children 3–12 years of age, 1 "history of involuntary sexual contact" (p. 662)	The complete sample consisted of 15 children from 21 months to 12 years. In a subsequent letter to the editor (Shore & Winkelstein, 1972), the authors note that "In each of our cases, a careful investigation by a skilled public health nurse and a physician was performed in order to rule out the possibility of sexual contact as the mode of transmission" (p. 193).
6. Allue, Rubio, & Riley (1973), 6 children 3–13 years of age, "sexual contact was admitted" in 2 cases (p. 585).	The complete sample consisted of 15 children from birth to 13 years. Sexual contact was "strongly suspected" in another case, and the authors "presumed" sexual abuse in all six cases of children 3 and older (p. 585).
7. Tomeh & Wilfert (1973), 9 children 4–15, 1 "admitted to sexual contact" and 1 "was known to have any sexual contact" (p. 110)	The complete sample consisted of 19 children from birth to 15 years.
8. Todaro, Controni, & Puig (1974), 31 children 3–11, at most 6 "cases of known sexual assault" (p. 320)	The complete sample consisted of 39 children from 1–11 years. The number of sexual assaults is reported as "at most" 6 because an unspecified proportion of the 6 may have been the children under 3.

(continued)

TABLE 3.1 (*Continued*)
Studies Reporting Rates of Confirmed Sexual Abuse Among Children With Gonorrhea

Study	Notes
9. Dajani (1975), 147 children 4 and older, at most "[p]ositive information for definite sexual contact was elicited from 24 cases" (p. 756).	The complete sample consisted of 222 children as young as neonates. The number of sexual contacts is reported as "at most" because an unspecified proportion may have been under 4. The number of children four and over was derived from bar graphs of the age groups (figure 1, p. 756).
10. Folland, Burke, Hinman, & Schaffner (1977), 43 children 4–9 years of age, at most "history of sexual contact was elicited" from 18 (p. 154).	The complete sample consisted of 73 children from birth to 9 years of age. The authors report whether a history of abuse was obtained only from the 53 children with urethritis or vaginitis. The number of sexual contacts is reported as "at most" because an unspecified proportion may have been under 4. The number of children 4–9 years of age with urethritis or vaginitis was derived from a bar graph (p. 154).
11. Low, Cho, & Dudding (1977), 7 children 3–9 years of age, 1 "admitted sexual abuse" (p. 625)	The complete sample consisted of 11 children 1 month old to 9 years of age. The authors reported "probable sexual abuse" in another case due to a diagnosis of gonorrhea in an uncle (p. 625).
12. Felman, William, & Corsaro (1978), 30 children 3–14 years of age, 29 "seem to have been acquired from direct sexual activity" (p. 253).	In concluding that the source of the infection was sexual, the authors relied on evidence other than disclosure. The authors note that "[a]lthough exposure histories did not always seem accurate, all nine boys apparently acquired their infections through direct sexual activity," and conclude that several girls were abused because of an infection in an older brother from whom "[t]hey were suspected of being infected" (p. 253).
13. Potterat, Markewich, & Rothenberg (1978), 3 children 3–4 years of age, all sexual contact denied.	The complete sample consisted of 4 2–4 year old children.
14. Frewen & Bannatyne (1979), 18 children 2–10 years of age, "definite history of sexual assault or molestation" in 3 cases (p. 492)	

(continued)

TABLE 3.1 (Continued)
Studies Reporting Rates of Confirmed Sexual Abuse Among Children With Gonorrhea

Study	Notes
15. Sgroi (1979), 15 children 4–12 years of age, "direct history of sexual contact was obtained from the infected child" in 8 cases (p. 78)	
16. Meek, Askari, & Belman (1979), 35 children 4–9 years of age, 19 "sexual act or abuse" was "probable or definite" source of infection.	The complete sample consisted of 45 children 1 to 9 years of age.
17. Wald, Woodward, Marston, & Gilbert (1980), 28 children 21 months to 10 years of age, "presumed child abuse" in 24 (p. 42).	The complete sample consisted of 319 children 21 months to 18 years of age. The authors note that "A case was considered to have resulted from sexual abuse when the mother's cultures were negative and the child did not share a bed with an infected parent or sibling" (p. 42).
18. Farrell, Billmire, Shamroy, & Hammond (1981), 46 children from 6 months to 11 years, "history" of "sexual assault" or "sexual play" in 24 (p. 152).	
19. Ingram, White, Durfee, & Pearson (1982), 28 children from 3–12 years of age, "history" of sexual contact in no more than 15 cases (p. 995).	The complete sample consisted of 31 children from 1–12 years of age. The number of children under 3 was calculated by reference to a bar chart (p. 994). The number of sexual contacts is reported as "no more than" because an unspecified proportion may have been under 3.
20. Ingram, Everett, Lyna, White, & Rockwell (1992), 38 children 3–12 years of age, "history" of sexual contact elicited from the child in 33 cases (Fig. 2, p. 946).	The complete sample consisted of 1,538 1–12 year old children evaluated for "possible sexual abuse" (p. 946), and 41 1–12 year old children with gonorrhea (Fig. 2, p. 946).
21. Shapiro, Schubert, & Myers (1993), 22 girls 1–9 years of age, no more than 11 disclosed abuse (p. 343).	The complete sample consisted of 622 girls under 12 seen for suspected sexual abuse or diagnosed with an STD. The rate of disclosure is "at most" 11 of 22 because it cannot be determined if the child whose chief complaint was abuse disclosed or if the history was obtained from another person.

disclosures and that children had in disclosing abuse (Folland, Burke, Hinman, & Schaffner 1977, p. 156:"an accurate history is usually unobtainable"). Ingram, White, Durfee, & Pearson (1982): refer to "difficulties in interviewing young children" and "children and families who were afraid to disclose information because of threats of violence by the male contacts" (p. 996); Nazarian, 1967, p. 374: [i]t is not easy to obtain detailed or honest information on the source of infection in children"; Shapiro et al., 1993, p. 343: '[o]lder children may refuse to disclose abuse because it was a secret that they had agreed to keep or because they may have been threatened with punishment if they made a disclosure"]

The disclosure rate is much lower than that in "substantiated" cases of sexual abuse reviewed by London and colleagues, suggesting that suspicion bias and substantiation bias affected their analysis. Suspicion bias was minimized in most of the studies reviewed here due to the process by which samples were constructed: children with STDs were identified, rather than children who were suspected of being abused.

Suspicion bias was not always avoided, however. If suspicions of sexual abuse are predominantly aroused by disclosure, then samples of children suspected of being abused will have inflated rates of disclosure. Suspicion bias will affect disclosure rates even in children ultimately found to exhibit medical evidence of abuse. Moreover, if medical evaluation is the result of suspicions of sexual abuse (which themselves are raised by disclosure) (e.g., Ingram et al., 1992), then one will see an artificially high rate of disclosure among children with STDs. For example, in Heger, Ticson, Velasquez, and Bernier's (2002) study, of the sample of children with diagnostic medical evidence of sexual abuse, 82% were referred for medical evaluation only *after* disclosing abuse. Ingram et al. (1992) selected children "being evaluated for possible sexual abuse" (p. 945), and reported that a high percentage of children with gonorrhea (87%: 33/38) eventually disclosed abuse. (As discussed below, multiple interviews may have also played a part in these relatively high rates of disclosure.)

WHAT QUESTIONS WERE ASKED? WHAT ANSWERS EQUALED DISCLOSURE?

There was a great deal of variability among the gonorrhea studies in rates of disclosure. Since this cannot be attributable to different rates of true abuse, one must ask what else affected disclosure. One reason has already been discussed: the studies differ in their definition of what qualifies as a history of abuse. A second reason is that there is no standardization of interviewing practices across studies. The lack of specificity regarding the questions asked or the statements made by children make it difficult to determine the role that direct and potentially suggestive interviewing played in affecting disclosure rates. These problems plague not only the gonorrhea studies reviewed here but also virtually all the research on disclosure, including that reviewed by London and colleagues.

In some studies, disclosure rates may have been inflated by the use of interviewing techniques that have been criticized as unduly leading. In an acknowledgement of what is currently known as "interviewer bias" (Bruck, Ceci, & Hembrooke, 1998), Sgroi (1979) admitted that "[t]he interviewer's and consultants' presumption that child sexual assault is a causative factor in the transmission of pediatric gonorrhea undoubtedly influenced the results" (p. 81). Drawings and dolls have been criticized as potentially eliciting false reports from children who have not been abused (Bruck, Ceci, & Francouer, 2000; Bruck, Ceci, Francouer, & Renick, 1995; Bruck, Melnyk, & Ceci, 2000). Farrell, Billmire, Shamroy, & Hammond (1981) accepted as disclosures drawings and doll play among children too young to provide a verbal history, and Ingram et al. (1992) interviewed children with the assistance of anatomically correct dolls. Branch and Paxton (1965) interviewed children (or their parents) "by showing a diagram of the anatomy and explaining the mechanism by which he or she became infected" (p. 349) (cf. Folland et al, 1997, who characterized Branch and Paxton's approach as "intensive interviews").

Repeated interviewing has also been criticized as unduly leading (Bruck, Ceci, & Hembrooke, 1998). Although most of the studies do not report the number of interviews, it is clear that gradual or incremental disclosure was quite common among children who ultimately disclosed. Sgroi (1979) noted that "[s]everal interviews may be necessary to enlist the confidence of the child to a degree that will permit the child to share the 'secret' of his/her sexual behavior with someone else" (p. 82). Similarly, Ingram et al (1992) "extensively interviewed" children on one or more visits in order to elicit a history of sexual contact, and emphasized that "[i]t may take multiple interviews over years to obtain this history" (p. 948).

In three studies one can calculate rates of incremental disclosure. In Farrell et al. (1981), 24 children ultimately provided a history of sexual contact. At most, 7 children disclosed sexual contact when seen in the emergency room.[3] Hence, of those children who ultimately disclosed, at least 71% (17/24) failed to disclose abuse when first questioned. As the authors conclude, "Our data support that of other investigators that a history of exposure to gonorrhea is infrequently obtained during the initial interview. We have demonstrated that when these same children are hospitalized and interviewed repeatedly by a skilled and sympathetic social worker, they often do give a history of exposure" (p. 152). Similarly, in Ingram et al. (1982), no more than 5 of the 29 girls with gonorrhea named a sexual contact during the first interview, whereas 13 had done so after "further interviews" (p. 995). Hence, of those who ultimately disclosed, at least 62% (8/13) did not do so initially. In Shapiro et al. (1993),

---

[3] Specifically, the researchers report that a "history of exposure to gonorrhea . . . was elicited during the initial emergency room interview in only seven of the 46 children" (p. 152). A history could mean a disclosure, but it could also mean identification of another family member with gonorrhea.

the authors noted that of the 10 children whose chief complaint was vaginitis at the initial visit but who ultimately disclosed abuse, only 1 of the 10 disclosed at the initial emergency room visit (p. 343).

In sum, the studies examining nondisclosure among children with gonorrhea present convincing evidence that a large percentage of sexually abused children do not disclose abuse, even when questioned, and that high rates of disclosure in some studies can be attributed to suspicion bias, substantiation bias, and differences both in what constitutes appropriate interviewing and in what equals disclosure. Furthermore, the studies support the proposition that although abused children may initially deny abuse, repeated interviewing may eventually elicit disclosures. Unfortunately, these disclosures may have been elicited in some cases through the use of interviewing techniques that risk false allegations, necessitating further work on non-leading techniques for overcoming reluctance to disclose.

It is important to keep in mind that the *ultimate* rate of disclosure should be quite high, even assuming sexual abuse accommodation. The argument is not that abused children will never disclose abuse when interviewed but rather that multiple interviews may be necessary. Research that has traditionally been cited as supporting accommodation finds high rates of ultimate disclosure. In the Lawson and Chaffin (1992) sample of children with STDS, most of whom did not initially disclose, Chaffin and colleagues (1997) found that four of the five nondisclosers they were able to locate had eventually disclosed abuse.

The research on childhood gonorrhea is also consistent with other research in which abuse is initially suspected and verified without reliance on the child's disclosure. Muram, Speck and Gold (1992) medically examined girls for whom suspicions of abuse had not arisen but who were siblings or associates of girls known to have been abused. Of the 35 girls with medical findings specific to abuse (such as hymenal tears), 51% (18/35) disclosed abuse when questioned. Sjöberg and Lindblad (2002) examined the disclosure histories of ten children who had not been suspected of being abused but whose abuse was documented on videotapes made by the perpetrator. Half (5/10) of the children disclosed sexual abuse in a forensic interview. Cederborg, Lamb, and Laurell (chapter 9, this volume) have examined the possible reasons for nondisclosure in this sample and conclude that it can be attributed largely to immaturity and fear.

THE CONSEQUENCES OF FOCUSING ON THE FALSE POSITIVE PROBLEM

I have argued elsewhere that the research on disclosure supports child sexual abuse accommodation (Lyon, 2002) and have reiterated and elaborated on some of those arguments here. London and colleagues (this volume) review much of the same literature, and arrive at the opposite conclusion. What explains our differences? I believe that our different interpretations and conclusions are primarily attributable to differing approaches to the false positive problem, suspicion bias, and substantiation bias. London and colleagues justifiably worry about the false positive problem but do not take account of suspicion bias or substantiation bias; indeed, their approach accentuates the effects of these biases on disclosure rates. The failure to take account of suspicion bias is illustrated by London et al's criticism that Lawson and Chaffin (1992) selected cases without suspicions of abuse; however, selecting cases on the grounds that abuse *is* suspected accentuates suspicion bias. Moreover, London et al's concern with the false positive problem is not balanced by recognition of the possibility of substantiation bias; selecting cases on the basis of substantiation accentuates substantiation bias.

Our different approaches are reflected in our respective analyses of disclosure rates among children with corroborative evidence of abuse. I have argued that if certain conditions are satisfied, corroborative evidence may enable us to avoid the false positive problem, suspicion bias, and substantiation bias. In contrast, London and colleagues consider corroborative evidence relevant in considering the false positive problem only. They note that because "classification of abuse was often based in part upon children's disclosures . . . the conclusion that abused children do disclose abuse during formal interviews may be circular," and cite three studies to support the notion that "when children are classified as abused based on medical evidence or on other nonchild factors (confession, material evidence) . . . most of these children do disclose abuse" (London et al., chapter 2, this volume).

All three cited studies (Dubowitz et al., 1992; Elliott & Briere, 1994; Gordon & Jaudes, 1996) were based on samples of children suspected of having been sexually abused. In Gordon and Jaudes (1996), the sample was particularly selective: All children had been "identified by the screening interview as probably victims of sexual abuse" (p. 316). Because of suspicion bias, the resulting disclosure rates are likely to be inflated. Unfortunately, none of the studies report the overall percentage of children who had disclosed prior to the first evaluation.

These three studies do provide an opportunity to reduce the false positive problem and substantiation bias, however. Of course, to truly correct for the false positive problem, the evidence must be truly corroborative. London and colleagues warn that some types of medical evidence are weak evidence of abuse. As noted above, erythema or redness of the genitalia is weak evidence, whereas STDs can be very strong evidence. In order to correct for substantiation bias, the corroborative evidence should be independent of disclosure. Disclosure should not make it more likely that the corroborative evidence will be produced, and the corroborative evidence should not make it more likely that the child will disclose. As I've argued above, medical evidence is likely to be less dependent on disclosure than many other types of corroborative evidence, such as a confession or a criminal conviction.

One can compare overall rates of disclosure with rates of disclosure among cases with independent corroborative evidence in order to determine if the false positive problem exists or if there is substantiation bias. If false suspicions are a serious problem, leading to lower rates of disclosure, then focusing on cases with strongly corroborative medical evidence ought to lead to higher rates of disclosure. This is because false cases (for which disclosure rates will be lower than for true cases) will be weeded out. On the other hand, if substantiation bias is a serious problem, then focusing on cases with convincing evidence ought to lead to lower rates of disclosure. This is because true cases will not be excluded simply because the child failed to disclose.

As with the research on disclosure rates among children with gonorrhea, we do not know what questions were asked in these studies and have limited information regarding the nature of children's disclosures. We should pay close attention to what constitutes a disclosure, and the definition of disclosure should remain consistent when considering cases with and without external evidence of abuse. For example, disclosure should not be defined more liberally when considering cases with external evidence, and more stringently when considering cases without such evidence.

The Gordon and Jaudes (1996) study, in fact, reveals the effects of substantiation bias on disclosure rates. Gordon and Jaudes found that children were significantly more likely to have disclosed in cases substantiated by the state, consistent with substantiation bias. Moreover, children were significantly less likely to have disclosed when they were diagnosed with an STD, which is also consistent with substantiation bias and inconsistent with the false positive problem. At the investigative interview, 43% (6/14) of the children with an STD disclosed sexual abuse, compared to the 74% disclosure rate calculated by London and colleagues (103/141) (Gordon & Jaudes, 1996, table 2, p. 319). Discussing the low rates of disclosure among children with STDs, Gordon and Jaudes conclude "[t]his is consistent with observations by Lawson and Chaffin (1992)" (p. 320).

London and colleagues' interpretation of Gordon and Jaudes's data obscures these differences. They report a 78% disclosure rate among children with medical evidence of abuse, but medical evidence included erythema, which has little diagnostic value. Moreover, the 78% figure exaggerates disclosure because it included a "history" of abuse, which, as London and colleagues emphasize when calculating recantation rates, could mean a report of abuse provided by the parent at the emergency room visit. (This problem is reminiscent of the difficulties in interpreting "history" percentages in the gonorrhea research.)

Elliott and Briere (1994) do not report results for medical evidence specifically, but they include medical findings along with confessions, eyewitnesses, and other evidence, all of which are likely to be somewhat dependent upon disclosure. Nevertheless, their results suggest that substantiation bias inflates disclosure rates because they find a disclosure rate of 67% among children with external evidence of abuse (79/118) compared to a rate of 85% (209/248) among what London and colleagues call "substantiated cases." London and colleagues report an 84% disclosure rate among children with external evidence of abuse, obscuring this difference. As with the results of Gordon and Jaudes (1996), London et al. calculate disclosure rates among the external evidence group more liberally than among the substantiated group; children who had "previously" disclosed were counted as disclosers when calculating disclosure rates for children with external evidence of abuse but not when calculating disclosure rates for children with substantiated abuse.[4]

In Dubowitz, Black, & Harrington (1992), there was little evidence of substantiation bias, and no evidence of the false positive problem. However, the rates of disclosure were quite low. Whereas 49% (31/63) of what London and colleagues' called "substantiated" cases involved a "clear verbal disclosure" of abuse, 46% (13/28) of cases with medical evidence of abuse were accompanied by a clear verbal disclosure.[5] These low rates of disclosure contrast with the disclosure rates reported by London and colleagues for the same sample: 83% among substantiated cases and 75% among cases with medical evidence. The explanation is that London and colleagues counted as disclosures what Dubowitz et al (1992) characterize as "suggestive doll play or an inconclusive account of alleged abuse" (p. 690). Whether these would be considered disclosures given today's standards is questionable.

Across the three studies, the disclosure rate drops when one focuses on more probative medical or other external evidence of abuse. This is consistent with the substantiation bias problem leading to elevated disclosure rates, and inconsistent with the false positive problem. Moreover, nondisclosure rates are quite high in these studies, despite the fact that the samples were comprised of children evaluated for suspicions of abuse and thus subject to suspicion bias. Even using a liberal definition of disclosure in the Dubowitz et al (1992) study, 25% of children with medical evidence of abuse did not disclose.

DISCUSSION

I have argued in this chapter that nondisclosure of sexual abuse among truly abused children is a real and serious phenomenon. When suspicion bias and substantiation bias are minimized, only about half of abused children questioned about abuse disclosed. Because rates of denial are substantially higher

---

[4] London and colleagues count as disclosures both what Elliott and Briere (1994) referred to as "credible" disclosures and as "partial" disclosures. If one limits one's consideration to "credible" disclosures, they occurred among 43% of the children with external evidence of abuse (51/118), compared to 60% of the substantiated cases (149/248).

[5] The strength of the medical evidence is somewhat unclear. The authors refer to medical evidence "indicative" of sexual abuse, although they found no cases of STDs and no acute trauma.

than zero, denial is neither conclusive nor particularly compelling evidence that a child was not abused. This does not mean that a child's denial is irrelevant. As long as nonabused children are more likely to deny abuse than abused children, a denial of abuse is some evidence that abuse did not occur. But to the extent that denial rates are surprisingly high, an expert can justifiably testify that denials are surprisingly weak evidence against abuse.

The methodological analysis here can be utilized in considering other controversies regarding sexual abuse accommodation. For example, how common is recantation among children? London and colleagues make the same argument that they make with respect to initial rates of disclosure: High rates of recantation are attributable to high rates of false allegations. Hence, the 22% rate of recantation in Sorensen and Snow (1991) is attributable to the authors' suggestive questioning practices, which likely led nonabused children to disclose and then recant, whereas the 4% rate of recantation in Bradley and Wood (1996) is attributable to the care with which cases were substantiated as true. However, a review of the numbers cited by London and colleagues reveals support for the effects of substantiation bias on recantation rates: the overall rate of recantation in Elliott and Briere (1994) was 17% among cases with external evidence of abuse, more than twice as high as the rate among substantiated cases (8%). The original research paper makes the substantiation problem explicit: Recantations were *always* excluded from the substantiated group unless there was external evidence of abuse (Elliott & Briere, 1993). Hence, substantiation reduces the apparent rate of recantation, whereas examining cases with corroborating evidence of abuse provides a fairer estimate.

I would hasten to add, however, that reluctance among abused children does not justify suggestive questioning techniques. Suspected abuse samples are made up of children unusually ready and willing to disclose when questioned—most of them have disclosed abuse before. As Lamb and his colleagues have demonstrated, when children in these samples disclose, most are able to do so without suggestive questioning (Lamb, Sternberg, Orbach, Esplin, Stewart, & Mitchell, 2003; Sternberg, Lamb, Orbach, & Esplin, 2001).

The pressing issue is what to do about the 20% of children who have heretofore been excluded from Lamb and colleagues' samples because they failed to disclose. If we believe that true disclosure is close to 100%, then we are not inclined to worry about them. They would most appropriately be considered cases of unfounded suspicions or false allegations. If we recognize that reluctance is real, however, and that a truly representative sample is likely to include children who were abused but deny it when questioned, then we must worry. We can utilize methods we know to be suggestive, but we risk increasing false allegations without being sure that our methods elicit more true reports. Alternatively, we can expend more energy researching means of overcoming reluctance. Fortunately, this volume reflects a growing awareness among child witness researchers of the significance of reluctance and false denials.

REFERENCES

Allue, X., Rubio, T., & Riley, H. D. (1973). Gonococcal infections in infants and children: Lessons from fifteen cases. *Clinical Pediatrics, 12,* 584–88.

American Academy of Pediatrics Committee on Child Abuse & Neglect (1998). Gonorrhea in prepubertal children. *Pediatrics, 101,* 134–35.

Anderson, J., Martin, J., Mullen, P., Romans, S., & Herbison, P. (1993). Prevalence of childhood sexual abuse experiences in a community sample of women. *Journal of the American Academy of Child and Adolescent Psychiatry, 32,* 911–19.

Beilin, L. M. (1931). Gonorrheal urethritis in male children (with some observations on their sexual impulses). *Journal of Urology, 25,* 69–84.

Bradley, A. R. (1995). *How do children tell? The disclosure process in child sexual abuse.* Unpublished Master's Thesis, University of Texas at El Paso.

Bradley, A. R., & Wood, J. M. (1996). How do children tell? The disclosure process in child sexual abuse. *Child Abuse & Neglect, 9,* 881–91.

Branch, G., & Paxton, R. (1965). A study of gonococcal infections among infants and children. *Public Health Reports, 80,* 347–52.

Bruck, M. (1999). A Summary of an Affidavit Prepared for Commonwealth of Massachusetts v. Cheryl Amirault LeFave. *Applied Developmental Science, 3,* 110–27.

Bruck, M., & Ceci, S. J. (2004). Forensic developmental psychology: Unveiling four common misconceptions. *Current Directions in Psychological Science, 13,* 229–32.

Bruck, M., Ceci, S. J., & Francouer, E. (2000). Children's use of anatomically detailed dolls to report genital touching in a medical examination: Developmental and gender comparisons. *Journal of Experimental Psychology: Applied, 6,* 74–83.

Bruck, M., Ceci, S. J., Francouer, E., & Renick, A. (1995). Anatomically detailed dolls do not facilitate preschoolers' reports of a pediatric examination involving genital touching. *Journal of Experimental Psychology: Applied, 1,* 95–109.

Bruck, M., Ceci, S. J., & Hembrooke, H. (1998). Reliability and credibility of young children's reports: From research to policy and practice. *American Psychologist, 53,* 136–51.

Bruck, M., Melnyk, L., & Ceci, S. J. (2000). Draw it again Sam: The effect of drawing on children's suggestibility and source monitoring ability. *Journal of Experimental Child Psychology, 77,* 169–96.

Burry, V. F., & Thurn, A. N. (1971). Goncoccal infections in prepubertal children. *Missouri Medicine, 68,* 691–92.

Chaffin, M., Lawson, L., Selby, A., & Wherry, J. N. (1997). False negatives in sexual abuse interviews: Preliminary investigation of a relationship to dissociation. *Journal of Child Sexual Abuse, 6,* 15–29.

Cohn, A., Steer, A., & Adler, E. L. (1940). Gonococcal vaginitis: A preliminary report on one year's work. *Venereal Disease Information, 21,* 208–20.

Conte, J. R., & Berliner, L. (1981). Sexual abuse of children: Implications for practice. *Social Casework, 61,* 601–6.

Dajani, A. S. (1975). Symptomatic gonococcal infections of children: A seven year experience in metropolitan Detroit. *Michigan Medicine, 74,* 755–63.

Davis, G., Hoyano, L, Keenan, C., Maitland, L, & Morgan, R. (1999). *The admissibility and sufficiency of evidence in child abuse prosecutions.* Home Office Research and Statistics Department Research Findings No. 100.

De Francis, V. (1969). *Protecting the child victim of sex crimes committed by adults.* Denver, CO: American Human Association.

DeJong, A. R., Emett, G. A., & Hervada, A. R. (1982). Sexual abuse of children. *American Journal of Diseases of Children, 136*, 129–34

DiPietro, E. K., Runyan, D. K., & Fredrickson, D. D. (1997). Predictors of disclosure during medical evaluation for suspected sexual abuse. *Journal of Child Sexual Abuse, 6*, 133–42.

Dubowitz, H., Black, M., & Harrington, D. (1992). The diagnosis of child sexual abuse. *American Journal of Diseases of Children, 146*, 688–93.

Elliott, D. M., & Briere, J. (1994). Forensic sexual abuse evaluations of older children: Disclosures and symptomatology. *Behavioral Sciences and the Law, 21*, 261–77.

Emans, S. J., Woods, E. R., Flagg, N. J., & Freeman, A. (1987). Genital findings in sexually abused, symptomatic and asymptomatic girls, *Pediatrics, 79*, 78–785.

Everson, M. D., & Boat, B. W. (1989). False allegations of sexual abuse by children and adolescents. *Journal of the American Academy of Child and Adolescent Psychiatry, 28*, 230–35.

Faller, K. C., & Henry, J. (2000). Child sexual abuse: A case study in community collaboration. *Child Abuse & Neglect, 24*, 1215–25.

Farrell, M. K., Billmire, E., Shamroy, J. A., & Hammond, J. G. (1981). Prepubertal gonorrhea: A multidisciplinary approach. *Pediatrics, 67*, 151–53.

Felman, Y. M., William, D. C., & Corsaro, M. C. (1978). Gonococcal infections in children 14 years and younger. *Clinical Pediatrics, 17*, 252–54.

Fergusson, D. M., Horwood, L. J., & Woodward, L. J. (2000). The stability of child abuse reports: A longitudinal study of the reporting behaviour of young adults. *Psychological Medicine, 30*, 529–44.

Fink, C. W. (1965). Gonococcal arthritis in children. *Journal of the American Medical Association, 194*, 123–24.

Finkelhor, D. (1979). *Sexually victimized children.* New York: Free Press.

———. (1980). Risk factors in the sexual victimization of children. *Child Abuse & Neglect, 4*, 265–73.

Fleming, J. M. (1997). Prevalence of childhood sexual abuse in a community sample of Australian women. *Medical Journal of Australia, 166*, 65–68.

Folland, D. S., Burke, R. E., Hinman, A. R., & Schaffner, W. (1977). Gonorrhea in preadolescent children: An inquiry into source of infection and mode of transmission. *Pediatrics, 60*, 153–53.

Frewen, T. C., & Bannatyne, R. B. (1979). Gonococcal Vulvovaginitis in prepubertal girls. *Clinical Pediatrics, 18*, 491–93.

Gagnon, J. H. (1965). Female child victims of sex offenses. *Social Problems, 13*, 176–92.

Gersten v. Senkowski, 299 F.Supp.2d 84 (S.D.N.Y. 2004).

Gordon, S., & Jaudes, P. K. (1996). Sexual abuse evaluations in the emergency department: Is the history reliable? *Child Abuse & Neglect, 20*, 315–22.

Gray, E. (1993). *Unequal justice: The prosecution of child sexual abuse.* New York: Free Press.

Hanson, R. F., Resnick, H. S., Saunders, B. E., Kilpatrick, D. G., & Best, C. (1999). Factors related to the reporting of childhood rape. *Child Abuse & Neglect, 23*, 559–69.

Haskett, M. E., Wayland, K., Hutcheson, J. S., & Tavana, T. (1995). Substantiation of sexual abuse allegations: Factors involved in the decision-making process. *Journal of Child Sexual Abuse, 4*, 19–47.

Heger, A., Ticson, L., Velasquez, O. & Bernier, R. (2002). Children referred for possible sexual abuse: medical findings in 2384 children. *Child Abuse & Neglect, 26*, 645–59.

Ingram, D. L., Everett, V. D., Lyna, P. R., White, S. T., & Rockwell, L. A. (1992). Epidemiology of adult sexually transmitted disease agents in children being evaluated for sexual abuse. *Pediatric Infectious Disease Journal, 11,* 945–50.

Ingram, D. L., White, S. T., Durfee, M. F., & Pearson, A. W. (1982). Sexual contact in children with gonorrhea. *American Journal of Diseases of Children, 136,* 994–96.

Kovera, M. B., & Borgida, E. (1997). Expert testimony in child sexual abuse trials: The admissibility of psychological science. *Applied Cognitive Psychology, 11,* S105-29.

Lamb, M. E., Sternberg, K. J., Orbach, Y., Esplin, P. W., Stewart, H., & Mitchell, S. (2003). Age differences in young children's responses to open-ended invitations in the course of forensic interviews. *Journal of Consulting & Clinical Psychology, 71,* 926–34.

Landis, J. T. (1956). Experiences of 500 children with adult sexual deviation. *Psychiatric Quarterly Supplement, 30,* 91–109.

Laumann, E. O., Gagnon, J. H., Michael, R. T., & Michaels, S. (1994). *The social organization of sexuality: Sexual practices in the United States.* Chicago: University of Chicago Press.

Lawson, L., & Chaffin, M. (1992). False negatives in sexual abuse disclosure interviews: Incidence and influence of caretaker's belief in abuse in cases of accidental abuse discovery by diagnosis of STD. *Journal of Interpersonal Violence, 7,* 532–42.

London, K., Bruck, M., Ceci, S. J., & Shuman, D. W. (2005). Disclosure of child sexual abuse: What does the research tell us about the ways that children tell? *Psychology, Public Policy, and the Law. 11,* 194–226.

Low, R. C., Cho, C. T., & Dudding, B. A. (1977). Gonococcal infections in young children: Studies on the social, familial, and clinical aspects of 11 instances. *Clinical Pediatrics, 16,* 623–26.

Lyon, T. D. (2002). Scientific support for expert testimony on child sexual abuse accommodation in J. R. Conte (Ed.), *Critical issues in child sexual abuse* (pp. 107–38). Newbury Park, CA: Sage.

Mason, M. A. (1995). The child sex abuse syndrome: The other major issue in State of New Jersey v. Margaret Kelly Michaels. *Psychology, Public Policy, & Law, 1,* 399–410.

Meek, J. M., Askari, A., & Belman, A. B. (1979). Prepubertal gonorrhea. *Journal of Urology, 122,* 532–34.

Mullen, P. E., Martin, J. L., Anderson, J. C., Romans, S. E., & Herbison, G. P. (1993). Childhood sexual abuse and mental health in adult life. *British Journal of Psychiatry, 163,* 721–32.

Muram, D., Speck, P. M., & Gold, S. S. (1991). Genital abnormalities in female siblings and friends of child victims of sexual abuse. *Child Abuse & Neglect, 15,* 105–10.

Nazarian, L. F. (1967). The current prevalence of gonoccoccal infections in children. *Pediatrics, 39,* 372–77.

Paine, M. L., & Hansen, D. J. (2002). Factors influencing children to self-disclose sexual abuse. *Clinical Psychology Review, 22,* 271–95.

Pollack, F. (1909). The acquired venereal diseases in children: A report of 187 children treated in the women's venereal department of the Johns Hopkins Hospital Dispensary. *Johns Hopkins Hospital Bulletin, 218,* 142–49.

Pottertat, J. J., Markewich, G. S., & Rothenberg, R. (1978). Prepubertal infections with Neisseria gonorrhoeae: Clinical and epidemiological significance. *Sexually Transmitted Disease, 5,* 1–3.

Rice, J. L., Cohn, A., Steer, A., & Adler, E. L. (1941). Recent investigations on gonococcic vaginitis. *Journal of the American Medical Association, 117,* 1766–69.

Rimsza, M. E., & Niggemann, M. S. (1982). Medical evaluation of sexually abused children: A review of 311 cases. *Pediatrics, 69*, 8–14.

Russell, D. E. H. (1983). The incidence and prevalence of intrafamilial and extrafamilial sexual abuse and female children. *Child Abuse and Neglect, 7*, 133–46.

Sgroi, S. M.(1979). Pediatric gonorrhea beyond infancy. *Pediatric Annals, 8*, 73–87.

Shapiro, R. A., Schubert, C. J., & Myers, P. A. (1993). Vaginal discharge as an indicator of gonorrhea and chlamydia infection in girls under 12 years old. *Pediatric Emergency Care, 9*, 341–45.

Shore, W. B., & Winkelstein, J. A. (1971). Nonvenereal transmission of gonococcal infections in children. *Journal of Pediatrics, 79*, 661–63.

———. (1972). Gonococcal infections in children: Reply. *Journal of Pediatrics, 81*, 193.

Sjöberg, R. L., & Lindblad, F. (2002). Limited disclosure of sexual abuse in children whose experiences were documented by videotape. *American Journal of Psychiatry, 159*, 312–14.

Sternberg, K. J., Lamb, M. E., Orbach, Y., & Esplin, P. (2001). Use of a structured investigative protocol enhances young children's responses to free-recall prompts in the course of forensic interviews. *Journal of Applied Psychology, 86*, 997–1005.

Stroud, D. D., Martens, S. L., & Barker, J. (2000). Criminal investigation of child sexual abuse: A comparison of cases referred to the prosecutor to those not referred. *Child Abuse and Neglect, 24*, 689–700.

Summit, R. C. (1983). The child sexual abuse accommodation syndrome. *Child Abuse & Neglect, 7*, 177–93.

———. (1992). Abuse of the child sexual abuse accommodation syndrome. *Journal of Child Sexual Abuse, 1*, 153–63.

Todaro, J. L., Controni, G., & Puig, J. R. (1974). Gonorrhea in prepubertal children. *Clinical Proceedings of the Children's Hospital National Medical Center, 30*, 317–24.

Tomeh, M. O., & Wilfert, C. M. (1973). Venereal diseases of infants and children at Duke University Medical Center. *North Carolina Medical Journal, 34*, 109–13.

United States v. Rouse 2004 DSD 14 (D.S.D. 2004) (available at http://www.sdbar.org/opinions/DSD/2004/2004dsd014.htm).

Wald, E. R., Woodward, C. L., Marston, G., & Gilbert, L. M. (1980). Gonorrheal disease among children in a university hospital. *Sexually Transmitted Disease, 7*, 41–43.

II
NEW DATA AND PERSPECTIVES ON WHEN AND WHY CHILDREN FAIL TO DISCLOSE ABUSE

4

Individual and Family Variables Associated with Disclosure and Nondisclosure of Child Abuse in Israel

Irit Hershkowitz
School of Social Work, University of Haifa, Israel

Dvora Horowitz
Ministry of Labour and Social Affairs, Jerusalem

Michael E. Lamb
University of Cambridge, United Kingdom

When alleged victims fail to report their abuse when questioned about it, it is more difficult to protect both them and other children from further victimization, provide appropriate mental health services when those are warranted, or punish perpetrators. As a result, it is extremely important to determine both how often and why suspected victims do not disclose abuse when interviewed and also what distinguishes those who do disclose from those who do not. Estimates of the number of suspected victims who are actual victims vary widely, however, for a variety of reasons. Firstly, most studies involve small, selective, and unrepresentative samples, and this impedes generalization, particularly because the results reported by different researchers are often widely discrepant (London et al., chapter 2, this volume). Secondly, the way children are interviewed may powerfully influence whether they make allegations. For example, there is convincing evidence that leading and coercive practices, repeated questioning, or reliance on anatomically detailed dolls substantially affect what children say (e.g., Ceci & Bruck, 1995). Most studies of disclosure and nondisclosure do not provide sufficient information about the types of interviewing involved, but some professionals (e.g., London et al., chapter 2, this volume; Poole & Lindsay, 1998) have sharply criticized the interviewing procedures used in some of the most widely cited studies (Gonzalez, Waterman, Kelly, McCord, & Oliveri, 1993; Sorensen & Snow, 1991) arguing that they make it hard to determine whether the disclosures were valid. The present study is distinguished by its reliance on a complete national data set comprising all investigations conducted during a five-year period using a single standardized investigative interview protocol.

In the last decade, researchers have learned a great deal about the factors and conditions that influence the accuracy and reliability of children's reports of abuse (see Pipe, Lamb, Orbach, & Esplin, 2004, and Poole & Lamb, 1998, for reviews). This progress has facilitated attempts to develop investigative protocols that guide interviewers to employ "best practices" when interviewing alleged victims. One of those protocols, the NICHD investigative interview protocol (Orbach, Hershkowitz, Lamb, Sternberg, Esplin, & Horowitz, 2000), was partially developed and field-tested in Israel, and its use has been mandatory nationwide for investigations of child sexual abuse since 1995 and for investigations of physical child abuse since 1998.

The NICHD protocol guides interviewers in detail through all phases of the investigative interview. In the introductory phase, the interviewer introduces himself or herself, clarifies the child's task, and explains the ground rules and expectations. The rapport-building phase that follows comprises two sections. The first is designed to create a relaxed, supportive environment for children and to establish rapport between the child and the interviewer. In the second, children are prompted to describe at least one neutral experienced event in detail so that the child understands his or her role as a crucial informant and can become familiar with the open-ended investigative strategies and techniques used to explore the alleged abuse.

The "getting the allegation" phase initiates the substantive parts of the interview using a graded series of prompts, progressing if necessary from open to focused, in an effort to identify the target event or events under investigation. The free recall phase follows as soon as the child mentions an incident that might be considered abusive. This phase begins with the main invitation ("Tell me everything that happened, from the beginning to the end, as best you can remember"). Follow up open-ended prompts and paired invitations are then used to elicit details about the alleged incident or incidents from free recall memory. Only after the open-ended questioning has been exhausted do interviewers move to focused questions. Suggestive utterances, which communicate what response is expected, are avoided throughout the interview.

A NATIONAL DATA BASE

The results reported below involve all child abuse investigations conducted in Israel between January 1, 1998, and December 31, 2002, during which time all youth investigators used the NICHD protocol in the course of their investigations. A total of 26,325 3- to 14-year-old alleged victims of sexual and physical abuse were involved. All the children were interviewed using the 1998 version of the National Institute of Child Health and Human Development (NICHD) protocol described by Orbach et al. (2000). A total of 140 experienced and trained youth investigators conducted all the investigative interviews.

FACTORS ASSOCIATED WITH DISCLOSURE AND NONDISCLOSURE

Just under two-thirds (17,174, 65.2%) of the children interviewed made an allegation during the investigative interview whereas a little over a third (9,151, 34.8%) did not. Children were significantly less likely to make allegations when physical (9,362, 60.9%) rather than sexual (7,813, 71.3%) abuse was suspected ($p < .0001$). Table 4.1 summarizes the data on sexual abuse cases as a function of the variables explored in this study while table 4.2 summarizes the data on physical abuse cases.

Children's Age and Gender

Rates of disclosure varied significantly depending on the children's gender. In general, boys (36.9%) were slightly more likely than girls (32.9%) not to make a disclosure when interviewed ($p < .0001$), but a closer examination of the data revealed that the difference was only significant when sexual abuse was suspected ($p < .002$). Even more impressive than the gender differences were the differences by age ($p < .0001$). More than half (52.4%) of the 3- to 6-year-olds interviewed made no allegation, compared with nearly a third (32.9%) of the 7- to 10-year-olds, and about a quarter (26.4%) of the 11- to 14-year-olds. Age differences were evident with respect to both physical and sexual ($p < .0001$ for both) abuse suspicions.

Children's Level of Intellectual Functioning

Allegation rates also varied depending upon the children's perceived level of mental functioning ($p < .0001$ for both sexual and physical abuse) which was evaluated by the interviewers using the following categorical scale: above average, average, below average, and very deviant. Nonallegation rates were lowest for "above average" children: 19.0% for sexual and 25.1% for physical abuse. The corresponding rates for "average" children were 27.6% and 39%; for "below average" children, 38.5% and 43.9%; and for "very deviant"

TABLE 4.1
Allegation and Nonallegation Rates of Sexual Abuse in Relation to
Individual and Family Characteristics

		No Allegation		Allegation		Total
		n	%	n	%	N
Age	3–6	1,160	52.5	1,049	47.5	2,209
	7–10	1,208	28.1	3,095	71.9	4,303
	11–14	808	18.1	3,668	81.9	4,476
Gender	Male	1,052	30.8	2,366	69.2	3,418
	Female	2,125	28.0	5,452	72.0	7,577
Child's mental functioning	Above average	62	19.0	264	81.0	326
	Average	2,519	27.6	6,610	72.4	9,129
	Below average	501	38.5	801	61.5	1,302
	Very deviant	82	46.6	94	53.4	176
Previous sexual abuse	Previous abuse	214	25.3	633	74.7	847
	No previous abuse	800	18.5	3,528	81.5	4,328
	Unknown	2,150	37.2	3,629	62.8	5,779
Sibling order	Oldest	2,160	36.0	3,838	64.0	5,998
	Middle	2,267	39.9	3,421	60.1	5,688
	Youngest	1,618	43.8	2,074	56.2	3,692
Family structure	Two parents	1,194	25.4	5,853	74.6	7,847
	Other	1,183	37.6	1,965	62.4	3,148
Displacement from home	No displacement	2,780	28.2	7,095	71.8	9,875
	Displacement	387	35.6	700	64.4	1,087
Relationship to suspect	Parent	2,312	79.1	612	20.9	2,924
	Nonparent	865	10.7	7,206	89.3	8,071

children, 46.6% and 53.9%. Evidently, there was a clear association between level of functioning and the children's tendency to allege that they had been abused: Children with the most pronounced mental handicaps were least likely to make allegations whereas those perceived to be most competent intellectually were most likely to do so.

Previous Experiences of Abuse

Children who had and had not made allegations in the past also differed with respect to the likelihood that they would make allegations when formally questioned, although there were important differences between those whose

TABLE 4.2
Allegation and Non-Allegation Rates of Physical Abuse in Relation to
Individual and Family Characteristics

		No Allegation		Allegation		Total
		n	%	n	%	N
Age	3–6	1,924	52.4	1,739	47.5	3,663
	7–10	2,572	36.4	4,493	63.6	7,065
	11–14	1,565	33.4	3,127	66.6	4,692
Gender	Male	3,503	39.5	5,366	60.5	8,869
	Female	2,560	39.0	3,996	60.5	6,556
Child's mental functioning	Above average	91	25.1	272	74.9	363
	Average	5,113	39.0	8,014	61.0	13,127
	Below average	756	43.9	967	56.1	1,723
	Very deviant	84	53.9	69	45.1	153
Previous physical abuse	Previous abuse	776	23.0	2,602	77.0	3,378
	No previous abuse	979	37.5	1,629	62.5	2,608
	Unknown	4294	45.6	5,115	54.4	9,409
Sibling order	Oldest	1,125	29.5	2,695	70.5	3,820
	Middle	1,104	26.0	3,143	74.0	4,247
	Youngest	917	32.2	1,933	67.8	2,850
Family structure	Two parents	3,845	40.5	5,648	59.5	9,493
	Other	2,218	37.4	3,714	62.6	5,932
Displacement from home	No displacement	5,640	39.5	8,633	60.5	14,273
	Displacement	405	36.3	710	63.7	1,115
Relationship to suspect	Parent	5,665	39.5	8,681	60.5	14,346
	Nonparent	398	36.9	681	63.1	1,079

alleged maltreatment involved sexual abuse and those whose alleged abuse involved physical abuse. Specifically, children who had previously alleged sexual abuse were less likely to make new allegations than other children (74.7% vs. 81.5%; $p < .0001$), whereas children who had made previous allegations of physical abuse were more likely to make new allegations than other children (77.0% vs. 62.5%; $p < .0001$).

Birth Order

Of the family variables studied (family structure, displacement from home, birth order), sibling status accounted for the greatest proportion of variance in allegation rates ($p < .0001$ for both sexual and physical abuse), even after controlling for the children's age. Last-born children failed to make allegations more frequently (43.8% for sexual and 32.2% for physical abuse) than middle (39.9% and 26%) or first-born children (36% and 29.5%). Children without siblings failed to disclose suspected sexual abuse more often (37.9%) than children living in larger families (27.2%–27.9%; $p < .0001$). When physical abuse was suspected, however, only children failed to disclose less often (35.8%) than children with siblings (38.6%–40%; $p < .005$).

Family Structure

The likelihood that children would make allegations also varied depending on family structure ($p < .0001$ for sexual and physical abuse). Whereas about a quarter of the children living with both parents failed to disclose sexual abuse when interviewed, more than a third of the children living in other family configurations failed to disclose, and almost half of the children whose parents were divorced failed to disclose sexual abuse when this was suspected. When physical abuse (typically by parents) was suspected, children living with both parents failed to disclose slightly more often (40.5%) than children living in other family configurations (37.4%). Children living with their fathers and partners were much more likely to disclose physical abuse; only 28.3% of them failed to make allegations when interviewed.

Displacement From Home

Children who had been removed from their homes and were thus no longer living with one or both parents failed to disclose more frequently (35.6%) than children living at home (28.2%; $p < .0001$) when sexual abuse was suspected but less frequently (36.3%) than children living at home (39.3%; p < .019) when physical abuse was suspected.

Relationship Between Children and Suspects

The likelihood that children would make allegations when interviewed also varied dramatically depending on the relationship between the children and the suspects, although it was inherently difficult to identify suspects when the children failed to make allegations. The data provided here reflect the investigators' attempts to identify the likely suspects using all available information. When the investigators suspected that children had been abused by their parents but the children made no allegations, the cases were referred to the Child Protection Agency, which only has jurisdiction when within-family abuse is suspected. When the children did not identify suspects, as a result, we used referral to CPA as the criterion when defining suspects as either parents or nonparents.

Most suspects were parents (including stepparents, adoptive parents, and foster parents), and children were much more likely to make allegations when the suspect was not a parent or parent figure. Small cell sizes prompt caution generalizing from these results, but the data also show greatest unwillingness among the youngest children to make allegations against parents or parent figures ($p < .0001$). The unwillingness to make accusations about parents or parent figures as opposed to other suspected perpetrators was especially marked when the alleged offenses were sexual in nature ($p < .0001$ for sexual and $p < .036$ for physical abuse), although in both cases the willingness to make allegations increased with age ($p < .0001$ for both types of abuse; log linear $p < .0001$).

In each age group, boys were less likely than girls to make allegations when sexual abuse by parents or parent figures was suspected, whereas there were no gender differences where physical abuse was concerned. Rates of sexual abuse disclosure by sons were 12.9%, 16.9%, and 11.9% for the 3- to 6-, 7- to 10-, and 11- to 14-year-old age groups, respectively, compared with 18.4%, 23.3%, and 32%, respectively, for daughters in the same age groups ($ps < .017, .009, .0001$, respectively). Gender differences in disclosure rates were largely accounted for by this unwillingness on the part of sons (especially adolescent sons) to make allegations of sexual abuse by their parents or parent figures. Again, however, caution is warranted when interpreting these data because suspects were often not clearly identified when children did not make allegations.

DISCUSSION AND CONCLUSION

According to the statistics reported here, about two-thirds of the interviews with young suspected victims of abuse yielded allegations of abuse. Once suspicions were reported to the authorities, in other words, alleged victims were quite likely to provide reports that substantiated those suspicions. Especially impressive is the disclosure rate for sexual offenses—a little over 71% of these suspicions were confirmed when the alleged victims were formally interviewed by youth investigators. Compared to previous studies involving cases in which suspicions were not substantiated in other ways, this rate is at the high end of the range (percentile = 94) with just one study reporting a slightly higher disclosure rate (74%, Gordon & Jaudes, 1996).

In many of those other studies, the forensic interviews were presumably not as carefully structured as those we studied. Indeed, the relatively high disclosure rate obtained in the current study may reflect, at least in part, the nationwide reliance on a single empirically validated investigative tool, the NICHD Investigative Interview Protocol. The protocol includes a systematic effort to establish rapport with children and prepare them for their role as witnesses, thereby enhancing their willingness and capacity to be informative. Compared with interviews not guided by the protocol, protocol-guided interviews yield information that is more likely to be accurate (Orbach et al., 2000, Sternberg, Lamb, Orbach, Esplin, & Mitchell, 2001) and facilitate judgments regarding credibility or validity (Hershkowitz, Fisher, Lamb, & Horowitz, in press). As a result, it is possible that nationwide use of the NICHD protocol enhanced the willingness of children included in this study to disclose abuse.

The high disclosure rate reported here is also consistent with findings from another recent study conducted in the United States. Examining data compiled by a single agency, Pipe and her colleagues (2003) reported that 81% of the suspected victims interviewed using the NICHD protocol disclosed abuse.

The statistics reported here indicate that rates of disclosure vary systematically depending on a number of factors. Overall, children were less likely to make allegations when physical rather than sexual abuse was suspected, and in the case of both physical and sexual abuse, children were extremely unwilling to accuse their parents or parent figures. Because parents or parent figures were the suspected perpetrators in about one quarter of all alleged sexual abuse incidents, compared with almost all (93%) of the physical abuse incidents, the desire to avoid making allegations against parents or parent figures may well explain why children were less likely to make allegations when physical abuse is suspected.

Gender differences in disclosure rates were also affected by the alleged perpetrators' identity. Specifically, although there was no gender difference in the disclosure of physical abuse, boys were more reluctant than girls to make allegations of sexual abuse. Similar gender differences have been reported by other researchers (Ghetti, Alexander, & Goodman, 2002; Gries, Goh, & Cavanaugh, 1996).

Likewise, other researchers have reported that rates of disclosure vary depending on the age of the children interviewed, with preschoolers less likely to make allegations than older children (DiPietro, Runyan, & Fredrickson, 1997; Gries et al., 1996; Keary & Fitzpatrick, 1994; Wood, Orsak, Murphy, & Cross, 1996). We were able to confirm this trend in the large national data set available to us and showed that the relationship between age and disclosure rate continues into adolescence. Regardless of the type of abuse suspected or the relationship with suspected perpetrators, adolescents and pre-adolescents were more likely to disclose abuse than school-aged children, who were in turn, less reluctant than preschoolers.

A surprisingly large proportion of young (3- to 6-year-old) children did not allege abuse when questioned. Although it is possible that some of these interviews were triggered by unwarranted suspicions, the magnitude of the age differences we found suggests that both cognitive and motivational factors may be involved as well. In particular, it may be that the youngest children are disproportionately likely to misunderstand the purpose and focus of the investigative interview or the abuse itself, thereby failing to report abuse experiences that they remember and would be willing to discuss if they recognized the investigators' interest. This possibility is supported by the link we found between the children's level of functioning and their tendency to disclose abuse when questioned. Nonallegation rates were higher for children whose cognitive functioning appeared poorer than for children who seemed more competent intellectually.

The fact that the very young children more readily make allegations against familiar nonfamily members and strangers while avoiding allegations about parents or stepparents, however, suggests that many of the nonallegations may indeed be motivated, perhaps by threats or fears about possible repercussions. This possibility is strengthened by the fact that older children likewise avoided making allegations of sexual abuse against parents or parent figures.

The data presented here also highlight differences in family structure that are associated with variations in the rates of disclosure and non-disclosure, especially rates of disclosure of physical abuse by parents or guardians. Specifically, these Israeli children were less willing to disclose abuse when they lived at home with their biological parents rather than in other settings (e.g., foster families, boarding schools, institutions); children living with both parents were least likely to disclose. The greater dependence of such children on their parents, the children's greater sense of responsibility for protecting the integrity of the family, or direct and indirect pressure by the parents may all explain why children living with their parents are least likely to disclose abuse.

The presence of siblings seems to further motivate children to avoid disclosing physical abuse, with children especially unlikely to allege abuse when they have older siblings. In part, this finding may reflect the age differences discussed earlier, but in addition it appears that older siblings may be perceived by younger children as authorities who inhibit disclosure in much the same way that parents do.

Although the large sample size and the fact that all interviews were conducted in a standardized fashion increase the reliability of the findings reported here, their interpretation is still limited because we do not know how valid the children's allegations and nonallegations were. As a result, we do not know how likely real victims are to report their abuse, or how often false allegations are made. In addition, our analyses only involved cases that had come to the attention of official agencies, so we have no idea how many or how few cases of abuse take place without ever triggering any kind of official investigation.

Despite these limitations, the findings are noteworthy because they include all reported cases in an entire country (Israel) over a five-year period and thus provide more representative data than any other report to date. In particular, our study yielded invaluable information about the frequency with which suspected child abuse victims disclosed abuse when interviewed, and about the characteristics of suspected victims who were more or less likely to make disclosures when interviewed. As discussed earlier, we found that nearly two-thirds of suspected victims made allegations when questioned and that children were more likely to make allegations when sexual rather than physical abuse was suspected, perhaps in part because physical abuse was more likely than sexual abuse to involve the parents as suspected perpetrators, and children of all ages were unlikely to name parent perpetrators. We also found a clear association between age and the likelihood that allegations would be made, with preschoolers most unlikely to make allegations when interviewed. Further research is clearly needed to determine why these developmental differences exist, and thus whether different interviewing strategies might be necessary when suspicions about young children arise.

REFERENCES

DiPietro, E .K., Runyan, D. K., & Fredrickson, D. D. (1997). Predictors of disclosure during medical evaluation for suspected sexual abuse. *Journal of Child Sexual Abuse, 6,* 133–42.

Ghetti, S., Alexander, K. W., & Goodman, G. S. (2002). Legal involvement in child sexual abuse cases consequences and interventions. *International Journal of Law and Psychiatry, 25,* 235–51.

Gonzalez, L. S., Waterman, J., Kelly, R., McCord, J., & Oliveri, K. (1993). Children's patterns of disclosures and recantations of sexual and ritualistic abuse allegations in psychotherapy. *Child Abuse & Neglect, 17,* 281–89.

Gordon, S., & Jaudes, P. K. (1996). Sexual abuse evaluation in the emergency department: Is the history reliable? *Child Abuse & Neglect, 20,* 315–22.

Gries, L. T., Goh, D. S., & Cavanaugh, J. (1996). Factors associated with disclosure during child sexual abuse assessment. *Journal of Child Sexual Abuse, 5,* 1–20.

Hershkowitz, I., Fisher, S., Lamb, M. E., & Horowitz, D. (in press). Improving credibility assessment in child sexual abuse allegations: The role of the NICHD investigative interview protocol. *Child Abuse and Neglect.*

Keary, K., & Fitzpatrick , C. (1994). Children's disclosure of sexual abuse during formal investigation. *Child Abuse & Neglect, 18,* 543–48.

Lamb, M. E., Sternberg, K. J., Orbach, Y., Hershkowitz, I., & Esplin, P. W. (1999). Forensic interviews of children. In A. Memon & R. Bull (Eds.). *Handbook of the psychology of interviewing* (pp. 253–77). New York: Wiley.

London, K., Bruck, M., Ceci, S. J., & Shuman, D. W. (2005). Disclosure of child sexual abuse: What does the research tell us about the ways that children tell?. *Psychology, Public Policy, & Law, 11,* 194–226.

Orbach, Y., Hershkowitz, I., Lamb, M. E., Sternberg, K. J., Esplin, P. W., & Horowitz, D. (2000). Assessing the value of structured protocols for forensic interviews of alleged child abuse victims. *Child Abuse & Neglect. 24,* 733–52.

Pipe, M. E., Lamb, M. E., Orbach, Y., & Esplin, P. W. (2004). Recent research on children's testimony about experienced and witnessed events. *Developmental Review, 24,* 440–68.

Pipe, M. E., Stewart, H. L., Sternberg, K. J., Lamb, M. E., & Esplin, P. W. (2003, August). Non-disclosures and alleged abuse in forensic interviews. *Paper presented to a conference on non-disclosure and delayed disclosure of child sexual abuse, Satra Bruk, Sweden.*

Poole, D. A., & Lamb, M. E. (1998). *Investigative interviews of children: A guide for helping professionals.* Washington, DC: American Psychological Association.

Poole, D. A., & Lindsay, D. S. (1998). Assessing the accuracy of young children's reports: Lessons from the investigation of child sexual abuse. *Preventive Psychology,* 1–26.

Sorensen, T., & Snow, B. (1991). How children tell: The process of disclosure in child sexual abuse. *Child Welfare, 19,* 3–17.

Sternberg, K. J., Lamb, M. E., Orbach, Y., Esplin, P. W., & Mitchell, S. (2001). Use of a structured investigative protocol enhances young children's responses to free recall prompts in the course of forensic interviews. *Journal of Applied Psychology, 86,* 997–1005.

Wood, B., Orsak, C., Murphy, M., & Cross, H. J. (1996). Semi-structured child sexual abuse interviews: Interview and child characteristics related to credibility of disclosure. *Child Abuse & Neglect, 20,* 81–92.

5

Factors Associated With Nondisclosure of Suspected Abuse During Forensic Interviews

Margaret-Ellen Pipe
Brooklyn College, CUNY

Michael E. Lamb
University of Cambridge, United Kingdom

Yael Orbach, Kathleen J. Sternberg
National Institute of Child Health and Human Development

Heather L. Stewart
Children's Justice Center, Salt Lake City

Phillip W. Esplin
Independent Practice

When a child does not disclose suspected sexual abuse in a formal investigative interview, how should we interpret this nondisclosure? As London, Bruck, Ceci, and Shuman, and Lyon have discussed in some detail (chapters 2 and 3, this volume), the answer to this question is far from simple. Nondisclosure may indicate that the suspicions of abuse were unfounded, but it may also reflect the child's failure, intentional or otherwise, to disclose abuse that has occurred. Erroneous selection of either interpretation can have serious consequences. The risks associated with the overzealous pursuit of reported abuse, in combination with inappropriate interviewing strategies, are now well recognized (Bruck & Ceci, 1999; Ceci & Bruck, 1993; Ceci & Friedman, 2000; Poole & Lamb, 1998; Schaaf, Alexander, Goodman, Ghetti, Edelstein & Castelli, 2002). Indeed, research examining the conditions under which children are more likely to recount false details or entire events that they never experienced (false positives) has burgeoned over the past two decades. In contrast, the conditions that favor false negatives have been relatively neglected. The failure to detect abuse that has occurred is also dangerous, however, because it may leave children in abusive situations and place other children at risk of becoming victims.

As London and colleagues point out in chapter 2 (see also London, Bruck, Ceci, & Shuman, 2005), estimates of the number of undisclosed cases of childhood sexual abuse range from 4% (Bradley & Wood, 1996) to 76% (Sorenson & Snow, 1991). Reported rates of denial and recantation are similarly varied (London et al., 2005, this volume; Schaaf et al., 2002), but the reasons why these estimates vary so widely remains poorly understood. Among the factors affecting estimates of nondisclosure are sample selection biases, defined by differences in the reasons why children were interviewed and in what context (therapy, formal forensic interview, and so on), how they came to the attention of authorities (e.g., Goodman, Ghetti, Quas, et al., 2003; Goodman-Brown, Edelstein, Goodman, Jones, & Gordon, 2003; Paine & Hansen, 2002; Schaaf et al., 2002), and how the interviews were conducted (see London et al., chapter 2, this volume). Further, to the extent that the failure to disclose abuse may be associated with variables relating to the child (e.g., age, gender), the relation between the child and the alleged perpetrator, and the nature of the alleged abuse (e.g., in terms of severity), across-study differences with respect to these variables may also add "noise" to the overall picture. In order to take such variables into account, we need to know how they influence disclosure rates.

There is consistent evidence that variables such as age, prior disclosure, and independent validation of abuse affect reported disclosure rates. With respect to age, a developmental increase in disclosure rate (and, conversely, higher rates of *non*disclosure for younger than for older children) appears to be reliable (see Hershkowitz, Horowitz, & Lamb, chapter 4, this volume, and 2005; London et al., chapter 2, this volume; Paine & Hansen, 2002; Schaaf et al., 2002, but see Bradley & Wood, 1996, for contrasting findings). Interestingly, disclosures by older children are more likely to be delayed significantly longer than those by younger children (Goodman-Brown et al., 2003), perhaps because at least some of the nondisclosing younger children later become delayed disclosers in older age groups. As several authors have pointed out, such age differences may reflect a variety of cognitive and motivational issues (see also Bussey & Grimbeek, 1995; Goodman-Brown et al., 2003; London et al., 2005). In comparison with older children, for example, very young children may be less likely to interpret abuse as abuse (and hence also more likely to accidentally disclose it, see Schaaf et al., 2002, and Cederborg, Lamb, & Laurell, chapter 9, this volume), more vulnerable to requests to keep secrets and conceal information (e.g., Bottoms, Goodman, Schwartz-Kenney, & Thomas, 2002; Pipe & Goodman, 1991), and more fearful of the consequences for their relationship to the suspect and hence less likely to disclose abuse that has occurred. It is also possible, however, that abuse is more likely to be suspected among younger children even when none has occurred because of difficulties in language and communication, with initial "disclosures" or behavior misinterpreted, or because younger children are more susceptible to misleading or suggestive questioning. Researchers have not yet examined factors underlying the observed age differences in nondisclosure rates.

Disclosure rates are also higher when there is independent validation of the abuse (e.g., by medical evidence or suspect confession) or when there was a disclosure prior to the investigative interview, for example, as reported by a caregiver or child protection worker (London et al., chapter 2, this volume, but see Lyon, chapter 3, this volume, for a contrasting view). A number of children do not, however, disclose when interviewed, despite independent evidence of abuse or reports of a prior disclosure. What are the circumstances surrounding these failures to disclose? In particular, is a failure to disclose abuse when formally interviewed, following a prior disclosure, likely to reflect recantation of the abuse allegation or the unreliability of the prior reported disclosure? In general, researchers have not examined the conditions under which inconsistencies occur, which in turn might shed light on reasons for them. One variable of particular interest is the identity of the person reporting that the child disclosed abuse prior to the interview—whether a potentially "interested party" such as a parent, or disinterested person such as schoolteacher or friend (Paine & Hansen, 2002). In the study described here, we examine case characteristics, including to whom the child's reported prior disclosure was made, in relation to inconsistencies in children's disclosure of abuse.

As far as a number of other variables related to nondisclosure of abuse are concerned, the evidence is inconsistent and further studies are needed. For example, Summit (1983) predicted that abuse by a close family member would be associated with nondisclosure or delayed and incomplete disclosure and retraction. London et al. (2005; chapter 2, this volume), however, identified only two recent studies supporting these predictions (excluding the more recent reports by Hershkowitz et al, in press and chapter 4, this volume), and three that did not (but see discussion by Lyon, chapter 3, this volume). Similarly, there have been mixed findings with respect to gender, with some studies showing males less likely to disclose (e.g., Hershkowitz et al., 2005) but others failing to find this difference (e.g., Goodman-Brown et al., 2003; London et al., chapter 2 this volume). Nor has the relation between type and severity of abuse and disclosure been consistent across studies; whereas some have found both minor and very severe abuse less likely to be disclosed (e.g., Sauzier, 1989), others have found only the most severe abuse is less likely to be reported (e.g., Arata, 1998; Paine & Hansen, 2002; see Schaaf et al., 2002, for review).

One limitation of the extant research is that the *combined* influence of variables such as age, type of abuse, and relation of perpetrator to suspect has not been examined, not least because the samples of nondisclosing children have been too small, and information relating to multiple variables has not been available in the same studies. Interactions are likely to both occur and magnify across-study differences in disclosure rates, however. For example, because younger children are particularly likely to keep secrets when asked (e.g., see Pipe & Goodman, 1991), to be very dependent on caregivers, and to have fewer alternative confidantes or sources of support than older children, the relation between victim and suspect may affect disclosure by younger children more. Older children may, in turn, disclose to a wider range of confidants than younger children. One of the objectives of the present study was, therefore, to examine rates of nondisclosure in a large sample of children interviewed about suspected sexual abuse, and to determine how the joint effects of age and relationship to suspect, prior disclosure, independent validation of abuse, and so on, are associated with rates of nondisclosure.

A second objective was to examine rates of disclosure and nondisclosure when children are interviewed using the National Institute of Child Health and Human Development (NICHD) protocol for investigative interviews. In the majority of previous studies, the ways in which children were interviewed was not described. The contribution of the interview to across-study differences in disclosure rates thus remained a matter of speculation. The NICHD protocol emphasizes open-ended questioning (see Sternberg, Lamb, Orbach, Esplin, & Mitchell, 2001; Orbach, Hershkowitz, Lamb, Sternberg, Esplin, & Horowitz, 2000) and some practitioners have expressed concern that such approaches may lead to low disclosure rates and, in particular, high rates of false negatives. In this chapter, we examine rates of nondisclosure when interviews followed the NICHD interview protocol. Since all interviews were recorded and transcribed, we knew exactly how the interviews were conducted.

Finally, we explore nondisclosures in relation to a number of variables that might help understand patterns of nondisclosure of suspected abuse but that have received little attention to date. For example, suspicions of abuse are often based on a lengthy chain of events, initiated by such triggers as age-inappropriate sexual behavior, physical signs, a verbal disclosure, or an ambiguous comment. Are disclosures of abuse more likely in the context of some initial triggers than others? Previous research suggests that prior verbal disclosures should be highly correlated with disclosure during formal interviews, although the recipient of the prior disclosures has hitherto been examined in very few studies (e.g., Sauzier, 1989). Moreover, extremely little is known about other factors that arouse suspicions and thus prompt formal investigative interviews.

In sum, we compare the characteristics of cases in which children who did not allege abuse in formal, investigative interviews conducted by interviewers trained to use the NICHD interview protocol. First, we report nondisclosure rates for interviews conducted with the NICHD protocol, and second, we examine variables associated with nondisclosure. If nondisclosures are generally true negatives, they should, for example, be characterized by the absence of corroborative evidence, ambiguous and unclear allegations, and by prior 'disclosures' reported by persons with a vested interest in reporting such disclosures and perhaps triggering investigations.

On the basis of previous studies, we expected that older children would be more likely than younger to make allegations in the formal interview, and that children of all ages would be more likely to make allegations when there had been prior verbal reports to someone else, and corroborative evidence, such as suspect confessions. We further predicted that children (especially younger children) would be less likely to allege abuse in the investigative interview when the suspects were close family members (Hershkowitz et al., chapter 4, this volume, and 2005; Summit, 1983; Paine & Hansen, 2002, p. 276). Among older children who disclose abuse, longer delays are likely (Goodman-Brown et al., 2003).

METHODOLOGY

The study involved forensic interviews conducted at a children's advocacy centre in Salt Lake City by forensic interviewers who had agreed to participate in the research and had undergone training in the use of the NICHD protocol. A total of 397 interviews with suspected victims of childhood sexual abuse, aged between 4 years 0 months and 13 years 11 months, were conducted between 1997 and 2000. (Children who were suspected of having been physically abused were few in number ($n = 22$) and were excluded from the present study). Only children suspected of being victims of, rather than witnesses to, sexual abuse were included. In each case, the interview was the child's first formal interview at the center where the interviews were conducted.

The NICHD interview protocol includes a presubstantive phase in which children are reminded to tell the truth, to correct the interviewer's mistakes, and ask for clarification when necessary. The presubstantive phase includes rapport building and training in episodic retrieval. The interviewer then shifts the focus to substantive issues, using nonsuggestive prompts designed to avoid interviewer input about a possible incident while allowing the child to introduce the topic. Other nonsuggestive prompts follow if the child does not make an allegation. If an allegation is made, the child is given an open "invitation" to give details about the incident, following which additional open-ended probes and cues (which request clarification about something the child had previously mentioned) are used as appropriate. Focused, nonsuggestive questions are asked only if some crucial information is still missing after exhaustive open-ended questioning. If the child mentions multiple incidents, the interviewer asks the child to describe each incident separately (see Orbach et al., 2000; Sternberg et al., 2001, for more detailed descriptions).

From police reports, information available at the children's advocacy center (where most of the interviews were conducted), and transcripts of the forensic interviews, we coded the following information about the child, the abuse, and the suspect:

Child related information included age at time of interview, gender, and with whom the child lived at the time of the interview.

Information relating to the disclosure included the initial triggering event, that is, the reason why abuse was suspected. This was categorized as disclosure to another person; suspicion raised by immediate family member (e.g., stepparent or sibling living with the child, or biological parent whether or not living with the child); suspicion raised by other relative, not living with the child; suspicion raised by friend, peer or neighbor; suspicion raised by community member (e.g., teacher or minister); suspicion raised by mandated reporters (e.g., child protection worker, therapist); suspect confession; or an anonymous informant. Whether the child had reportedly told someone else about the abuse (whether or not this was the initial trigger) and who the child was reported to have told were coded separately.

Information relating to the abuse included the type of alleged abuse coded as penetration (digital or penile), touch under clothing, touch over clothing, and exposure. There was also a category of "other" which included ambiguous suspicions such as sexual advances made to other children and other sexual activity. Whether there was a single incident or repeated occurrences, and the delay between the last known incident and the interview, where this could be determined, were also coded.

Information relating to the suspect included age, gender, whether he or she was suspected of abusing multiple victims, and his or her relationship to the victim, namely immediate family, other family, familiar nonfamily, unfamiliar (as defined for triggering events, above). Whether the suspect had confessed to the entire abusive incident(s) or to a substantial part of it (e.g., suspect confesses that the child touched him but not that he touched the child, when the child alleges both) was also coded.

Information relating to the interview included whether the interviewer had adhered to the NICHD interview protocol and whether a disclosure was made during the interview.

All of the No Allegation cases were coded twice, with average percent agreement of 90%. Of Allegation cases, 70% of cases were coded twice, and average percent agreement was 91%. All differences were resolved by discussion until consensus was achieved.

RESULTS

Allegation Rates

Based on the sample of all 397 interviews (males = 136; females = 261), the disclosure rate for the complete age range was 83%, and across the age groupings of 4–5, 6–8, and 9–13 years, rates were 75%, 82%, and 88%, respectively. However, not all interviews adhered to the NICHD protocol; in 31 cases, children disclosed "spontaneously" before the interviewer had completed the presubstantive phase of the interview, and in a further 72 cases the interview deviated from the interview protocol in some way (e.g., the name of the suspect was introduced by the interviewer, or suggestive questions were used early in the interview). Although children who made spontaneous disclosures are also interesting, as are children who made an allegation when the interviewers did not follow the protocol, these cases raise questions outside the scope of the present paper. In this chapter we focus on those children who did not make an allegation (n = 68) and those who did make an allegation (n = 226) when interviewed following the NICHD interview protocol.

Table 5.1 summarizes the descriptive characteristics of these cases. In those interviews following the protocol in which there was no spontaneous disclosure, the disclosure rate was 77%, with approximately the same percentage of males (73%) and females (79%) making an allegation when interviewed.

Age and Disclosure Rates

As table 5.1 shows, disclosure rates increased across age groups from 63% to 85%. Nondisclosure rates are, of course, the inverse and were 37%, 24%, and 15% across age groups. Because these rates exclude children who made spontaneous allegations or made an allegation when the interviewers deviated from the protocol, they are conservative estimates of disclosure rates.

Type of Abuse and Disclosure

In a significant proportion of cases, the alleged or suspected abuse related to the most intrusive types of abuse, namely penetration or touching under clothes, and in general, when abuse of this type was suspected, children were highly likely to make allegations during the interview (table 5.1). Allegations (or suspicions) of exposure, although relatively infrequent, were almost always associated with an allegation in the interview as well. In contrast, cases in which the suspected abuse was uncertain or ambiguous were relatively infrequent and were rarely associated with allegations during the interview. In only 4 of the 17 cases classified as "ambiguous suspicion" was an allegation made in interview. Further, there was no support for the prediction that younger children would be interviewed on the basis of the more ambiguous or less certain

TABLE 5.1
Sample Characteristics and Numbers of Children Who Did or Did Not Make an Allegation When Interviewed

	4–5 years		6–8 years		9–13 years		Overall	
Mean Age	NA 5.05	A 5.13	NA 7.56	A 7.32	NA 10.97	A 10.87	NA 7.95	A 8.55
	n	n (%)	n	n (%)	n	n (%)	n	n (%)
Gender								
Male	10	14 (58)	10	27 (73)	7	32 (82)	27	73 (73)
Female	15	29 (66)	13	52 (80)	12	73 (86)	40	154 (79)
Type of Abuse								
Penetration	6	15 (71)	2	22 (92)	2	42 (96)	10	79 (89)
Touch un/clothes	12	20 (63)	14	39 (74)	8	31 (80)	34	90 (73)
Touch ov/clothes	2	5 (71)	1	13 (93)	5	24 (83)	8	42 (84)
Exposure	0	2 (100)	2	5 (71)	0	5 (100)	2	12 (86)
Other	5	1 (17)	4	0 (0)	4	3 (43)	13	4 (24)
Perpetrator Familiarity								
Immediate Family	15	12 (44)	14	32 (70)	6	45 (88)	35	89 (72)
Other Family	1	7 (88)	2	17 (90)	4	16 (80)	7	40 (85)
Familiar	9	23 (72)	7	29 (81)	8	39 (83)	24	91 (79)
Unfamiliar	0	1 (100)	0	1 (100)	0	5 (100)	0	7 (100)
TOTAL	25	43 (66)	23	79 (78)	19	105 (85)	67	227

Note: Percentage making an allegation is shown in brackets.

suspicions than older children. Indeed, such suspicions seldom triggered interviews, regardless of age, and were seldom associated with allegations during the formal interviews.

Suspect–Victim Relationship

The suspects were unfamiliar in only seven cases, and in all of these cases, children made allegations when interviewed. Five of these cases involved children in the oldest age group, and there was one from each of the other two age groups. Because there were so few unfamiliar suspects (as in prior studies), these cases were not included in many of the more detailed comparisons below.

There was a tendency for children (combined across age groups) to be less likely to make allegations when the suspects were immediate family members (72%), than otherwise (81%), chi sq = 3.50, p <.06 (Table 5–1). When biological fathers were suspected, 57% of the children made allegations, compared to 81% for all other categories, and this difference was statistically significant, chi sq = 13.14, p <.001.[1]

However, as shown in figure 5.1, the relation between disclosure and suspect familiarity depended on age; it was strongest for the youngest children and was not evident in the oldest age group. When the suspect was an immediate family member, disclosure rates were 44%, 70%, and 88% across age groups, and for other suspects (combined), 76%, 82%, and 83%. Chi-sq comparisons conducted separately for each age group showed that significant differences in disclosure rates between immediate family members and other suspects (categories combined) for the 4–5 -year- old children, chi sq = 6.80, p < .01, but not for either of the two older age groups, chi sq = 2.20 and < 1, respectively. When the suspect was a biological father, disclosure rates were 41%, 47%, and 92% across age groups, compared to 71%, 82% and 85% for all other suspect categories (combined). For the two youngest groups, there was a significant association between suspect relationship (biological father versus all other suspects, combined) and disclosure, chi sq = 4.74, p < .03, and 9.81, p < .01, respectively, but not for the oldest group, chi sq = <1.

Although younger children were less likely to allege abuse by an immediate family member than the older children were, it is important to note that the probability of immediate family members being suspects did not differ across the three age groups. Immediate family members were suspects in 40% of the cases (allegation and no-allegation cases, combined) for the youngest children, 45% for the middle age group, and 42% for the oldest (table 5.1). Thus, immediate family members were no more (or less) likely to be suspected abusers of younger children than older children, but younger children were less likely than older children to disclose abuse by immediate family members.

---

[1] Chi squares were conducted on raw numbers, although percentages are reported for ease of interpretation.

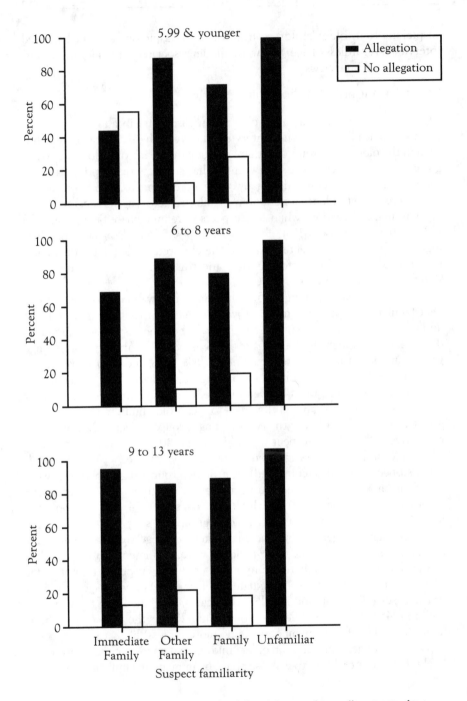

Figure 5.1 Proportion of children who did or did not make an allegation in the formal interview, separately for each victim–suspect relationship.

TABLE 5.2
Allegation Rate in Interview as a Function of Whether or Not There Had Been a
Disclosure Prior to Interview

	Prior Disclosure (%)	No Prior Disclosure (%)
4–6 years	75	20
6–8 years	91	6
9–13 years	98	26

Prior Disclosure in Relation to Allegation in Interview

Previous studies suggest that a verbal disclosure prior to a formal interview is predictive of an allegation in interview (see London et al., chapter 2, this volume). The probability of a prior disclosure did not differ as a function of age; 78% of 4–6 year olds, 83% of 6–8 year olds, and 82% of 9–13 year olds had (reportedly) made a prior disclosure. Table 5.2 shows the proportion of children who, having made verbal disclosures prior to the investigative interviews, also made allegations during the interviews. Whereas 75% of the children in the youngest age group who had made a prior disclosure also disclosed in the interview, 98% of the oldest children did so. That is, the older children were more likely to be consistent from prior allegation to allegation in interview. Depending on definition, the inconsistencies of the younger children could be considered evidence of recantation. However, although this age difference in consistency may reflect the younger children's unwillingness to disclose abuse that has occurred when interviewed, it may also reflect over-zealous reporting of prior disclosures by a concerned caregiver or others, an issue we consider below.

Table 5.2 also shows that, in each age group, a small but not insignificant proportion of children who had never made a prior, verbal disclosure of abuse but for whom abuse was nonetheless suspected made allegations during the formal investigative interview (see Keary & Fitzpatrick, 1994, for similar findings).

When children disclosed prior to the interview, did the prior disclosure and to whom the disclosure was (reportedly) made influence the probability of within-interview disclosure? Table 5.3 shows the number of children disclosing to an immediate family member, other family member, a familiar person, or "other" (community person such as teacher, minister, or child protection case worker). Across all age groups, children were reportedly most likely to disclose to an immediate family member, followed by another family member outside the home (table 5.3). Only 8% (n = 4/53) of the youngest children disclosed to someone outside the family (such as peer or neighbor) compared to 20% and 24% for the two older age groups, respectively. Disclosure in interview, following a prior disclosure (to *anyone*), was least likely for the youngest children and almost 100% for the older children (table 5.3), and this pattern did not depend on to *whom* the prior disclosure had been made. Disclosure in interview was

TABLE 5.3
Proportion of Children Reported to Have Disclosed Prior to Interview Who Also
Disclosed in Interview as a Function of Relationship Between Child and Confidante

	Immediate Family	Other Family	Other
4–6 (n = 53)	77% (43)	83% (6)	50% (4)
6–8 (n = 85)	93% (61)	100% (7)	76% (17)
9–13 (n = 101)	99% (74)	100% (3)	96% (24)

Note. The number reporting prior to interview, on which proportions are based, is shown in brackets.

least likely following prior disclosure to someone outside of the family for children in the youngest groups (see table 5.3).

What Was the "Trigger" for the Investigation?

In many cases, a complex series of events triggered the investigative interview, and the initiating event or "trigger" was coded for each case. In the majority of cases, the initial trigger was either the child's disclosure as reported by another person or the concern of an immediate family member (table 5.4). Immediate family members were more likely to trigger suspicions for the younger children overall and accounted for 40% of the cases in which children made allegations, compared to only 12% of allegations by the oldest children (see table 5.4).

TABLE 5.4
Initial Trigger (Percent of Each Age Group) Separately for Allegation and
Nonallegation Cases

Initial Trigger	4–6 years (%)		6–8 years (%)		9–13 years (%)	
	n/a n = 25	a n = 43	n/a n = 24	a n = 78	n/a n = 19	a n = 105
Child's (prior) disclosure	16	47	21	53	5	66
Immediate family	32	40	42	27	32	12
Other family	16	2	13	3	—	1
Peer, neighbor	20	2	21	9	16	14
Community, teacher, minister	—	2	—	—	5	2
CP, therapist	12	—	—	—	11	1
Suspect confession	—	5	4	9	26	2
Anonymous	4	2	—	—	5	2
Total	100	100	101	100	101	100

Concern raised by familiar persons (not relatives), such as peers or neighbors, increasingly triggered suspicions as children grew older.

An alternative way of looking at these data is to ask: Given a particular initial trigger, what is the likelihood that an allegation will be made during the interview? When the initial trigger was the child's prior disclosure, a family member outside the immediate family, or a familiar person, the proportion of children making an allegation in the interview increased with age (table 5.5). In contrast, regardless of age, children made allegations two-thirds of the time when immediate family members first raised a suspicion. Thus, although an immediate family member was most likely to *trigger* the investigation for the youngest children, there was no age difference in the probability of disclosure when the child was formally interviewed.

Delay Since the Most Recent Alleged/Suspected Incident

The delay between suspected incident and time of interview is potentially important, especially for the youngest children. In extreme instances, long delays for these children could mean that the alleged events occurred before the

TABLE 5.5
Percentages of Cases Initiated by Each Trigger That Led to an Allegation

Initial Trigger	4–5 years (%)	6–8 years (%)	9–13 years (%)
Prior disclosure	83 (24)	89 (46)	99 (70)
Immediate family	68 (25)	68 (31)	68 (19)
Other family	20 (5)	40 (5)	100 (1)
Peer, neighbor	17 (6)	58 (12)	83 (18)
Community, teacher	100 (1)	—	67 (3)
CP, therapist	— (3)	—	33 (3)
Suspect confession	100 (2)	88 (8)	29 (7)
Anonymous	50 (2)	—	67 (3)

Note: The number in brackets is the total number of cases on which the percentage is based.

TABLE 5.6
Proportion of Children for Whom Abuse Was Suspected and Delay
Since Last Suspected or Alleged Incident

	4–6 years (%)	6–8 years (%)	9–14 years (%)
<1	71	34	43
1–6	19	35	19
6–12	7	12	12
1	3	8	13
>1	—	11	14
Total	100	100	101

period of childhood amnesia ended, in which case we would not expect the incidents to be remembered or reported.

Table 5.6 shows that for the youngest children the majority of suspected incidents of abuse (allegation and no allegation cases combined) had occurred in the past month and a full 90% within six months; none were suspected to have occurred two years (or more) before the interview. In contrast, almost a third of the cases involving 6- to 8-year-old and 9- to 13-year-old children involved abuse that last occurred more than six months before the formal disclosure and sometimes more than two years before the interview. It is also interesting to note that, despite the decreasing number of children suspected of having been abused as delay increased, particularly in the youngest group, the allegation rate (proportion of children who made an allegation when interviewed) did not change; across increasing delays, 81%, 81%, 84%, 75%, and 80% of the children (three age groups combined) made allegations about suspected abuse.

Figure 5.2 shows the proportions of children making an allegation in an interview as a function of delay since the last incident separately for each suspected victim–suspect category (immediate family, other family, familiar, unfamiliar). Delays to interview tended to be longer when the allegations related to members of the child's family although, contrary to Summit's (1983)

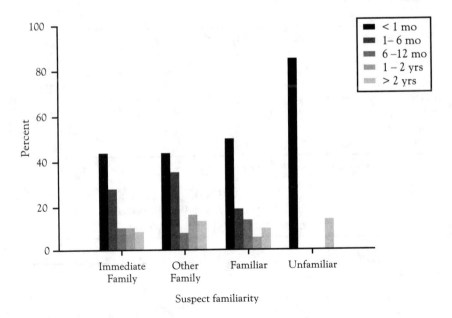

Figure 5.2 Delay to disclosure in interview as a function of the relation between the victim and suspect (proportion of cases for each suspect-victim relation falling into each delay interval).

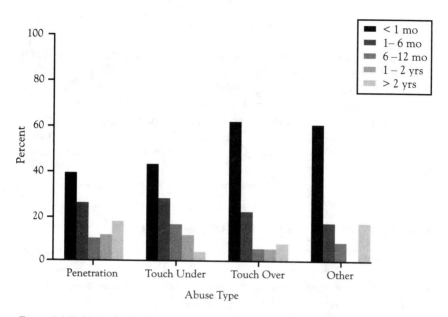

Figure 5.3 Delay to disclosure as a function of type of abuse (proportion of cases for each abuse category falling into each delay interval).

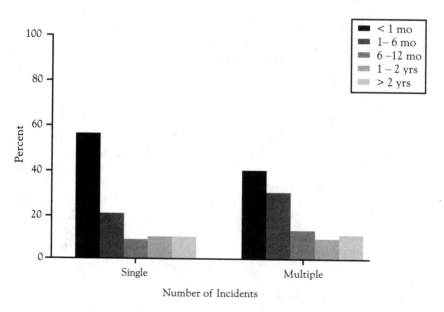

Figure 5.4 Delay to disclosure for single and multiple instances of abuse (proportions falling into each delay interval).

prediction, this was not different for members of the immediate family (see figure 5.2).

When we looked at delay in relation to type of abuse, we found that children were more likely to delay disclosure of the more severe categories of abuse (penetration and touch under clothing) (see figure 5.3). Further, when the abuse was alleged to have occurred on multiple occasions, there were longer delays between the last incident and the interview than when it was alleged to have occurred a single time (see figure 5.4). Again, age was an important variable, however. This pattern of delayed disclosure, particularly disclosure of penetration, was strongest for children age six years or older; as noted earlier, the youngest children tended to disclose all types of abuse within six months (when they disclosed at all).

Suspect Confession and Rate of Allegations

Confessions were recorded in 19%, 37%, and 35% of the cases involving children in the three age groups, respectively (allegation and no-allegation cases, combined). On average, suspects confessed in 18% of cases in which no allegation was made in the formal interview and in 36% of cases in which an allegation was made. If the suspect had confessed, a disclosure was more likely (87%) than when the suspect had not confessed (72%).

Across age groups, the proportions of children who made an allegation when the suspect had confessed were 77%, 95%, and 84%. The unexpectedly lower rate for the oldest children is attributable to one perpetrator who confessed to multiple instances of abuse that had occurred many years earlier. When there was no confession, disclosure rates were 60%, 66%, and 85%. Thus, the age difference in disclosure rate was evident whether or not the suspect had confessed.

DISCUSSION

These findings make clear that most (80%) of the children interviewed using an interview protocol that emphasized open-ended questioning made an allegation of abuse in the formal investigative interview. Although a high disclosure rate might be expected in the present sample because the children had been brought in for formal forensic interviews, not all children had disclosed the abuse previously and the bases for suspicion varied. The results reported here are consistent with many of those reported in previous studies, falling at neither extreme. Importantly, they highlight variables likely to affect observed disclosure rates, and interactions between them, and may thus help explain the wide-ranging rates of nondisclosure reported by other researchers.

As in several previous studies based on formal interviews with suspected victims, age was an important variable, and disclosure rates were highest for the oldest children (DiPietro, Runyan, & Frederickson, 1997; Gris, Goh, & Cavanaugh, 1996; Hershkowitz et al., 2005 and chapter 4, this volume; Keary

& Fitzpatrick, 1994). However, many of the older children had delayed disclosing, sometimes over very long time periods. Although Goodman-Brown et al. (2003) did not find a direct relation between age and delay to disclosure in their model predicting delays to disclosure, both fear of negative consequences and the perception of responsibility for the abusive incidents were associated with long delays, and both of these variables were significantly linked to age. Whether the older children in our study would have disclosed had they been asked about the abuse earlier we can not know from these data. It is possible, however, that some of the younger, nondisclosing children in the present sample may disclose later, thereby becoming delayed disclosers. That is, it is likely that our sample included not only children who had been abused and disclosed the abuse but also children who had been abused but chose not to disclose. Some evidence for this is discussed below in the context of the imperfect association between disclosure and confession.

Age also interacted with other variables in its association with disclosure. In particular, the relationship between the suspect and the victim was related to disclosure rate for the younger children but not for those the oldest age group (9- to13-year-olds). Although immediate family members were no more likely to be suspects in cases involving the younger children than in those involving older children, the younger children were much less likely to make allegations when the suspects were immediate family members, and particularly when the suspects were the biological fathers. Therefore, the youngest children were *selectively* less likely to make allegations than older children, specifically when the suspected abusers were close family members (see also Hershkowitz et al., chapter 4, this volume; 2005).

Consistent with several other studies, disclosures were more likely to be delayed when the suspect was a family member. However, this was the case when family member was defined very narrowly to include only immediate family members or was defined broadly to include, for example, grandparents. Goodman-Brown and colleagues similarly found that delayed disclosure was more common in cases of intrafamilial than extrafamilial abuse, a difference that is perhaps easy to understand in terms of loyalties, fear of consequences to the family, and the opportunity for repeated instances of abuse, to name but a few. However, we found no support for the more specific prediction that children would be more likely to delay disclosure in the context of abuse by a parent figure living with the child or an immediate family member (cf., Summit, 1983).

Members of the children's immediate families were more likely to have raised initial concerns when the children were younger, but this age difference was evident with respect to cases in which children made an allegation in the interview rather than cases in which there was no allegation. Specifically, whereas immediate family members raised initial suspicion in 40% of the cases in which 4–6-year-old children had made allegations, the comparable figure for 9- to13-year-olds was 12%. When children did not make allegations when interviewed, however, immediate family members were the initial trigger in 32%, 42%, and 32% of the cases, respectively, across age groups.

The younger children were not only less likely than older children to make allegations when formally interviewed but they were also less likely to do so following a prior disclosure. Of course, the prior disclosures were reported by other people, and the reliability of these secondhand reports may be questioned, especially when the reporters were not "disinterested." It appears, however, that if the person to whom the child had reportedly made the prior disclosure was an immediate family member, presumably those most likely to have a strong interest, children were no less (or more) likely to make an allegation in the formal interview.

Although the suspect confessed to the abusive incident or incidents in fewer than a third of all cases, confessions were not always associated with an allegation. Somewhat surprisingly, several of the older children did not make an allegation in the interview, when the suspect's confession had been triggered suspicion in the first place. More detailed examination showed, however, that in these cases the abusive incident or incidents had occurred several years earlier, and (or) the nature of the abuse was such that the child might not have interpreted it as abuse at the time, as discussed by Cederborg, Lamb, and Laurell (chapter 9, this volume). Nonetheless, to the extent that suspect confession is corroborative evidence, we can conclude that there were children in all age groups who had been abused but did not report the abuse. The reasons for the nondisclosure are many and varied and are likely to differ developmentally, as a function of the nature of the abuse, and the circumstances surrounding it.

In sum, in this sample of children, it was the youngest children who were least likely to make an allegation of abuse in the formal investigative interview. The finding that younger children are less likely to allege abuse is not specific to the open-ended interviewing style characterizing the NICHD interview protocol; to the contrary, the disclosure rates reported here compare very favorably with those from other studies. We found no basis for suspecting that fewer of the younger children had indeed been abused, and hence that the lower allegation rate reflected a lower rate of abuse amongst this age group; suspicions were no more likely to be based on ambiguous evidence than in the older age groups, verbal disclosures prior to the investigative interview were no less likely than in the older groups, and confessions as corroborative evidence were no less likely among the youngest group. Although an immediate family member was more likely to trigger the suspicion in the first instance for the younger children, this is readily understood in terms of the more restricted social milieu of the younger children; the older children had more outside confidantes and contacts, and perhaps people more familiar with them and their activities. Rather, it appears that the youngest children were less likely to disclose abuse when interviewed, despite reportedly having made a verbal allegation prior to the formal interview, and the low rate of disclosure was strongly associated with an immediate family member as a suspect. These findings point to the need for further refinement of techniques for interviewing of the youngest children to ensure that those who have been abused are able to disclose the abuse when formally interviewed.

ACKNOWLEDGMENTS

Special thanks to Kyiah Butler, Veronica Chavez, Katie Hrapzinski, Melanie Pienknagura, Kathleen Sullivan, and Nina Thomas for help with coding, data analysis, and preparation of this paper.

REFERENCES

Arata, C. M. (1998). To tell or not to tell: Current functioning of child sexual abuse survivors who disclosed their victimization. *Child Maltreatment: Journal of the American Professional Society on the Abuse of Children, 3,* 63–71.

Berliner, L., & Conte J. R. (1995). The effects of disclosure and intervention on sexually abused children. *Child Abuse and Neglect, 19,* 371–84.

Bidrose, S., & Goodman, G. S. (2000). Testimony and evidence: A scientific case study of memory for child sexual abuse. *Applied Cognitive Psychology, 14,* 197–213.

Bottoms, B., Goodman, G., Schwartz-Kenney, & Thomas, S. (2002). Understanding children's use of secrecy in the context of eyewitness reports. *Law and Human Behavior, 26,* 285–313.

Bradley, A. R., & Wood, J. M. (1996). How do children tell? The disclosure process in child sexual abuse. *Child Abuse & Neglect, 9,* 881–91.

Bruck, M., & Ceci, S. J. (1999). The suggestibility of children's memory. *Annual Review of Psychology, 50,* 419–39.

Bussey, K., & Grimbeek, E. J. (1995). Disclosure processes: Issues for child sexual abuse victims. In K. Rotenberg (Ed.), *Disclosure processes in children and adolescents* (pp. 166–203). NY: Cambridge University Press.

Ceci, S. J., & Bruck, M. (1993). Suggestibility of the child witness: A historical review and synthesis. *Psychological Bulletin, 113,* 403–39.

Ceci, S. J., & Friedman, R. D. (2000). The suggestibility of children: Scientific research and legal implications. *Cornell Law Review, 86,* 34–108.

DeVoe, E. R., & Faller, K. C. (1999). The characteristics of disclosure among children who may have been sexually abused. *Child Maltreatment, 4,* 217–27.

DiPietro, E. K., Runyan, D. K., & Frederickson, D. D. (1997). Predictors of disclosure during medical evaluations for suspected sexual abuse. *Journal of Child Sexual Abuse, 6,* 133–42.

Goodman, G. S., Ghetti, S., Quas, J. A., Edelstein, R. S., Weede Alexander, K., Redlich, A. D., Cordon, I. M., & Jones, D. P. H. (2003). A prospective study of memory for child sexual abuse. *Psychological Science, 14,* 113–18.

Goodman-Brown, T. B., Edelstein, R. S., Goodman, G. S., Jones, D. P. H., & Gordon, D. S. (2003). Why children tell: A model of children's disclosure of sexual abuse. *Child Abuse & Neglect, 27,* 525–40.

Hershkowitz, I., Horowitz, D., & Lamb, M. E. (2005). Trends in children's disclosure of abuse in Israel: A national study. *Child Abuse and Neglect, 29,* 1203–1214.

Keary, K., & Fitzpatrick, C. (1994). Children's disclosure of sexual abuse during formal investigation. *Child Abuse & Neglect, 18,* 543–48.

Lawson, L., & Chaffin, M. (1992). False negatives in sexual abuse disclosure interviews: Incidence and influences of caretaker's belief in abuse in cases of accidental abuse discovery by diagnosis of STD. *Journal of Interpersonal Violence, 7*, 532–42.

London, K., Bruck, M., Ceci, S. J., & Shuman, D. W. (2005). Disclosure of Child Sexual Abuse: What Does the Research Tell Us About the Ways That Children Tell? *Psychology, Public Policy, & Law, 11*, 194–226.

Orbach, Y., Hershkowitz, I., Lamb, M. E., Sternberg, K. J., Esplin, P. W., & Horowitz, D. (2000). Assessing the value of structured protocols for forensic interviews of alleged child abuse victims. *Child Abuse and Neglect, 24*, 733–52.

Paine, M. L., Hansen, D. J. (2002) Factors influencing children to self-disclose sexual abuse. *Clinical Psychology Review, 22*, 271–95.

Pipe, M.-E., & Goodman, G. (1991). Elements of secrecy: Implications for children's testimony. *Behavioral Sciences and the Law, 9*, 33–41.

Poole, D. A., & Lamb, M. E. (1998). *Investigative interviews of children: A guide for helping professionals.* Washington, DC: American Psychological Association.

Sauzier, M. (1989). Disclosure of child sexual abuse: For better or for worse. *Psychiatric Clinics of North America, 12*, 455–69.

Schaaf, J. M., Alexander, K. W., Goodman, G. S, Ghetti, S., Edelstein, R. S., & Castelli, P. (2002). Children's eyewitness memory: True disclosures and false reports. In B. L. Bottoms, M. K. Bull, & B. D. McAuliff (Eds.), *Children, social science, and the law* (pp. 342–77). New York: Cambridge University Press.

Sorenson, T., & Snow, B. (1991). How children tell: The process of disclosure in child sexual abuse. *Child Welfare, 70*, 3–15.

Sternberg, K. J., Lamb, M. E., Orbach, Y., Esplin, P., & Mitchell, S. (2001). Use of a structured investigative protocol enhances young children's responses to free-recall prompts in the course of forensic interviews. *Journal of Applied Psychology, 86*, 997–1005.

Summit, R. C. (1983). The child sexual abuse accommodation syndrome. *Child Abuse & Neglect, 7(2)*, 177–93.

6

Suspected Victims of Abuse Who Do Not Make Allegations: An Analysis of Their Interactions With Forensic Interviewers

Irit Hershkowitz
University of Haifa, Israel

Yael Orbach, Kathleen J. Sternberg, Margaret-Ellen Pipe
National Institute of Child Health and Human Development

Michael E. Lamb
University of Cambridge, United Kingdom

Dvora Horowitz
Israeli Ministry of Labour and Social Affairs, Jerusalem, Israel

It is widely recognized that many victims fail to disclose that they have been abused. Clear understanding of the reasons why they behave this way when interviewed is seriously impeded by a lack of information about the way these children were interviewed (London, Bruck, Ceci, & Shuman, 2005; chapter 2 this volume; Pipe, Stewart, Sternberg, Lamb, & Esplin, 2003). In particular, there is substantial reason to believe that the way children are interviewed—especially the use of leading and coercive practices, repeated questioning, or the reliance on anatomically detailed dolls—may affect what they say. Most studies of disclosure and nondisclosure rates do not provide sufficient information about investigative and interviewing practices, however. Critics have argued (London et al., chapter 2 this volume; Poole & Lindsay, 1998) that interviewing procedures in some of the widely cited studies (Gonzalez, Waterman, Kelly, McCord, & Oliveri, 1993; Sorensen & Snow, 1991) were seriously flawed, leaving ambiguity about whether the disclosures were valid. The present study was designed to explore differences between interviews in which 4- to 13-year-old children made allegations of abuse during forensic interviews and those in which children of the same age did not make allegations despite previous disclosures or strong evidence of abuse. The research was facilitated by the fact that all interviewers were guided by the same interviewing protocol and were thus striving to interview all children in similar ways.

In the last decade, many professionals have described the best ways to interview alleged child abuse victims (e.g., American Professional Society on the Abuse of Children [APSAC], 2002; Bull, 1992; Lamb, Sternberg, & Esplin, 1998; Memorandum of Good Practice, 1992; Poole & Lamb, 1998; Raskin & Esplin, 1991). Recognizing the remarkable agreement among professional groups and researchers with respect to optimal practices, researchers at the National Institute of Child Health and Human Development (NICHD) operationalized these recommendations in the form of an investigative interview protocol comprising specific and concrete guidelines that forensic interviewers can follow (Orbach, Hershkowitz, Lamb, Sternberg, Esplin, & Horowitz, 2000). Introduction of the NICHD Investigative Protocol has facilitated systematic research on the dynamics of interviews with alleged abuse victims and has permitted researchers to show how much information can be elicited, even from quite young children, when they are interviewed in accordance with "best practice" guidelines (Aldridge, Lamb, Sternberg, Orbach, Esplin, & Bowler, 2004; Lamb, Orbach, Sternberg, Esplin, & Hershkowitz, 2002; Lamb, Sternberg, Orbach, Esplin, Stewart, & Mitchell, 2003; Orbach et al., 2000; Sternberg, Lamb, Orbach, Esplin, & Mitchell, 2001). To date, however, studies using the NICHD Investigative Protocol have been limited to interviews with cooperative alleged victims who have made specific allegations of abuse during the forensic interview. As a result, we do not know about the dynamics of interviews with reluctant victims who do not disclose abuse. The current study was the first to examine closely the dynamics of interviews with nondisclosing children, selected for study because there were good objective reasons to believe that they had actually been abused. The study was designed to explore differences between protocol-guided interviews with suspected child-victims in which children made allegations and those in which children did not make allegations despite strong evidence of abuse or previous disclosures.

Approximately a third of the alleged victims interviewed in Israel do not disclose abuse during forensic interviews, despite some evidence that abuse might have occurred (Hershkowitz, Horowitz, & Lamb, chapter 4 this volume). Victims who withhold information or deny that they were abused presumably do so in order to protect familiar perpetrators, especially family members (Paine & Hansen, 2002; Yuille, Tymofievich, & Marxsen, 1995), or because they yield to requests for secrecy (DeYoung, 1988; Goodman-Brown, 1995), assume some responsibility or blame (Lyon, 2002; Sjöberg & Lindblad, 2002), feel ashamed or embarrassed (Lyon, 1995; Saywitz, Goodman, Nicholas, & Moan, 1991), or fear threatened or imagined negative outcomes (Berliner & Conte, 1995; DeYoung, 1988; Paine & Hansen, 2002; Palmer, Brown, Rae-Grant, & Loughlin, 1999). In addition, young victims may not understand that they have been abused and may have failed to encode or remember experiences that did not appear salient to them (Cedeborg, Lamb, & Laurell, chapter 9, this volume).

Because children are typically somewhat shy in initial encounters with unfamiliar adults, forensic interviewers are routinely advised to establish rapport with children and to prepare them in other ways before turning attention to the possible abuse, so as to maximize their willingness and capacity to be informative (Poole & Lamb, 1998; Saywitz & Goodman, 1996; Sternberg, Lamb, Hershkowitz, Yudilevitch, Orbach, Esplin, & Hovav, 1997). Interviewers using the NICHD Protocol instruct children to tell the truth, to report personally experienced events only, and to admit lack of knowledge or lack of understanding, correcting the interviewer when necessary (Orbach et al., 2000; Poole & Lamb, 1998; Sternberg et al., 2001). Explicit rules of communication are also explained in order to diminish confusion and inaccuracy while maximizing the resistance to suggestion. To further motivate them, children are typically reminded that they are unique sources of information and are encouraged to practice reporting information from episodic memory by describing other personally meaningful events (Fivush & Shukat, 1995). Clear expectations are conveyed to the children regarding the amount of details and level of spontaneous elaboration expected of them in order to increase the amounts of event-specific information they provide.

Recent field research on forensic interviewing practices has shown that use of the NICHD investigative interview protocol improves retrieval in both the presubstantive and substantive phases of the interview (Lamb, Sternberg, Orbach, Esplin, Stewart, & Mitchell, 2003; Orbach et al., 2000; Sternberg et al., 2001). Because free-recall prompts are more likely than recognition prompts to elicit accurate information (Dale, Loftus, & Rathbun, 1978; Dent & Stephenson, 1979; Hutcheson, Baxter, Telfer, & Warden, 1995; Oates & Shrimpton, 1991), protocol-guided interviews are characterized by greater reliance on such prompts than non-protocol interviews are (Orbach et al., 2000; Sternberg et al., 2001). As a result, children interviewed using the protocol provide more information in response to free-recall prompts than do children interviewed using other approaches (Orbach et al., 2000; Sternberg et al., 1997, 2001). Recognition prompts (including yes/no and forced-choice questions that introduce information provided by the interviewer rather than the child and are known to raise the risk of eliciting erroneous information) are minimized and are delayed as much as possible in NICHD-protocol interviews.

The present study was designed to explore differences in interview dynamics between forensic interviews in which children made allegations and those in which children did not make allegations. To assess these differences, we compared the interviewers' prompts and the children's responses during the presubstantive and "getting the allegation" phases of forensic interviews. Interviews in the allegation and nonallegation groups were matched with respect to age of child, abuse type, perpetrator familiarity, and, where possible, strength of the suspicion that triggered the investigation. The variables explored included the interviewers' eliciting utterance types (invitations, directive, option-posing, and suggestive), which were also categorized with respect to the type of memory retrieval prompted (recall [free- and cued-] and recognition), the interviewers' supportive and nonsupportive verbal behavior, and the children's responses to the interviewers' prompts, categorized as informative, uninformative, or denials.

As in interviews with young suspects or perpetrators (Hershkowitz, Horowitz, Lamb, Orbach, & Sternberg, 2004), we expected that interviewers might use more focused and even coercive strategies while withholding support from children who were reluctant to provide information. We thus predicted that interviewers would use more recognition than free-recall prompts and would be less supportive and more confrontational when interviewing children who did not make allegations. We expected that children in "no-allegation" interviews would show their reluctance by giving more uninformative (e.g., omission, "don't know," "don't want to talk," "don't remember"), digressive (e.g., reversions to nonsubstantive responses or issues), and denial (e.g., "never happened") responses during the "getting the allegation" phase than children who made allegations of abuse.

THE INTERVIEWS

A total of 100 forensic interviews with 4- to 13-year-old alleged victims (M = 8.8 years, SD = 2.99; 57 boys and 43 girls) were examined. The 50 interviews of suspected victims who did not allege abuse during the interview were matched with the same number of forensic interviews of alleged victims who made allegations of sexual or physical abuse. Interviews were matched with respect to age, abuse type (sexual, n = 19; physical, n = 31), perpetrator familiarity (parent, n = 66; non-parent, n = 34), and basis for suspicion (strong evidence, n = 32; prior disclosure, n = 18). Children were divided into two age groups (4 to 8 and 9 to 13 years). All interviews were conducted between 1998 and 2003 by trained youth investigators, who are the only officials who can formally question child victims, witnesses, and suspects under the age of 14 in Israel; their recommendations have a major impact on the interventions attempted by courts and social service agencies (see Sternberg, Lamb, & Hershkowitz, 1996, for further information about the Israeli system).

All interviews were rated with respect to the strength of evidence or the basis for suspicion using the "Ground Truth" scheme described by Lamb and his colleagues (Lamb, Sternberg, Esplin, Hershkowitz, & Orbach, 1997; Lamb, Sternberg, Esplin, Hershkowitz, Orbach, & Hovav, 1997). Only cases in which there was substantial reason to believe that abuse had taken place (i.e., medical evidence, clear disclosure to a non-interested person such as a teacher or psychologist, reports by disinterested eyewitnesses, or perpetrator confessions) were included in the study.

Procedure

All interviews were conducted using the NICHD investigative interview protocol (see Orbach et al., 2000). As explained earlier, protocol interviews open with a presubstantive phase designed to establish rapport with the interviewees, prepare child-witnesses for their role as information providers, and teach narrative responsive styles while exploring neutral experienced events. Interviewers then switch focus to substantive issues in a nonsuggestive fashion, giving priority to free-recall, in a structured series of "getting the allegation" prompts. Increasingly focused nonsuggestive recognition prompts follow if "free-recall" prompts fail to elicit a disclosure.

Audio-taped recordings of the interviews were transcribed and checked to ensure their completeness and accuracy. Native Hebrew speakers then coded the presubstantive and "getting the allegation" phases of the interviews. Two raters coded interviewers' utterances with respect to type and supportiveness, categorized children's response types, and tabulated the number of details conveyed in the children's responses.

Inter-rater Reliability

The coders were trained on an independent set of transcripts until they agreed 98% of the time in their categorization of interviewers' utterance types, supportiveness, and insistence, as well as the children's responses and the number of details reported. During the course of training, 20% of the transcripts were independently recoded by two or more of the raters to ensure that they remained equivalently reliable. In these assessments, raters agreed regarding the classification of at least 98% of the interviewer utterances and 95% of the children's responses and details.

Coding Interviewer Behavior

All interviewers' utterances (defined as "turns" in the discourse) in both the presubstantive and the substantive phases of the interview were classified as either information-requesting prompts or noninformation-requesting utterances. All information-requesting prompts were further categorized, based on the extent of interviewer input, using the four exhaustive and mutually exclusive categories introduced by Lamb and his colleagues (Lamb, Hershkowitz, Sternberg, Boat, & Everson, 1996; Lamb, Hershkowitz, Sternberg, Esplin, Hovav, & Manor, 1996), i.e., invitations, directive, option-posing, and suggestive. These four categories are often considered with respect to the type of memory tapped, i.e., recall (invitations and directive prompts) and recognition (option-posing and suggestive). Noninformation-requesting utterances involving introductory comments (procedural) as well as unfinished and unclear utterances were also noted. In addition to these interviewer utterance types, interviewers' comments inserted within any type of utterance in either the presubstantive and substantive phases of the interview were coded for supportiveness.

Information-Requesting Prompts

1. *Invitations* prompted free-recall responses from the child. Such utterances provided a general invitation to report what happened during the investigated event or event components, without limiting the child's focus except in a general way (e.g., "Tell me everything that happened") or used details disclosed by the child as cues (e.g., "You mentioned that you touched him. Tell me everything about the touching").

2. *Directive prompts* refocused on details or aspects of the alleged incident that the child had previously mentioned and provided a category for additional information, typically in the form of "wh–" questions (e.g., "When did it happen?" when the child disclosed that something happened).

3. *Option-posing prompts* focused the child's attention on details or aspects of the alleged incident that the child had not previously mentioned. These utterances prompted the child to affirm, negate, or select among investigator-given options, using recognition memory processes (i.e., yes/no and "forced-choice" questions) but did not imply that a particular response was expected (e.g., "Did she touch you over or under your clothes?" when the child mentioned being touched).

4. *Suggestive prompts* were stated in such a way that the interviewer strongly communicated what response was expected (e.g. "He forced you to do that, didn't he?") or assumed details that had not been disclosed by the child (e.g., Child: "We laid on the sofa." Interviewer: "You laid on her or she laid on you?").

Interviewers' utterances that did not request information were not included in the utterance type analyses.

Noninformation-Requesting Utterances

Noninformation-requesting utterances provided procedural information during the interview but did not prompt the interviewees for information. In addition, all unfinished and unclear interviewer utterances were included in this category.

Interviewer Supportiveness

Supportive comments involved comments anywhere in the interview intended to unconditionally encourage children to disclose information. *Supportive comments* were categorized using four exhaustive and mutually exclusive categories:

1. *Nonsuggestive positive reinforcement* involved positive responses to the children's behavior during the interview (e.g., "You are telling very well").

2. *Addressing the child in a personal way* involved using names or terms of endearment (e.g., "Dan, tell me everything about that").

3. *References to the child's emotions* involved expressions of empathy in response to the children's expressions of positive or negative emotion during the interview (e.g., "I understand that it is very difficult for you to tell me this").

4. *Facilitators* involved nonsuggestive encouragement—by saying "ok," "Aha," or by echoing the children's last few words—to continue talking.

By contrast, *unsupportive comments* were interviewer's comments anywhere in the interview exerting pressure on children to respond by challenging information they provide or criticizing their behavior. *Unsupportive comments* were categorized using four exhaustive and mutually exclusive categories:

1. In *confrontations*, interviewers challenged the information provided by the children by referring to an external source (e.g., ". . . but I heard from the police officer that [details] happened"), a physical mark on the child's body ("You said that nothing had happened, so how do you explain this burn on your hand?"), or the implausibility of the child's statement (or contradiction).

2. *Reference to positive outcomes* involved conditional statements that positive outcomes would follow if the children cooperated (e.g., "If you tell me, you'll feel better"; "If you tell me, we can help you").

3. *Warnings about negative outcomes* involved conditional statements that negative outcomes would follow if the children did not cooperate (e.g., "We cannot help children who do not talk").

4. *Negative references to the child's behavior* involved criticism of the children's behavior during the interview (e.g., "You're looking away"; "Don't touch the tape-recorder"; "Sit still!"; "You are talking too softly, I can't hear you").

Coding Children's Responses

The children's responses were categorized using three exhaustive and mutually exclusive categories: *informative, uninformative,* and *denials.*

In *informative responses,* children provided the information requested in the eliciting utterance. *Informative details* were thus defined as words or phrases identifying or describing individuals, objects, or events (including actions) that were related to the topics being investigated (Lamb, Hershkowitz, Sternberg, Esplin, et al., 1996). Details were used as units to measure the amount of information reported and were only counted when they were new and added to understanding of the topic discussed. As a result, restatements were not counted.

Uninformative responses did not provide the information requested in the eliciting utterance and were classified using the following five exhaustive and mutually exclusive categories:

1. *Omissions* involved failing to respond informatively, omitting any response (i.e., no answer), providing unclear, inaudible, or unfinished responses, excusing an inability to provide an informative response (e.g., "don't know," "don't remember," "not sure"), or requesting clarification (e.g., "What do you mean?").

2. *Digressions* involved responses that were unrelated to the eliciting content (e.g., Interviewer: "How old are you?" Child: "My friend did not behave well at school").

3. *Displacements* involved unexpected and irrelevant allegations in response to any of the "getting the allegation" prompts (e.g., Interviewer: "Do you know why you are here today?" Child: "A kid in my class threw a stone at me") or implausible explanations in response to questions about bruises or injuries (e.g., Interviewer: "I have a doctor's report showing that you have serious burns on your . . ." Child: "I fell on a hot plate").

4. *Resistance* involved verbal expressions or actions indicating that the children were unwilling to provide information or be interviewed (e.g., verbal responses such as "I don't want to tell"; action responses like unplugging the microphone or leaving the interview room).

5. *Denials* involved claims that an investigated event, a previous interaction, or an earlier disclosure never happened, or admissions that a previous disclosure was false.

FINDINGS

Interviewers' Behavior

Overall, interviewers posed more questions to nondisclosing children than to children who made allegations ($t_{(98)} = -5.646$, $p < .000$). Interviewers posed fewer invitations ($t_{(98)} = -5.671$, $p < .000$) and proportionally more option-posing ($t_{(98)} = 4.203$, $p < .000$) and suggestive ($t_{(98)} = -5.606$, $p < .000$) prompts when interviewing children who did not make allegations as opposed to children who did (see table 6.1). They also made fewer supportive comments ($t_{(98)} = 3.09$, $p < .003$) to children who did not disclose than to those who made allegations.

Children's Responses

As expected, children who did not make allegations gave fewer informative responses during the presubstantive phase of the interview than their counterparts ($t_{(98)} = -6.356$, $p < .000$, see table 6.1). Only 17.4% of the children who

TABLE 6.1
Interviewers' Utterances and Children's Responses

	Nondisclosers		Disclosers	
	Mean	SD	Mean	SD
Interviewers' utterances				
Total number of utterances	53.40	21.83	29.52	20.47
Information requesting prompts (proportions)				
Invitations	.53	.17	.72	.17
Directive	.16	.16	.12	.11
Option-posing	.21	.09	.13	.10
Suggestive	.08	.08	.01	.02
Interviewers' supportiveness				
Proportion of supportive comments	.416	.158	.526	.214
Proportion of non-supportive comments	.029	.041	.015	.050
Children's responses (proportions)				
Informative	.566	.191	.812	.194
Uninformative	.298	.226	.159	.176
Denial	.135	.090	.027	.048
Average number of details per response				
Average response	3.70	4.65	7.60	6.88
Response to invitations	6.27	9.43	9.23	8.21
Response to directive prompts	2.61	2.46	5.57	13.12
Response to option-posing prompts	1.26	2.70	1.25	1.98
Response to suggestive prompts	1.47	2.89	5.19	6.62

did not disclose gave informative responses to all the prompts posed by the interviewers in the episodic memory training phase, compared to 56.5% of the disclosing children. A logistic regression analysis revealed that the proportion of informative responses significantly predicted whether children would make allegations ($X2_{(1)} = 15.71; p < .001$). The overall predictive probability was 69.6%, with partial informativeness predicting nondisclosure in 82.6% of the cases and full informativeness predicting disclosure in 56.5% of the cases. Partially informative children were about 6 times less likely to make allegations than fully informative children were ($Exp_{(B)} = 6.175$).

Nondisclosing children also gave more uninformative responses than disclosing children did ($t_{(98)} = 3.410, p < .001$), offering more responses that involved omissions ($t_{(98)} = 2.391, p < .019$), displacements ($t_{(98)} = 2.799, p < .006$), and denials ($t_{(98)} = 7.337, p < .000$), and tended to offer more physical and verbal resistance ($t_{(98)} = -1.833, p < .070$). They also provided fewer details ($t_{(83)} = -1.983, p < .053$)—particularly spontaneous details ($t_{(98)} = -3.315, p < .001$)—than children who made allegations. Compared with children in the allegation group, children in the nonallegation group provided significantly fewer details on average in response to each interviewer prompt ($t_{(98)} = 3.31, p < .001$) and in responses to suggestive prompts ($t_{(98)} = 3.022, p < .004$). They also tended to provide fewer details in responses to invitations ($t_{(98)} = -1.669, p < .098$) and to directive ($t_{(98)} = 1.970, p < .051$) prompts.

Interestingly, all children, regardless of disclosure group, provided more details in their average responses to invitations than in their average responses to directive, option-posing or suggestive prompts ($F(3,11) = 9.361; p < 000$ and $F(3,11) = 6.272; p < 001$ for allegation and nonallegation interviews, respectively).

Effects of the Source of Suspicion

An ANOVA revealed a near significant main effect of the source of suspicion (previous disclosure or evidence) on the interviewers' supportiveness ($F_{(1,100)} = 3.18; p < .077$) and a significant interaction between the source of suspicion and disclosure with respect to the interviewer's supportiveness $F_{(1,100)} = 5.02, p < .027$). Interviewers were in general more supportive of children who previously disclosed than of children for whom there was evidence ($M = .51$, $SD = .20$ vs. $M = .44, SD = .18$). When interviewing disclosing children, however, interviewers were more supportive of children who previously disclosed than of those for whom there was evidence ($M = .62$, $SD = .20$ vs. $M = .47$, $SD = .20$), whereas when interviewing nondisclosers, interviewers were less supportive of children who previously disclosed than of children for whom there was evidence ($M = .40, SD = .15$ vs. $M = .42, SD = .16$).

Age Differences

In other multivariate analyses, the children's ages were significantly associated with the proportions of responses that were informative and uninformative. Children up to nine years of age provided fewer informative ($M = .61$, $SD = .24$ vs. $M = .77$, $SD = .17$; $F_{(1,97)} = 20.30$, $p < .0001$) and more uninformative responses than older children did ($M = .30$, $SD = .24$ vs. $M = .15$, $SD = .13$; $F_{(1,97)} = 15.64$, $p < .0001$).

Age and disclosure interacted in their effect on the proportion of denial responses. Whereas older children in the nonallegation group provided more denial responses than younger children did ($M = .14$, $SD = .09$ vs. $M = .12$, $SD = .08$), older children in the allegation group provided fewer denial responses than younger children did ($M = .01$, $SD = .01$ vs. $M = .04$, $SD = .06$; $F_{(1,97)} = 4.37$, $p < .039$).

Type of Abuse

Main effects for type of abuse (sexual vs. physical) were apparent in the interviewers' behavior. Interviewers posed more invitations ($M = .66$, $SD = .17$ vs. $M = .60$, $SD = .21$; $F_{(1,97)} = 5.691$, $p < .080$) and fewer directive prompts ($M = 10$, $SD = .06$ vs. $M = .17$, $SD = .17$; $F(1,97) = 4.588$, $p < .035$) to suspected sexual abuse victims than they did to suspected physical abuse victims although they were equally supportive of children in both groups. The type of abuse and disclosure interacted in their effect on the proportion of prompts that were option-posing questions. When interviewing nondisclosers, interviewers posed more option-posing prompts to suspected victims of physical abuse than to suspected victims of sexual abuse ($M = .19$, $SD = .08$ vs. $M = .14$, $SD = .10$ and $M = .25$, $SD = .10$ vs. $M = .10$, $SD = .10$; $F_{(1,97)} = 6.415$, $p < .013$, for physical and sexual abuse, respectively).

Children reacted differentially depending on the type of abuse suspected. Suspected victims of sexual abuse provided more informative ($M = .65$, $SD = .24$ vs. $M = .75$, $SD = .17$; $F_{(1,97)} = 7.41$, $p < .008$) and fewer uninformative responses than suspected victims of physical abuse did ($M = .27$, $SD = .24$ vs. $M = .14$, $SD = .11$; $F_{(1,97)} = 9.84$, $p < .002$). Suspected victims of sexual abuse also provided more details on average in response to each interviewer prompt than suspected victims of physical abuse did ($M = 7.34$, $SD = 7.25$ vs. $M = 4.70$, $SD = 5.25$; $F_{(1,97)} = 4.80$, $p < .031$).

The type of abuse suspected and disclosure interacted in their effect on the proportion of responses that were denials. Specifically, whereas nondisclosers denied more than disclosers overall, the difference was especially marked among suspected victims of sexual abuse ($M = .17$, $SD = .09$ vs. $M = .01$, $SD = .05$) as opposed to physical abuse ($M = .11$, $SD = .08$ vs $M = .03$, $SD = .04$) abuse ($F_{(1,97)} = 6.65$, $p < .011$).

Gender Effects

Interviewers posed proportionally more invitations ($M = .68$, $SD = .15$ vs. $M = .58$, $SD = .21$; $F_{(1,97)} = 5.554$, $p < .021$) and fewer directive questions ($M = .10$, $SD = .09$ vs. $M = .18$, $SD = .14$; $F_{(1,97)} = 6.176$, $p < .015$) to girls than to boys. They also tended to be more supportive of girls than of boys ($M = .45$, $SD = .20$ vs. $M = .39$, $SD = .11$; $F_{(1,97)} = 3.427$, $p < .067$).

Statistical interactions between gender and disclosure were apparent with respect to the children's responsiveness $F_{(1,97)} = 6.05$, $p < .016$) and unresponsiveness ($F_{(1,97)} = 4.73$, $p < .032$). Girls in the allegation group were more informative than boys ($M = .91$, $SD = .10$ vs. $M = .72$, $SD = .21$), whereas there were no differences between girls and boys in the nonallegation group ($M = .57$, $SD = .20$ vs. $M = .57$, $SD = .17$ for girls and boys, respectively. Compared to boys, girls in the nonallegation group also offered slightly fewer uninformative responses ($M = .28$, $SD = .04$ vs. $M = .29$ $SD = .05$) whereas girls in the allegation group offered considerably fewer uninformative responses ($M = .07$, $SD = .08$ vs. $M = .23$, $SD = .20$).

Overall, girls provided more details per response than boys ($M = 7.29$, $SD = 6.85$ vs. $M = 4.50$, $SD = 5.40$; $F_{(1,97)} = 4.65$, $p < .034$) but there was a near-significant interaction between gender and disclosure on the number of details ($F_{(1,97)} = 3.42$, $p < .067$). Whereas girls provided slightly more details than boys in nonallegation interviews ($M = 3.96$, $SD = 4.56$ vs. $M = 3.61$, $SD = 4.84$), they provided considerably more details than boys in allegation interviews ($M = 10.18$, $SD = 7.26$ vs. $M = 5.50$, $SD = 5.89$).

The Effects of Relationship to the Suspect

Fewer invitations ($M = .59$, $SD = .20$ vs. $M = .68$, $SD = .16$; $F (1,99) = 3.758$ $p < .055$) were addressed to children suspected of having been abused by their parents than to children who were suspected victims of abuse by other individuals. Children who were suspected victims of parental abuse provided proportionally fewer informative responses ($M = .65$, $SD = .24$ vs. $M = .75$, $SD = .18$; $F (1,99) = 5.340$, $p < .023$) and more uninformative responses ($M = .26$, $SD = .23$ vs. $M = .16$, $SD = .14$; $F (1,99) = 5.854$, $p < .017$) than children who were suspected victims of nonparental perpetrators. They also provided fewer details per response than did counterparts believed to have been abused by individuals other than their parents ($M = 7.31$, $SD = 7.39$ vs. $M = 4.68$, $SD = 5.12$; $F(1,93) = 3.91$, $p < .051$).

DISCUSSION

The descriptive analyses reported here make clear that forensic interviews that yielded allegations of child abuse were characterized by quite different dynamics than interviews with children who seemed equivalently likely to have been abused but chose not to make allegations during the interview. When interviewing nondisclosers, the interviewers adhered less closely to the NICHD protocol with respect to both memory-elicitation strategies and expressions of support. The interviewers thus made less frequent use of free-recall prompts and offered fewer supportive comments when interviewing nondisclosers than when interviewing children who made allegations of abuse. In nonallegation interviews, interviewers tended to use more recognition memory prompts in an effort to elicit information. In most allegation interviews, by contrast, interviewers did not have to proceed to recognition prompts before the children made allegations. The protocol recommends starting with more open prompts before resorting to more focused prompts, so when disclosing children began providing narrative accounts, interviewers did not have to resort to the more focused prompts. By contrast, when interviewers failed to elicit allegations using open-ended means, they had to resort to more focused recognition prompts when interviewing nondisclosing children. Interestingly, as in the case of young offenders (Hershkowitz et al., 2004), the nondisclosers behaved like cooperative "disclosing" children in the presubstantive phase of the interview to the extent that they were more responsive and informative in response to free-recall invitations than in response to recognition prompts, although the interviewers relied on proportionally more of the latter.

Although reluctant children probably needed more rather than less emotional support, nondisclosers were given less support than children who made allegations. These experienced interviewers acted as though they were unaware of how important it is to be supportive and maintain rapport, especially when children may have emotional and motivational reasons to avoid disclosing their experiences. Interviewers were remarkably less supportive of nondisclosers who disclosed to someone before the interview but refused to tell in the interview. This finding suggests that interviewers' reacted to their own frustration rather than to the children's needs. Whether nondisclosers were affected by feelings of guilt, shame, commitment, or fear, reluctant children are likely to experience forensic interviews as stressful and to perceive the interviewers as threatening.

In a previous report (Hershkowitz, Horowitz, & Lamb, 2005) we emphasized the association between interviewers' supportiveness and children's informativeness during different phases of the interviews. Although interviewers provided equal amounts of support to disclosers and nondisclosers during the first phase of the interview, they tended to gradually withdraw their support from nondisclosers as the children became less informative, which in turn, may have influenced the children's motivation to disclose. These findings are consistent with previous findings (Carter, Bottoms, & Levine, 1996; Davis & Bottoms, 2002; Goodman, Bottoms, Schwartz-Kenney, & Rudy, 1991; Imhoff & Baker-Ward, 1999) demonstrating that interviewer supportiveness has a positive effect on the amount of information provided by children.

Interviewers also used less appropriate techniques (using more recognition memory prompts than free-recall prompts) when interviewing less

informative eyewitnesses, i.e., boys rather than girls, suspected victims of physical abuse rather than of sexual abuse, and victims of parental rather than of
non-parental perpetrators.

The findings also suggest that the likelihood to disclose can be assessed
with reasonable validity by noting children's responsiveness and engagement
during the presubstantive rapport building. Such assessments may help investigators decide whether to proceed with the substantive phase of forensic
interviews. Using this simple, easy to apply, predictive indicator of informativeness, many reluctant disclosers can apparently be identified and given additional rapport building and support before substantive issues are broached. If
nonreluctant children are incorrectly identified as reluctant, we assume that
no harm will be caused by the additional rapport building and support. It is
possible that some children may need to be interviewed on another occasion
and that investigators need to consider ending the interview without addressing substantive issues. Our results suggest that intrusive and confrontational
means certainly do not help reluctant children disclose abuse.

ACKNOWLEDGMENTS

The authors are grateful to the youth investigators who conducted the interviews and collected the corroborative evidence, as well as Carmit Katz and
Talma Manor for assistance coding the interviews and compiling ground truth
information. Unfortunately, Kathleen J. Sternberg died before the research
could be completed.

REFERENCES

Aldridge, J., Lamb, M. E., Sternberg, K. J., Orbach, Y., Esplin, P. W., & Bowler, L. (2004).
    Using a human figure drawing to elicit information from alleged victims of child sex-
    ual abuse. *Journal of Consulting and Clinical Psychology. 72,* 304–16.
American Professional Society on the Abuse of Children. (2002). *Guidelines for psychosocial
    evaluation of suspected sexual abuse in young children.* Chicago,IL: American Professional
    Society on the Abuse of Children.
Berliner, L., & Conte, J. R. (1995). The effects of disclosure and intervention on sexually
    abused children. *Child Abuse & Neglect, 19,* 371–84.
Bull, R. (1992). Obtaining evidence expertly: The reliability of interviews with child wit-
    nesses. *Expert Evidence, 1,* 5–12.
Carter, C. A., Bottoms, B. L., & Levine, M. (1996). Linguistic and socioemotional influ-
    ences on the accuracy of children's reports. *Law and Human Behavior, 20,* 335–58.
Cederborg, A.-C., Lamb, M. E. & Laurell, O. (2004, March 5). *Delay of disclosure, mini-
    mization and denial when the evidence is unambiguous: A multivictim case.* Paper presented
    in a symposium on Delayed and Non-disclosure of Child Sexual Abuse in Forensic In-
    terviews at the American Psychology-Law Society conference, Scottsdale, AZ.

Dale, P. S., Loftus, E. F., & Rathbun, L. (1978). The influence of the form of the question of the eyewitness testimony of preschool children. *Journal of Psycholinguistic Research, 74*, 269–77.

Davis, S. L., & Bottoms, B. L. (2002). The effects of social support on the accuracy of children's reports: Implications for the forensic interview. In I. B. Weiner (Ed.), *Personality and clinical psychology series* (pp. 437–57). Chichester, England: Wiley.

Dent, H. R., & Stephenson, G. M. (1979). An experimental study of the effectiveness of different techniques of questioning child witnesses. *British Journal of Social and Clinical Psychology, 18*, 41–51.

DeYoung, M. (1988). Issues in determining the veracity of sexual abuse allegations. *Children's Health Care, 17*, 50–57.

Fivush, R., & Shukat, J. R. (1995). Content, consistency, and coherence of early autobiographical recall. In M. S. Zaragoza, J. R. Graham, G. C. N. Hall, R. Hirschman, & Y. S. Ben-Porath (Eds.), *Memory and testimony in the child witness* (Vol. 1, pp. 5–23). Thousand Oaks, CA: Sage.

Gonzalez, L. S., Waterman, J., Kelly, R., McCord, J., & Oliveri, K. (1993). Children's patterns of disclosures and recantations of sexual and ritualistic abuse allegations in psychotherapy. *Child Abuse & Neglect, 17*, 281–89.

Goodman, G. S., Bottoms, B. L., Schwartz-Kenney, B. M., & Rudy, L. (1991). Children's testimony about a stressful event: Improving children's reports. *Journal of Narrative and Life History, 1*, 69–99.

Goodman-Brown, T. B. (1995). Why children tell: A model of children's disclosure of sexual abuse (Doctoral dissertation, California School of Professional Psychology, 1995). *Dissertation Abstracts International, 56*, 2325.

Hershkowitz, I., Horowitz, D., & Lamb, M. E. (2005). Trends in children's disclosure of abuse in Israel: A national study. *Child Abuse and Neglect, 29*, 1203–1214.

Hershkowitz, I., Horowitz, D., Lamb, M. E., Orbach, Y., & Sternberg, K. J. (2004). Interviewing youthful suspects in alleged sex crimes: A descriptive analysis. *Child Abuse & Neglect, 28*, 423–38.

Hershkowitz, I., Orbach, Y., Lamb, M. E., Pipe, M. E, Sternberg, K. J., & Horowitz, D. (2006). Dynamics of forensic interviews with suspected abuse victims who do not disclose abuse. *Child Abuse & Neglect, 30*, 753–770.

Hutcheson, G. D., Baxter, J. S., Telfer, K., & Warden, D. (1995). Child witness statement quality: Question type and errors of omission. *Law and Human Behavior, 19*, 631–48.

Imhoff, M. C., & Baker-Ward, L. (1999). Preschooler's suggestibility: Effects of developmentally appropriate language and interviewer supportiveness. *Journal of Applied Developmental Psychology 20*, 407–29.

Lamb, M. E., Hershkowitz, I., Sternberg, K. J., Boat, B., & Everson, M. D. (1996). Investigative interviews of alleged sexual abuse victims with and without anatomical dolls. *Child Abuse and Neglect, 20*, 1251–59.

Lamb, M. E, Hershkowitz, I., Sternberg, K. J., Esplin, P. W., Hovav, M., & Manor, T., et al. (1996). Effects of investigative utterance types on Israeli children's responses. *International Journal of Behavioral Development, 19*, 627–37.

Lamb, M. E., Orbach, Y., Sternberg, K. J., Esplin, P. W., & Hershkowitz, I. (2002). The effects of forensic interview practices on the quality of information provided by alleged victims of child abuse. In H. L. Westcott, G. M. Davies, & R. Bull (Eds.), *Children's testimony: A handbook of psychological research and forensic practice* (pp.131–45). Chichester, England: Wiley.

Lamb, M. E., Sternberg, K. J., Esplin, P. W. (1998). Conducting investigative interviews of alleged sexual abuse victims. *Child Abuse & Neglect, 22,* 813–23.

Lamb, M. E., Sternberg, K. J., Esplin, P. W., Hershkowitz, I., & Orbach, Y. (1997). Assessing the credibility of children's allegations of sexual abuse: A survey of recent research. Learning and Individual Differences, 9, 175–94.

Lamb, M. E., Sternberg, K. J., Esplin, P. W., Hershkowitz, I., Orbach, Y., & Hovav, M.(1997). Criterion-based content analysis: A field validation study. *Child Abuse & Neglect, 21,* 255–64.

Lamb, M. E., Sternberg, K. J., Orbach, Y., Esplin, P. W., Stewart, H. L., & Mitchell, S. (2003). Age differences in young children's responses to open-ended invitations in the course of forensic interviews. *Journal of Consulting and Clinical Psychology, 71,* 926–34.

London, K., Bruck, M., Ceci, S. J., & Shuman, D. W. (2005). Disclosure of child sexual abuse: What does the research tell us about the ways that children tell? *Psychology, Public Policy, and the Law, 11,* 194–226.

Lyon, T. D. (1995). False allegations and false denials in child sexual abuse. *Psychology, Public Policy, and Law, 1,* 429–37.

———. (2002). Scientific support for expert testimony on child sexual abuse accommodation. In J. R. Conte (Ed.), *Critical issues in child sexual abuse* (pp.107–38). Newbury Park, CA: Sage.

Memorandum of Good Practice (1992). London: Her Majesty's Stationery Office.

Oates, K., & Shrimpton, S. (1991). Children's memories for stressful and non-stressful events. *Medical Science and the Law, 31,* 4–10.

Orbach, Y., Hershkowitz, I., Lamb, M. E., Sternberg, K. J., Esplin, P. W., & Horowitz, D. (2000). Assessing the value of structured protocols for forensic interviews of alleged child abuse victims. *Child Abuse and Neglect, 24,* 733–52.

Paine, M. L., & Hansen, D. J. (2002). Factors influencing children to self-disclose sexual abuse. *Clinical Psychology Review, 22,* 271–95.

Palmer, S. E., Brown, R. A., Rae-Grant, N. I., & Loughlin, M. J. (1999). Responding to children's disclosure of familial abuse: What survivors tell us. *Child Welfare, 78,* 259–82.

Pipe, M. E., Stewart, H. L., Sternberg, K. J., Lamb, M. E., & Esplin, P. W. (2003, August). Non-disclosures and alleged abuse in forensic interviews. *Paper presented to a conference on Non-disclosure and delayed disclosure of child sexual abuse, Satra Bruk, Sweden.*

Poole, D. A., & Lamb, M. E. (1998). Investigative interviews of children: A *guide for helping professionals.* Washington, DC: American Psychological Association.

Poole, D. A., & Lindsay, D. S. (1998). Assessing the accuracy of young children's reports: Lessons from the investigation of child sexual abuse. *PreventivePsychology,* 1–26.

Raskin, D. C., & Esplin, P. W. (1991). Statement validity assessments: Interview procedures and content analyses of children's statements of sexual abuse. *Behavioral Assessment, 13,* 265–91.

Saywitz, K. J., & Goodman, G. S. (1996). Interviewing children in and out of court: Current research and practice implications. In J. Briere, L. Berliner, J. A. Bulkley, C. Jenny, & T. Reid (Eds.), *The APSAC handbook on child maltreatment* (pp. 297–318). Thousand Oaks, CA: Sage.

Saywitz, K. J., Goodman, G. S., Nicholas, E., & Moan, S. F. (1991). Children's memories of a physical examination involving genital touch: Implications for reports of child sexual abuse. *Journal of Consulting and Clinical Psychology, 59,* 682–91.

Sjöberg, R. L., & Lindblad, F. (2002). Delayed disclosure and disrupted communication during forensic investigation of child sexual abuse: A study of 47 corroborated cases. *Acta Paediatrica, 91,* 1391–96.

Sorensen, T., & Snow, B. (1991). How children tell: The process of disclosure in child sexual abuse. *Child Welfare, 19,* 3–17.

Sternberg, K. J., Lamb, M. E., & Hershkowitz, I. (1996). Child sexual abuse investigations in Israel. *Criminal Justice & Behavior, 23,* 322–37.

Sternberg, K. J., Lamb, M. E., Hershkowitz, I., Yudilevitch, L., Orbach, Y., Esplin, P. W., & Hovav, M. (1997). Effects of introductory style on children's abilities to describe experiences of sexual abuse. *Child Abuse & Neglect, 21,* 1133–46.

Sternberg, K. J., Lamb, M. E., Orbach, Y., Esplin, P. W., & Mitchell, S. (2001). Use of a structured investigative protocol enhances young children's responses to free recall prompts in the course of forensic interviews. *Journal of Applied Psychology, 86,* 997–1005.

Yuille, J. C., Tymofievich, M., & Marxsen, D. (1995). The nature of allegations of child sexual abuse. In T. Ney (Ed.), *True and false allegations of child sexual abuse: Assessment and case management* (pp. 21–46). New York, NY: Brunner/Mazel.

7

Reluctant Disclosers of Child Sexual Abuse

Yael Orbach, Hana Shiloach
National Institute of Child Health and Human Development

Michael E. Lamb
University of Cambridge, United Kingdom

Most researchers agree that the manner in which children are questioned has profound implications for what is "remembered" (Ceci & Bruck, 1995; Brainerd & Ornstein, 1991; Dent & Stephenson, 1989; Jones, 1989; Lamb, Sternberg, & Esplin, 1998; Poole & Lamb, 1998; Quinn, White, & Santilli, 1989). Because victims are frequently the only available sources of information, it is especially important that forensic investigators use interviewing strategies that are most likely to elicit accurate and complete accounts. There is a broad consensus that the amount and quality of information obtained from young children is affected by the types of prompts used by interviewers, with free-recall prompts eliciting more detailed and more accurate information than recognition memory prompts in both laboratory and forensic contexts (e.g., Dale, Loftus, & Rathbun, 1978; Dent, 1986; Dent & Stephenson, 1979; Goodman & Aman, 1990; Goodman, Bottoms, Schwartz-Kenney & Rudy, 1991; Hutcheson, Baxter, Telfer, & Warden, 1995; Lamb & Fauchier, 2001; Oates & Shrimpton, 1991; Orbach & Lamb, 2001; Ornstein, Gordon, & Larus, 1992). Whereas most open-ended prompts are formulated as invitations (to "tell everything that happened") or as directive "wh–" questions, which focus on disclosed information and request additional elaboration, recognition prompts are typically formulated as option-posing (yes/no or forced choice) or suggestive prompts (implying the expected responses), which introduce undisclosed information and request confirmation, rejection, or selection among investigator-given options. Young children, particularly preschoolers, are especially vulnerable to such suggestion and implicit coercion. As a result, many experts

115

and professional groups have recommended interview practices that empha-size open-ended strategies for eliciting rich and accurate accounts from alleged victims (e.g., American Professional Society on the Abuse of Children [APSAC], 1990, 1997; Bull, 1992, 1995; Fisher & Geiselman, 1992; Jones, 1992; Lamb, Sternberg, & Esplin, 1998; Lamb, Sternberg, Orbach, Her-shkowitz, & Esplin, 1999; Memorandum of Good Practice, 1992; Poole & Lamb, 1998; Saywitz & Goodman, 1996; Walker & Warren, 1995; Yuille, Hunter, Joffe, & Zaparniuk, 1993). These recommendations have been incor-porated into the National Institute of Child Health and Human Development (NICHD) Investigative Interview Protocol (Orbach, Hershkowitz, Lamb, Sternberg, Esplin, & Horowitz, 2000; Orbach & Lamb, 2001).

The NICHD protocol emphasizes reliance on free-recall probes and re-trieval cues, and instructs interviewers to give children practice responding to such prompts when describing neutral events in the presubstantive phase of forensic interviews, before their attention is turned to the alleged abuse. In-terviewers are guided to elicit disclosures and allegations using free- and cued-recall prompts as much as possible, and to introduce focused prompts (i.e., yes/no questions), providing carefully graduated "hints" about possible abuse, to prompt those who failed to disclose in response to the recall prompts. To minimize contamination, the NICHD interview protocol further recommends that interviewers delay recognition prompts until open-ended prompts have been exhausted, and pair them with open-ended prompts. Using the protocol, interviewers elicit much more information, even from very young children, in response to open-ended prompts than do interviewers using "standard" inter-viewing practices (Aldridge, Lamb, Sternberg, Orbach, Esplin, & Bowler, 2004; Lamb, Sternberg, Orbach, Esplin, Stewart, & Mitchell, 2003; Lamb, Or-bach, Sternberg, Esplin, & Hershkowitz, 2002; Orbach et al., 2000; Sternberg, Lamb, Orbach, Esplin, & Mitchell, 2001).

To disclose sexual abuse, children need an adequate memory of the inves-tigated event and the communicative skills necessary to report it (Bussey & Grimbeek, 1995). These necessary conditions do not guarantee disclosure, however. Although alleged victims of sexual abuse can provide substantial amounts of information about their experiences, many children either fail to disclose abuse or are reluctant to do so (Hershkowitz, Horowitz, & Lamb, chapter 4, this volume; Kuehnle, 1996; Poole & Lamb, 1998) for a variety of cognitive, emotional, or motivational reasons (Bandura, 1965; Sauzier, 1989; Sjöberg & Lindblad, 2002). Children may be reluctant to talk with an unfa-miliar interviewer about sensitive or embarrassing issues, such as socially pro-scribed forms of intimate touching (Ceci, Leichtman, & Nightingale, 1993) or to acknowledge "coercive, repeated abuse that can instill high levels of fear, shame, and mistrust" (Saywitz, Goodman, Nicholas, & Moan, 1991, p. 691). Victims may be motivated to withhold information or deny that they were abused because they wish to protect familiar perpetrators, especially family members (Paine & Hansen, 2002; Yuille, Tymofievich, & Marxsen, 1995), yield to requests for secrecy (DeYoung, 1988; Goodman-Brown, 1995), assume responsibility or blame (Lyon, 2002; Sjöberg & Lindblad, 2002), feel ashamed or embarrassed (Lyon, 1995; Saywitz, et al., 1991), or fear negative outcomes (Berliner & Conte, 1995; DeYoung, 1988; Paine & Hansen, 2002; Palmer, Brown, Rae-Grant, & Loughlin, 1999).

Age may also affect disclosure by child witnesses. Younger children, who are not aware of the norms regarding sexual activity, may unwittingly disclose abuse by casually mentioning the incident (Finkelhor, Williams, & Burns, 1988) or by enacting sexual behavior they learned (Friedrich, 1993; Friedrich, Fisher, Dittner, Acton, Berliner, Butler, et al., 2001). Young victims may not understand that they have been abused and may fail to encode experiences that did not appear salient to them (Cederborg, Lamb, & Laurell, chapter 9, this volume, 2004; DeVoe and Faller, 1999), leaving them unable to retrieve related memories when later interviewed. Older children, by contrast, are more likely to disclose verbally and intentionally, regulating their disclosure by choosing to whom they disclose and the amount of information they are willing to provide. Because they have been socialized more extensively and know more about sexual behavior, however, older children seem to recognize that their experiences were inappropriate and are more aware of the potential consequences of disclosure, and thus have the cognitive capacity to purposefully inhibit disclosure (Campis, Hebden-Curtis, & DeMaso, 1993). In addition, young children provide less information about their experiences in both field/forensic and laboratory settings, perhaps because they have less developed retrieval strategies and poorer communicative abilities (Baker-Ward, Gordon, Ornstein, Larus, & Clubb, 1993; Dietze & Thompson, 1993; Goodman & Reed, 1986; Hershkowitz, Orbach, Lamb, Sternberg, Horowitz, & Hovav, 1998; Lamb, Hershkowitz, Sternberg, Boat, & Everson 1996; Lamb, Hershkowitz, Sternberg, Esplin, et al., 1996; Lamb et al., 2003; Ornstein et al., 1992; Peterson & Bell, 1996; Saywitz, Snyder, & Lamphear, 1996; Sternberg, Lamb, Hershkowitz, Esplin, Redlich, & Sunshine, 1996). As a result, many professionals have suggested that younger children need more focused prompting than older children do (Clarke-Stewart, Thompson, & Lepore, 1989; DeVoe & Faller, 1999; Gries, Goh, & Cavanaugh, 1996; Keary & Fitzpatrick, 1994; Saywitz, et al., 1991; Terry, 1990; Wood, Orsak, Murphy, & Cross, 1996).

Most of the published research on forensic interviewing has focused on interviews with cooperative alleged victims who were ready to disclose, had often made specific allegations of abuse prior to the formal investigation, and were especially responsive to open-ended prompts. A diverse array of factors, including veiled disclosure to nonprofessionals (e.g., family members and teachers) or to professionals (e.g., medical doctors, CPS workers or police officers), as well as suspicions that the child was abused, may trigger formal investigative interviews with children who are unwilling to disclose. Unlike cooperative informants, children who are reluctant to disclose may be less responsive to open-ended prompts and may require more guidance and more fo-cused prompts before making allegations of abuse. As a result, those inter-viewing them face an inevitable tension between the desire to initiate the disclosure of information about what actually happened and the need to avoid contaminating the memories by suggestively implanting information (even prompting false allegations) by using leading and suggestive prompts. The goal is to minimize the amount of information provided by the interviewer, rather than the child, especially during the crucial early stages of the interview.

The first field study to explore the dynamics of forensic interviews with re-luctant victims (Hershkowitz, Orbach, Lamb, Sternberg, Pipe, & Horowitz, chapter 6, this volume) compared reluctant disclosers who did not disclose abuse in the course of forensic interviews, despite strong evidence that abuse occurred, with children who disclosed abuse. Hershkowitz and her colleagues showed that forensic interviews that yielded allegations of abuse were charac-terized by quite different dynamics than interviews with children who seemed equally likely to have been abused but did not make allegations during the in-terview. Nondisclosers were somewhat uncooperative, offered less informa-tion, and gave more uninformative responses, even in the presubstantive rapport-building phase of the interview, before the interviewers focused on substantive issues and before the interviewers themselves began to behave dif-ferently. Moreover, the children's informativeness or uninformativeness in the presubstantive phase of the interview was indicative of the likelihood that they would disclose. Hershkowitz and colleagues also demonstrated that interview-ers addressed nondisclosers and disclosers differently, offering fewer free-recall prompts to nondisclosers than to disclosers.

The present study was designed to explore differences in the dynamics of interviews with reluctant and nonreluctant disclosers, all of whom disclosed sexual abuse during protocol-guided forensic interviews. Half of the children in the present study (nonreluctant disclosers) made allegations of abuse in re-sponse to the interviewers' open-ended free-recall prompts. The other half (re-luctant disclosers) failed to disclose abuse in response to free-recall prompts and made allegations only when prompted in a more focused—sometimes even suggestive—fashion, using recognition memory prompts.

The present study was the first designed to explore variations in the chil-dren's apparent willingness to disclose and to describe experiences of abuse when questioned systematically by investigative interviewers in the course of forensic interviews. We examined the relationship between the children's ini-tial reluctance to make allegations and the total amount of information they provided about the investigated incident in the substantive phase following disclosure, as well as in the rapport-building phase, when discussing neutral topics, prior to the substantive questioning. We also examined whether inter-viewers addressed nonreluctant and reluctant disclosers differently.

We expected that children who disclosed in response to focused recogni-tion prompts would remain reluctant to provide information about the alleged abuse even after making allegations. We thus expected that nonreluctant disclosers would provide more abuse-related information overall, more central (i.e., allegation crucial) information, more information in response to free-recall prompts, and more information in response to each invitational prompt than reluctant disclosers would.

We also expected to find continuity in levels of cooperativeness in the presubstantive and the substantive phases, which would be reflected in significant correlations between the amount of information provided by children when discussing neutral topics in the presubstantive rapport building phase and the amount of abuse-related information provided in the substantive phase. We thus expected that reluctant disclosers would provide less information than nonreluctant disclosers even before abuse-related issues were introduced.

As in interviews with young suspects (Hershkowitz, Horowitz, Lamb, Orbach, & Sternberg, 2004), we expected that interviewers might use more recognition prompts, fewer free-recall prompts, and more prompts overall to elicit substantive information from reluctant than from nonreluctant disclosers.

PARTICIPANTS

The 70 interviews included in the study were drawn from a pool of 365 investigative interviews conducted, using the NICHD protocol, by professional investigators in the United Kingdom and the United States. The children (48 girls and 22 boys) were 4- to 12-years old at the time of interview ($M = 6.89$ years, $SD = 2.26$; 22 boys and 48 girls). For the purpose of analysis, we distinguished between 35 interviews in which children made their allegations in response to one of the open-ended "getting the allegation" prompts (i.e., nonreluctant disclosers) and 35 interviews in which children did not make allegations in response to the initial open-ended prompts and only disclosed when asked more focused (option-posing and suggestive) prompts (i.e., the reluctant group; see appendix for a complete list of "getting the allegation" prompts). Interviews in the two disclosure groups were individually matched by age and abuse type. All interviews were also divided into two age groups by median split; children in the younger age group ($n = 35$) were 4 to 6.40 years old, whereas children in the older age group ($n = 35$) were 6.41 years and older.

The alleged crimes included anal or genital penetrations ($n = 14$), genital touching ($n = 33$), genital fondling from outside the clothes ($n = 17$), sexual exposure ($n = 2$) and physical abuse ($n = 4$). Thirty-three of the children reported single events, and 37 reported multiple events. All the perpetrators were familiar to the victims prior to the alleged abusive events. Twenty-eight of the perpetrators were members of the victims' immediate families (i.e., biological mothers, fathers, or siblings, stepparents and including mothers' boyfriends and fathers' girlfriends), 12 were other family members (e.g., grandfathers, uncles, cousins) who lived with the family, or biological parents or siblings not living with the family, and 30 were familiar, unrelated acquaintances of the child (e.g., friends, teachers, nonresident boyfriend or girlfriend of a parent).

PROCEDURE

As explained earlier, the NICHD structured investigative protocol is designed to maximize the use of open-ended probes and retrieval cues (Orbach et al., 2000). Alleged child victims are encouraged to provide as much information as possible from free-recall and to report event-specific rather than generic information. The initial presubstantive phase serves introductory, preparatory, and rapport-building goals. Interviewers explain the importance of telling the truth, and clarify communication rules (e.g., encourage children to correct the interviewers when they are incorrect and instruct children to seek clarification when necessary). In the rapport-building phase, investigators pose open-ended questions about the children and their families before asking the children to describe recent events in detail ("Tell me about it from the beginning to the end as best you can remember"). In addition, children are prompted using follow-up invitations (i.e., "And then what happened?" or "Tell me more about that"), cued invitations ("You said something about X. Tell me about that"), and temporal cues ("What happened after he came in?"), based on disclosed information, as part of an effort to familiarize children with open-ended interview strategies and with the expected level of detail. Following the presubstantive phase, the interviewers shift focus to substantive issues, using a sequence of prompts designed to facilitate disclosure nonsuggestively. The interviewers follow this sequence until the children make references to abuse. The first prompts in this sequence are open-ended, introducing no information. If the children do not make allegations in response to open-ended prompts, interviewers use increasingly focused prompts that hint at the possibility of abuse. The interviewers only used focused prompts (first option-posing and then, if necessary, suggestive) after exhausting the open-ended prompts. The appendix lists the probes in sequence.

When children make allegations of abuse, investigators offer an open-ended invitation ("Tell me everything that happened to you from the beginning to the end, as best you can remember"), which is followed by follow-up open-ended prompts ("Tell me more about it," or "And then what happened?") and cued invitations ("Tell me more about [something mentioned by the child]") as needed. The open-ended prompts are designed to elicit free recall accounts of the alleged incidents. If some crucial information was missing after exhaustive open-ended questioning, the interviewers were instructed to use more focused, nonsuggestive questions. If the children mentioned multiple incidents, the interviewers asked them to give separate accounts of each incident. Further details about the protocol are provided by Orbach et al. (2000) and Sternberg et al. (2002).

For the purposes of the present study, children who made allegations in response to NICHD "getting the allegation" prompts numbered 1, 2, or 3 were classified as having responded to open-ended free-recall prompts. Those who made allegations in response to prompts 4, 5, or 6 were classified as having responded to focused recognition prompts. None of the children made allegations in response to prompts 7, 8, or 9.

CODING INTERVIEWER STRATEGIES

Interviews were transcribed and checked for accuracy. Two trained raters independently reviewed each of the transcripts, categorizing each utterance made by the interviewers in both the presubstantive and substantive phases of the interview. Four categories introduced by Lamb and his colleagues (Lamb, Hershkowitz, Sternberg, Boat, et al., 1996; Lamb, Hershkowitz, Sternberg, Esplin, et al., 1996) were used to characterize the interviewer utterances (defined as "turns" in the discourse or conversation) as invitations, directives, option posing prompts, or suggestive prompts.

1. Invitations. Utterances, including questions, statements, or imperatives, prompting free recall responses from the child (for example, "Tell me everything that happened"). Some invitations used details disclosed by the child as cues (for example, "You mentioned that he kissed you. Tell me everything about the kiss").

2. Directive utterances. These refocus the child's attention on details or aspects of the alleged incident that the child has already mentioned, providing a category for requesting additional information using "wh–" questions (cued recall), (for example, "Where did he touch you?" when the child mentioned "he touched me").

3. Option-posing utterances. These utterances draw the child's attention to details or aspects of the alleged incident that the child has not mentioned, asking the child to affirm, negate, or select investigator-given options (tapping recognition memory processes) but do not imply that a particular response is expected (e.g., "Did he say anything to you?").

4. Suggestive utterances. These utterances are stated in such a way that the interviewer strongly communicates what response is expected (e.g., "He touched you under your clothes, didn't he?"), or they assume details that have not been revealed by the child (e.g., "Where did he touch you?" when the child has not mentioned being touched).

Nonsuggestive encouragements to continue with ongoing responses (i.e., "facilitators") were not considered as independent utterances. The details provided following facilitators were attributed to the previous utterance.

CODING CHILDREN'S RESPONSES

The amount of information provided by the children was quantified by two raters using the informative detail as the smallest unit of information. By definition, a detail involved mentioning, identifying, or describing individuals, objects, events, locations, times, actions, emotions, or thoughts and sensations, that are part of an alleged incident, as well as any of their features (e.g., appearances, temporal attributes, sound, smell and texture). All details pertaining to the alleged sexual/physical allegation were identified and counted. Allegation-crucial details were coded as "central details." Details were counted in specific statements that express recollection of personal episodic memories of alleged incidents (occurring at a specific time and specific location), as well as in generic statements that referred in general to something that happened during a single incident or summarize more than one incident with the same suspect.

Raters were trained on an independent set of transcripts until they reached 95% inter-rater agreement before coding the transcripts included in the study. During the course of the coding, 20% of the transcripts were coded by both raters to ensure that they remained reliable. In these assessments, raters agreed regarding the classification of at least 98% of the interviewer prompts and 95% of the children's response types and informative details.

THE FINDINGS

Multivariate analyses of variance (MANOVAs) were used to explore the effect of disclosure group and age on the amount of information provided by children in response to prompts of different types. Subsequent univariate analyses of variance (ANOVAs) were computed where appropriate to specify the variables on which the groups differed.

A 2 (disclosure status: non-reluctant, reluctant) X 2 (Age: older, younger) MANOVA with the number of details provided during the presubstantive and the substantive phases of the interview in response to prompts of the four main types (invitation, directive, option-posing, suggestive) as dependent variables revealed significant multivariate effects for both disclosure status and age ($F_{7,60} = 4.37; p < .001$ and $F_{7,60} = 3.86, p = .002$ for disclosure status and age, respectively), as well as in the number of details reported per prompts of each type ($F_{7,60} = 2.44, p = .029$ and $F_{7,60} = 3.81, p = .002$ for disclosure status and age, respectively).

Subsequent ANOVAs revealed that nonreluctant disclosers provided more details in total in both the presubstantive and the substantive phases of the interview (see table 7.1). No significant differences were evident, however, in the number and proportion of details provided in responses to prompts of each type and in the number provided per prompt of each type in the presubstantive phase, although nonreluctant disclosers tended to provide more information in response to pre-substantive invitations than reluctant disclosers did. In the substantive phase, however, in addition to providing more substantive information overall, nonreluctant disclosers provided more central details and more details in response to invitations, directive, and option-posing prompts than reluctant disclosers did. They also provided more details per invitation, directive, and option-posing prompts and tended to provide more details in response to suggestive prompts than reluctant disclosers did (see table 7.1).

With respect to age, subsequent ANOVAs revealed that in both the presubstantive and the substantive phases, older children provided more details and significantly more forensically relevant information in total than younger children did. There was a significant interaction, however, between age and disclosure group in the total number of details reported in the presubstantive phase ($F_{1,66} = 4.25$, $p = .043$), with more details reported by older than by younger children in the nonreluctant group and more details reported by younger than by older children in the reluctant group ($M_{younger} = 116.13$, $M_{older} = 207.95$ and $M_{younger} = 113.68$, $M_{older} = 106.69$ for nonreluctant and reluctant children, respectively).

There were significant correlations between the total number of details provided by children, the number of details elicited in response to invitation, directive, and option-posing prompts in the presubstantive and substantive phases, and the average number of details elicited per invitation, directive, and option-posing prompt in the presubstantive and the substantive phases (see table 7.2).

A 2 (disclosure status: non-reluctant, reluctant) X 2 (Age: older, younger) MANOVA with the number of interviewer prompts of each of the four main types (invitations, directive, option-posing, suggestive) as dependent variables revealed no significant differences for disclosure status or age on the total number of prompts posed by interviewers in the presubstantive and the substantive phases of the interview, although there were significant effects for disclosure status in the number of prompts of each type ($F_{7,60} = 2.59$; $p = .021$) posed to children in the two disclosure groups.

Subsequent ANOVAs revealed no significant differences in the total number of prompts and the number of prompts of each type posed by interviewers to children in the two disclosure groups in the presubstantive and substantive phases. In the substantive phase of the interview, however, interviewers posed absolutely and proportionally more directive ($F1,68 = 9.45$, $p = .003$, for proportions) and fewer suggestive ($F1,68 = 13.33$, $p = .001$, for proportions) prompts to nonreluctant than to reluctant disclosers. No differences were evident in the numbers or proportions of invitation and option-posing prompts posed to children in the two disclosure groups (see table 7.3).

TABLE 7.1
Mean Number of Details Provided by Nonreluctant and Reluctant Disclosers in Response to Prompts of Each Type

Eliciting prompt	Number of details				Average number of details per each prompt type			
	Nonreluctant (n = 35)	Reluctant (n = 35)	F_a	p	Nonreluctant (n = 35)	Reluctant (n = 35)	F_a	p
Pre-substantive phase								
Total # of details	165.97 (130.32)	110.49 (67.32)	4.69b	.034*	—	—	—	—
Invitation	122.34 (91.24)	87.31 (61.83)	3.54	.064	19.14 (16.10)	13.38 (16.49)	2.18	.144
Directive	34.06 (69.85)	18.37 (33.75)	1.43	.236	13.58 (49.39)	3.49 (4.66)	1.45	.233
Option-Posing	5.20 (16.07)	2.34 (7.61)	.90	.345	1.74 (4.44)	.67 (1.33)	1.83	.180
Suggestive	4.11 (10.20)	2.31 (4.80)	.893	.348	2.59 (5.55)	1.44 (2.61)	1.23	.271
Substantive phase								
Total # of details	179.89 (172.06)	77.34 (69.02)	10.34b	.002*	—	—	—	—
# central details	105.63 (72.74)	50.46 (45.96)	14.24b	.000*	—	—	—	—
Invitation	101.09 (113.54)	33.91 (40.22)	10.89	.002*	7.44 (6.93)	2.26 (2.70)	16.97	.000*
Directive	46.54 (69.95)	19.54 (20.25)	4.81	.032*	2.37 (1.93)	1.52 (1.17)	4.99	.029*
Option-Posing	24.89 (23.15)	12.14 (8.14)	9.44	.003*	2.10 (1.29)	1.12 (.64)	16.48	.000*
Suggestive	5.37 (6.76)	9.94 (13.43)	3.24	.076	2.38 (3.98)	2.24 (4.85)	.018	.893

Note: Numbers in parentheses are standard deviations.
*Indicates a significant difference.
a df = 1,68
b df = 1,66

TABLE 7.2

Correlations Between the Number of Details Provided by Children in the Presubstantive and Substantive Phases in Response to Prompts of Each Type

Eliciting prompt	Number of details				Average number of details per each prompt type			
	Pre-substantive phase	Substantive phase	r	p	Pre-substantive phase	Substantive phase	r	p
Total # of details	138.23 (106.69)	128.61 (140.01)	.61	.000*	—	—	—	—
Invitation	104.83 (79.35)	67.50 (91.07)	.43	.000*	16.26 (16.44)	4.85 (5.95)	.47	.000*
Directive	33.04 (52.89)	26.21 (55.03)	.55	.000*	8.54 (35.19)	1.95 (1.64)	.25	.039*
Option-Posing	3.77 (12.57)	18.51 (18.38)	.53	.000*	1.21 (3.30)	1.61 (1.12)	.54	.000*
Suggestive	3.21 (7.96)	7.66 (10.80)	−.08	.516	2.01 (4.34)	2.31 (4.40)	−.06	.601

Note: Numbers in parentheses are standard deviations.
*Indicates a significant difference.

TABLE 7.3
Mean Number of Prompts Posed by Interviewers to Nonreluctant and Reluctant

Eliciting prompt	Nonreluctant (n = 35)		Reluctant (n = 35)		F^a	p
Presubstantive phase						
Total number of prompts	11.60	(6.39)	12.94	(9.14)	.27b	.608
Invitations	7.46	(3.58)	8.17	(5.71)	.39	.533
Directive	2.89	(3.55)	3.31	(5.03)	.17	.682
Option-Posing	.89	(1.37)	.91	(1.62)	.006	.937
Suggestive	.37	(.69)	.54	(1.12)	.594	.443
Total recall	10.34	(5.63)	11.49	(7.68)	.50	.480
Total recognition	1.26	(1.72)	1.46	(2.28)	.17	.680
Substantive phase						
Total number of prompts	46.06	(21.08)	44.57	(15.56)	.14b	.706
Invitations	14.94	(7.55)	16.60	(8.70)	.72	.398
Directive	17.69	(13.27)	11.86	(6.47)	5.46	.022*
Option-Posing	11.46	(6.15)	11.37	(4.98)	.004	.949
Suggestive	1.97	(1.72)	4.74	(4.47)	11.69	.001*
Total recall	32.63	(16.42)	28.46	(11.96)	1.48	.229
Total recognition	13.43	(7.18)	16.11	(6.45)	2.73	.103

Note: Numbers in parentheses are standard deviations.
*Indicates a significant difference.
[a] $df = 1,68$
[b] $df = 1,66$

DISCUSSION

The results reported here reveal compelling differences in the dynamics of interviews with nonreluctant and reluctant disclosers with respect to both the children's and interviewers' behavior. There were significant relationships between the children's initial willingness to make allegations and the total amount of information they provided about the investigated incidents in the substantive phase following disclosure. As expected, reluctant disclosers who failed to provide information in response to open-ended free-recall prompts and disclosed only when given additional focused recognition memory prompts reported fewer abuse-related details in the substantive interview following disclosure than nonreluctant disclosers did. Moreover, reluctant disclosers were already somewhat uncooperative when discussing neutral topics in the presubstantive phase of the interview.

Differences in children's willingness to disclose information about abuse when questioned systematically by investigative interviewers in the course of forensic interviews were measured in the present study using the number and types of interviewers' prompts that were necessary to elicit allegations. The amount of information disclosed, evident in the total number of details, the number and proportion of details provided in response to prompts of each type, and the average number of details provided per prompts of each type, reflect the quantitative characteristic on which nonreluctant and reluctant disclosers differed. Information provided by reluctant and nonreluctant disclosers also differed qualitatively with respect to the types of prompts used to trigger retrieval, which may have had a direct effect on accuracy (Dale et al., 1978; Dent & Stephenson, 1979; Hutcheson et al., 1995; Lamb & Fauchier, 2001; Oates & Shrimpton, 1991; Orbach & Lamb, 1999; Orbach & Lamb, 2001). Whereas reluctant disclosers made their allegations by confirming details offered by the interviewers, nonreluctant disclosers made allegations in response to open-ended invitational prompts. Thus, reluctant disclosers not only received more prompts in total as well as more focused prompts but were also reluctant both prior to and following the introduction of abuse-related issues by the interviewers. They were already unwilling to provide much information when asked to talk about themselves, family, school, and related neutral events in the presubstantive phase, and provided much less abuse-related information than nonreluctant disclosers did following disclosure.

We also found significant similarities between the substantive and presubstantive phases of the interview with respect to the total amount of information as well as information provided in response to all prompt types, except suggestive, indicating the children were consistent in their willingness to provide information, regardless of interview phase. Moreover, a significant statistical interaction between age and disclosure group indicates that children in the reluctant group provided so little information in the presubstantive phase that the expected difference between older and younger children in the number of details reported totally disappeared. Additionally, although they did not differ from reluctant disclosers with respect to the average number of details provided per prompt of each type in the presubstantive phase, nonreluctant disclosers provided significantly more details on average per invitation, directive, and option-posing prompt in the substantive phase.

As expected, nonreluctant disclosers provided significantly more details overall, as well as more central details than reluctant disclosers did, although proportionally there were no group differences. A post hoc analysis also revealed that more of the interviewers' prompts elicited information from nonreluctant than from reluctant disclosers, indicating that the reluctant children were more likely than nonreluctant disclosers to give uninformative responses, or not to respond at all.

Despite their difficulties eliciting disclosures from reluctant disclosers, however, the interviewers did not offer more prompts overall and in each of the two phases of the interview to reluctant than to nonreluctant disclosers. Interviewers differed, however, with respect to the number of prompts of each type posed to children in the two disclosure groups. Whereas there were no differences in the number of prompts posed by interviewers to reluctant and nonreluctant disclosers in the presubstantive phase, interviewers adhered less closely to the NICHD protocol with respect to memory elicitation strategies when interviewing reluctant disclosers about substantive issues. They addressed reluctant disclosers with fewer free-recall and more recognition prompts, particularly more suggestive prompts, than they did nonreluctant disclosers. To a great extent, this was because the interviewers used more prompts including recognition memory prompts in the "getting the allegation" sequence when interviewing reluctant disclosers. When interviewing nonreluctant disclosers, by contrast, interviewers did not have to proceed to the recognition prompts because allegations were made earlier in response to open-ended prompts. Contrary to our expectations, based on research including forensic interviews with young suspects (Hershkowitz et al., 2004) and nondisclosers (Hershkowitz et al., chapter 6, this volume), the interviewers did not use more focused recognition prompts to counter the children's resistance. The higher number of directive prompts addressed to nonreluctant disclosers, by contrast, may be explained by the larger amount of free-recall information provided by children in this group that could be used as cues for directive refocusing.

In summary, these data suggest that reluctant witnesses were less communicative than nonreluctant witnesses even in the nonsubstantive portions of the interview, before the introduction of abuse-related issues, and remained reluctant to provide information about the alleged abuse even after making their initial allegations. They provided less information overall, fewer central details, fewer details in response to invitations, and more uninformative and omission responses than nonreluctant disclosers did. Unlike nonreluctant disclosers, reluctant disclosers provided more information in response to recognition than to recall prompts. Interviewers modified their strategies only in the substantive phase, apparently reacting when the reluctant disclosers failed to respond informatively to recall prompts.

Further research is needed to explore alternative ways for motivating reluctant victims of abuse to disclose their abusive experiences in the course of forensic interviews. As suggested by their research on nondisclosers (Hershkowitz et al., chapter 6, this volume), increasing supportive techniques and avoiding confrontation may enhance rapport building and facilitate the creation of retrieval conditions that better help suspected victims of abuse to describe their abuse experiences during investigative interviews, even when they are reluctant to do so.

ACKNOWLEDGMENTS

The authors are grateful to Renee DeBoard, Sarah Jensen, and Monique Mendoza for their help managing and preparing the data for statistical analysis and to Jessica Norris for performing the statistical analyses.

REFERENCES

Aldridge, J., Lamb, M. E., Sternberg, K. J., Orbach, Y., Esplin, P. W., & Bowler, L. (2004). Using a human figure drawing to elicit information from alleged victims of child sexual abuse. *Journal of Consulting and Clinical Psychology.*

American Professional Society on the Abuse of Children. (1990, 1997). *Guidelines for psychosocial evaluation of suspected sexual abuse in young children.* Chicago: American Professional Society of the Abuse of Children.

Baker-Ward, L., Gordon, B. N., Ornstein, P. A., Larus, D. M., & Clubb, P. A. (1993). Young children's long-term retention of a pediatric examination. *Child Development, 64,* 1519–33.

Bandura, A. (1965). Influence of models' reinforcement contingencies on the acquisition of imitative responses. *Journal of Personality and Social Psychology, 1,* 589–95.

Berliner, L., & Conte, J. R. (1995). The effects of disclosure and intervention on sexually abused children. *Child Abuse & Neglect, 19,* 371–84.

Brainerd, C., & Ornstein, P. A. (1991). Children's memory for witnessed events: The developmental backdrop. In J. Doris (Ed.), *The suggestibility of children's recollections* (pp. 10–20). Washington, DC: American Psychological Association.

Bull, R. (1992). Obtaining evidence expertly: The reliability of interviews with child witness. *Expert Evidence, 1,* 5–12.

———. (1995). Innovative techniques for the questioning of child witnesses, especially those who are young and those who are with learning disability. In M. S. Zaragoza, J. R. Graham, G. C. N. Hall, R. Hirschman, & Y. S. Ben-Porath (Eds.), *Memory and testimony in the child witness* (pp. 179–94). Thousand Oaks, CA: Sage.

Bussey, B. & Grimbeek, E. J. (1995). Disclosure processes: Issues for child sexual abuse victims. Disclosure processes in children and adolescence. *Cambridge Studies in Social and Emotional Development,* 166–203.

Campis, L. B., Hebden-Curtis, J., & DeMaso, D. R. (1993). Developmental differences in detection and disclosure of sexual abuse. *Journal of American Academy of Child and Adolescent Psychiatry, 32,* 920–24.

Ceci, S. J., & Bruck, M. (1995). *Jeopardy in the courtroom: A scientific analysis of children's testimony.* Washington, DC: American Psychological Association.

Ceci, S. J., Leichtman, M. D., & Nightingale, M. N. (1993). The suggestibility of children's recollections. In D. Cicchetti & S. Toth (Eds.), *Child abuse, child development, and social policy* (pp. 117–37). Norwood, NJ: Albex.

Cederborg, A-C, Lamb, M. E. & Laurell, O. (2004, March). *Delay of disclosure, minimization and denial when the evidence is unambiguous: A multivictim case.* Paper presented in a symposium on Delayed and Non-disclosure of Child Sexual Abuse in Forensic Interviews at the American Psychology-Law Society conference, Scottsdale, AZ.

Clarke-Stewart, A., Thompson, W., & Lepore, S. (1989). *Manipulation of children's interpretation through interrogation.* Paper presented at the biennial meeting of the Society for Research in Child Development, Kansas City, MO.

Dale, P. S., Loftus, E. F., & Rathbun, L. (1978). The influence of the form of the question on the eyewitness testimony of preschool children. *Journal of Psycholinguistic Research, 7,* 269–77.

Dent, H. R. (1986). Experimental study of the effectiveness of different techniques of questioning mentally handicapped child witnesses. *British Journal of Clinical Psychology, 25,* 13–17.

Dent, H. R., & Stephenson, G. M. (1979). An experimental study of the effectiveness of different techniques of questioning child witness. British Journal of Social and Clinical Psychology, 18, 41–51.

———. (1989). An experimental study of the effectiveness of different techniques of questioning child witnesses. British Journal of Social and Clinical Psychology, 18, 41–51.

DeVoe, E. R., & Faller, K. C. (1999). The characteristics of disclosure among children who may have been sexually abused. Child Maltreatment , 4, 217–27.

DeYoung, M. (1988). Issues in determining the veracity of sexual abuse allegations. Children's Health Care, 17, 50–57.

Dietze, P. M., & Thompson, D. M. (1993). Mental reinstatement of context: A technique for interviewing child witnesses. Applied Cognitive Psychology, 7, 97–108.

Finkelhor, D., Williams, L. M., & Burns, N. (1988). Disclosure and detection. In D. Finkelhor, & L. M. Williams (Eds.), Nursery Crimes: Sexual abuse in day care (pp. 99–113). Newsbury Park, CA: Sage.

Fisher, R. P., & Geiselman, R. E. (1992). Memory-enhancing techniques for investigative interviewing: The cognitive interview. Springfield, IL: Charles C. Thomas.

Friedrich, W. N. (1993). Sexual victimization and sexual behavior in children: A review of recent literature. Child Abuse & Neglect, 17, 59–66.

Friedrich, W. N., Fisher, J. L., Dittner, C. A., Acton, R., Berliner, L., Butler, J., Damon, L., Davies, W. H., Gray, A., Wright, J. (2001). Child Sexual Behavior Inventory: Normative, psychiatric, and sexual abuse comparisons. Child Maltreatment, 6, 37–49.

Goodman, G. S., & Aman, C. (1990). Children's use of anatomically detailed dolls to recount an event. Child Development, 61, 1859–71.

Goodman, G. S., Bottoms, B. L., Schwartz-Kenney, B. M., & Rudy, L. (1991). Children's testimony about a stressful event: Improving children's reports. Journal of Narrative and Life History, 1, 69–99.

Goodman, G. S., & Reed, D. S. (1986). Age differences in eyewitness testimony. Law and Human Behavior, 10, 317–37.

Goodman-Brown, T. B. (1995). Why children tell: A model of children's disclosure of sexual abuse (Doctoral dissertation, California School of Professional Psychology, 1995). Dissertation Abstracts International, 56, 2325.

Gries, L. T., Goh, D. S., & Cavanaugh, J. (1996). Factors associated with disclosure during child sexual abuse assessment. Journal of Child Sexual Abuse, 5, 1–20.

Hershkowitz, I., Horowitz, D., Lamb, M. E., Orbach, Y., & Sternberg, K. J. (2004). Interviewing youthful suspects in alleged sex crimes: A descriptive analysis. Child Abuse and Neglect, 28, 423–38.

Hershkowitz, I., Lamb, M. E., Sternberg, K. J., & Esplin, P. W. (1997). The relationships among interviewer utterance type, CBCA scores, and the richness of children's responses. Legal and Criminological Psychology, 2, 169–76.

Hershkowitz, I., Orbach, Y., Lamb, M .E., Sternberg, K. J., Horowitz, D., & Hovav, M. (1998). Visiting the scene of the crime: Effects on children's recall of alleged abuse. Legal and Criminological Psychology, 3, 195–207.

Hutcheson, G. D., Baxter, J. S., Telfer, K., & Warden, D. (1995). Child witness statement quality: Question type and error of omission. Law and Human Behavior, 19, 631–48.

Jones, D. (1989). Some reflections on the Cleveland affair. Association of Child Psychology Newsletter, 11, 13–18.

Jones, D. P. H. (1992). Interviewing the sexually abused child. Oxford: Gaskell.

Keary, K., & Fitzpatrick, C. (1994). Children's disclosure of sexual abuse during formal investigation. *Child Abuse & Neglect, 18,* 543–48.

Kuehnle, K. (1996). *Assessing allegations of child sexual abuse.* Sarasota, FL: Professional Resource Exchange.

Lamb, M. E., & Fauchier, A. (2001). The effects of question type on self-contradictions by children in the course of forensic interviews. *Applied Cognitive Development, 15,* 483–91.

Lamb, M. E., Hershkowitz, I., Sternberg, K. J., Boat, B., & Everson, M. D. (1996). Investigative interviews of alleged sexual abuse victims with and without anatomical dolls. *Child Abuse and Neglect, 20,* 1239–47.

Lamb, M. E., Hershkowitz, I., Sternberg, K. J., Esplin, P. W., Hovav, M., Manor, T., & Yudilevitch, L. (1996). Effects of investigative utterance types on Israeli children's responses. *International Journal of Behavioral Development, 19,* 627–37.

Lamb, M. E., Orbach, Y., Sternberg, K. J., Esplin, P. W., & Hershkowitz, I. (2002). The effects of forensic interview practices on the quality of information provided by alleged victims of child abuse. In H. L. Westcott, G. M. Davies, & R. Bull (Eds.), *Children's testimony: A handbook of psychological research and forensic practice* (pp. 131–45). Chichester, England: Wiley.

Lamb, M. E., Sternberg, K. J., & Esplin, P. W. (1998). Conducting investigative interviews of alleged sexual abuse victims. *Child Abuse and Neglect, 22,* 813–23.

Lamb, M. E., Sternberg, K. J., Orbach, Y., Esplin, P. W., Stewart, H., & Mitchell, S. (2003). Age differences in young children's responses to open-ended invitations in the course of forensic interviews. *Journal of Consulting and Clinical Psychology, 71,* 926–34.

Lamb, M. E., Sternberg, K. J., Orbach, Y., Hershkowitz, I., & Esplin, P. W. (1999). Forensic interviews of children. In A. Memon & R. A. Bull (Eds.), *Handbook of the psychology of interviewing* (pp. 253–77). Chichester, England: Wiley.

Lyon, T. D. (1995). False allegations and false denials in child sexual abuse. *Psychology, Public Policy, and Law, 1,* 429–37.

———. (2002). Scientific support for expert testimony on child sexual abuse accommodation. In J. R. Conte (Ed.), *Critical issues in child sexual abuse* (pp.107–38). Newbury Park, CA: Sage.

Memorandum of Good Practice. (1992). London: Her Majesty's Stationery Office.

Oates, K., & Shrimpton, S. (1991). Children's memories for stressful and non-stressful events. *Medical Science and Law, 31,* 4–10.

Orbach, Y., Hershkowitz, I., Lamb, M. E., Sternberg, K. J., Esplin, P. W., & Horowitz, D. (2000). Assessing the value of structured protocols for forensic interviews of alleged abuse victims. *Child Abuse and Neglect, 24,* 733–52.

Orbach, Y., & Lamb, M. E. (1999). Assessing the accuracy of a child's account of sexual abuse: A case study. *Child Abuse and Neglect, 23,* 91–98.

———. (2001). The relationship between within-interview contradictions and eliciting interviewer utterances. *Child Abuse and Neglect, 25,* 323–33.

Ornstein, P. A., Gordon, B. N., & Larus, D. M. (1992). Children's memory for a personality experienced event: Implications for testimony. *Applied Cognitive Psychology, 6,* 49–60.

Paine, M. L., & Hansen, D. J. (2002). Factors influencing children to self-disclose sexual abuse. *Clinical Psychology Review, 22,* 271–95.

Palmer, S. E., Brown, R. A., Rae-Grant, N. I., & Loughlin, M. J. (1999). Responding to children's disclosure of familial abuse: What survivors tell us. *Child Welfare, 78,* 259–82.

Peterson, C., & Bell, M. (1996). Children's memory for traumatic injury. *Child Development*, *67*, 3045–70.

Poole, D. A., & Lamb, M. E. (1998). *Investigative interviews of children: A guide for helping professionals*. Washington, DC: American Psychological Association.

Quinn, K. M., White, S., & Santilli, G. (1989). Influences of an interviewer's behaviors in child sexual abuse investigations. *Bulletin of the American Academy of Psychiatry and Law*, *17*, 45–52.

Sauzier, M. (1989). Disclosure of child sexual abuse: For better or for worse. *Psychiatric Clinics of North America*, *12*, 455–69.

Saywitz, K. J., & Goodman, G. S. (1996). Interviewing children in and out of court: Current research and practice implications. In J. Briere, L. Berliner, J. A. Bulkly, C. Jenny, & T. Reid (Eds.), *The APSAC handbook on child maltreatment* (pp. 297–318). Thousand Oaks, CA: Sage.

Saywitz, K. J., Goodman, G. S., Nicholas, E., & Moan, S. F. (1991). Children's memories of a physical examination involving genital touch: Implication for reports of child sexual abuse. *Journal of Consulting and Clinical Psychology*, *59*, 682–91.

Saywitz, K. J., Snyder, L., & Lamphear, V. (1996). Helping children tell what happened: A follow-up study of the narrative elaboration procedure. *Child Maltreatment*, *1*, 200–212.

Sjöberg, R. L., Lindbland, F. (2002). Limited disclosure of sexual abuse in children whose experiences were documented by videotape. *American Journal of Psychiatry*, *159*, 312–14.

Sternberg, K. J., Lamb, M. E., Hershkowitz, I., Esplin, P. W., Redlich, A., & Sunshine, N. (1996). The relation between investigative utterance types and the informativeness of child witnesses. *Journal of Applied Developmental Psychology*, *17*, 439–51.

Sternberg, K. J., Lamb, M. E., Orbach, Y., Esplin, P. W., & Mitchell, S. (2001). Use of a structured investigative protocol enhances young children's responses to free recall prompts in the course of forensic interviews. *Journal of Applied Psychology*, *86*, 997–1005.

Terry, W. T. (1990). *Perpetrator and victim accounts of sexual abuse*. Paper presented at the San Diego Conference on Responding to Child Maltreatment, San Diego, CA.

Walker, A. G., & Warren, A. R. (1995). The language of the child abuse interview: Asking the questions, understanding the answers. In T. Ney (Ed.), *True and false allegations of child sexual abuse: Assessment and case management* (pp. 153–62). New York: Brunner/Mazel.

Wood, B., Orsak, C., Murphy, M., & Cross, H. J. (1996). Semistructured child sexual abuse interviews: Interview and child characteristics related to credibility of disclosure. *Child Abuse & Neglect*, *20*, 81–92.

Yuille, J. C., Hunter, R., Joffe, R., & Zaparniuk, J. (1993). Interviewing children in sexual abuse cases. In G. S. Goodman & B. L. Bottoms (Eds.), *Child victims, child witnesses: Understanding and improving testimony* (pp. 95–115). New York: Guilford Press.

Yuille, J. C., Tymofievich, M., & Marxsen, D. (1995). The nature of allegations of child sexual abuse. In T. Ney (Ed.), *True and false allegations of child sexual abuse: Assessment and case management* (pp. 21–46). New York, NY: Brunner/Mazel.

APPENDIX

"Getting the allegation" prompts in the NICHD investigative interview protocol used in this study

The series of open-ended prompts in the NICHD investigative protocol begins with general invitations:

1. "Now that I know you a little better, I want to talk to you about why are you here today. Tell me why you came to talk to me." [This is an open-ended question designed to motivate the child, who understands why he or she is being interviewed, to disclose].

2. "It is important for me to understand why you came to talk to me today." [This is similar to the previous prompt but trying to emphasize the importance of understanding as a way to help the child to focus on the alleged abuse].

If children do not make allegations of abuse, the interviewers continue with increasingly more focused prompts:

3. "I heard you saw a policeman [social worker, doctor, etc.] last week [yesterday]. Tell me what you talked about." [This prompt tries to remind the child of a recent conversation he or she had with a professional. It is designed to motivate the child by indicating that the interviewer knows that he or she previously talked about the alleged event and to provide an input-free cue to children who are not sure why they are being interviewed].

4. "As I told you, my job is to talk to kids about things that might have happened to them. It's very important that I understand why you are here. Tell me why you think your mom [your dad, etc.] brought you here today."

5. "Is your mom [dad, etc.] worried that something may have happened to you? [Wait for a response; if it is affirmative say: Tell me what they are worried about"].

6. "I heard that someone has been bothering you. Tell me everything about the bothering."

7. "I heard that someone may have done something to you that wasn't right. Tell me everything about that, everything you can remember." [This prompt implies that something might have happened, without mentioning the alleged perpetrator, actions, or location. By posing the prompt as formulated in the protocol, the interviewer avoids interjecting assumption or biases about what might have happened].

If children fail to disclose abuse in response to the previous open-ended prompts, the interviewers introduce incident-related external input:

8. "I heard that something may have happened to you at [location of the alleged incident.] Tell . . ." [This prompt is designed for children who either do not know why they are being interviewed or are unwilling to disclose information about the abuse. Focusing on the location might cue children by reinstating the context of the alleged event].

If the first suggestive prompt fails, interviewers may choose to introduce even more specific prompts,which involve a summary of the allegation without mentioning the name of the perpetrator:

9. "I heard that someone may have [brief summary of the allegation]. Tell . . ." (Sternberg et al., 2001).

8

The Influence of the Interviewer-Provided Social Support on Children's Suggestibility, Memory, and Disclosures

Bette L. Bottoms
The University of Illinois at Chicago

Jodi A. Quas
University of California, Irvine

Suzanne L. Davis
R&D Strategic Solutions, Houston

As the chapters in this book reveal, a significant number of actual child abuse victims never disclose childhood abuse experiences at all, or they disclose in ways that do not lead to formal investigation. If there is an investigation, a victim's disclosure during a forensic interview must be accurate, detailed, and specific for abuse to be substantiated. Without detailed disclosures, children cannot be protected from further abuse and offenders cannot be prosecuted. It is critically important, then, for researchers to identify factors that encourage both informal disclosures prior to legal investigations as well as formal disclosures during forensic interviews. Several chapters in this book focus on well-defined cognitive-based techniques for conducting interviews (i.e., the National Institute of Child Health and Human Development [NICHD] protocol) and developmental and cognitive factors linked to disclosure during forensic interviews (Pipe, Lamb, Orbach, Stewart, Sternberg, & Esplin, chapter 5, this volume; Hershkowitz, Orbach, Lamb, Horowitz, & Sternberg, chapter 6, this volume). But social psychological factors—that is, situational and socioemotional contextual factors—also exert an important influence on whether children disclose and on the accuracy of their eyewitness reports (Bottoms, Goodman, Schwartz-Kenney, & Thomas, 2002; Goodman & Schwartz-Kenney, 1992).

In this chapter, we focus on one social psychological factor: social support. A considerable amount of research has revealed that social support can affect a range of outcomes in both children and adults, including health, performance, and memory (e.g., Burleson, Albrecht, Goldsmith, & Sarason, 1994; Hilmert, Kulik, & Christenfeld, 2002). In particular, and as we will discuss in detail, social support provided by an interviewer during a forensic interview can improve the quality of a child's report. Interviewer demeanor (supportive or otherwise) is more controllable than characteristics intrinsic to children such as age, cognitive abilities, and temperament. Thus, investigating the effects of social support on the accuracy of children's reports provides insight into practical interventions that can facilitate children's disclosures of abusive experiences.

Our chapter is organized as follows: First, we provide a general overview of theory regarding social support. Second, we review literature addressing the effect of social support on children's memory and suggestibility. Finally, we discuss new directions in the study of social support in forensic contexts: (a) the study of individual difference characteristics that predispose certain children to be particularly sensitive to social support manipulations, and (b) explorations of how adult observers, such as potential jurors, view socially supportive versus nonsupportive interview techniques. Throughout, we highlight findings from new studies in our own laboratories.

Before continuing, we must be clear about two important issues. Thus far, with only one exception which we describe later (Hershkowitz et al., this volume), the studies we review are so-called analogue studies, in which child participants are interviewed about nonabusive past events. Thus, it is difficult to draw definitive conclusions about the influence of support on disclosures of actual child abuse. Even so, whenever possible, we make informed inferences and pose predictions about how social support might affect the disclosure of child abuse. Second, we review no studies in which social support was provided to children contingent upon expected or desired answers. Specific and persistent reinforcement for incorrect answers (which might or might not be perceived by a child as socially supportive) is a highly leading, undesirable interview tactic that is associated with increases in young children's suggestibility (Garven, Wood, Malpass, & Shaw, 1998). A review of the consequences of highly leading techniques is beyond the scope of this paper (for discussion of that topic, see Poole & Lindsay, 2002).

SOCIAL SUPPORT AND ITS INFLUENCE ON CHILDREN'S EYEWITNESS REPORTS

Social support has been of interest to researchers across disciplines such as psychology, sociology, and communications, where it is conceptualized as a form of verbal or nonverbal interaction or communication between people that fosters a feeling of well-being in a target (Burleson et al., 1994). Social support has been operationally defined in varied ways, such as informational support (e.g., providing advice), emotional support (e.g., providing affection and nurturance), network support (e.g., being a part of a group of emotionally and supportive friends or family members), and esteem support (e.g., the bolstering of self-esteem over time by others) (Burleson & MacGrorge, 2002; Burleson et al., 1994; Cutrona & Russell, 1990; Hilmert et al., 2002; Tardy, 1994; Zelkowitz, 1989). Perceived social support is associated with a host of positive outcomes, including better physical and emotional health, reduced physiological reactivity, more fulfilling social relationships, and improved performance on cognitive tasks (e.g., Gerin, Milner, Chawla, & Pickering, 1995; Sarason, Sarason, & Pierce, 1990; Tardy, 1994; Uchino, Cacioppo, & Kiecolt-Glaser, 1996).

Researchers have investigated the effects of social support on children's memory and suggestibility because pretrial forensic interviews and courtrooms can be either socially supportive or intimidating places for children, depending on the demeanor and interview strategies of the adults in those venues. For example, forensic interviewers, attorneys, and judges can be warm and friendly, or they can be intimidating in their professional neutrality. Defense attorneys and others argue that children who are interviewed in a socially supportive manner may want to give answers that will please their friendly interrogator rather than answers that are accurate (e.g., Underwager & Wakefield, 1990). This intuition is occasionally bolstered by media coverage of cases involving young witnesses. For example, in a Chicago case several years ago, two very young suspects were wrongly suspected of killing a playmate. During their interviews with the child suspects, police officers used socially supportive techniques such as giving the children food and talking with them in a friendly manner. The children made statements that placed them at the crime scene and were interpreted as confessions. When the real (adult) killer was identified, public outrage focused on the policemen's child-friendly interview techniques. In fact, the first author was contacted for expert consultation by a party exploring the feasibility of a lawsuit against the city based on the argument that the socially supportive interview techniques were inappropriate. She declined, informing the caller that, as we review next, empirical evidence supports precisely the opposite conclusion.

Today, most child welfare professionals recommend child-friendly interview techniques (e.g., Wood, McClure, & Birch, 1996), reasoning that social support will be emotionally calming and thus encourage children to give accurate reports of past events. This is consistent with current developmental theories that stress the importance of environmental support for children to perform at their maximum levels of cognitive performance (e.g., Fischer, 1980; Vygotsky, 1934/1978). Perceived social support has been found to enhance adolescents' and adults' psychological well-being and perceived ability to cope with life stress (for reviews, see Cohen & Wills, 1985; Wolchik, Sandler, & Braver, 1990), grade school students' academic performance (Rosenthal & Jacobson, 1968), and the accuracy of students' short-term recall (Kelley & Gorham, 1988). On the basis of such psychological theory and empirical evidence, psychologists interested in socially supportive interviewing techniques have hypothesized that social support would similarly benefit children in forensic interview contexts. To test this prediction, they have conducted studies of children's memory and suggestibility using a standard mock eyewitness testimony paradigm wherein children experience an event and are interviewed either immediately or after a delay with open-ended free-recall questions (noncued prompts) or detailed questions that are misleading (suggestive of incorrect answers) or specific (cued, but not suggestive or coercive). Across studies, social support has been manipulated in three distinct ways, each of which is relevant in actual forensic settings: (a) the presence of child peers during an interview (Cornah & Memon, 1996; Greenstock & Pipe, 1996; Greenstock & Pipe, 1997; Moston & Engelberg, 1992); (b) the familiar identity of an interviewer (mother as opposed to stranger, Goodman, Sharma, Thomas, & Constadine, 1995; Ricci, Beal, & Dekle, 1996); and (c) the demeanor and actions of an interviewer (supportive or nonsupportive). In this chapter, we focus exclusively on the third type of manipulation. (For a review of the other work, see Davis & Bottoms, 2002b).

In the first published study of the effects of interviewer-provided social support on children's eyewitness abilities, 3- to 4-year-olds and 5- to 7-year-olds received routine (but stressful) inoculations at a medical clinic (Goodman, Bottoms, Rudy, & Schwartz-Kenney, 1991). Children were interviewed two and/or four weeks later about their clinic visit with free recall questions, specific questions, and misleading questions. Children in the socially supportive interview condition were interviewed by a woman who acted in a supportive manner by giving the children a snack, smiling frequently, and complimenting them at specific times without regard for accuracy. The remaining children were interviewed without these snacks, smiles, or compliments, in what could be characterized as a neutral rather than intimidating manner. Based on developmental theories that stress the importance of environmental support for children to perform at their "optimal level" (e.g., Fischer, 1980), Goodman and colleagues predicted that children in the supportive interview would be most accurate overall. Results indicated that social support reduced the number of inaccuracies in children's free recall generally. Further, after a four-week (but not a two-week) delay, social support also reduced younger children's errors in response to misleading questions and to questions that incorrectly suggested that abuse had occurred at the clinic. In fact, with socially supportive interviewing, 3- to 4-year-olds were as accurate when answering the misleading questions as were 5- to 6-year-olds. Goodman and colleagues speculated that interviewer-provided support decreased the extent to which children were intimidated, which in turn decreased their suggestibility. There was only one negative effect of social support: It increased the number of omission errors in younger children's responses to misleading questions about peripheral characteristics of the clinic setting (such as the color of the walls in the room).

Carter, Bottoms, and Levine (1996) investigated the effects of interviewer-provided social support on 5- to 7-year-olds' immediate eyewitness reports of a nonstressful interaction with an unfamiliar adult. Social support versus intimidation (rather than neutrality as in Goodman et al., 1991) was operationalized in terms of specific behaviors noted in the clinical literature to convey emotional warmth or a lack thereof (Mehrabian, 1969; Kelley & Gorham, 1988). In the supportive condition, the interviewer built rapport with the child, used a warm and friendly voice, gazed and smiled at the child often, and assumed a relaxed body position. In the nonsupportive condition, the interviewer withheld these behaviors. This manipulation, in which conditions were arguably better differentiated than those in the Goodman et al. (1991) study, produced more specific effects. That is, although support had no effect on children's responses to free recall or specific questions, children in the supportive condition were more resistant to misleading questions than were children in the nonsupportive condition. Expanding on Goodman et al.'s (1991) interpretation, Carter and colleagues theorized that interviewer-provided support increased children's resistance to misleading information by decreasing children's anxiety, lessening intimidation, and increasing feelings of empowerment.

In a study by Imhoff and Baker-Ward (1999), 3-and 4-year-olds witnessed a classroom demonstration in small groups. Two weeks later, they were individually interviewed about what happened by either a supportive or nonsupportive interviewer. Supportive interviewing had no effect on children's responses to specific or misleading questions, perhaps because Imhoff and Baker-Ward's nonsupportive interview was at most neutral and possibly even mildly supportive, albeit not to the extent as in the supportive condition. Specifically, the nonsupportive interviewers sometimes smiled at the children and complimented them on their performance.

Davis and Bottoms (2002a) examined 6- and 7-year-olds' memory for games and activities with a confederate "babysitter" (e.g., the children laid down on a giant piece of paper and had their bodies traced with a crayon). In interviews conducted immediately afterwards, interviewers were supportive or intimidating using the operationalization devised by Carter et al. (1996). Children questioned by a supportive person were significantly more resistant to misleading suggestions than children questioned by a nonsupportive person.

As in Carter et al.'s study, there were no effects on free recall, specific questions, or questions about whether abuse had occurred (on which children were already highly accurate). A unique aspect of Davis and Bottoms' research was their focus on two potential mechanisms, anxiety and perceived self-efficacy, by which social support might affect children's performance. First, the researchers tested the possibility that social support reduces children's anxiety, which in turn facilitates children's memory and resistance to false suggestions (as suggested by Carter et al., 1996, and Greenstock & Pipe, 1996, 1997). Results indicated that support was indeed associated with lower anxiety during the mock forensic interview (as measured by the State-Trait Anxiety Inventory, Spielberger, 1979), but anxiety was not in turn associated with suggestibility and thus did not mediate the effect of interviewer support on resistance to suggestion. Even so, the authors cautioned that it would be premature to rule out anxiety as a mediator under all circumstances, because their child participants were probably not terribly anxious in the first place.

Second, the researchers tested the predicted mediation of "Resistance Efficacy," defined as children's perceived self-efficacy (Bandura, 1982, 1997) for being able to resist misleading questions; that is, children's feelings of confidence about telling an adult he or she is wrong. For the older (but not younger) children in the sample, social support increased children's perceived Resistance Efficacy, which in turn increased their resistance to misleading questions. Therefore, one mechanism by which social support decreases older children's compliance in response to misleading interview questions is by increasing children's Resistance Efficacy.

With colleagues Kari Nysse-Carris, Tamara Haegerich, and Andrew Conway, Davis and Bottoms have now performed an additional study concerned with the effects of social support on children's memory and suggestibility, reinterviewing the children who participated in the Davis and Bottoms (2002a) study one year later. Specifically, the researchers tested whether the positive effects of supportive interviewing would be obtained even if the interview occurred long after the original event, as happens when children's disclosures are delayed (e.g., Bottoms, Rudnicki, & Epstein, chapter 10, this volume; Goodman-Brown, Edelstein, Goodman, Jones, & Gordon, 2003; Hanson, Resnick, Saunders, Kilpatrick, & Best, 1999; Lyon, chapter 3, this volume; Lyon, 2002; Pipe et al., this volume). As in the original study, the new interviewer behaved either supportively or nonsupportively. Children recalled a great deal of accurate information after even one year. Compared to children in the nonsupportive condition, children questioned by the supportive interviewer freely recalled significantly more correct and less incorrect information, and made significantly fewer commission errors in response to both misleading and specific questions. Thus, social support had positive effects even after one year, when children's memory for the original event was less strong.

Other than the study just described, only Goodman et al. (1991) found effects of social support on the amount of information retrieved using free recall questions, and theirs was the only other study that included a significant delay between the event and the interview. In fact, the effects of support in Goodman et al.'s study were strongest at the longest delay (four weeks). Studies using no delay have shown no effects of support on recall (Carter et al., 1996; Davis & Bottoms, 2002a), perhaps because of a ceiling effect; that is, memory for the event was already so strong that support could not improve it further. Also, with the exception of Imhoff and Baker-Ward (1999), who operationalized support-ive and nonsupportive interviewing in a mildly differentiated manner, all other researchers have found that suggestibility is reduced when children are ques-tioned by a supportive rather than a nonsupportive interviewer.

Together these findings illustrate that social support has two-pronged ef-fect. First, it decreases children's suggestibility or social compliance, which is not wholly dependent on memory (as illustrated by similar effects on mislead-ing, suggestive questions in studies with or without interview delay). That is, although it is easier to mislead people about events for which memory is weak (Loftus, 1979), compliance can occur regardless of the underlying memory strength. Compliance is the social psychological process of agreeing with an-other's request or directive due to a desire to comply with perceived social pressure (Aronson, 1999). In the present case, the request is implicit in the in-terviewer's misleading question: to agree publicly with the suggested inaccu-rate information regardless of one's actual memory for the event. The compliance-reducing aspect of social support is the aspect that is likely to be mediated by psychological constructs such as perceived Resistance Efficacy.

Second, in some studies social support enhanced children's memory per-formance, as illustrated by effects on free recall performance and on responses to specific questions in studies that included a delay. When memory is weak, support might increase accuracy by helping children calmly focus on their memories for past events and in turn recall more information. Thus, we theo-rize that the memory-enhancing effects of social support are likely to be medi-ated by psychological constructs such as anxiety reduction or attentional focus, although this has yet to be tested in a study involving delay.

A final, recent study conducted by Hershkowitz et al. (chapter 6, this vol-ume) represents the most ecologically valid test thus far of effects of socially supportive interviewing. They examined the interviews of 100 actual sus-pected child abuse victims in Israel. The interviews studied were chosen to create a set of cases wherein half of the interviews resulted in disclosures of abuse and half resulted in no disclosure. Cases were otherwise matched with respect to factors such as child age and gender, perpetrator identity, abuse type, etc. In all cases, there was considerable corroborative evidence of abuse. Chil-dren ranged in age from 4 to 14 years and were interviewed by official investi-gators trained in the NICHD interview protocol, which recommends socially supportive interviewing. Hershkowitz and colleagues found that interviewers displayed more socially supportive behaviors and fewer negative behaviors to-ward children during the interviews that resulted in disclosure than in interviews that resulted in nondisclosure. When interviewers acted in non-supportive ways, children were less responsive and offered more denials. More-over, the interviewers' nonsupportive behaviors began even during the rapport-building stage of interviews, before substantive questioning. Of course, the real world nature of this study is both its triumph and downfall: It is im-possible to disentangle the direction of causality in these effects. We do not know whether the children's resistance provoked the interviewers' unsupport-ive behaviors, or whether the interviewers' nonsupportive techniques fostered children's resistance and nondisclosure (consistent with research showing that adults get defensive when interaction partners are perceived to be cool and de-tached, Civickly, Pace, & Krause, 1977). It is likely that the interviews being studied involved a complex and dynamic interaction process, wherein inter-viewers and children reacted to and reflected each other's demeanor and ac-tions (Gilstrap, 2004).

In summary, in five of the six studies reviewed, interviewer-provided social support had a positive effect on children's reports of past events by increasing resistance to misleading suggestions and by facilitating free recall after a delay. Furthermore, and of importance, none of the studies revealed adverse effects of supportive interviewing on memory or suggestibility, with a single exception: Support led to increases in the number of omission errors in response to ques-tions about peripheral details in the Goodman et al. (1991) study, a finding that has not been replicated. Hershkowitz and colleagues' (chapter 6, this vol-ume) findings suggest that disclosures of actual child abuse may also be facili-tated by supportive rather than unsupportive interview techniques, with little risk of increased false disclosures. Overall, we believe that the available evi-dence illustrates that socially supportive interviewing is unlikely to have ad-verse effects on children's performance, and therefore, the evidence supports the recommendation made by many (e.g., Bottoms & Davis, 2002b; Sorenson, Bottoms, & Perona, 1997; Wood et al., 1996) that forensic interviewers should behave in a socially supportive rather than an intimidating manner during forensic interviews.

INDIVIDUAL DIFFERENCES IN RESPONSIVENESS TO SOCIAL SUPPORT

Although we can confidently conclude that, in general, social support has pos-itive effects (and few if any adverse effects), numerous important questions re-main concerning the precise conditions under which social support improves the accuracy of children's reports. One such question concerns individual dif-ferences in children's performance, which have been the focus of a growing number of child eyewitness studies (e.g., Eisen, Goodman, Davis, & Qin, 1999; Merrit, Ornstein, & Spicker, 1994; Quas, Bauer, & Boyce, 2004). As Bottoms and Davis (2002a, 2002b) have suggested, individual differences probably moderate the effects of social support on memory and suggestibility.

Psychologists who have studied social support in other domains (e.g., adult relationships) find that correlations between outcomes such as physical health and *perceived* (felt) social support are stronger than those with *actual* (directly observable) social support (Bersheid & Reis, 1998). This suggests that there may be dispositional sensitivities to social support. For example, people who are dysphoric and have negative expectations do not recognize supportive behaviors in relationships as well as people who are more positively oriented (Lakey & Cassidy, 1990).

Researchers are just beginning to address this interesting issue in child witness research. As we review next, individual child characteristics that appear to moderate the effects of interviewer-provided social support include preexisting social support reserves, attachment style, working memory ability, and physiological reactivity. A host of other temperament and personality factors might also be involved.

Social Support Reserves. Carter et al. (1996) theorized that social support reserves (i.e., the amount of social support generally existing in a child's life) would moderate the effects of interviewer-provided support. Specifically, children having less contact with supportive friends and family members would feel less empowered generally, and in turn would be more sensitive to social support and perhaps benefit more from interviewer-provided social support than children who enjoy more preexisting social support from other people. Davis and Bottoms (2002a) tested this prediction by measuring children's support reserves with the parent form of the Zelkowitz (1989) Social Support Inventory, on which mothers reported interactions between their children and family members and friends. Results provided some, but not pervasive, support for the hypotheses: Children low in support reserves made more commission errors to specific questions when they had a nonsupportive interviewer, as compared to a supportive interviewer, whereas children who were already high in support reserves were unaffected by interviewer support. Surprisingly, there were no effects on responses to misleading questions, however. The authors called for research using a more sensitive measure of support reserves, arguing that parents might not be able to (or want to) accurately represent their children's feelings of support from others.

Attachment Style. Child witness researchers have also become interested in the relation between testimonial accuracy and individual differences in the quality of children's emotional attachment to significant others (Goodman, Quas, Batterman-Faunce, Riddlesberger, & Kuhn, 1997; see also Alexander, Quas, & Goodman, 2002). Attachment quality (or style) might be related to children' s reactions to a nonsupportive interviewer, and in turn their resistance to misleading questions asked by such an individual. Specifically, the emotional quality of a forensic interview (supportive or nonsupportive) may make attachment issues salient. Insecurely attached children, who are generally more apprehensive and less trusting of others during social interactions (Bowlby, 1973), could be more sensitive to interviewer supportiveness than securely attached children, who are generally at ease during social interactions. Also, compared to securely attached children, insecurely attached children might experience more distress during confusing, potentially stressful interactions with unfamiliar adults (e.g., Alexander et al., 2002). To the extent that a nonsupportive, emotionally unavailable interviewer is distressing to children, insecurely attached children might react especially negatively and have the most difficulty contradicting interviewers and resisting false suggestions.

In the same experiment described above with 6- and 7-year-olds (Davis & Bottoms, 2002a) but in analyses not yet published, Davis, Bottoms, Guererro, Shreder, and Krebel (1998) tested these interesting possibilities. Because there is often a correspondence between parental and child attachment style (Bartholomew, 1990; Shaver & Hazan, 1993), parental attachment style was used as a proxy for children's attachment. Using Bartholomew and Horowitz's (1991) measure of adult attachment, parents classified themselves as either secure, anxious–ambivalent, avoidant, or dismissing–avoidant in their romantic relationships. We collapsed anxious–ambivalents, avoidants, and dismissing–avoidants into one "insecure" category, consistent with prior research (e.g., Bradshaw, Goldsmith, & Campos, 1987). As expected, attachment and support condition interacted to affect children's rate of commission errors to misleading questions. Children whose parents classified themselves as insecurely attached made significantly more errors in the nonsupportive than the supportive condition, but secure children were unaffected by the support manipulation. These preliminary results are consistent with the possibility that insecurely attached children are more vulnerable to suggestion than secure children during nonsupportive forensic interviews, and that socially supportive interviewing may buffer against problems associated with insecure attachment. Replication is, of course, needed, especially with research that explores relations among children's own attachment, interviewer behaviors, and children's memory and suggestibility, including the specific mechanisms by which attachment style affects children's responses during forensic interviews.

Working Memory. Davis and Bottoms, along with colleagues Conway, Nysse-Carris, and Haegerich, also examined working memory as another potentially important moderator of social support. Historically, psychologists have thought of working memory only from a capacity standpoint, but more recent theorists (e.g., Conway & Engle, 1996) conceptualize working memory as a mixture of storage (i.e., capacity) and control processes. Working memory is thought to be a dynamic system used to operate on information that is currently the focus of attention. Control processes (or executive functions) determine what information gets into working memory. Individuals with high working memory capacity are thought to have more efficient control processes, leaving more resources available for storage. They are good at controlling, regulating, and actively maintaining task-relevant information, even in the face of distracters. Individuals with low working memory capacity have less efficient control processes, which reduces their ability to actively maintain task-relevant information and ignore distracting and irrelevant information, which, in turn, allows extraneous information to enter working memory (Conway & Engle, 1996).

We predicted that, compared to children with higher working memory capacity, children with lower working memory capacity would have difficulty ignoring misleading information provided by an interviewer and focusing on the central content of questions, thus becoming more suggestible. We expected that children with higher working memory capacity would be better able to focus and concentrate on the central content of questions and to respond more accurately. We tested these predictions in the one-year follow-up to the Davis and Bottoms (2002a) study described earlier. Specifically, after the mock forensic interview, we measured children's working memory ability (high or low) using a counting span task (Case, Kurland, & Goldberg, 1982) that was computer administered and modified to included distracters. Overall, compared to children with high working memory capacity, children with low working memory were more suggestible to misleading questions. However, when correlations between working memory and suggestibility were computed separately for children in the supportive and nonsupportive interview conditions, an interesting picture emerged: For children in the nonsupportive condition, working memory capacity was significantly (and relatively strongly, $rs > -.40$) negatively correlated with commission errors in response to misleading and specific questions, indicating that those children low in working memory capacity made more errors. In the supportive condition, however, there was no significant relation between working memory capacity and interview performance.

These data suggest not only that our theories about the relation between suggestibility and working memory were correct but also that socially supportive interviewing moderates the otherwise negative effects of a preexisting cognitive individual difference. When interviewed in a supportive manner, children with low working memory capacity performed as well as those with high working memory capacity. But when interviewed in an intimidating manner, children with low working memory capacity were disadvantaged. Children with low working memory needed the support of a friendly, encouraging interviewer more. This is particularly interesting because some cognitive theorists view working memory capacity as a stable characteristic that may be affected by task factors but not by social factors, which presumably do not change the demands of the task itself.

Physiological Reactivity. Physiological reactivity has also been studied as a potentially important individual-difference characteristic with implications for the relations between social support and memory and suggestibility. Physiological reactivity refers to children's tendency to experience heightened (versus moderate or brief) physiological responses when faced with situations that are stressful and challenging. Physiological reactivity is believed to be a relatively stable characteristic in children. It has been measured using a variety of indices reflecting sympathetic, parasympathetic, and hypothalamic pituitary adrenal axis activation. Traditionally, reactivity has been viewed as a risk factor for a variety of physical, emotional, and cognitive problems in childhood (e.g., Johnston-Brooks, Lewis, Evans, & Whalen, 1998). Findings from empirical studies, however, have not yielded consistent results: Heightened reactivity is associated with increased risk in some studies, is unrelated to risk in others, and is associated with reduced risk in still others (Boyce, Chesney, Alkon, Tschann, Adams, Chesterman, et al., 1995; Fabes, Eisenberg, & Eisenbud, 1997; Gunnar, Tout, de Haan, Pierce, & Stansbury, 1997).

To explain these variable results, some researchers have reconceptualized physiological reactivity not as a risk factor but instead as a form of biological sensitivity to social context (e.g., Boyce & Ellis, 2005). When the context is stressful or challenging, physiologically reactive individuals need to devote attention and resources to self-regulation at the expense of attending to potentially important environmental information. However, when the context is socially warm, nurturing, and supportive, reactive individuals' increased sensitivity should enable them to benefit fully from the positive context. Findings from several naturalistic studies of physiological reactivity in childhood support this conceptualization, at least when social context is examined broadly in terms of life stressors. For instance, consistent with traditional views of reactivity, high heart rate reactivity was associated with frequent respiratory problems in 3- to 6-year-olds but only when parents also reported high levels of family conflict. When parents reported low levels of family conflict, highly reactive children actually had low levels of respiratory problems. The frequency of illnesses among nonreactive children was unrelated to parent-reported conflict (Boyce et al., 1995).

Consistent with the conceptualization of reactivity as a form of sensitivity to social context, Quas and colleagues (2004a) predicted a link between physiological reactivity and sensitivity to socially supportive interviewing. We were specifically interested in whether high- versus low-stress social contexts differentially affected reactive and nonreactive children's memories for novel, challenging experiences. We hypothesized that, in the high stress environment of a nonsupportive interview, physiologically reactive children would have limited ability to attend to environmental information (i.e., the questions being asked), which would then lead to poorer memory performance relative to (a) nonreactive children in the high stress environment (nonsupportive interview) and (b) reactive children in the high support environment (supportive interview). Furthermore, because nonreactive children are less sensitive to changes in their social environment, we predicted that the social support manipulation would not affect the nonreactive children's performance as much as it would affect the reactive children's performance.

We tested these predictions on 4- to 6-year-olds who first came to our laboratory and completed a series of mildly challenging laboratory tasks during which their physiological arousal (i.e., autonomic reactions) was continuously monitored. Physiological reactivity scores were calculated based on children's level of autonomic arousal during the tasks relative to their arousal while listening to neutral stories. After a two-week delay, children were interviewed about what happened during the previous session with free-recall and direct (including both misleading and specific) questions. Interviewers behaved in either a highly supportive or nonsupportive manner using the manipulation procedures employed by Davis and Bottoms (2002a). Findings confirmed expectations: Physiologically reactive children questioned in a supportive manner provided more correct responses to the direct questions than did reactive children questioned by a nonsupportive interviewer. Among nonreactive children, however, social support was generally unrelated to performance. We thus found, for the first time, that characteristics of children indeed moderated the effects of socially supportive interviewing techniques on children's memory.

Quas and Lench (in press) have now extended these initial findings in a second investigation that tested children's memory for fear-eliciting emotional information. During a visit to a research laboratory, 5- and 6-year-olds completed a range of challenging laboratory tasks, one of which involved watching a brief videoclip that elicited mild fear responses. After a week's delay, children returned for an interview about the video. Interviewers behaved in either a socially supportive or nonsupportive manner, again using the manipulation employed by Davis and Bottoms (2002a). Children's physiological arousal was monitored while children watched the initial video and while they were interviewed. Differences scores were computed by subtracting children's baseline heart rate (obtained while children were engaged in relatively neutral, nonchallenging activities) from their heart rate during the video and during the memory interview.

Analyses revealed that the relation between children's physiological arousal and their memory performance varied depending on whether arousal at encoding versus retrieval was considered, the latter of which further interacted with interviewer demeanor. First, greater heart rate while watching the fear video was associated with later enhanced memory. Second, consistent with former findings, when arousal at retrieval was considered, the supportive interviewer benefited children who were especially aroused at the time of the interview. More specifically, children who were highly aroused during the interview (i.e., large interview-baseline difference scores) and who were questioned by a nonsupportive interviewer evinced poorer memory for the fear video than did children who were not aroused, regardless of interviewer support, and children who were aroused and questioned by a supportive interviewer. The highly aroused children questioned in a nonsupportive manner may have been unable to attend to the interviewer and retrieve negative, fear-related information while concurrently try to regulate their arousal, an interpretation consistent with limited resource models of cognition (e.g., Case, 1991) and with former studies, including the work described above on working memory and other research on physiological arousal, attention, and memory in children (e.g., Bugental, Blue, Fleck, Rodriguez, & Cortex, 1992; Quas et al., 2004).

Together, these studies demonstrate the complex array of factors that might be important when evaluating not only the effects of social support on memory but also when attempting to identify which children may be particularly vulnerable to adverse effects of a nonsupportive interviewer or, conversely, which children are most in need of highly supportive interviewers.

Other Potentially Important Individual Difference Factors. We know of no other tests of individual differences in sensitivity to interviewer-provided social support, but there are theoretical reasons to predict that a number of other individual-difference characteristics would be fruitful for study. For example, dispositional shyness, which is believed to reflect high physiological reactivity, might be a marker of sensitivity to social support. In addition, Davis and Bottoms (2002b) reasoned that children who are low in self-esteem may doubt their abilities more than children who are high in self-esteem (Harter & Pike, 1984) and thus could be more sensitive to interviewer-provided social support. Social support might help such children to relax and answer questions to their maximum capability, when they might otherwise be intimidated and withdrawn. This is a particularly interesting potential mediator because low self-esteem is associated with childhood abuse (Kaufman & Cicchetti, 1989), and thus might characterize many of the children actually questioned in forensic settings. There could also be cultural differences that predispose some children to recognize and/or benefit more from social support than other children. For example, there is some evidence that American parents use more supportive communication styles with their children than do Chinese parents (Miller, Wiley, & Fung, 1997). This might have implications for sensitivity to varying interviewer communication styles.

Also, some researchers speculate that there exists a trait-like "suggestibility" characteristic in children (and adults); that is, a relatively stable tendency to acquiesce to an interviewer's suggestions or pressure (e.g., Gudjonsson, 1984; Scullin & Ceci, 2001). The manifestation of such a trait might be affected by interviewer support. When children are not comfortable contradicting an interviewer's suggestions (i.e., when an interviewer behaves in a nonsupportive manner), they might be consistent in their acquiescence regardless of the strength of their actual memory. However, when children feel at ease with an interviewer (i.e., when the interviewer is supportive), they might be more comfortable answering questions, saying "I don't know" when they truly do not know an answer, and contradicting false statements and suppositions. This might result in less stability in children's errors when questioned about different events. Evidence from one of our labs is consistent with such a possibility. In a study of children's memory and suggestibility about two separate events, children's errors in response to specific questions about the two events were significantly positively correlated when the interviewer behaved nonsupportively. The correlation was nonsignificant, however, when the interviewer behaved supportively, such that the number of errors made about each event was unrelated (Quas, Wallin, Papini, Lench, & Scullin, 2005). Thus, interviewer support appeared to moderate the manifestation of trait suggestibility within children.

Summary

The studies we have reviewed represent a small portion of a broader line of research investigating individual differences that predict children's memory and suggestibility (e.g., Goodman et al., 1997). What is uniquely important about these studies is that they extend this broader range of research by focusing on interactions between individual and social-contextual characteristics. The results offer a more complicated, but also more accurate, depiction of the mechanisms underlying children's memory and reporting capabilities and the processes by which some children might be more as opposed to less accurate in forensic interview situations. More research is needed, especially on children's willingness to disclose personal, potentially traumatic information such as abuse. None of the studies of individual differences in sensitivity to support have been conducted with suspected abuse victims, but this could be accomplished by, for example, adding individual difference measures to studies like that conducted by Hershkowitz and her colleagues (chapter 6, this volume).

This individual-difference research is of obvious theoretical value but also of practical significance. The results highlight the fact that the effects of social support on performance are not consistent across children. Instead, certain characteristics, such as low working memory or a propensity to exhibit exaggerated physiological reactions to stress, predispose some children to be particularly sensitive to manipulations of social support in interview contexts. It would be useful for interviewers to be aware of individual children's propensities and needs when conducting forensic interviews with alleged victims. Although it is unlikely that some individual differences (physiological reactivity) could be assessed in legal contexts to identify those children who would most benefit from socially supportive interviewing, it might be possible to assess other individual differences (e.g., support reserves or shyness). In any case, because research indicates that socially supportive interviewing carries no apparent risks, it should be used with all children, ensuring that the most needy can reap its benefits. Perhaps in the future, as individual difference assessment becomes more feasible, special techniques could be developed for the children most likely to perform poorly in interviews.

ADULTS' PERCEPTIONS OF SOCIALLY SUPPORTIVE INTERVIEWS

Finally, a second new line of research in this area focuses on how manipulations of interviewer support affect adults' *perceptions* of children's credibility. This is of great practical concern in a forensic context. If a child makes a disclosure of abuse, adults must deem that disclosure to be credible before any action will be taken to remove a child from harm or bring a perpetrator to justice. Specifically, legal and/or social service professionals will evaluate the credibility of a child's report and decide whether to pursue an investigation. If the case comes to trial, attorneys, judges, and jurors will also make judgments about the child's credibility. Adults have considerable difficulty discerning the actual accuracy of children's testimony (Goodman, Bottoms, Herscovici, & Shaver, 1989; Leippe, Manion, & Romanczyk, 1992), and as a result, decisions about children's credibility can be influenced by people's pre-existing beliefs and biases (Bottoms, 1993), perhaps including beliefs about the effects of interview techniques on children's accuracy. Little is known about adults' perceptions of children's testimony derived from socially supportive as opposed to nonsupportive interviews. Adults might be skeptical of supportive interviewing, viewing such techniques as coercive: "If you are nice to children, they will just say whatever they think you want to hear." Adults might sympathize with and believe children who are interviewed in an unsupportive manner. Or, adults might intuit the integrity of supportive techniques and favor reports resulting from such interviews.

Bottoms, Rudnicki, and Nysse-Carris (2004) have recently completed a study of this in the laboratory. A large, ethnically diverse group of college-aged men and women viewed videotapes of 7- to 8-year-old boys' and girls' answers to questions that were asked during the mock forensic interviews in the previously discussed one-year follow-up study to the Davis and Bottoms (2002a) study. Half of the adults watched the interview of 1 of 10 children who had been interviewed in a socially-supportive manner; the other half watched the interview of 1 of 10 children who had been interviewed in a socially-unsupportive manner. In other words, the adults each watched and rated one child, and approximately a dozen adults watched each of the 20 children. (This methodology reduces the influence of idiosyncratic differences among particular children.) Interview style had no impact on adults' ability to discern children's actual accuracy or inaccuracy. In fact, adults rated children interviewed in a nonsupportive manner as accurate more often than children interviewed in a supportive manner, even though children were actually more accurate in the supportive than the nonsupportive condition. Analyses of judgment bias indicated that adults who viewed nonsupportive interviews were more biased to believe children than adults who watched supportive interviews. Finally, the adults rated the children interviewed in a nonsupportive manner to be more credible and less nervous generally than children who had been interviewed in a supportive manner.

Thus, although socially supportive interviewing has positive effects on the actual accuracy of children's reports, this research reveals that socially supportive interviewing techniques have the potential to disadvantage child witnesses in terms of their perceived credibility. Replication is clearly needed, but this study provides an important first step toward understanding the effects that interview style can have on the perceptions that adults form when evaluating children's testimony. If the finding holds, it will indicate the need for educating judges, attorneys, jurors, and others who are in positions to evaluate child witnesses about the influences of social psychological factors on the accuracy of children's reports, as well as the biases that they themselves might bring to the task of evaluating children's credibility.

CONCLUSIONS

Several global conclusions are warranted based on our review of research on socially supportive interviewing techniques. First, a socially supportive interviewer can enhance children's eyewitness reports by reducing their suggestibility (compliance) and by aiding memory recall after a delay. Second, even when no benefits of social support emerge, support does not adversely affect children's performance. Thus, concerns about negative consequences of highly supportive interviewers simply are not warranted. Third, when questioned by an unsupportive interviewer, certain children might be particularly vulnerable to negative performance, especially those who are low in social support reserves, insecurely attached, low in working memory capacity, and high in physiological reactivity to stress and challenge. Further research is likely to reveal other dispositional characteristics that moderate the effects of supportive interviewing. Fourth, despite the actual advantages of supportive interviewing, supportive interviews might increase adults' skepticism of the children's reports, leading to the unintended consequence of reduced credibility. This indicates a need for educating adults in the legal system about the research we have reviewed in this chapter.

Although many of the studies we reviewed did not include suspected abuse victims as participants, we believe that similar findings would have been obtained if actual victims had been studied. That is, based on the consistent finding that children's accuracy is either enhanced or unaffected by highly supportive interviewers, we believe that supportive interviewers would probably elicit more true disclosures but not more false disclosures. Tentative evidence supporting our belief comes from Lyon and colleagues' studies of the effects of truth-induction techniques on maltreated children's disclosures of transgressions. One truth-induction technique involves supportively reassuring children that it is "OK to disclose" the transgression. In some research, the alleged transgression is explicitly mentioned during the reassurances (e.g., "It is OK if you played with the toy house") (Lyon & Dorado, 2004), whereas in other research the transgression is not explicitly mentioned (Lyon, Malloy, Talwar, & Quas, 2004). Further, and of particular note, although the target event was a mock transgression (i.e., the children either played or did not play with a forbidden toy), the participants were children removed from home because of substantiated maltreatment. Thus, the studies' findings are particularly relevant to the actual populations who are likely to be interviewed about suspected abuse. Supportive reassurances often increased children's true disclosures of the transgression when they actually played with the toy. However, reassurance sometimes had negative effects on children who had not transgressed, particularly when the reassurance specifically mentioned the transgression or was coupled with suggestive questions. Despite Lyon and colleagues' studies not being direct tests of the effects of social support per se on disclosures, insofar as reassuring children during forensic interviews fosters feelings of interpersonal warmth and reduces children's distress, findings suggest that such support, so long as it is general, can facilitate maltreated children's disclosures, a pattern also supported by Hershkowitz and colleagues' results concerning children's actual abuse disclosures (chapter 6, this volume).

Forensic interviewers and other legal and social service professionals who come into contact with child victim/witnesses need to be aware of empirical research so that they use the best possible interview techniques and, in turn, obtain the best possible information from children. This will help accomplish the complementary goals of forensic investigation: protecting children who are in abusive situations from further harm, prosecuting actual offenders, and guarding against false accusations of abuse against innocent persons (Perona, Bottoms, & Sorenson, 2006). Social scientists have a duty to make their results accessible to legal and child protection professionals for such purposes (Reppucci, 1985). We hope this chapter is a step toward fulfilling that duty and also a useful resource for scientists wishing to conduct further research in this important area.

ACKNOWLEDGMENTS

The research we summarize in this chapter was supported by funding to the authors from the American Psychology-Law Society (Davis), the National Institute of Health (Bottoms, Quas), and the MacArthur Foundation (Quas). For their substantial contributions to the new studies we have reported, we thank our collaborators: Amy Bauer, Thomas Boyce, Kari Nysse-Carris, Andrew Conway, Tamara Haegerich, Heather Lench, and Aaron Rudnicki. We also thank the many individuals who participated in our research and research assistants who helped with data collection, including Abbey Alkon, Jason DeCaro, Holly Eibs, Monique Ewig, Krissie Fernandez, Lauren Goldstein, Rosalie

B. Guerrero, Sarah Kay, Christie Kollmar, Andrea L. Krebel, Danielle Lemon, Debra Matthiews, Richard T. Reyes, Jason P. Rohacs, Stephanie Schenk, Anisha Shetty, Elaine A. Shreder, Alon Stein, and Mimi Wolff.

REFERENCES

Aronson, E. (1999). *The social animal.* (8th Edition). New York: Worth.

Bandura, A. (1982). Self-efficacy mechanism in human agency. *American Psychologist, 37,* 122–47.

———. (1997). *Self efficacy: The exercise of control.* New York: Freeman.

Bersheid, E., & Reis, H. (1998). Attraction and close relationships. In D. T. Gilbert, S. T. Fiske, & G. Lindzey (Eds.), *The handbook of social psychology, Vol. 1.* (pp. 193–281). Boston: McGraw-Hill.

Bottoms, B. L. (1993). Individual differences in perceptions of child sexual assault cases. In G. S. Goodman & B. L. Bottoms (Eds.), *Child victims, child witnesses* (pp. 229–61). Newbury Park, CA: Sage.

Bottoms, B. L., Davis, S., Nysse, K. L., Haegerich, T. M., & Conway, A. (2000, March). *Effects of social support and working memory capacity on children's eyewitness memory.* In B. L. Bottoms & M. B. Kovera (Chairs), Individual and contextual influences on adults' perceptions of children's reports. Symposium conducted at the biennial meeting of the American Psychology/Law Society, New Orleans, LA.

Bottoms, B. L., Goodman, G. S., Schwartz-Kenney, B. M., & Thomas, S. F. (2002). Children's use of secrecy in the context of eyewitness reports. *Law and Human Behavior, 26,* 285–313.

Bottoms, B. L., Rudnicki, A. G., & Nysse-Carris, K. L. (2004, Mar.). *The influence of socially supportive interviewing on adults' perceptions of children's report accuracy.* Presentation at the biennial meeting of the American Psychology/Law Society, Austin, TX.

Bowlby, J. (1973). *Attachment and loss, Vol. 2.* Separation: Anxiety and anger. NY: Basic Books.

Boyce, W. T., Chesney, M., Alkon, A., Tschann, J. M., Adams, S., Chesterman, B., Cohen, F., Kaiser, P., Folkman, S., & Wara, D. (1995). Psychobiologic reactivity to stress and childhood respiratory illnesses: Results of two prospective studies. *Psychosomatic Medicine, 57,* 411–22.

Boyce, W. T., & Ellis, B. J. (2005). Biological sensitivity to context: I. an evolutionary-developmental theory of the origins and functions of stress reactivity. *Development and Psychopathology, 17,* 271-301.

Burleson, B. R., Albrecht, T. L., Goldsmith, D. J., & Sarason, I. G. (1994). Introduction: The communication of social support. In B. R. Burleson, T. L. Albrecht, & I. G. Sarason (Eds.), *Communication of social support* (pp. xi–xxx). Thousand Oaks, CA: Sage.

Burleson, B. R., & MacGrorge (2002). Supportive communication. In M. L. Knapp & J. A. Daley (Eds.), *Handbook of interpersonal communication* (3rd Ed.) (pp. 374–424). Thousand Oaks, CA: Sage.

Carter, C. A., Bottoms, B. L., & Levine, M. (1996). Linguistic and socioemotional influences on the accuracy of children's reports. *Law and Human Behavior, 20,* 335–58.

Case, R., Kurland, M. D., & Goldberg, J. (1982). Operational efficiency and the growth of short-term memory span. *Journal of Experimental Child Psychology, 33,* 386–404.

Cohen, S., & Wills, T. (1985). Stress, social support, and the buffering hypothesis. *Psychological Bulletin, 98,* 310–57.

Conway, A. R. A., & Engle, R. W. (1996). Individual differences in working memory capacity: More evidence for a general capacity theory. *Memory, 4*, 577–90.

Cornah, D., & Memon, A. (1996). *Improving children's testimony: The effects of social support.* Presentation made at the biennial meeting of the American Psychology-Law Society, Hilton Head, TX.

Cutrona, C. E., & Russell, D. W. (1990). Type of social support and specific stress: Toward a theory of optimal matching. In S. R. Sarason, I. G. Sarason, & G. R. Pierce, (Eds.), *Social support: An interactional view* (pp. 319–66). New York: Wiley.

Davis, S. L. (1998). Social and scientific influences on the study of children's suggestibility: A historical perspective. *Child Maltreatment, 3*, 186–194.

Davis, S. L., & Bottoms, B. L. (2002a). Effects of social support on children's eyewitness reports: A test of the underlying mechanism. *Law and Human Behavior, 26*, 185–215.

———. (2002b). Social support and children's eyewitness testimony. In M. L. Eisen, J. A. Quas, & G. S. Goodman (Eds.) *Memory and suggestibility in the forensic interview* (pp. 437–57). Mahwah, NJ: Lawrence Erlbaum Associates.

Davis, S. L., Bottoms, B. L., Guererro, R. B., Shreder, E. A., & Krebel, A. L. (1998, May). *Attachment style, social support, and children's eyewitness reports.* Presentation at the annual meeting of the Midwest Psychological Association, Chicago, IL.

Eisen, M. E., Goodman, G. S., Davis, S. L., & Qin, J. (1999). Individual differences in maltreated children's memory and suggestibility. In L. M. Williams & V. Banyard (Eds.), *Trauma and memory*. Thousand Oaks, CA: Sage.

Fabes, R. A., Eisenberg, N., & Eisenbud, L. (1993). Behavioral and physiological correlates of children's reactions to others in distress. *Developmental Psychology, 29*, 655–63.

Fischer, K. W. (1980). A theory of cognitive development: The control and construction of hierarchies of skills. *Psychological Review, 87*, 477–531.

Garven, S., Wood, J. M., & Malpass, R. S., & Shaw, J. S. (1998). More than suggestion: The effect of interviewing techniques from the McMartin Preschool case. *Journal of Applied Psychology, 83*, 347–59.

Gerin, W., Milner, D., Chawla, S., & Pickering, T. G. (1995). Social support as a moderator of cardiovascular reactivity in women: A test of the direct effects and buffering hypotheses. *Psychosomatic Medicine, 57*, 16–22.

Gilstrap, L. L. (2004). A missing link in suggestibility research: What is known about field interviewers' behavior in unstructured interviews with young children. *Journal of Experimental Psychology: Applied, 10*, 13–24.

Goodman, G. S., Bottoms, B. L., Herscovici, B. B., & Shaver, P. R. (1989). Determinants of the child victim's perceived credibility. In S. J. Ceci, D. F. Ross, & M. P. Toglia (Eds.), *Perspectives on children's testimony* (pp. 1–22). New York: Springer-Verlag.

Goodman, G. S., Bottoms, B. L., Rudy, L., & Schwartz-Kenney, B. M. (1991). Children's testimony about a stressful event: Improving children's reports. *Journal of Narrative and Life History, 1*, 69–99.

Goodman, G. S., & Quas, J. A. (1996). Trauma and memory: Individual differences in children's recounting of a stressful experience. In N. L. Stein, C. Brainerd, P. A. Ornstein, & B. Tversky (Eds.), *Memory for everyday and emotional events* (pp. 267–94). Hillsdale, NJ: Lawrence Erlbaum Associates.

Goodman, G. S., Quas, J. A., Batterman-Faunce, J. M., Riddlesberger, M. M., & Kuhn, G. (1997). Children's reactions to and memory for a stressful event: Influences of age, anatomical dolls, knowledge, and parental attachment. *Applied Developmental Science, 1*, 54–75.

Goodman, G. S., & Schwartz-Kenney, B. M. (1992). Why knowing a child's age is not enough: Effects of cognitive, social, and emotional factors on children's testimony. In R. Flin & H. Dent (Eds.), *Children as witnesses* (pp.15–32). London: Wiley.

Goodman, G. S., Sharma, A., Thomas, S. F., & Constadine, M. G. (1995). Mother knows best: Effects of relationship status and interviewer bias on children's memory. *Journal of Experimental Child Psychology, 60*, 195–228.

Goodman-Brown, T. B., Edelstein, R., Goodman, G. S., Jones, D., & Gordon, D. S. (2003). Why children tell: A model of children's disclosures of sexual abuse. *Child Abuse and Neglect, 27*, 525–40.

Greenstock, J., & Pipe, M. E. (1996). Interviewing children about past events: The influence of peer support and misleading questions. *Child Abuse and Neglect, 20*, 69–80.

———. (1997). Are two heads better than one? Peer support and children's eyewitness reports. *Applied Cognitive Psychology, 11*, 461–83.

Gunnar, M., Tout, K., de Haan, M., Pierce, S., & Stansbury, K. (1997). Temperament, social competence, and adrenocortical activity in preschoolers. *Developmental Psychobiology, 31*, 65–85.

Hanson, R. F., Resnick, H. S., Saunders, B. E., Kilpatrick, D. G., & Best, C. (1999). Factors related to the reporting of childhood rape. *Child Abuse and Neglect, 23*, 559–69.

Imhoff, M. C., & Baker-Ward, L. (1999). Preschoolers' suggestibility: Effects of developmentally appropriate language and interviewer supportiveness. *Journal of Applied Developmental Psychology, 20*, 407–29.

Johnston-Brooks, C. H, Lewis, M. A., Evans, G. W., & Whalen, C. K. (1998). Chronic stress and illness in children: The role of allostatic load. *Psychosomatic Medicine, 60*, 597–603.

Kaufman, J., & Cicchetti, D. (1989). Effects of maltreatment on school-age children's socioemotional development: Assessments in a day-camp setting. *Developmental Psychology, 25*, 516–24.

Kelley, D. H., & Gorham, H. (1988). Effects of immediacy on recall of information. *Communication Education, 37*, 198–207.

Lakey, B., & Cassidy, P. B. (1990). Cognitive processes in perceived social support. *Journal of Personality and Social Psychology, 59*, 337–43.

Leippe, M., Manion, & Romanczyk, A. (1992). Eyewitness persuasion: How and how well do fact finders judge the accuracy of adults' and children's memory reports? *Journal of Applied Psychology, 63*, 181–97.

Loftus, E. F. (1979). *Eyewitness testimony*. Cambridge, MA: Harvard University Press.

Lyon, T. D. (2002). Scientific support for expert testimony on child sexual abuse accommodation. In J. R. Conte (Ed.), *Critical issues in child sexual abuse*. Newbury Park, CA: Sage.

Lyon, T. D., & Dorado, J. (2004). *The effects of the oath and reassurance on maltreated children's true and false reports of a minor transgression*. Submitted manuscript.

Lyon, T. D., Malloy, L., Talwar, V., & Quas, J. A. (2004, March). *Truth-induction: Reducing children's lies and secrets*. Paper presented at the Biennial conference of the American Psychology-Law Society, Scottsdale, AZ.

Mehrabian, D. (1969). Some referents and measures of nonverbal behavior. *Behavioral Research Methods and Instruments, 1*, 213–17.

Merrit, K. A., Ornstein, P. A., & Spicker, B. (1994). Children's memory for a salient medical procedure: Implications for testimony. *Pediatrics, 94*, 17–23.

Miller, P. J., Wiley, A. R., & Fung, H. (1997). Personal storytelling as a medium of socialization in Chinese and American families. *Child Development, 68*, 557–68.

Moston, S. (1992). Social support and children's eyewitness testimony. In H. Dent & R. Flin (Eds.), *Children as witnesses* (pp. 33–46). Chicester: Wiley.

Moston, S., & Engelberg, T. (1992). The effects of social support on children's eyewitness testimony. *Applied Cognitive Psychology, 6*, 61–75.

Perona, A., Bottoms, B. L., & Sorenson, E. (2006). Research-based guidelines for child forensic interviews. *Journal of Aggression, Maltreatment, and Trauma, 12*, 81-130.

Poole, D. A., & Lindsay, D. S. (2002). Children's suggestibility in the forensic context. In M. Eisen, J. A. Quas, & G. S. Goodman (Eds.), *Memory and suggestibility in the forensic interview* (pp. 355–82). Mahwah, NJ: Lawrence Erlbaum Associates.

Quas, J. A., Bauer, A B., & Boyce, W. T. B. (2004). Emotion, Reactivity, and Memory in Early Childhood. *Child Development, 75*, 797–814.

Quas, J. A., & Lench, H. C. (in press). Arousal at encoding, arousal at retrieval, interviewer support, and children's memory for a mild stressor. *Applied Cognitive Psychology.*

Quas, J. A., Wallin, A., Papini, S., Lench, H., & Scullin, M. (2005). Suggestibility, social context, and memory for a novel experience in young children. *Journal of Experimental Child Psychology, 91*, 315–341.

Reppucci, N. D. (1985). Psychology in the public interest. In A. M. Rogers & C. J. Sheirer (Eds.), *The G. Stanley Hall Lecture Series* (Vol. 5). Washington, DC: American Psychological Association.

Ricci, C. M., Beal, C. R., & Dekle, D. J. (1996). The effect of parent versus unfamiliar interviewers on children's eyewitness memory and identification accuracy. *Law and Human Behavior, 20*, 483–500.

Rosenthal, R., & Jacobson, L. (1968). *Pygmalion in the classroom: Teacher expectation and student intellectual development.* New York: Holt, Rinehart, & Winston.

Sarason, I. G., & Sarason, B. R. (1986). Experimentally provided social support. *Journal of Personality and Social Psychology, 50*, 1222–25.

Sarason, B. R., Sarason, I. G., & Pierce, G. R. (Eds.). (1990). *Social support: An interactional view.* New York: Wiley.

Shaver, P. R., & Hazan, C. (1993). Adult romantic attachment: Theory and evidence. In D. Perlman & W. H. Jones (Eds.), *Advances in personal relationships* (Vol. 4, pp. 29–70). London: Jessica Kingsley.

Sorenson, E., Bottoms, B. L., & Perona, A. (1997). *Intake and forensic interviewing in the children's advocacy center setting: A handbook.* Washington, D.C.: National Network of Children's Advocacy Centers.

Spielberger, C. D. (1979). *State-trait anxiety inventory for children.* Palo Alto, CA: Consulting Psychologists Press.

Tardy, C. H. (1994). Counteracting task-induced stress: Studies of instrumental and emotional support in problem-solving contexts. In B. R. Burleson, T. L. Albrecht, & I. G. Sarason (Eds.), *Communication of Social Support: Messages, Interactions, Relationships, and Community* (pp. 71–87). Thousand Oaks, CA: Sage.

Uchino, B. N., Cacioppo, J. T., & Kiecolt-Glaser, J. K. (1998). The relationship between social support and physiological processes: A review with emphasis on underlying mechanisms and implications for health. *Psychological Bulletin, 119*, 488–531.

Underwager, R., & Wakefield, H. (1990). *The real world of child interrogations.* Springfield, IL: Thomas.

Vygotsky, L. (1934/1978). *Mind in society: The development of higher psychological processes.* Cambridge, MA: Harvard University Press.

Wolchik, S. A., Sandler, I. N., & Braver, S. L. (1990). Social support: its assessment and relation to children's adjustment. In N. Eisenberg (Ed.), *Contemporary topics in developmental psychology,* (pp. 319–349). New York: Wiley & Sons.

Wood, J. M., McClure, K. A., & Birch, R. A. (1996). Suggestions for improving interviews in child protection agencies. *Child Maltreatment, 1,* 233–30.

Zelkowitz, P. (1989). Parents and children as informants concerning children's social networks. In D. Belle (Ed.), *Children's social networks and social supports* (pp. 221–37). New York: Wiley.

9

Delay of Disclosure, Minimization, and Denial of Abuse When the Evidence Is Unambiguous: A Multivictim Case

Ann-Christin Cederborg
Linkoping University, Sweden

Michael E. Lamb
University of Cambridge, United Kingdom

Ola Laurell
Prosecutor, Uppsala, Sweden

Controversy about whether and how children disclose that they have been abused has stoked a heated debate about the best way of obtaining information from those who appear reluctant to be informative. As indicated elsewhere in this book, although most alleged victims reveal that they have been abused within a first or second interview, many children do not (see chapters 3, 4, and 5). We do not know, however, why some children are reluctant to tell of their experiences, perhaps even denying that something has happened to them.

Memory related factors may be part of the explanation. Once encoded in memory, stressful and traumatic events can often be recounted in detail after considerable delays (Fivush, McDermott Sales, Goldberg, Bahrick, & Parker, 2004; Cordon, Pipe, Liat, Melinder, & Goodman, 2004). Traumatic or not, however, experiences differ from one another and their recollection and retrieval can be affected by many factors, including the number of times they were repeated, the age of the child, when the events happened, their personal significance, and whether they have been discussed in the interim (Cordon et al., 2004). Younger children are typically less informative than older children and appear to forget more rapidly (Baker-Ward et al., 1991; Ornstein, Gordon, & Larus, 1992; Schneider & Bjorklund, 1998). The delays between the abuse and interviews about it also affect retrieval (Salmon & Pipe, 2000) although recollection of stressful events does not appear to depend on when interviews occur following delays of up to six weeks (Meritt, Ornstein, & Spicker, 1994). With increasing age, children recall more information regardless of delay (Lamb, Sternberg, & Esplin, 2000), and children who experience several similar events seem to recall more information than those who experienced single events (Hershkowitz et al., 1998; Powel & Thomson, 1996; Sternberg et al., 1996). Children may forget some traumatic experiences; however, memory is not the whole story, or perhaps even a large part of it. Several other factors influence children's willingness to disclose abuse.

To gain further insight into the determinants of (non)disclosure, we studied a Swedish case in which a pedophile had videotaped his abuse of twelve different children. A previous analysis of this case described a significant tendency among these children to deny and minimize their experiences (Sjöberg & Lindblad, 2002). Sjöberg and Lindblad also reported that the children did not want to disclose, and that they could not adequately understand and describe what they had experienced. In this study, we explored some possible reasons for these findings. The prosecutor (one of the authors) and the police officers dealing with this case allowed us to study all of the documents from the investigative process, including the videotaped interviews with the children, the court files, and the actual videotaped abuse scenes.

In order to ensure that none of the victims can be recognized, every child is referred to as a boy, and each is identified by a number. All names, personal details, and places that may signal identity have been removed. These changes do not affect the conclusions reported here.

BACKGROUND

When the police officers discovered the perpetrator's sex crimes, he was living with a woman and her children in a middle-sized Swedish town. The man was a trained child care provider and had worked for several months at a day care center where he met three of the children. He systematically planned the sexual abuse of these children, and in an interview he said he had tried to do the least possible harm when abusing them. His crimes could have resulted in many years of imprisonment but because the court concluded that he was a pedophile, he was instead confined to a psychiatric institution for many years.

The perpetrator was convicted of having sexually abused 11 identified victims. Altogether, the police investigation identified 116 different videotaped incidents of abuse involving the 10 children in this study. No child had disclosed abuse before the police investigation. Two were, for different reasons, not interviewed and are therefore excluded from this study. From a legal as well as a research perspective, this case is unique because the perpetrator videotaped his abuse of the children and kept the tapes in his study. The videotapes were found when the police officers raided the man's home for other reasons.

As shown in table 9.1, the children were between 3 and 11.1 years of age when abused and between 4.1 and 12.7 years when interviewed (M = 6.11). The mean delay between first incident and interview was 2.2 years and between last incident and interview, 1.2 years. The length of the recorded incidents of abuse ranged from 2 to 342 minutes and the number of videotaped incidents from 1 to 74. Four of the children were abused on tape only once, one was recorded twice, one 3 times, one 4 times, one 6 times, one 23 times, and one 74 times. As described more fully below, four of the children might not have categorized the abusive experiences as sexual abuse, and the abuse is thus described here as "not severe" (see table 9.1). In contrast, six of the children experienced incidents that should have been recognized by them as abuse, and these incidents are labeled "severe" in table 9.1.

The alleged crimes varied from filming the children's genitals in natural settings to forcible penetration of the children's anuses. Most of the incidents of abuse took place in or near the children's or the perpetrator's homes. Twenty of the incidents occurred in the children's homes, 59 in the perpetrator's home, 27 in or near the home of the perpetrator's parents, and 10 at the day care center where the perpetrator worked.

EVALUATION OF INFORMATIVENESS

The first analyses involved evaluation of 12 interviews with the 10 victims of sexual abuse (children 2 and 9 were interviewed twice). All interviews with the children were transcribed from video recordings and transcriptions were checked to ensure their completeness and accuracy. One native Swedish speaker identified substantive utterances (those related to the investigated incident) and tabulated the number of new details concerning the investigated event using a technique developed by Yuille and Cutshall (1986, 1989; Cutshall & Yuille, 1990) and elaborated by Lamb and his colleagues (1996). Details were defined as words or phrases identifying or describing individuals, objects, or events (including actions) related to the investigated incident. Details were only counted when they were new and added to an understanding of the target incidents and their disclosure. As a result, restatements were not counted.

The coder also reviewed the transcripts and categorized each interviewer utterance, defined by a "turn" in the discourse or conversation, using the

TABLE 9.1
Summary of the Children's Experiences

Child	Duration of videotaped abuse. minutes	Age when abused (yr.mo) first	last	Age when interviewed (yr.mo)	Delay between abuse and interview (yr.mo) first	last	Number of incidents	Nature of experience	Nature of relationship
1	4	3.0	—	4.8	1.8	1.8	1	not severe	relative
2	2	3.7	—	4.1	0.6	0.6	1	not severe	familiar
3	23	3.1	3.8	5.4	2.3	1.8	6	not severe	familiar
4	4	5.4	—	7.0	1.8	1.8	1	not severe	relative
5	342	4.2	5.3	5.9	1.7	0.6	74	severe	relative
6	15	6.8	7.6?*	7.8	0.10	0.2	2	severe	relative
7	33	6.0	6.0	7.8	1.8	1.8	3	severe	familiar
8	131	4.4	5.2	6.6	2.2	1.4	23	severe	familiar
9	9	6.	10	7.11	1.1	1.1	1	severe	familiar
10	188	4.6?	11.1	12.7	8.1?	1.6	4	severe	relative
Total M =	751	4.9	5.8	6.11	2.2	1.2	116		

? = unspecified

categories developed by Lamb et al. (1996). For the purpose of these ratings, we did not distinguish between questions and statements.

Interviewer statements made during the portion of the investigative interviews concerned with substantive issues were placed in one of the following categories (Lamb et al., 1996):

1. *Invitations. Utterances,* including questions, statements, or imperatives, prompting free-recall responses from the child. Such utterances do not delimit the child's focus except in a general way (for example, "Tell me everything that happened") or use details disclosed by the child as cues (for example, "You mentioned that he touched you. Tell me everything about the touching.").

2. *Directive utterances.* These refocus the child's attention on details or aspects of the alleged incident that the child has already mentioned, providing a category for requesting additional information using "Wh–" questions (cued recall).

3. *Option-posing utterances.* These focus the child's attention on details or aspects of the alleged incident that the child has not previously mentioned, asking the child to affirm, negate, or select an investigator-given option using recognition memory processes, but do not imply that a particular response is expected.

4. *Suggestive utterances.* These are stated in such a way that the interviewer strongly communicates what response is expected (for example, "He forced you to do that, didn't he?") or they assume details that have not been revealed by the child (for example, *Child:* "We laid on the sofa." *Interviewer:* "He laid on you or you laid on him?").

The rater, who was fluent in both Swedish and English, was trained on an independent set of English transcripts until she reached 90% agreement with

TABLE 9.2
Types and Number of Alleged Crimes per Child

Types of Crimes	Number of Incidents	Number of Children Involved
Filming genitals	5	3
Touching	7	4
Urinating	15	1
Emptying the bowels	5	1
Measuring the penis	1	1
Masturbation	34	7
Oral intercourse	40	5
Anal penetration	9	4
Total	116	

American raters regarding the identification of details and utterance types. This level of proficiency was reached before she began coding the Swedish transcripts included in the study. The Swedish rater remained reliable (> 95%) with American raters who independently coded transcripts of interviews in English during the period that the Swedish interviews were being coded.

The mean number of investigative utterances in the substantive portions of the interviews was 101.2. The relative prominence of the different utterance types is displayed in table 9.3.

The prosecutor in these cases had instructed the 5 (1 male, 4 female) police interviewers not to press the children for disclosure because he already had access to the perpetrator's video tapes and thus did not need to rely upon the children's testimony to prove that the abuse had taken place. Despite this, the police officers mostly used directive (52%) and option-posing (39%) prompts to elicit information from the children. There were few invitations (2%) but also few suggestive utterances (7%).

On average, the children gave substantive details in their interviews (M = 144), although the number of details varied from 624 to as few as 24 (see table 9.4). Two of the children, numbers 9 and 10, provided much more information than the others, and they were also the ones who were asked the most questions, mostly directive utterances, about their experiences. The proportion of details elicited by the different utterance types closely paralleled the proportion of interviewer utterances. On average, 2% of the details provided by the children were elicited by invitations. Most of the details (52%) came in response to directive utterances, 40% were elicited by option-posing questions, and 6% were elicited by suggestive prompts.

Variations in the amount of information provided may have reflected differences in the children's ages, differences in the number of incidents and type of abuse experienced, and differences in the children's motivation or willingness to discuss their abuse. To gain a deeper understanding of the children's motives for providing or not providing information, we looked more closely at each of the cases.

Examination of the Videotaped Abuse Scenes in Relation to Disclosure

This analysis involved an inductive, qualitative attempt to understand the children's informativeness in relation to their age, length of delay between the last known incident and the interview, the nature of the relationship with the perpetrator, and the nature of their experiences (see table 9.5). A qualitative analysis of all the videotaped abuse sequences was carried out by watching the films, transcribing all spoken words verbatim, and coding possible reasons for not disclosing in relation to the nature of the abuse. The transcribed police

TABLE 9.3
Number and Proportion of Utterances of Each Type

Child	Invitations Number	%	Directives Number	%	Option-posing Number	%	Suggestive Number	%	Total Number	%
1	2	6%	17	48%	15	43%	1	3%	35	100%
2	0	0	31	62	8	16	11	22	50	100
3	0	0	12	31	24	61	3	8	39	100
4	1	2	22	37	35	59	1	2	59	100
5	0	0	54	67	24	30	2	3	80	100
6	1	2	39	62	23	36	0	0	63	100
7	1	3	13	34	20	53	4	10	38	100
8	3	2	114	60	62	33	9	5	188	100
9	12	6	122	59	53	26	19	9	206	100
10	5	2	153	60	79	31	17	7	254	100
Mean	2.5	2	57.7	52	34.3	39	6.7	7	101.2	100

TABLE 9.4
Total Number and Proportion of Details Provided by Each Child

Child#	Number	%
1	30	2
2	24	2
3	53	4
4	56	4
5	112	8
6	91	6
7	42	3
8	150	10
9	258	18
10	624	43
Mean	144	100

TABLE 9.5
Reasons for Minimization and Nondisclosure

Child #	Guilt-Shame	Secrecy Pact	Fear of Disbelief	Fear of Reprisals	Immaturity	Not memorable
1					X	X
2					X	X
3					X	X
4						X
5		X	X	X		
6		X	X	X		
7		X				
8		X				
9			X	X		
10	X					

interviews, documents from the police investigations and the court files were also studied.

As summarized in table 9.5, this analysis made clear that there were several reasons why the children may have failed to provide more information about their experiences.

Child #1, a boy, was 3 years old when he was exploited briefly on a single occasion during which the perpetrator filmed the boy's genitals while instructing him how to swim safely. The boy was a relative of the pepetrator and he disclosed very little in the interview, which took place more than a year and a half after the abuse. Because of his youth and immaturity, the boy may not have understood that he was being abused. The incident may not have been salient. In addition, the lengthy delay between incident and interview may have allowed the child to forget the incident.

Child #2 was 3.7 years old when abused on a single occasion and 4.1 when interviewed. The boy was familiar with the perpetrator who masturbated the boy while asking him if he needed to urinate. The abuse lasted less than two minutes. In the interview, the boy confirmed that he had been touched. The child's age may explain the small number of details he provided. In addition, the abuse did not appear unpleasant and the incident was brief. As a result it may not have been very memorable.

Child #3 was between 3.2 and 3.8 years of age when he was abused six times. About two years passed before he was interviewed at 5.4 years of age. In the first recorded incident, the boy was masturbated by the perpetrator at the day care center while the perpetrator was changing his diaper. The boy was lying on a changing table and his face was hidden behind a cloth. The next abusive events happened over four consecutive days when the perpetrator was babysitting. The perpetrator told the boy that he wanted to see if the child had any grit on his penis or if it was injured.

This boy disclosed very little in the interview. When asked if the man had done something he did not like, he said "No". As with the first two children, these incidents were not unpleasant and the child may well not have understood that he was being abused. In addition, there was an extended delay between the incidents and the interview and this, too, may contribute to the explanation of why this child provided so little information and denied that he had been abused.

Child #4 was abused once when he was 5.4 years old. He was interviewed 1.8 year later. In the recorded incident, the child was bathing naked outdoors when the perpetrator invited him to visit his house nearby in order to find some equipment. Filming him from behind when the boy was searching for some equipment, the perpetrator briefly touched the boy's genitals while talking to him in a friendly manner. When interviewed, however, the boy provided little information and did not mention being filmed or touched. Again, it is possible that this incident happened so long before and was so brief and benign that it was not memorable.

Child #5, in contrast, was subjected to 74 different videotaped incidents of abuse over a period of slightly more than one year. This child was between 4.2 and 5.3 years of age during this period of abuse. The interval between the first incident and the interview was 1.7 years, and between the last incident and the interview, 6 months. Judging from the videotapes, many of the experiences should have been memorable, especially those in which the child was coerced to participate as well as threatened. At least eight times, the perpetrator was recorded telling the child to keep the abuse secret. The child did not disclose a great deal in the interview about what he experienced and he denied that the perpetrator had been unkind to him.

This child's parents did not meet his needs for parental support and the perpetrator, who was a relative, largely controlled and cared for him. Fearing punishment and perhaps further abuse if he told anyone, the boy appeared to have chosen not to tell more than he did.

Child #6 was abused twice when he was 6.8 and about 7.6 years old. The delays between the two incidents and the interview were 10 and 2 months respectively. It is possible that the boy did not perceive the first videotaped sexual abuse as such because he was simply filmed while bathing naked. The second time, however, the child was severely abused. Although he was quiet and the film did not show his face, it seems unlikely that he was asleep. In one of the interviews, interestingly, the perpetrator said the boy "had pretended" to be asleep.

In the interview, the child was reluctant to disclose and said that the perpetrator had told him not to tell. Like child number 5, this child was dependent on the perpetrator and had been punished during the years he had known him without being supported by his single mother. The perpetrator told him not to discuss his experiences. The boy may have feared not being believed by his parent and being punished by the perpetrator if he told.

Child #7 was 6 years old when he was abused three times on two consecutive days. He was interviewed when he was 7.8 years old. The boy first met the perpetrator at day care and this man later served as babysitter. It is not certain that this boy knew what was happening on the first occasion because the perpetrator, while abusing him, talked about the need to remove grit from the child's penis. The second time, however, when being masturbated, the child was instructed twice not to tell anyone about the perpetrator's conduct. This boy, apparently, did what the man told him to do.

During the interview the boy continued to deny that anything exceptional had happened even when the police officer explicitly asked him about details of abuse. In this case, the boy had been instructed not to talk and this may have prevented him from telling.

Child #8 was exploited over a year long-period when he was between 4.4 and 5.2 years of age and was videotaped 23 times. The delay between the first incident and the interview was 2.2 years and between the last incident and the interview 1.4 years.

The child was first abused at day care and thereafter abused while the perpetrator was babysitting in the child's home. The child was bribed and told that the perpetrator loved him at the same time as he was being subjected to painful abuse. Additionally, the child was told that the activities were forbidden. The perpetrator was recorded seven times telling the child not to tell anyone about the perpetrator's activities. The instructions may have prevented the child from saying more than he did.

In the case of **Child #9,** the perpetrator was babysitting the child, who was 6.10 years old at the time of the single, nine-minute-long filmed incident. The boy was interviewed 1.1 year after this incident. The boy was familiar with the perpetrator and the perpetrator cared for him frequently. The perpetrator's masturbation of the child was obvious and they communicated about what was going on. At times during the incident the boy told the perpetrator that he did not want to participate but he seemed coerced to follow the perpetrator's instructions.

In the first interview, when he was 7.11 years old, the boy said the perpetrator was stupid and had slapped him when he was disobedient. The boy admitted that the perpetrator had filmed his penis one time but he did not say anything about the masturbation even when the police officer tried to get him to tell more.

The child's minimized version can be explained by the fact that he had reasons to fear reprisals from the perpetrator and that this child could not rely on his parents' support. For unrelated reasons, this child was taken into the custody of the local social agency after the sexual abuse incident six months before being interviewed about the sexual abuse.

Child #10 was a relative who was abused for the first time when he was about 4.6 years of age, and the perpetrator was 13 years of age. The delay between the first incident and the interview was more than eight years. Altogether, the child participated in four different videotaped incidents that involved oral intercourse and anal penetration. The child was almost 11 years old when the perpetrator (then aged 20 years) videotaped the last three abuse acts. The last time this boy was abused was about one and a half years before the interview.

This boy was the one who gave the most details when interviewed although he was not specific about what happened on each occasion and instead blended information from the different incidents. He underestimated both the length of the incidents and what actually happened each time. He said he did not think about telling, he did not dare to tell, he was afraid and did not know how to tell either. He said he tried to forget his experiences.

The boy considered the perpetrator to be a "fairly good friend" and described the experiences as unpleasant. Nine times during the interview, he said he did not want to participate in the sexual abuse, and he said ten times that he did not understand what was going on between him and the perpetrator. During the actual incidents, however, the boy also played an active role, even offering suggestions about what they should do.

Even though this boy gave the most details, he still revealed little about his actual experiences. This minimization appeared to reflect the boy's assumption of responsibility for what happened—he appeared to feel ashamed because of his active role in the incidents.

DISCUSSION

This study helps explain why some children minimize, delay disclosure, and even deny their experiences of sexual abuse. At least six of the children we studied experienced abusive incidents which should have been memorable. Some of them refused to admit that sexual abuse had occurred, however. Four children seem to have been unaware of what happened and could not "remember" or provide specific details about their abuse. These four were also young when abused, and this too may have affected their ability to understand and encode the events. They may have been enticed to participate without realizing they were being abused.

Close relationships with the perpetrator may have prevented the children from disclosing; consistent with this, children may be less likely to disclose abuse the more closely related they are to the perpetrator (DiPietro, Runyan, & Fredrickson., 1997; Smith et al., 2000; Wyatt & Newcomb, 1990). All of the children knew this man and were dependant on him in important ways. He was a powerful figure in their lives. Of the six children who experienced memorable or severe abuse, three were relatives and three were familiar with the perpetrator after he cared for them at day care or as a babysitter at home. Bussey, Lee, and Grimbeek (1993) have shown that children can refrain from describing their experiences when they fear reprisals by the perpetrator, and this appeared to be true for three of the children.

The perpetrator also concealed his intentions by frequently arranging his activities so that the children could not understand what he was doing. Children may also resist disclosure when they feel responsible and thereby guilty or ashamed for having participated in sexual activities. The perpetrator undoubtedly made use of his power as an adult in order to satisfy his objectives, but in one case (number 10) the interactions with the boy were negotiated, and the boy even made suggestions about how he and the perpetrator might behave. Even if he did not want to participate, the boy may afterwards have felt responsible for what he had experienced. Only two years after the last incident, when the boy became aware that he was viewed by the authorities as a victim rather than as a responsible participant, did this boy feel comfortable describing some of the sexual abuse.

Instructions to keep a secret can have a powerful effect on 5- to- 6-year old children (Bottoms, Goodman, Schwartz-Kenney, & Thomas, 2002; Pipe & Wilson, 1994), and three of the children who had memorable experiences were encouraged by the perpetrator to keep their interactions secret. These three were between 5 and 6 years of age when the last abuse happened. A fourth child told the police that he was instructed to keep the activities secret, but an examination of the data suggested that he was really at risk for being punished by the perpetrator. In this case, as in the case of child number 5, the combination of fear and demands to secrecy could have induced the children to minimize their abuse.

SUMMARY

We know from research that children can give accurate, detailed, and reliable information about their experiences of abuse (Orbach & Lamb, 1999; Lamb & Fauchier, 2001; Bidrose & Goodman, 2000), but we cannot be sure they will be motivated enough to disclose their experiences. Even when reports are delayed or inconsistent, furthermore, we should not consider them to be unreliable (Bottoms et al., 2002; Pipe & Goodman, 1991). Our findings show that children can have different reasons for not specifically reporting their experiences. It is important that interviewers recognize that they cannot expect children to disclose when they are not mature enough to understand what they experienced or when the incidents were innocuous and not especially memorable. Children may also minimize, delay disclosure or deny abuse when they are in a secrecy pact with the perpetrator, when they feel responsible for participating, or if they fear punishment by the perpetrator if they tell about their experiences. They may also fear not being believed by their parents.

Children are as unique as their experiences. Elicitation of information depends on understanding individual circumstances in order to facilitate disclosure. In order to obtain accurate and complete information, interviewers must adapt their techniques to the circumstances and motivations of individual victims. In addition, children who have been threatened with reprisals by a manipulative perpetrator and fear their parents will not be supportive must be reassured that they will be protected if they do disclose what has happened to them.

REFERENCES

Baker-Ward, L., Gordon, B. N., Ornstein, P. A., Larus, D. M., & Cubb, P. A. (1993). Young children's long term retention of a pediatric examination. *Child Development, 64,* 1519–33.

Bidrose, S., & Goodman, G. S. (2000). Testimony and evidence: A scientific case study of memory for child sexual abuse. *Applied Cognitive Psychology, 14,* 197–213.

Bottoms, B. L., Goodman, G, S., Schwartz-Kenney, B. M., & Thomas, S. N. (2002). Understanding children's use of secrecy in the context of eyewitness reports. *Law and Human Behaviour, 26(3),* 285–313.

Bussey, K., Lee, K., & Grimbeek, E. J. (1993). Lies and secrets: Implications for children's reporting of sexual abuse. In G. S. Goodman & B. L. Bottoms (Eds,). *Child victims, child witnesses. Understanding and improving children's testimony* (pp. 147–68). New York: Guilford.

Cordon, I. M., Pipe, M. E., Liat, S., Melinder, A., & Goodman, G. S (2004). Memory of traumatic experiences in early childhood. *Developmental Review, 24,* 101–132.

Cutshall, J. & Yuille, J. C. (1990). Field studies of eyewitness memory of actual crimes. In D. C. Raskin. *Psychological methods in criminal investigation and evidence.* (pp 97–124). New York: Spring Publishing Company.

DiPietro, E. K., Runyan, D. K., & Fredrickson, D.D. (1997). Predictors of disclosure during medical evaluation for suspected sexual abuse. *Journal of Sexual Abuse, 6,* 133–42.

Fivush, R., Sales, J., Goldberg, A., Bahrick, L., & Parker, J. (2004). Weathering the storm: Children's long-term recall of Hurricane Andrew. *Memory, 12,* 104–118.

Hershkowitz, I., Orbach, Y., Lamb, M. E., Sternberg, K. J.,Horowitz, D., & Hovov, M. (1998). Visiting the scene of the crime: Effects on children's recall of alleged abuse. *Legal and Criminological Psychology, 3,* 195–207.

Lamb, M. E.& Fauchier, A. (2001). The effects of question type on self contradiction by children in the course of forensic interviews. *Applied Cognitive Development, 15,* 483–91.

Lamb, M. E, Hershkowitz, I., Sternberg, K. J., Esplin, P.W., Hovav, M., Manor, T., & Yudilevitch, L (1996). Effects of investigative utterance types on Israeli children's responses. *International Journal of Behavioral Development, 19,* 627–37.

Lamb, M. E., Sternberg, K. J., & Esplin, P. W. (2000). Effects of age and delay on the amount of information provided by alleged sex abuse victims in investigative interviews. *Child Development, 71,* 1586–96.

Meritt, K. A., Ornstein, P. A., & Spicker, B. (1994). Children's memory for a silent medical procedure: Implications for testimony. *Pediatrics, 94*(1), 17–23.

Orbach, Y., & Lamb, M. E. (1999). Assessing the accuracy of child's account of sexual abuse: A case study. *Child Abuse and Neglect, 23,* 91–98.

Ornstein, P. A., Gordon, B. N., & Larus, D, M. (1992). Children's memory for a personally experienced event: Implications for testimony. *Pediatrics, 94,* 17–23.

Pipe, M. E., & Goodman, G. S. (1991). Elements of secrecy: Implications for children's testimony. *Behavioral Sciences and the Law, 9,* 33–41.

Pipe, M. E., Wilson, J.C. (1994). Cues and secrets: Influences on children's events reports. *Developmental Psychology, 30,* 515–25.

Powel, M .B., & Thomson, D. M. (1996). Children's memory of an occurrence of a repeated event: Effects of age, repetition, and retention interval across three question types. *Child development, 67,* 1988–2004.

Salmon, K., & Pipe, M. (2000). Recalling an event one year later: The impact of props, drawing and a prior interview. *Applied Cognitive Psychology, 14,* 99–120.

Saywitz, K. J., Goodman, G, S., Nicholas, E., & Moan, S.F. (1991). Children's memories of a physical examination involving genital touch: Implications for reports of child sexual abuse." *Journal of Consulting & Clinical Psychology, 59:* 682–91.

Schneider, W., & Bjorklund, D. F. (1998). Memory. In D. Kuhn & R. S. Siegler (Eds.), W. Damon (Series Ed.), Handbook of child psychology: Vol. 2. *Cognition, perception and language* (5th ed., pp. 467–521). New York: Wiley.

Sjöberg, R. & Lindblad, F. (2002). Limited disclosure of sexual abuse in children whose experiences were documented by videotape. *American Journal of Psychiatry, 159,* 312–14.

Smith, D. W., Letournrau, E. J., Saunders, B. E., Kilpatrick, D.G., Resnick, H. S., & Best, C. L. (2000). Delay in disclosure of childhood rape: Results from a national survey. *Child Abuse & Neglect, 2,* 273–87.

Sternberg, K. J., Lamb, M. E., Hershkowitz, I., Esplin, P., Redlich, A., & Sunshine, N. (1996). The relation between investigative utterance types and the informativeness of child witnesses. *Journal of Applied Developmental Psychology, 17,* 439–51.

Wyatt, G. E., & Newcomb, M. D. (1990). Internal and external mediators of women's sexual abuse in childhood. *Journal of Consulting and Clinical Psychology, 58,* 758–67.

Yuille, J. C., & Cutshall, J. L. (1986). A case study of eyewitness memory of a crime. *Journal of Applied Psychology, 71*: 291–301.

———. (1989). Analysis of the statements of victims, witnesses and suspects. In J. C. Yuille. *Credibility assessment, 47*, 175–91. Dordrecht, Netherlands: Kluwer Academic Publishers.

10

A Retrospective Study of Factors Affecting the Disclosure of Childhood Sexual and Physical Abuse

Bette L. Bottoms, Aaron G. Rudnicki
Michelle A. Epstein
The University of Illinois at Chicago

Although the number is declining, there are still approximately a million substantiated cases of child maltreatment in a given year in the United States, and about three times that many cases are reported to authorities (Jones & Finkelhor, 2003). These figures, however, are surely underestimates of the actual incidence of abuse. That is, as the chapters in this book reveal, many children, adolescents, and adults hide the fact of their childhood abuse, never telling anyone about their experiences. Little is known about the factors associated with nondisclosure of childhood maltreatment. In this chapter, we address this issue by examining the prevalence and correlates of nondisclosure of sexual and physical childhood abuse in a sample of young adults.

The data reported here were collected as a part of a larger retrospective study of abuse and other trauma described by Epstein and Bottoms (2002). Specifically, in an anonymous survey, we determined the form of abuse women had suffered and asked the victims if they had ever disclosed that abuse to others at any time up to the moment they completed our survey. The survey also included questions designed to measure characteristics of the abuse experience, including the frequency of the experience and the identity of and victim's emotional relationship with the perpetrator. Further, we measured victim characteristics, including the perceived emotional distress at the time of the experience and at present, age at time of the experience, tendency to self-label as a victim of abuse, and individual differences in attachment style and in the use of avoidant psychological coping styles. In this chapter we report the results of analyses that allow us to construct a profile of factors related to the tendency of victims to disclose or not disclose childhood maltreatment to others.

A number of unique aspects of our research ensure that our findings add to the extant literature in significant ways. For example, we measured disclosure not only of sexual abuse, which has been the focus of most other studies in this literature, but also of physical abuse. In addition, our sample is diverse in terms of ethnicity and socioeconomic status, and it was collected from several geographical regions. We also included measures of factors that have not been previously studied in relation to disclosure, such as individual differences in psychological coping mechanisms and attachment style.

Because the extant literature on factors linked to disclosure has already been thoroughly reviewed by others in this volume (see, in particular, chapters by London, Bruck, Ceci, & Shurman, chapter 2, this volume; and Lyon, chapter 3, this volume), we forgo an extensive literature review and move directly to a description of our study. We refer readers to relevant findings from related research as we present our hypotheses and results and discuss their implications.

METHOD

Sample

Our full sample consisted of 1,411 young women who completed our anonymous survey in return for psychology course credit at colleges and universities in Illinois (77%), California (15%), and Virginia (7%). The students attended a session and filled out the survey without prior knowledge of the study. After being informed of the nature of the study, they were free to opt out of the study completely or leave survey items blank, although very few did. Of the total sample, 619 (44%) had experienced some form of physical abuse, sexual abuse, and/or emotional-verbal abuse.[1]

Our subsample of victims is among the most ethnically diverse of all existing studies of disclosure of abuse: 27% self-identified as African-American, 19% as Asian-American, 33% as Caucasian, 16% as Hispanic/Latino, and 5% as "other." Participants were on average 22 years of age (range = 18 to 58 years old). Of our sample, 37% were in their first year of college, 25% were in their sophomore year, 25% were in their junior year, and 13% were in their senior

---

[1] This number excludes one physical abuse victim who reported abuse that occurred prior to the age of offset of infantile amnesia (there were no sexual abuse victims who did this), and 25 teenaged sexual abuse victims who reported sexual abuse that was perpetrated by a romantic partner or boyfriend.

year. We measured annual parental income (a proxy for the students' own socio-economic status) by asking participants to choose from among nine categories of per-annum income, ranging in ten thousand dollar increments from 0–$9999 to over $80,000. The median response was $40,000–49,000, with a broad distribution of responses.

Measures of Abuse Experiences

There were three separate sections of our anonymous survey, one each for experiences of childhood sexual abuse, physical abuse, and emotional abuse. In this chapter, we focus on the experiences of physical and sexual abuse only, and only on those victims who told us whether they had disclosed their abuse prior to completing our survey.

Sexual abuse was assessed with the following question: *When you were 17 years old or younger, did you ever have any of the following experiences with someone at least 5 years older than you? (Note: this could mean that you did these things to someone or someone did them to you)*. Respondents answered by choosing one

TABLE 10.1
Percentage of Abuse Victims Who Chose Each of the Specific Forms of Abuse Listed in the Abuse Screening Questions

% of Abuse Victims	Item From Abuse Screening Question
Sexual abuse (N = 319)	
7	Viewed or took part in child pornography
32	Exhibitionism (inappropriately exposed to adult's genitals)
77	Fondling (touching) genitals, breasts, or buttocks directly or through clothing
22	Oral sex (mouth/genital contact)
7	Anal sex (penetration of anus with genitals, fingers, or other object)
30	Attempted vaginal intercourse (with penis, fingers, or other object)
27	Completed vaginal intercourse (penetration with penis, fingers, or other object)
17	Other sexual abuse
Physical abuse (N = 352)	
71	You were spanked, beaten, or whipped and it resulted in welts, bruises, bleeding, or other physical injuries
30	You were slapped or choked and it resulted in welts, bruises, bleeding, or other physical injuries
22	You were punched, kicked, or beaten up and it resulted in welts, bruises, bleeding, or other physical injuries
41	You were hit with an object and it resulted in welts, bruises, bleeding, or other physical injuries
25	Other physical abuse

Note: Percentages do not add to 100% because victims could have experienced more than one form of sexual activity within their abusive experience or more of the specific items listed in table 10.1. Our definition of sexual abuse was modeled after others used in the literature (e.g., Finkelhor, 1979) and is ecologically valid in terms of ages of victim and perpetrator, as per laws in states such as Illinois and California. This objective "checklist" method of measuring abuse is arguably more accurate than subjective measures that require victims to self-label as victims of abuse without specifying types of events experienced. Of the 1,411 subjects who completed our survey, 26% (N = 367) of respondents reported at least one instance of sexual abuse, which is consistent with prior estimates [e.g., Finkelhor, Hotaling, Lewis, & Smith, 1990 (27%); Martin et al., 1993 (25%)]. Of those victims, 48 failed to answer the disclosure question (described below) and were not, therefore, included in further comparisons in this chapter. Table 10.1 shows the percentage of the remaining sexual abuse victims (N = 319) who indicated each of the specific types/forms of sexual abuse. These percentages do not add to 100% because victims could have experienced more than one form of sexual activity within their abusive experience. Separately, we asked if victims had suffered multiple sexual abuses (distinct abuse events at the hands of different perpetrators), and if so, they were asked to complete the survey about "the experience you feel was most traumatic."[2]

Physical abuse was assessed with the following question (based on work by Straus & Gelles, 1988): "*When you were 17 years old or younger, did you ever have any of the following experiences where someone at least 5 years older than you used excessive physical force on you that resulted in welts, bruises, bleeding, or other physical injuries?*" Respondents answered by choosing one or more items from among those listed in table 10.1. Of the total sample, 27% (N = 385), reported physical abuse. Of those, 33 who failed to answer the disclosure question were dropped from additional analyses. Table 10.1 shows

---

[2] Defining sexual abuse is a controversial task. We were sensitive to the issue of our sample including cases of older teenagers involved romantically with the perpetrator (such as a 17 year old with a 22 year old). Although some would argue that any case captured with our definition would be abuse (and it would be legally defined as such in some states), others would argue that these types of cases are not abusive. Given the controversy, we chose to exclude cases in which the perpetrator was specified to be a romantic partner or boyfriend. In addition, we conducted an additional series of analyses matching those we report in this paper but dropping the 42 sexual abuse victims who were older than 16 years old. The pattern of results was very similar to those we report in this paper. For example, the percentage of disclosure, perhaps the most important variable in this study, differed by only one percent, with 79% of sexual abuse victims and 66% of physical abuse victims disclosing. Finally, some might argue that some forms of abuse on our checklist, especially exposure to child pornography (if viewed only) and exhibitionism, might not be as traumatic as other forms of abuse and might affect disclosure rates. Of all victims who answered the disclosure question, only one was exposed to child pornography without also experiencing some other form of sexual abuse, and only 18 were exposed to exhibitionism without experiencing some other form of sexual abuse. Analyses revealed that removing these victims from our sample had no impact on disclosure rates.

the percentage of the remaining victims ($N = 352$) who indicated each specific type of physical abuse. Respondents who had suffered multiple physical abuses answered the remainder of survey questions about the most traumatic experience.

Measure of Disclosure

We measured our key grouping variable, disclosure, with the following question, "Did you ever tell anyone about your abuse experience?" Table 10.2 reveals that although disclosure was more likely than nondisclosure for both types of abuse, a substantial minority of victims failed to ever tell anyone about their abuse prior to completing our survey: 22% of sexual abuse victims and 33% of physical abuse victims. Our nondisclosure rate for sexual abuse (22%) is much lower than the 46% rate found by Ussher and Dewberry (1995) in a British magazine survey study. Our rate is closer to but still lower than (a) the 28% rate found by Smith and collegues (2000), who asked adults in the community via a national telephone survey whether they had ever disclosed their abuse; (b) the 33% rate found by Finkelhor, Hotaling, Lewis, and Smith (1990); and (c) the 31% rate found by Arata (1998), whose study is perhaps the closest to ours in terms of methodology and college sample. Note that Arata asked victims to indicate if they disclosed at the time of the abuse; thus, one would expect our nondisclosure rate to be lower because our victims had a more extended time period following the incident to tell someone about the abuse. We do not know why our rate is somewhat lower than the community samples. College students might be, on average, more educated and of higher SES, and one might speculate that education could give victims more courage or opportunity to discuss issues of abuse openly.

RESULTS

Next, we present a descriptive profile of the circumstances surrounding the disclosure of abuse (i.e., to whom victims disclosed, what happened as a result of the disclosure). Then, we present a series of analyses examining factors that

TABLE 10.2

Percentage (and Number) of Victims Who Disclosed and Did Not Disclose
Their Abuse to Others, as a Function of Abuse Type

	Abuse Type	
	Sexual	Physical
Disclosed	78% (248)	67% (236)
Did not disclose	22% (71)	33% (116)
Total Number	319	352

were associated with disclosure and nondisclosure. Specifically, we used t-tests and *chi* squared analyses, as appropriate, to compare the characteristics, experiences, and circumstances of victims who disclosed and victims who did not disclose their abuse. For these analyses, our sample comprised all victims who answered the disclosure question (see table 10.2). We conducted all analyses separately for sexual abuse victims and physical abuse victims because some victims experienced both sexual and physical abuse, which precludes direct statistical comparisons between the two forms of abuse.

Persons to Whom Victims Disclosed and Outcomes of Disclosure

We asked victims who disclosed their abuse to indicate the person(s) to whom they disclosed. As shown in table 10.3, victims were most likely to disclose to friends, followed by parents, other relatives, and significant others. Of particular interest, very few victims (9% or fewer) disclosed to any type of recognized authority figure. This low percentage of victims making a formal report of abuse is very close to the rates for sexual abuse reported by Arata (1998, 10%) and Smith and colleagues (2000, 12%), and it is troubling: It suggests that when child abuse is disclosed, it is not usually disclosed in a manner that leads directly to an official investigation of the abuse. In turn, abuse might not be interrupted and perpetrators are undeterred from future abuse.

TABLE 10.3
Percentage (and Number) of Victims Who Disclosed and Did Not Disclose Their Abuse to Others, as a Function of Abuse Type

	Abuse Type	
	Sexual (%)	Physical (%)
Persons to whom victims disclosed		
Friend	65	78
Parent	45	34
Other relative	29	35
Significant other	32	26
Therapist	17	19
Teacher/Clergy	8	8
Authorities	9	9
Other	2	3
Outcomes of disclosure		
Abuse stopped	28	25
Legal action ensued	8	5
Parents divorced	1	3
Abuser confessed	8	4
Nothing (i.e., abuse continued)	16	40
Other	63	31

To investigate this issue further, we asked victims to tell us what happened as a result of their disclosure. As reflected in the large percentage of victims choosing the "other" response category in table 10.3, this survey item failed to capture many of the outcomes of disclosure, which underscores the need for future research to explore the consequences of disclosure in victims' lives. Even so, the findings are interesting. Disclosure ended the abuse for only about a quarter of the sexual or physical abuse victims. Legal action and perpetrator confession were rare, occurring in less than 8% of either type of abuse case.

Physical abuse victims were particularly likely to indicate that nothing occurred as a result of their disclosure. This might reflect the greater extent to which some forms of physical abuse, especially parental corporal punishment, are accepted in American society (Straus, 1995; Straus & Gelles, 1988). Thus, even if these victims tell others about their abuse, nothing is likely to happen as a result. This highlights the importance of psychological research into the short- and long-term effects of physical abuse, and for public awareness about the potential negative effects on children's well being of physical abuse (Kolko, 2002) and severe corporal punishment (Gershoff, 2002).

Demographic Factors

Before conducting analyses comparing the circumstances and characteristics of abuse that was disclosed versus abuse that was not disclosed, we conducted analyses to ensure that there were no significant differences between disclosers and nondisclosers in terms of the demographic profile we discussed previously. Indeed, there were no differences in terms of parental income [for sexual abuse victims, $t(297) = .32$, ns; for physical abuse victims, $t(328) = 1.94$, ns], or victims' age when they completed the survey [for sexual abuse, $t(316) = 1.06$, ns; for physical abuse, $t(345) = 1.03$, ns]. Finally, a comparison of the four major categories of participant race/ethnicity described previously (excluding the "other" category) revealed no significant differences in terms of race or ethnicity [for sexual abuse, $X^2 (3, N = 302) = 5.09$, ns; for physical abuse, $X^2 (3, N = 329) = 1.02$, ns].

The lack of differences associated with ethnicity is particularly interesting because some argue that culture can affect disclosure rates (e.g., Fontes, 1993). As London et al. (chapter 2, this volume) note, other disclosure studies have generally failed to include diverse samples, even the large national sample study conducted by Smith and colleagues (2000). Thus, our study provides one of the first reasonable tests of relations between race/ethnicity and disclosure, and our results suggest that nondisclosure is no more or less likely for some racial or ethnic groups than for others. Of course, our results relate only to differences among different ethnicities within North American society, namely people of European (Caucasian), African American, Hispanic/Latina, and Asian descent. It is not a test of differences among other cultures within our society or cultures outside of our society, and it is a test that warrants replication with other samples.

Multiple Abuse Experiences

As mentioned previously, we asked participants whether they had experienced each type of abuse multiple times (i.e., separate abuse incidents at the hands of different perpetrators), and if so, to complete the survey about the experience they felt was most traumatic. We examined whether experiencing a form of abuse multiple times was related to disclosing the one target abuse experience that victims had in mind when completing our survey. For both sexual abuse and physical abuse, victims who disclosed were more likely than nondisclosers to have suffered multiple abuses. Specifically, 34% of sexual abuse victims who had disclosed had suffered multiple sexual abuse events, while only 11% of nondisclosers had suffered multiple sexual abuses, χ^2 ($N = 280$) = 11.65, $p < .001$. Thirty percent of victims who disclosed physical abuse reported multiple physical abuses, compared to 18% of non-disclosers, χ^2 ($N = 305$) = 4.84, $p < .05$.

Identity of and Relationship with Perpetrator

Abuse perpetrated by loved, trusted adults is theorized to be more psychologically severe than abuse by acquaintances or strangers, and is therefore less likely to be disclosed and, some suggest (Freyd, 1996), perhaps even likely to be repressed. Researchers such as Goodman-Brown and colleagues (2003), Sas (1993), Sauzier (1989), and Smith et al. (2000) have found that victims are less likely to disclose, or at least more likely to delay in disclosing, as emotional closeness to the perpetrator increases (especially if parents are the perpetrators). They generally explain this tendency in terms of victims' concerns about betraying loved ones and disrupting families by disclosing.

In our sample, as would be expected, physical abuse was usually perpetrated by trusted family members (i.e., parents, 72%; stepparents, 4%; and other family members, 14%), which probably reflects that much of this abuse stemmed from overzealous discipline. The perpetrator was rarely a nonfamilial trusted adult (5%), acquaintance (4%), or stranger (1%). The pattern for sexual abuse was different, but generally in keeping with the sexual abuse literature: Parents (4%) and stepparents (3%) were not commonly the perpetrator. Instead, most abuse was perpetrated by other relatives (35%) and trusted adults (30%). The perpetrator was an acquaintance in 18% of cases, and a stranger in 10% of cases.

We compared the rate of disclosure for victims abused by parents and stepparents versus all other perpetrators. There was no statistical difference for either sexual abuse, χ^2 (1, $N = 310$) = 2.74, ns, or physical abuse, χ^2 (1, $N = 341$) = .37, ns. Nor were there significant differences in disclosure for sexual abuse, χ^2 (1, $N = 310$) = .23, ns, or physical abuse, χ^2 (1, $N = 341$) = .07, ns, when the comparison was between victims abused by a broad category of "trusted adults" (parents, stepparents, other family members, friends, and trusted adults) and victims abused by acquaintances and strangers. Because of very small numbers of victims in some cells for these analyses, especially for sexual abuse victims, we also compared disclosure as a function of intra- versus extra-familial abuse. Again, there were no statistical differences for either sexual, χ^2 (1, $N = 310$) $= .85$, or physical abuse, χ^2 (1, $N = 341$) $= .24$.

In these types of analyses, we assign more emotional closeness to adults who are more closely related to the victim than to adults who are more distantly related to the victim. Although this is a widely accepted assumption, we also obtained victims' own ratings of their emotional closeness to the perpetrator. Specifically, we asked victims to indicate how emotionally close they felt to the perpetrator prior to the abusive incident, using a 7-point scale ranging from 1 (*not close at all*) to 7 (*extremely close*). Even with this subjective measure, however, our analyses failed to uncover significant differences in disclosure tendencies: Disclosers ($M = 3.34$) and nondisclosers ($M = 3.08$) of sexual abuse indicated feeling similarly close to their perpetrators, $t(313) = .95$, ns. For physical abuse, there was a difference that approached, but did not reach, significance: Disclosers ($M = 4.63$) reported being slightly less close to the perpetrator than nondisclosers ($M = 5.03$), $t(344) = 1.74$, $p = .08$.

To summarize, across several types of comparisons, we found no evidence of a link between disclosure and perpetrator identity. Our results are similar in this respect to those reported by Arata (1998). We also found no relation between subjectively rated emotional closeness and disclosure of sexual abuse, although there was a trend for the nondisclosure of physical abuse to be linked to feelings of emotional closeness. This is consistent with the theory that victims protect trusted abusers, who, in physical abuse cases, were often the parent or other relatives. Alternatively, this trend might also reflect a tendency for some physical abuse victims to not consider the actions abusive but instead to be a part of parental discipline, and therefore, they would see no need for disclosure. We consider the issue of self-labeling as an abuse victim next.

Tendency to Self-Label as a Victim

Some individuals fail to self-label as victims even though they have had experiences that would be considered abusive by most researchers and professionals in the field of child maltreatment and that would be considered abuse by legal definitions. People who self-label as victims differ in some ways from those who do not self-label (Epstein & Bottoms, 2002; Martin, Anderson, Romans, Mullen, & O'Shea, 1993; Silvern, Waelde, Baughan, Karel, & Kaersvang, 2000). There has been little discussion of this issue in the disclosure literature, perhaps because few if any researchers have included both objective and subjective measures of victimization. We expected that victims who did not think they were abused would be less likely to disclose their experiences than victims who self-labeled as victims. This is because those who do not self-label would probably see little reason for disclosing: If a victim does not think an action is abusive, she probably would not believe that others would be motivated to stop the action even if informed about it. Also, such victims might even think that they deserved or instigated the actions. Victims are likely to believe all of these things in cases of parentally inflicted severe corporal punishment or in cases of sexual abuse where the victim has been carefully groomed by a perpetrator to believe that the experience is a special and positive event.

We tested our hypothesis by asking respondents, after they had completed the objective measure of abuse experiences described earlier, "When you were 17 years old or younger, were you a victim of childhood [sexual abuse/physical] abuse?" Only 60% of sexual abuse victims and 44% of physical abuse victims self-labeled (surprisingly low proportions that have serious implications for defining child maltreatment). In support of our hypothesis, labeling was significantly related to disclosure tendencies for both sexual abuse, χ^2 (1, $N = 297$) $= 19.04$, $p < .001$, and physical abuse, χ^2 (1, $N = 336$) $= 27.06$, $p < .001$. Specifically, 67% of sexual abuse victims who disclosed labeled themselves as sexual abuse victims, while only 37% of those who did not disclose labeled themselves as victims. Similarly, 53% of physical abuse victims who disclosed labeled themselves as victims, but only 23% of those who did not disclose self-labeled.

Thus, victims do not label as abusive many experiences that researchers and the law would define as abuse. This finding suggests a need for more public awareness about the definitions of abuse, which might lead some victims to understand that their experiences are abusive, and perhaps, in turn, foster their disclosures. It might also lead more observers to recognize abuse when they encounter it.

Frequency of the Target Abuse

We asked victims to estimate the number of times their abuse experience occurred on a 6-point scale comprising the following intervals: 1 (*once*), 2 (*twice*), 3 (*3 to 5 times*), 4 (*6 to 10 times*), 5 (*11 to 20 times*), 6 (*21 or more times*). Sexual abuse victims who disclosed reported that their abuse occurred significantly more frequently ($M = 2.98$) than did nondisclosers ($M = 2.48$), $t(310) = 2.09$, $p < .05$. Physical abuse victims who disclosed also experienced more frequent abuse ($M = 3.91$) than did nondisclosers ($M = 3.09$), $t(330) = 4.12$, $p < .001$.

These mean differences stand in contrast to Smith et al.'s (2000) finding that higher frequency was related to delayed disclosure. Of course, our study is of disclosure versus nondisclosure during childhood instead of immediate versus delayed disclosure. We suspect that our results reflect a pragmatic tendency for more severe abuse to attract the attention of others and in turn lead to disclosure, even if that disclosure is not an active outcry from the victim, a possibility also suggested by Hanson, Resnick, Saunders, Kilpatrick, and Best

(1999). Future research should include measures of abuse circumstances that are more capable of testing this possibility (e.g., more specific questions about the nature of the abuse, such as whether the child received medical attention as a result of the abuse or whether injuries were noticed by persons such as teachers or friends). Alternatively, the more frequent the abuse, the greater the possibility that the victim would reach the point of being unable to stand it any longer, and disclose in an attempt to end the abuse. These explanations may also be relevant to understanding the finding reported earlier that disclosers were more likely than nondisclosers to suffer multiple incidences of abuse.

Victim Age

Some studies have shown that older children are less likely to delay in disclosing sexual abuse than are younger children (Goodman-Brown, Edelstein, Goodman, Jones, & Gordon, 2003; Smith et al., 2000); others have found no relation (e.g., Arata, 1998; Bradley & Wood, 1996). We did not measure age at disclosure, but we did measure victims' age at the time the abuse started and

TABLE 10.4
Mean Victim Age (in Years) and Ratings of Emotional Distress as a
Function of Abuse Type and Disclosure

	Abuse Type	
	Sexual	Physical
Age abuse began		
Disclosed	9.73	8.45
Did not disclose	9.70	7.76
Age abuse ended		
Disclosed	11.70	14.42
Did not disclose	10.81	12.78
Worry about serious injury at time of abuse		
Disclosed	2.49	3.23
Did not disclose	1.42	2.12
Emotional distress at time of abuse		
Disclosed	4.77	5.52
Did not disclose	3.65	4.48
Emotional distress at time of survey		
Disclosed	4.13	3.21
Did not disclose	3.46	2.47

Note: See text for the wording of all measures. Worry was measured with a Likert scale ranging from 1 (*no, not at all*) to 7 (*yes, very much*). Emotional distress was measured with a Likert scale ranging from 1 (*no, not at all upsetting*) to 7 (*yes, very upsetting*).

when it stopped. As table 10.4 reveals, there was no difference in the age abuse began for disclosers and nondisclosers of sexual abuse, $t(310) = .05$, ns, or physical abuse, $t(328) = 1.51$, ns. There was also no significant difference in the age at which sexual abuse ended, $t(310) = 1.53$, ns. There was, however, a significant but small difference in the age physical abuse ended: Disclosers were older than were nondisclosers when the abuse ended, $t(331) = 4.20, p < .001$.

The significant finding for physical abuse is counterintuitive in one sense: One would expect that disclosed abuse would have been cut short by the disclosure and therefore would have ended earlier than undisclosed abuse. But as we reported earlier, disclosure was unlikely to stop either form of abuse. Thus, we think it is more likely that these results are supportive of the idea we raised previously: that more severe abuse, which could be defined as abuse that continues longer and perhaps more likely to be noticed by others, is more likely to be disclosed than less severe abuse.

Perceived Emotional Impact of the Abuse

We included several measures of victims' emotional reactions to and feelings about the abuse, and explored their relation to disclosure and nondisclosure (see table 10.4). First, we asked participants, "When you experienced your [sexual/physical] abuse, did you worry about being seriously injured or killed?" Overall, the level of worry about such extreme injury was fairly low, but even so, sexual abuse victims, $t(314) = 4.38, p < .001$, and physical abuse victims, $t(345) = 4.87, p < .001$, who disclosed were significantly more worried than were those who did not disclose. Kellogg and Hoffman (1995) and Hanson et al. (1999) also found that sexual abuse involving threat of serious injury was associated with higher disclosure rates.

We also asked victims, "At the time it occurred, was your [sexual/physical] experience emotionally upsetting or distressing to you?" and "Is your [sexual/physical] experience emotionally upsetting or distressing to you now?" For physical abuse, the disclosers reported being significantly more upset at the time of the abuse and more upset at the time of the survey than did the nondisclosers, both $ts(> 344) > 3.12$, $ps < .01$. The same pattern held for sexual abuse victims, both $ts(> 315) > 2.15$, $ps < .05$.

Thus, according to multiple indicators, as subjective levels of distress increased, so did the likelihood of disclosure. These findings, like our abuse frequency findings, might indicate that more severe abuse is harder to hide and leads to disclosure, whether that disclosure is wanted by the victim or not. This disclosure could be initiated by the victim who cannot live with the severe abuse any longer or who cannot hide it any longer, or it might be initiated by someone else who observes the results of the severe abuse, which is harder to miss than less severe abuse. Even so, we note that our results are not consistent with many studies of delayed disclosure, which have found that increased abuse severity, in terms of more intrusive abuse and factors such as victims feeling fearful, leads to delayed disclosure and nondisclosure. Nor are our findings consistent with Arata's (1998) conclusion that "disclosure is least common for assaults that produce the greatest distress."

Temporary Forgetting

Is disclosure linked to memory for abuse? It might be argued that victims are less likely to disclose abuse if they experienced periods of time during which they did not remember their abuse. We asked victims, "Was there ever a time when you could not remember your sexual abuse experience?", an item similar to measures used by researchers such as Briere and Conte (1993), Feldman-Summers and Pope (1994), Melchert (1996), Melchert and Parker (1997), and Williams (1995). A marginally significant trend, χ^2 $(N = 317) = 3.05, p = .08$, indicated that sexual abuse victims who disclosed were somewhat less likely to report temporary forgetting (14%) than those who did not disclose (23%). In contrast, there was no significant difference in the percentage of disclosers (9.8%) and nondisclosers (10%) who reported temporary forgetting of physical abuse, χ^2 $(N = 344) = .00$, ns.

Thus, we uncovered only a marginally significant tendency for disclosers to report less temporary forgetting than nondisclosers, a trend that might reach significance in larger samples of victims who report forgetting. Arata (1998), in fact, did find a relation between forgetting and disclosing among sexual abuse victims. As we discuss elsewhere (Epstein & Bottoms, 2002), analyses of other measures included in this survey revealed that victims who reported temporary forgetting in response to this survey question rarely meant that they repressed the abuse totally and completely. Instead, they often meant that they failed to label the experience as abuse until later in life, or that they purposely tried to not think about the abuse. These would be consistent with failure to disclose: First, as we discussed previously, victims might be less likely to disclose experiences that they do not label as abusive. Second, victims would probably be less likely to discuss abuse that they are actively trying not to think about. This could be a mechanism for coping with the abuse (by avoiding it), an issue we take up more directly next.

Individual Differences in Coping and Attachment Styles

A unique feature of the present study is that we measured several individual difference factors, which we examined in relation to disclosure and non-disclosure of abuse.

Avoidant Coping. We measured three types of avoidant coping styles proposed by clinical and personality theorists (although there is some controversy about their construct validity, e.g., see Spanos, 1994, for discussion): repressive coping style, dissociation proneness, and fantasy proneness. Generally, avoidant coping styles are characterized by attempts to avoid acknowledgment of painful traumatic experiences and efforts to evade affect, memories, and retrieval cues associated with traumas (Briere, 1996; Maynes & Feinauer, 1994; Putnam, 1985). We reasoned that evading thoughts about trauma could lead to avoiding disclosure and discussion of trauma, and therefore that people who are prone to use avoidant coping styles would be more likely than others not to disclose their abuse.

First, we examined repressive coping style. People who use a repressive coping style ("repressors") tend to avoid acknowledging their own experiences of negative affect and avoid thoughts, information, and memories that are negative and stressful (Weinberger, 1990). We reasoned that, in turn, repressors would also avoid disclosure of traumas. In keeping with other research (e.g., Weinberger, 1990), we combined respondents' scores on the short forms of the Marlowe-Crowne Social Desirability Scale (MCSDS, Crowne & Marlowe, 1960; 1964) and the Taylor Manifest Anxiety Scale (Bendig, 1956) to obtain a measurement of repressive coping style.

Second, we studied dissociative coping style. People who are high in dissociative coping are said to lack an integration of thoughts, feelings, and experiences (Bernstein & Putnam, 1986) and to have disturbances in memory, awareness, and identity (Nemiah, 1980). We theorized that dissociative-prone individuals might use dissociation to escape thoughts and memories associated with abuse and therefore be less likely to disclose than nondissociative-prone individuals. Dissociative proneness was operationalized as scoring 30% or higher on the Dissociative Experiences Scale (Carlson & Putnam, 1993).

Finally, we studied fantasy proneness, which refers to a tendency to be deeply involved in fantasy and to avoid remembering memories of trauma, which is, for the highly fantasy prone, like vividly re-experiencing the traumatic events (Wilson & Barber, 1983). Thus, we expected that fantasy prone individuals would also avoid disclosing and discussing traumatic experiences because this would necessitate remembering and reliving the experience. We measured fantasy proneness with the Inventory of Childhood Memory and Imaginings (Wilson & Barber, 1983), where scores greater than or equal to 28 are considered high on the construct.

Our analyses revealed that the likelihood of disclosing abuse was unrelated to any of the three avoidant coping styles that we measured. Specifically, among sexual abuse victims, 76% of repressors and 78% of nonrepressors disclosed their abuse, χ^2 ($N = 317$) = .09, ns; 83% of the dissociative prone and 77% of the nondissociative-prone participants disclosed, χ^2 ($N = 317$) = .93, ns; and 83% of the fantasy prone victims and 76% of the nonfantasy-prone victims disclosed, χ^2 ($N = 316$) = 1.47, ns. Among physical abuse victims, 69% of repressors and 66% of non-repressors disclosed, χ^2 ($N = 350$) = .12, ns; 66% of dissociative prone and 67% of nondissociative-prone participants disclosed, χ^2 ($N = 351$) = .06; and 71% of fantasy prone and 66% of nonfantasy-prone disclosed, χ^2 ($N = 351$) = .87, ns.

To our knowledge, no other researchers have examined a link between disclosure and these individual differences in coping styles. At least two groups of researchers, however, have measured general psychological functioning. Specifically, neither Hanson and colleagues (1999) nor Arata (1998) (who used the SCL90-R and TSC-40 measures of psychological functioning) found a relation between disclosure and global measures of current psychological functioning. Our null findings for avoidant coping styles are consistent with this prior research to the extent that persons high in such coping strategies might also be less psychologically healthy generally.

Attachment Style. We also measured individual differences in participants' attachment style. The basic premise of attachment theory is that early life interactions with an infant's primary caregiver mold the infant's mental representations for others and for the reactions one can expect from others in close relationships (Bowlby, 1969/1980). For example, supportive, attentive parents foster secure relationship schemas in their children, which leads to the children expecting support and emotional stability from relationships with others (a secure attachment style). Hazan and Shaver (1987) provided the first evidence for the enduring nature of these relationship schemas, illustrating that adult romantic attachments often reflect early life attachment styles. According to Bartholomew and Horowitz (1991), there are four main types of adult attachment styles: secure, preoccupied, dismissing–avoidant, and fearful–avoidant. As described by Fraley and Shaver (1997), secure individuals are positive in their view of the self, trust in the responsiveness of others, and enjoy close relationships. Preoccupied individuals are insecure in their relationships with others and constantly worry that they are getting less from others than they give. People with a dismissing–avoidant attachment style tend to value emotional independence over close relationships and therefore avoid relationships. Individuals who are fearful–avoidant avoid, but want, relationships. They have low feelings of self worth and negative expectations of how responsive others will be to their needs.

A close, but imperfect, relation between adult and childhood attachment styles suggests that secure attachment in young adulthood results from supportive parenting. If so, then compared to insecurely attached adults, securely attached adults might have experienced a relatively high degree of perceived parental support during childhood. Throughout life, they also might have felt more emotionally close to others, more certain of others' emotional support for them, and therefore, we reason, more comfortable discussing close emotionally wrought issues such as childhood abuse. Thus, we hypothesized that securely attached individuals would be more likely to disclose abuse than insecurely attached individuals.

Respondents completed Bartholomew and Horowitz's (1991) measure of attachment style by choosing from among one of four descriptions of attachment styles. Analyses revealed no significant differences in disclosure tendencies among victims having the four various styles, and therefore no support for our hypothesis, for either sexual abuse victims, χ^2 ($N = 286$) = 5.18, ns, or physical abuse victims, χ^2 ($N = 312$) = 4.42, ns. Specifically, among sexual abuse victims, 79% of the securely attached, 76% of the preoccupied, 92% of the dismissing avoidant, and 74% of the fearful avoidant victims disclosed their abuse. For physical abuse victims, corresponding percentages were 72%, 63%, 56%, and 67%, respectively.[3] Thus, we uncovered no evidence of a link between attachment and disclosure in this sample.

CONCLUSION

The implications of our results must be considered in light of the study's limitations. As is true for any retrospective self-report study, we must rely on the victims' memories and reports, even though people are not always accurate in reflecting upon their past experiences, their motivations, or their cognitive processes (Azar, 1997). Furthermore, although our sample was large and diverse in terms of socioeconomic status and race/ethnicity, it comprised a nonclinical sample of young women only. Our findings might not represent the experiences of men or of individuals who suffered extremely severe abuse or emotional sequelae and who therefore are less likely to appear in a sample of highly functioning college students (e.g., Duncan, 1999).

These limitations notwithstanding, the study has a number of strengths, particularly in light of the paucity of research on this important topic. Our participants knew nothing about the study before coming to the survey session, potentially reducing the underestimation of nondisclosure that can arise when people respond to requests for abuse victims. Thus, our approach is more likely to include participants who have never disclosed their abuse. Other methods of estimating rates of nondisclosure, including studies of cases reported to authorities or therapists, would be less able to access and study victims who had never disclosed. A second strength of our study is its large, nonclinical sample, which is diverse in terms of ethnicity/race and socioeconomic status. The diversity allowed for testing relations between disclosure and race, and the large number of participants allowed us to have confidence in making statistical comparisons between relatively large numbers of victims who did and did not disclose their abuse. The nonclinical sample also provides more information

---

[3] Results did not differ when we analyzed a more sensitive measure of attachment style, on which respondents use a 7-point Likert scale to indicate the extent to which each style was like them.

than clinical samples about the relations among variables in the normal population at large.

Third, we defined abuse both objectively (with the checklist approach) and subjectively (with a question about perceived victimhood), an approach not used in previous studies. This allowed us to understand that disclosure is strongly linked to victims' own perceptions of the abusiveness of their experiences, with victims who self-labeled being approximately twice as likely to disclose abuse than were victims who did not self-label. This implies that many perpetrators of abuse are quite skilled in misleading their victims. It also suggests a need in our society for more education about physical and sexual abuse to help teachers, doctors, and parents, as well as victims themselves, recognize abuse.

Fourth, we examined patterns of disclosure and nondisclosure not only of sexual abuse, which is of course an important threat to children's well-being, but also of physical abuse, a more common form of child maltreatment. Our data provide insights concerning the extent to which physical maltreatment is not only undisclosed but also not even considered abusive by its victims. Research in the field of child maltreatment is entering a new era, in which forms of maltreatment other than sexual abuse are being given more attention. Future research should examine disclosure of all forms of maltreatment, including neglect (the most common form of child maltreatment, Myers et al., 2002) and emotional abuse. In fact, a significant minority of victims in our study reported traumatic experiences involving witnessing domestic violence and emotional/verbal abuse, forms of maltreatment that are gaining increasing recognition. We are currently examining our data to understand factors associated with the disclosure and nondisclosure of these forms of maltreatment.

Finally, our study is unique in examining the relation between disclosure and various psychological individual difference variables such as attachment style and avoidant coping style. That social and situational variables may be better predictors of disclosure than individual difference variables (at least the ones we measured) is a welcome finding given that social factors are likely to be easier to identify and change for children than individual difference factors. Social psychological and social developmental theories should be brought to bear on the problem of understanding the factors that lead to disclosure and nondisclosure so that child protection professionals will understand the conditions that facilitate disclosure.

In conclusion, our findings make an important contribution to a growing area of inquiry into the circumstances surrounding the disclosure and nondisclosure of childhood maltreatment. Our study reveals that a significant number of victims never disclose abuse at all, or they disclose in ways that do not lead to formal investigation and do not bring an end to their abuse (nor prevent the abuse of other children). Although it is of critical importance to ensure that investigation techniques guard against false disclosures of abuse, it is clear from the present study that techniques must also be sensitive to the huge societal problem of the under-reporting of child maltreatment. As psychologists, we must help front-line investigators of child maltreatment by providing tools that ensure better detection of actual abuse (for discussion, see other chapters in this volume by Bottoms, Quas, & Davis; Pipe, Lamb, Orbach, Stewart, Sternberg, & Esplin; and Hershkowitz, Orbach, Lamb, Sternberg, Pipe, & Horowitz). We move closer to realizing this goal by studying the factors that facilitate and hinder the disclosure of maltreatment.

ACKNOWLEDGMENTS

We thank John Briere and Sarah Ullman for comments on our survey instrument; Beth Schwartz, Gail Goodman, Jodi Quas, Simona Ghetti, and Maureen Smith for help with participant recruitment; and Matthew Badanek, Nadine Stevoff, Catherine Pelzman, Kara Doering, and Elaine Shreder for valuable research assistance. Portions of this research were supported by a grant to Michelle Epstein from the National Institute of Mental Health.

REFERENCES

Arata, C. M. (1998). Examining questionable child sexual abuse allegations in their environmental and psychodynamic contexts. *Journal of Child Sexual Abuse, 3*, 21–36.

Azar, B. (1997). Poor recall mars research and treatment: Inaccurate self-reports can lead to faulty research conclusions and inappropriate treatment. *The APA Monitor, 28*, 1.

Bartholomew, K., & Horowitz, L. (1991). Attachment styles among young adults: A test of a four-category model. *Journal of Personality and Social Psychology, 61*, 226–44.

Bernstein, E. M., & Putnam, F. W. (1986). Development, reliability, and validity of a dissociation scale. *The Journal of Nervous and Mental Disease, 174*, 727–35.

Bowlby, J. (1980). *Attachment and loss: Vol. 1. Attachment.* New York: Basic Books. Original work published 1969.

Bradley, A. R., & Wood, J. M. (1996). How do children tell? The disclosure process in child sexual abuse. *Child Abuse and Neglect, 20*, 881–91.

Briere, J. (1996). A self-trauma model for treating adult survivors of severe child abuse. In J. Briere, L. Berliner, J. Bulkey, C. Jenney, & T. Reid (Eds.), *The APSAC handbook of child maltreatment.* Newbury Park, CA: Sage.

Briere, J., & Conte, J. (1993). Self-reported amnesia for abuse in adults molested as children. *Journal of Traumatic Stress, 6*, 21–31.

Carlson, E. B., & Putnam, F. W. (1993). An update on the Dissociative Experiences Scale. Dissociation: *Progress in the Dissociative Disorders, 6*, 16–27.

Duncan, R. (1999). *Childhood maltreatment and college drop-out rates: Implications for researchers and educators.* Presented at the 7th Annual Colloquium of the American Professional Society on the Abuse of Children, San Antonio, TX.

Epstein, M. E., & Bottoms, B. L. (2002). Forgetting and recovery of abuse and trauma memories: Possible mechanisms. *Child Maltreatment, 7*, 210–25.

Feldman-Summers, S. & Pope, K. (1994). The experience of "forgetting" childhood abuse: A national survey of psychologists. *Journal of Consulting & Clinical Psychology. 62,* 636–39.

Finkelhor, D. (1979). *Sexually victimized children.* New York: Free Press.

Finkelhor, D., Hotaling, G., Lewis, I. A., & Smith, C. (1990). Sexual abuse in a national survey of adult men and women: Prevalence, characteristics, and risk factors. *Child Abuse and Neglect, 14,* 19–28.

Fontes, L. (1993). Disclosures of sexual abuse by Puerto Rican children: Oppression and cultural barriers. *Journal of Child Sexual Abuse, 2,* 21–35.

Fraley, C., & Shaver, P. (1997). Adult attachment and the suppression of unwanted thoughts. *Journal of Personality and Social Psychology, 73,* 1080–91.

Freyd, J. (1996). *Betrayal trauma: The logic of forgetting childhood abuse.* Cambridge, MA: Harvard University Press.

Gershoff, E. T. (2002). Corporal punishment by parents and associated child behaviors and experiences: A meta-analytic and theoretical review. *Psychological Bulletin, 128,* 539–79.

Goodman-Brown, T. B., Edelstein, R., Goodman, G. S., Jones, D., & Gordon, D. S. (2003). Why children tell: A model of children's disclosures of sexual abuse. *Child Abuse and Neglect, 27,* 525–40.

Hanson, R. F., Resnick, H. S., Saunders, B. E., Kilpatrick, D. G., & Best, C. (1999). Factors related to the reporting of childhood rape. *Child Abuse and Neglect, 23,* 559–69.

Hazan, C., & Shaver, P. (1987). Romantic love conceptualized as an attachment process. *Journal of Personality and Social Psychology, 59,* 511–24.

Jones, L. M., & Finkelhor, D. (2003). Putting together evidence on declining trends in sexual abuse: A complex puzzle. *Child Abuse & Neglect, 27,* 133–35.

Kellogg, N. D., & Hoffman, T. (1995). Unwanted and illegal sexual experiences in childhood and adolescence. *Child Abuse and Neglect, 19,* 1457–68.

Kolko, D. J. (2002). Child physical abuse. In J. E. B. Myers, L. Berliner, J. Briere, C. T. Hendrix, C. Jenny, & T. A. Reid. *The APSAC handbook on child maltreatment* (pp. 21–54). Thousand Oaks, CA: Sage.

Martin, J., Anderson, J., Romans, S., Mullen, P., & O'Shea, M. (1993). Asking about child sexual abuse: Methodological implications of a two stage survey. *Child Abuse and Neglect, 17,* 383–92.

Maynes, L. C., & Feinauer, L. L. (1994). Acute and chronic dissociation and somatized anxiety as related to childhood sexual abuse. *The American Journal of Family Therapy, 22,* 165–75.

Melchert, T. (1996). Childhood memory and a history of different forms of abuse. *Professional Psychology: Research & Practice, 27,* 438–46.

Melchert, T. & Parker, R. L. (1997). Different forms of childhood abuse and memory. *Child Abuse & Neglect, 21,* 125–35.

Myers, J. E. B., Berliner, L., Briere, J., Hendrix, C. T., Jenny, C., & Reid, T. (Eds.) (2002), *The APSAC handbook on child maltreatment* (pp. 269–91). Thousand Oaks, CA: Sage.

Nemiah, J. C. (1980). Dissociative disorders. In A. M. Freedman and H. I. Kaplan (Eds.), *Comprehensive textbook of psychiatry* (pp. 1544–61). Baltimore: Williams & Wilkins.

Putnam, F. W. (1985). Dissociation as a response to extreme trauma. In R. P. Kluft (Ed.), *The childhood antecedents of multiple personality.* Washington: American Psychiatric Press.

Sas, L. (1993). *Three years after the verdict.* London, Ont., Canada: London Family Court Clinic, Inc.

Sauzier, M. (1989). Disclosure of child abuse: For better or for worse. *Psychiatric Clinics of North America, 12,* 455–69.

Silvern, L., Waelde, L. C., Baughan, B. M., Karel, J., & Kaersvang, L. J. (2000). Two formats for eliciting retrospective reports of child sexual and physical abuse: Effects on apparent prevalence and relationships to adjustment. *Child Maltreatment, 5,* 236–50.

Smith, D.W., Letourneau, E., Saunders, B., Kilpatrick, D. G., Resnik, H. S., & Best, C. L. (2000). Delay in disclosure of childhood rape: Results from a national survey. *Child Abuse and Neglect, 24,* 273–87.

Spanos, N. P. (1994). Multiple identity enactments and multiple personality disorder: A sociocognitive perspective. *Psychological Bulletin, 116,* 143–65.

Straus, M. A. (1995). *Beating the devil out of them: Corporal punishment in American families.* New York: Lexington Books

Straus, M. A., & Gelles, R. J. (1988). How violent are American families? Estimates from the National Family Violence Survey and other studies. In G. T. Hotaling, D. Finkelhor, J. T. Kirkpatric, & M. A. Straus (Eds.), *Family abuse and its consequences: Violence in American families.* New York: Anchor/Doubleday.

Ussher, J. & Dewberry, C. (1995). The nature and long-term effects of childhood sexual abuse: A survey of adult women survivors in Britain. *British Journal of Clinical Psychology, 34,* 177–92.

Weinberger, D. A. (1990). The construct validity of the repressive coping style. In J. L. Singer (Ed.), *Repression and dissociation: Implications for personality theory, psychopathology, and health* (pp. 337–86). Chicago: University of Chicago Press.

Wilson, S. C., & Barber, T. X. (1983). The fantasy prone personality: Implications for understanding imagery, hypnosis, and parapsychological phenomena. In A. A. Sheikh (Ed.), *Imagery: Current theory, research, and application* (pp. 340–87). New York: John Wiley & Sons.

11

Canadian Criminal Court Reports of Historic Child Sexual Abuse: Factors Associated With Delayed Prosecution and Reported Repression

Deborah A. Connolly, J. Don Read
Simon Fraser University

Based on a very thorough review of the limited literature of delayed disclosure and nondisclosure of child sexual abuse (CSA), London, Bruck, Ceci, and Shuman (chapter 2, this volume) concluded that a majority of CSA victims do not disclose their abuse until long after it ends. Although the literature is reasonably consistent on the fact that most children delay disclosing CSA, there is far less consensus on the reasons for delayed disclosure. As reviewed by London et al., research on abuse characteristics that could help to explain delay include intrusiveness of the abuse, relationship between the perpetrator and the child, age of the child at the time of abuse, frequency of abuse, the presence of threats, and sex of the child. With very few exceptions, this research has been carried out with three distinct populations, university students, community participants, and clinical clients. Research on complainants who delay pursuit of a legal remedy is understudied. In this chapter, we discuss results of a large-scale study of criminal complaints of CSA that were alleged to have happened in the distant past. Research on a forensic population is important for at least three reasons. First, it gives emphasis to particular psychological and legal problems that arise when reports and prosecutions of CSA are delayed. Second, it provides unique insight into predictors of delayed prosecution. Third, it highlights many legal issues that psychologists are well suited to address. One such issue is claims of repression. In this chapter, we discuss each of these issues in turn.

Much of the extant research has focused on predictors of delayed disclosure. Relatively less attention has been devoted to the problems that arise when there has been a long delay in disclosing and prosecuting CSA. A long delay in disclosing CSA has important mental health implications as well as, in some jurisdictions, considerable legal costs. CSA can lead to significant psychological problems in adulthood: Browne and Finkelhor (1986) found higher incidence of depression, problems with parenting, self-destructive behaviors, as well as isolation and stigmatization among adult survivors of CSA; Quas, Goodman, and Jones (2003) reported self-blame and internalizing behaviors as sequelae of CSA (see also Beitchman et al., 1992; Briere & Runtz, 1988; Runyan, 1998). There is some consensus that CSA can lead to adult pathology; it is less clear, however, whether early disclosure ameliorates the effects. Arata (1998), for instance, reported that timing of disclosure was unrelated to global measures of current functioning among an adult sample of self-reported CSA survivors (for a similar conclusion with respect to socio-emotional functioning see Lamb & Edgar Smith, 1994). Other scholars reported healthier functioning among those who delayed disclosing CSA compared to those whose abuse was disclosed in a timely manner. Both Gomes-Schwatz et al. (1990) and Sauzier (1989) reported lower levels of anxiety and hostility among delayed disclosers compared to those who disclosed in a timely fashion. Still others reported healthier functioning on some measures if disclosure of CSA was timely compared to delayed. Arata (1998) reported fewer intrusive and avoidant symptoms among timely disclosers and Gries and colleagues (2000) reported lower externalizing scores among timely disclosers. Some of the ambiguity in this literature may be attributed to the reactions to the disclosure. That is, an important mediator in outcome of early disclosure of CSA appears to be the reaction of the confidant (Gries et al., 2000). A child who receives a negative reaction from the person to whom the abuse is disclosed may be at greater risk for adult pathology than a child who does not disclose the abuse at all (e.g., Hazzard, Celano, Gould, Lawry, & Webb, 1995; Lipton, 1997).

Notwithstanding the inconsistent findings with respect to clinical symptoms as sequelae of delayed disclosure of CSA, there is more consensus that children who do not disclose the abuse in a timely manner are themselves at risk of continued abuse, other children are at risk of being abused, and therapy for all affected children is delayed (Goodman-Brown et al., 2003; Sas & Cunningham, 1995). This, inter alia, led Paine and Hansen (2002) to conclude "prompt disclosure is second only to prevention in the goal of protecting children from sexual abuse" (290).

The important forensic implications of failing to disclose CSA in a timely manner are less ambiguous. Perhaps the one that most readily comes to mind is statutory law concerning how long a party has to commence a lawsuit (i.e., statutes of limitations). Very briefly, statutes of limitations prescribe that a legal proceeding must be commenced within a specific time from a triggering event (e.g., the harm was done, the complainant attained the age of majority, the injured party identified that he/she suffered harm etc.). In most American states there are statutes of limitations on criminal offences; however, there are several notable exceptions: In 11 states, statutes of limitations, if they exist, do not apply to cases involving sexual abuse of young children (Wyoming, Kentucky, Virginia, West Virginia, Alaska, Maryland, North Carolina, South Carolina, Rhode Island, Alabama, and Maine). In jurisdictions that have a statute of limitations that apply in CSA cases, the limitations period can be tolled (i.e., suspended) in certain circumstances. For instance, in almost all states that have a statute of limitations on sexual offences against children, it is tolled until the child reaches the age of majority (National Center for Victims of Crime, 1998; Shuman & Smith, 2000).

In Canada, as in England, Australia, and New Zealand, there are no limitation periods on indictable (roughly equivalent to felony) offences, except in very rare circumstances. Indeed, criminal prosecutions of CSA that occurred in the distant past (historic child sexual abuse, HCSA) have been the topic of discussion and policy debate in the United Kingdom (Home Affairs Committee, 2002). Thus, although our data are from Canadian trials, the phenomena and erudition the data provide are of international interest. In the balance of this chapter, we report data from a large-scale study of decisions involving criminal prosecutions of HCSA. In particular, we compare delayed and timely official reports of CSA and we review the role of non-continuous memory (often referred to as *repression*) in such cases.

THE FORENSIC SAMPLE

The data described in this chapter were obtained from judicial decisions in criminal prosecutions involving CSA that were alleged to have occurred in the distant past. As discussed above, this is an understudied sample and one that provides insight into the unique psychological and legal issues that arise when reporting and prosecuting CSA is delayed.

Quicklaw™ was used to identify relevant criminal cases. Quicklaw™ is a full-text database that contains, from 1986 forward, all Supreme Court of Canada decisions; written and oral decisions from provincial Courts of Appeal[1]; written decisions from the provincial Superior Courts; and written decisions from Provincial Courts that were forwarded to Quicklaw™ (forwarded at the discretion of the judge). Only English decisions were included

---

[1] The judge decides whether to release a decision orally or in writing. Generally, a judge will provide written reasons if an issue raised at trial is important or if the case is long and complex (B.C. Court Library, personal communication, July, 1997).

(i.e., we excluded all decisions from Quebec and some decisions from New Brunswick). The key words "child" (including variations) *and* the names of various sexual offences were used to locate relevant cases[2]. Each case was reviewed to confirm that the complainant was 19-years old or younger when the alleged offence began. Further, to meet the "historic" requirement, we included only those complaints for which two or more years had elapsed between the end of the alleged offence and the trial date. Our final database contained 2064 HCSA complainants.

Cases were coded on 35 variables. Intercoder reliability, defined as agreements / agreements + disagreements, was obtained on 10% of the complaints. For the variables described in this chapter, intercoder agreement ranged from 83% to 98%. Most of the variables are self-explanatory (e.g., age of the complainant when the alleged abuse began, duration, and frequency of abuse). Variables that require further explanation are described in appendices A and B at the end of this chapter.

DELAYED AND TIMELY OFFICIAL COMPLAINTS

We compared our HCSA data (median and modal year that the offence allegedly ended was 1978 and 1981, respectively) with timely official CSA complaints reported in 1981.[3] We used the Report of the Committee on Sexual Offences Against Children and Youths [Badgley Report] (1984) to obtain data on timely official reports of CSA.

Included in the Badgley investigation was a National Police Survey of all official CSA reports made to 28 police forces across Canada in 1981. It was difficult to identify the precise number of cases included in the Badgley analyses, but it appears to have been over 3,000 complaints. These timely reports were profiled along many of the dimensions that we use to describe the HCSA cases; however, some changes to the HCSA variables were necessary to

---

[2] Particular offences included in the search were "sexual offence(s)," "sexual assault," "sexual interference," "sexual intercourse," "gross indecency," "indecent assault," "incest," "rape," "bestiality," or "buggery." Gross indecency, indecent assault, and rape are no longer offences under the Canadian Criminal Code—the behaviors remain criminal offences but they will be charged under a different offence, often sexual assault. However, when a person is charged with an offence, the charged will comply with the Criminal Code that was in force at the time of the alleged offence. Because our interest is historical child sexual abuse, it was necessary to search for sexual offences that no longer exist.

[3] Of course, delayed prosecution does not necessarily mean delayed disclosure. We recoded whether the judge reported that the complainant had made an unofficial disclosure before reporting it to the authorities. In only 20% (413 complaints) of the cases was this reported to have occurred. In those cases, the median length of delay between disclosure to nonauthorities and disclosure to authorities was 6 years (the mode was 2 years and the mean was 8.96 years). In those cases the median, modal, and mean length of delay from the end of the abuse to the trial was 11 years, 5 years, and 12.65 years, respectively.

construct the HCSA data file to be comparable to the Badgley data. The following changes were made: (1) only complainants who were under 16-years old when the alleged abuse began were included in the analyses; (2) all exposure cases were omitted; and (3) the relationship variable was recombined as described below and in appendix B. (In the original coding of the HCSA data, 36 relationship categories were created. They were combined to create the four categories described in appendix A. The coding described in appendix A was used for all analysis of claims of repression reported later in this chapter). After making these changes, the data file contained 1382 HCSA complaints.

Comparisons between HCSA prosecutions and timely official complaints of CSA were possible on the following variables: age of the child at the time of the alleged abuse (under 7 years old, between 7 and 11 years old, between 12 and 13 years old, and between 15 and 16 years old), whether vaginal or anal intercourse was alleged to have been involved, claimed threats, claimed use of alcohol, and relationship between the child and the accused person. The relationship variable was coded into one of eight categories: incest, blood relative other than incest, a guardianship relationship (e.g., stepfather), a relationship of trust (e.g., teacher), a friend, some other person who was known to the child, or a stranger. A more complete description of the relationship variable is presented in appendix B.

The percentage of CSA and HCSA cases that fell into each level of several categories was compared. Chi-square analyses were used to identify significant differences (expected frequencies were calculated as the average of the two observed frequencies). As can be seen in table 11.1, the profiles of timely and delayed official complaints of CSA were quite different. As discussed in more detail below, abuse characteristics that may heighten children's vulnerability were associated with delayed official reports. Compared to the timely official reports, a greater percentage of delayed official reports involved young children who were subjected to more intrusive and intimidating abuse involving alcohol by persons who were close to them.

Strikingly, incest offenders, blood relatives, other family members, and those who held a position of trust or guardianship vis-à-vis the child comprised 84% of the accused persons in the HCSA data while they comprised only 26% of accused persons in the CSA data. As described by London et al., (chapter 2, this volume) a close relationship between the child and the perpetrator is inconsistently predictive of delayed disclosure. In these data, the relationship was strong and large. Perhaps we found such a strong relationship because we studied complainants who had made formal legal complaints against the perpetrators. Clearly, the implications of such complaints are vast and the effects may be more substantial when the relationship between the perpetrator and the child is close rather than distant. To the extent that this contributed to our results, it suggests that future researchers should consider the implications of the disclosure. The timing of disclosures that set in motion more serious

TABLE 11.1
Comparison of Percentages of Delayed (HCSA) and
Timely (Badgley) Official CSA Complaints

	HCSA %	Badgley %	X^2
Age of Female Complainant			
Under 7 years	29	18	2.71
7–11 years	48	29	4.55**
12–13 years	16	21	.69
14–15 years	7	32	15.62**
Age of Male Complainant			
Under 7 years	19	29	2.22
7–11 years	49	39	1.38
12–13 years	19	14	.69
14–15 years	13	18	.97
***Desc. Females**			
Vaginal penetration	35	17.6	5.87**
Anal Penetration	4	.6	3.09
***Desc. Males**			
Anal Penetration	20	8	5.27**
Threats			
Female	33	3	25.09**
Male	26	6	12.67**
Presence of Alcohol			
Female	23	12	3.92**
Male	12	7	1.18
Relation between complainant and accused			
Incest	21	9	4.58**
Other Blood Relative	15	4	5.75**
Guardianship	17	5	7.17**
Other Family Member	10	3	4.03**
Position of Trust	21	5	9.29**
Friend/Acquaint.	13	36	11.01**
Other Known Person	1	2	.13
Stranger	2	36	29.55**

*If a child experienced more than one type of abuse Badgley (1984) recorded each type of abuse, whereas only the most intrusive abuse was recorded for the HCSA data. Thus, only the most intrusive form of abuse is analyzed here.
   **$p < .05$.

consequences may be predicted by the relationship between the child and the perpetrator while disclosures that have less serious consequences may not.

The relationship between age of the child when the abuse began and timeliness of official complaint was complex. For male complainants, there was no association. For female complainants, on the other hand, age when the abuse began was sometimes associated with timeliness of the official complaint: Being between 7 and 11 years old when the abuse began was associated with a delayed complaint and being between 14 and 15 years old when the abuse began was associated with a timely complaint. London et al. (chapter 2, this volume) reported that a young age of the child victim is sometimes found to predict delayed disclosure and sometimes it is not. Although the data reported here represent a unique sample (i.e., criminal complainants), they may provide some guidance for future researchers. These data suggest that there may be an interaction between sex and delay such that age sometimes predicts delay for female victims but not for male victims. These data also suggest that, at least for female complainants, using age as a continuous variable may actually mask its predictive value. This could occur if some, but not all, ages are predictive of timeliness of complaints. These data suggest that early childhood and early adolescence are not predictive of delayed complaints for females. On the other hand, being in middle to late childhood or middle adolescence are both predictive of timeliness of complaint, although in opposite directions.

As can be seen in table 11.1, compared to timely complaints, complainants in the HCSA data were far more likely to have been subjected to very intrusive abuse involving penile penetration, threats, and alcohol. Indeed, the percentage of complaints involving vaginal or anal penetration was twice as large in the delayed complaints data compared to the timely complaints data. Moreover, compared to the percentage of timely complaints involving threats, the percentage of HCSA complaints involving threats was eleven times greater for females and more than four times greater for males. For female complainants, the presence of alcohol on the part of the accused was also associated with delayed complaints.

We studied each variable individually in terms of its association with timing of reports. Because we did not combine variables, it is possible that a variable in the HCSA data was associated with timing of disclosure because of its relationship with a third factor. For statistical and theoretical reasons we did not analyze more than one variable at a time. First, we only had access to summary information from the Badgley report and thus were restricted in terms of the types of analyses that were possible. Second, based on the current literature, we had no theoretical or empirical reason to combine abuse characteristics in particular ways. To provide readers with information needed to interpret the associations we found, in table 11.2 we present a correlation matrix of all variables that were included in the analyses.

As is clear from this table, some bivariate correlations were strong. Importantly, the three variables that were associated with seriousness of the offence were related. That is, the correlation between intrusiveness and threats was .24 and the correlation between threats and presence of alcohol was .11. Although each of these variables predicted delay when studied individually, the correlations suggest that they may not contribute independently to predicting

TABLE 11.2
Correlations Between Variables Associated With Delayed Disclosure

	Age (males)	Age (females)	Intrusive	Threats	Alcohol	Relation
Age (Males)	1.00	N/A				
Age (Females	N/A	1.00				
Intrusiveness	−.130**	.096**	1.00			
Threats	−.174**	−.061	.238**	1.00		
Alcohol	−.035	.021	.057*	.108**	1.00	
Relation	.252**	.096**	−.183**	−.053	−.076**	1.00

*p < .05. **p < .01.
Note: Coding of variables was as follows:
Intrusive, 1 = fondle, 2 = nonpenile penetration, 3 = penile penetration
Threats, 1 = no, 2 = yes
Alcohol, 1 = no, 2 = yes
Relation, 1 = incest, 2 = other blood relative, 3 = guardian, 4 = other family, 5 = position of trust, 6 = friend/acquaintance, 7 = other known person, 8 = stranger

delayed disclosure. More controlled research that studies co-occurring abuse characteristics is needed to disentangle the independent contribution of these three variables.

It is also interesting that as the age of the male complainant when the abuse began increased, the relationship between the complainant and the accused became more distant. And, for both males and females, a more distant relationship was correlated with less intrusive abuse. It would be premature to speculate on the reasons for these patterns of correlations. What we can say is that, at least in HCSA cases that go to trial, some offence characteristics tend to go together and the predictive power of some characteristics may be mediated through others.

In summary, three classes of variables reliably discriminated between timely and delayed official complaints of CSA. First, compared to timely complainants, there was a higher percentage of delayed complainants between the ages of 7 and 11 years when the alleged offence began and a smaller percentage of complainants who were between the ages of 14 and 15 years when the claimed abuse began. If this effect generalizes to other populations, it may help to explain the inconsistent effect of the child's age on timing of disclosure. Perhaps timing of disclosure is associated with particular ages and older and younger children predict timing in opposite directions. If this is the case, treating age as a continuous variable may actually mask its effect. Second, delayed complainants were subjected to very intrusive abuse including penetration, threats, and alcohol (for females only). Third, delayed complainants were more likely to have been abused by a family member or a person in a position of guardianship or trust. This latter effect may reflect the very serious implications of making a complaint to authorities and the heightened impact such a complaint may have if the child is closely associated with the accused. These hypotheses are offered cautiously because they are based on correlational data and bivariate analyses.

CLAIMED REPRESSION

By definition, delayed disclosure of CSA follows and requires a period of nondisclosure. In addition to the offence-related factors that have been studied as predictors of delayed disclosure (reviewed by London et al., chapter 2, this volume) there are subjective explanations provided by those who report having delayed disclosing their abuse. These subjective reasons include feelings of shame, feeling responsible, fear of being judged negatively, fear of not being believed, fear for others, threats or bribes, fear of the perpetrator, concern for the perpetrator, and memory failures (Badgley Report, 1984; Berliner & Conte, 1990; Gomes-Schwartz, Horowitz, & Cardarelli, 1990; Goodman-Brown et al., 2003; Ney, Moore, McPhee, & Trought, 1986; Roesler, 1994; Sas & Cunningham, 1995; Sauzier, 1989). Whereas these reasons vary widely, they consistently reflect the fact that the complainant was, apparently, always aware of the abusive experiences during the period of nondisclosure. For the complainants of interest in this section however, disclosure follows not so much a change of *willingness* to report but instead a change of one's *awareness* about the alleged abuse. In short, what was, apparently, previously unavailable to recall had, apparently, become available. It is certainly the case that altered awareness can reflect different understandings of events (such that what was not identified as sexual abuse later becomes so identified); however, we will focus here upon complainants whose awareness of the abusive events changed and who perceived an increase in their memory recall of CSA events. This kind of disclosure of CSA is qualitatively different from other disclosure patterns discussed because it is likely the change in mental, memory, or metacognitive state (in the extreme, from absolutely no awareness to detailed recall) that provides the foundation and perhaps motivation for the complainant's allegation. This stands in contrast to the complainant's need to overcome the previously described reasons in support of nondisclosure seen in continuous memory for CSA events.

The False Memory Debate: A Few Words of History

Readers are no doubt aware of the public and highly acrimonious "false memory" debate about *repressed* and *recovered* memories of abuse that has raged for the past 15 years, a debate between those who assert that many formerly repressed, recovered or *hidden memories* are false constructions or reconstructions of one's childhood, and those who assert that periods of a lack of awareness of abuse events are natural (if not inevitable) outcomes of CSA. Hundreds of academic research papers, books, and media communications have described this debate. The reader is referred to a number of resources for thorough, current, and differing perspectives on the debate (e.g., Brown, Scheflin, & Hammond, 1998; Conway, 1997; Davies & Dalgleish, 2001; Lynn & McConkey, 1998; Read & Lindsay, 1997). Our theoretical and scientific positions on the topic of repressed and recovered memories are neutral: Empirical evidence does support the reality of both false and recovered memories of abuse, an agreement only arduously achieved by the APA Working Group on Recovered Memories (1998).

It is safe to say that the concepts of *repression, memory recovery, dissociation,* and *trauma* were highly unfamiliar (and quite possibly foreign) to most experimental or cognitive psychologists before 1990. However, a number of events in academic and public arenas surfaced during the 1980s and '90s that piqued the experimentalists' interest in these concepts. First, society began to respond sympathetically to data on the surprisingly high prevalence rates of CSA, rates that far exceeded what had been considered accurate as late as the 1960s. Second, research exploring the effects of misleading information had well established the ease with which the details recalled of staged events could be altered in witnesses. Third, both the clinical and popular psychology literatures made frequent references to the memory-impairing consequences of certain kinds of experiences; however, on the basis of extant research many of these claims were judged by experimentalists to be unfounded, unsupportable, or egregiously in error. Fourth, allegations of frequent sexual activity in day care centers followed questionable child interviewing practices, an arena to which the misleading questions research could be easily applied. The fallout from these events affected all players in the ensuing debate: Well established experimental psychologists weighed in on the claims made about memory processes by clinical practitioners; individuals accused of CSA found support for their claims of innocence within the research studies; and support groups for both complainants and accused blossomed in response to the claims and counter-claims heard.

The contrast in professional responses to claims of continuous and non-continuous memories of abuse by complainants is absolutely striking. Complainants for whom recall of CSA events has always been (reportedly) available have received virtually no attention by memory psychologists. Indeed, many writers simply excluded discussion of continuous memory claims from the debate (Lindsay & Briere, 1997; Lindsay & Read, 1994, 1995). There is little doubt that these continuous memories, like all autobiographical experiences, contained both qualitative and quantitative errors, but their essential truth was never questioned by researchers, leaving that determination, if one was needed, to the courts instead. On the other hand, disclosures of CSA following memory-recovery activities (e.g., Brown et al, 1998; Corwin & Olafson, 1997; Pope, 1996) were received with skepticism and intense scrutiny (Loftus, 1993; Loftus & Guyer, 2002; Lindsay & Read, 1994). For these latter researchers, the focus was on the context in which recall occurred and whether it included "memory work" or suggestive interviewing (e.g., hypnosis and guided imagery) and retrieval (e.g. sodium amytal) techniques.

The context of greatest interest was that of psychotherapy because the possibility of suggestion and influence does exist within therapeutic interventions, and in the extreme, this context may foster the iatrogenic construction of an abuse history, cowritten by the client and therapist together. Indeed, early in the false memory debate, proponents of the repressed-memory perspective cited clinicians who sometimes encouraged the diagnosis of a "disguised presentation" for clients suspected of having been abused but who failed to report such histories (e.g., Gelinas, 1983). Some writers evidently took pride in revealing their sleuth-like abilities by announcing to clients that they knew their "secret" (Ellenson, 1985). Further, despite the absence of a reliable post-CSA syndrome, individual clinicians relied idiosyncratically upon favored symptoms as indicators of hidden or repressed memories of abuse (see Poole, Lindsay, Memon, & Bull 1994; Yapko, 1995). More recently, guidelines have been developed by numerous professional groups to assist therapists who treat clients with known or suspected abuse histories (see Grunberg & Ney, 1997).

In the U.S., the peak of legal activities involving accused abusers, complainants, and therapists appears to have been reached in 1994–95 (Lipton, 1999). Whether the subsequent decline reflects actual changes in therapeutic practices or in litigation strategies that seek to avoid the presentation of recovered memory testimony is unknown. For example, the principle of "delayed discovery" was used to toll civil statutes of limitation in regard to damages wrought by CSA with the initial effect being an increase in reports of repressed memories. Courts in the U.S. have more recently tested the scientific status of the concept of memory repression by the Daubert standard and have found it wanting (e.g., Gordon, 1998). As a result, fewer repressed memory cases are being heard (Lipton, 1999).

Followers of the false memory debate may have been led to believe that noncontinuous memories of abuse are normative in cases of CSA. Indeed, according to many writers (e.g., Brown et al., 1998) and the Supreme Court of Canada (M. K. v. M. H., 1992), memory impairment (*partial* or *complete amnesia*) is normative and to be expected in the majority of CSA victims. Closer inspection of the research data offered in support of this proposition, however, reveals other more mundane explanations for the reported high rates of memory impairment following CSA, including sampling and response biases as well as ordinary memory and inferential processes (see Read, 1999; Read & Lindsay, 2000; Schooler, Bendiksen, & Ambadar, 1997; Shobe & Schooler, 2001). Similarly, the APA Working Group concluded that most CSA victims remember all or part of their abuse experiences, and characterized conjunctions of complete amnesia and full recovery of CSA details as relatively rare (see also Andrews, 2001; Connolly & Read, 2003; Polusny & Follette, 1996).

Much debate has focused on the rates at which self-identified CSA victims report that they had forgotten or had impaired recall of the alleged abuse events. Unfortunately, these data are based upon respondents' retrospective assessments of what they did or did not remember at some point in the past (Schooler, Bendiksen, & Ambadar, 1997), and the frequent unreliability of retrospective judgments is well known both in psychology generally and specifically in clinical psychology. Furthermore, researchers have demonstrated the extent to which estimates of prior forgetting may be influenced by recent memory-retrieval activities, as may be found in therapeutic interventions (e.g., Belli, Winkielman, Read, Schwarz, & Lynn 1998; Brewin & Stokou, 2002; Read & Lindsay, 2000). That is, based upon an implicit theory of change or improvement resulting from memory-focused therapy (cf. Read & Lindsay, 2000; Ross, 1989), we can anticipate that when the quantity and quality of memories available at the end of therapy are compared with those seemingly available at the beginning of therapy, what was initially known will be seriously underestimated and interpreted as evidence of the memory-impairing effects of CSA events.

The HCSA Sample of Repressed Memories

The HCSA data may provide a window on the question of normativeness, but estimates of memory-impairment from these data must be tempered with the knowledge that complainants who are actually heard in court are but a small and nonrepresentative sample of all those who experienced CSA. Prosecution of a criminal charge of CSA would only be pursued to the court level if the victim pursued a criminal charge and if Crown believed there was a reasonable chance of conviction. Further, the HCSA data cannot fully inform us as to the factors that may have contributed to a report of impaired memory and, without information from the as-yet-unidentified individuals who are presently unaware of their abuse histories, we cannot discern how they differ from those for whom recall was eventually achieved. We can, however, examine the archival data to identify those variables that predict whether a complainant believes he or she was unaware of the alleged abuse for a substantial period of time. We recognize the limitations of these data: Information about disclosure data has been acquired in a second-hand fashion, through the eyes of a court, a body that neither questions the complainants' explanations for the purported memory difficulties nor seeks to arrive at a scientific explanation for such difficulties. For lack of a better word and to make contact with much of the literature, we will refer to these complainants who report noncontinuous memories as *repressed* memory complainants.

We coded complainants as having repressed memories on the basis of the written judgments. Repression was coded as present only if it was stated, explicitly or implicitly, that there was a time when the complainant would not have been able to recall the alleged abuse or that the complainant had "blocked out" critical and central details (e.g., identity of known perpetrator, for instance, a parent). All other cases were coded as repression absent (e.g., even if the complainant was unable to recall a subset of instances of the offence or some nonessential details of particular instances). Complainants for whom the court considered memory to have been completely absent were rare indeed: The majority of comments instead reflected the complainant's beliefs that periods of time existed in which portions of the abusive experiences and critical details (e.g., identity of the abuser) were unavailable to recall. Using this lenient criterion, 123 (6%) of all 2,064 complainants in our HCSA data set were coded as having reported repression.

The CSA literature identifies several variables that are anticipated to exacerbate the victim's emotional and cognitive responses to abuse, responses that may serve to reduce either the encoding or retrieval possibilities of memories for CSA experiences:

- the age of the complainant (as a result of infantile amnesia and impaired memory encoding) with younger ages thought to be more susceptible to impairment as a result of, *inter alia*, an inability to comprehend CSA experiences
- intrusiveness, frequency, and duration of abuse (with the greater intrusiveness or severity, frequency, and duration thought to lead to increased trauma, reduced encoding, and/or the memory impairment features of PTSD)
- the relationship of perpetrator to complainant (with more negative memorial consequences hypothesized for closer familial relationships as a result of denial, confusion, and thought avoidance)
- the use of physical or psychological threats and admonitions about secrecy (with the use of threat leading to thought avoidance and poorer recall)

To the extent that CSA features match the more extreme ranges or forms of abuse, the greater the likelihood that some form of psychotherapy may be sought. In addition, we included complainant sex because not only are males less likely to disclose sexual abuse experiences but also some researchers have found reported repression to be more prevalent among female than male complainants. There is inadequate space here to review the investigations of the roles these variables may play in memory repression. Suffice it to say that the outcomes have been mixed with, in our view, greater support for than against their predictive roles (for review, see Epstein & Bottoms, 1998, 2002).

Therapeutic intervention, of course, has been the whipping boy for memory-recovery claims. Some CSA memories may be false and a result of therapeutic intervention (and all agree that they can). On the other hand, it is also the case that if a person does have a repressed history of CSA, and a therapist is sought to assist with the individual's psychological adjustment, the therapy may certainly assist in the valid recovery of those CSA memories (and all agree that it could). Overall, 16% of our HCSA complainants were reported as having received therapy. Considering the central role of therapy and comparisons of clinical to nonclinical samples in the debate, we assigned complainants to either a Therapy ($n = 330$) or a No Therapy group ($n = 1,734$). Those complainants for whom the records omitted mention of therapeutic intervention comprised the latter category. An initial comparison of rates of reported repression in the two samples supported this dichotomy: Whereas 21% of the Therapy group reported repression, only 3% of the No Therapy group did so. Thus Therapy complainants were seven times more likely than No Therapy complainants to claim repression of CSA experiences.

Logistic regression was used to assess the relationships between claimed repression and the independent variables of sex and age of the complainant when the abuse began, intrusiveness, frequency, and duration of the abuse, relationship between the perpetrator and the complainant, and the presence of threats. For reasons discussed above, these regressions were completed separately for the Therapy and No Therapy samples. Overall, five variables proved to be significant ($p < .05$) or marginally significant ($p < .10$) for one or both samples. Neither the frequency of abuse nor relationship of perpetrator to complainant proved to be significant predictors in either sample.

Table 11.3 presents the percentages of therapy complainants who claimed repression for each of the variables that met the significance criteria. As may be seen, depending upon the specific level of the categorical variables represented, the percentage of complainants who claimed repression for abuse experiences ranged from 0.9% to 31.0%. Thus, of the seven variables explored and previously judged to be relevant to memory impairment, five were significant (or marginally so) within the Therapy sample and two significant (or marginally so) in the No Therapy group. Only sex of the complainant achieved statistical significance in both samples. Across samples, females were three to four times more likely than males to report repression.

The directions of the relationships were consistent with what has been predicted on the basis of other nonforensic samples. What is most striking about these outcomes is that it was only in the clinical subsample that the majority of previously identified "memory" variables predicted repression. In the No Therapy group, on the other hand, no features of the abuse predicted repression whereas sex of the complainant did so. In addition, complainant age was marginally predictive as may be seen in table 11.3 where the youngest age group demonstrated a substantially higher rate of reported repression than that reported by older children.

In summary, claims of repression in the Therapy Group but not in the No Therapy Group are predicted by both features of abuse and complainant. There are at least two broad perspectives on the interpretation of our data. First, from the skeptical view, one could argue that as a result of the therapeutic context, content, and experience, Therapy complainants developed specific beliefs about their memories and CSA. For example, the stereotypical view of CSA for some therapists may suggest that repression is most likely

TABLE 11.3

Percentage of Complainants in the Therapy and No Therapy Subsamples Who Claimed Repression of CSA Experiences

Variable	Therapy	No Therapy
Age		
1 to 6 years	31.0**	5.5*
7 to 9 years	13.2**	2.9*
10 to 12 years	21.7**	1.9*
13 to 19 years	10.9	3.2
Intrusiveness		
Expose/Fondle	13.7**	2.6
Penetration	13.2**	2.3
Penile Penetration	29.7	4.3
Sex		
Female	23.4**	3.7**
Male	7.3	0.9
Threat		
Present	28.1*	2.8
Absent	18.6	3.4
Duration		
.03 to 11 months.	12.2*	3.0
12 to 24 months.	16.9*	3.9
25 to 59 months.	30.4*	3.3
61 to 216 months.	21.0	1.5

Note: Variables determined to be significant predictors of repression are designated by $*p < .10$ and $**p < .05$.

when the abuse was severe, perpetrated against a young child, endured for a long time, and involved threats to maintain secrecy. As a result, the alleged abuse described in the legal process has features consistent with the therapist's view. A more general consequence of memory-recovery activities engaged in during therapy, however, may also provide an explanation for the higher rates of reported repression in the Therapy group. Specifically, given what CSA information was perceived as readily available in recall at the end of therapy, complainants may have inferred that recall must have been seriously impaired and their memories blocked or inhibited in some way at the beginning of therapy (see Brewin & Stokou, 2002 for a similar argument).

Alternatively, from the contrasting perspective, one could as easily argue that it is precisely those individuals who have suffered abuse at the earliest age and at the greatest severity who are in most need of therapeutic assistance and who, as result of CSA's memory-impairing effects most frequently reported repression. When we compared Therapy and No Therapy groups on the variables used to predict repression we found interesting patterns. Those who were in therapy were younger when the abuse began ($M = 8.93$ years) than were those who were not reported to have been in therapy (M = 9.47 years) and the abuse was alleged to have occurred for a longer duration among those in therapy (M = 49.88 months) than those not reported to have been in therapy (M = 37.70 months). Moreover, when comparing across the three levels of intrusiveness, there was a higher percentage of complainants who were in therapy in the most intrusive level than in the least intrusive level (the percentage of complainants who claimed abuse levels 1, 2, and 3 and who were in therapy was 9.29%, 16.91%, and 22.73%, respectively). Similarly, a higher percentage of females (18.09%) than males (11.13%) were in therapy and a higher percentage of complainants who alleged having been threatened (19.6%) than those who did not claim to have been threatened (15.85%) were in therapy. In other words, the variables that predicted claims of repression, also predicted whether a complainant would be in therapy. One might assume that comparisons of the Therapy and No Therapy groups on all demographic and abuse characteristics might inform us accurately as to pretherapeutic differences in complainants and abuse characteristics. Unfortunately, because all of our archival information derives from retrospective recall by complainants given in courts of law, there are no variables that can accurately reflect "ground truth". Even complainants' recall of their ages at the time of abuse may be over- or underestimated as a result of social context and expectation. Further, the written judgments only very rarely indicated at what point the complainant entered therapy or at what point the complainant "recovered" memories of CSA, before, during, or after therapy. Recent work by Andrews et al. (1999, 2000) as well as Brewin and Andrews (2001) of large samples of therapy clients in the United Kingdom suggests that whereas for a minority of clients (22%) there was an opportunity for an iatrogenic basis to their CSA memories, for the majority of clients there was not. However, if similar opportunities for the production of false memories existed within the Canadian therapy contexts and if claimed repression accompanied fabricated memories of abuse, our result that 21% of Therapy complainants reported repression is at least consistent with the Brewin and Andrews data and this possibility. In summary we are presently unable to discriminate between these two broad interpretations or variations on them. However, on the face of these data, concerns (e.g., Lindsay & Read, 1994; Loftus, 1993; McNally, 2004; Read & Lindsay, 2000) that the clinical samples reported in previous studies (e.g, Briere & Conte, 1994; Herman & Schatzow, 1987) are not representative of all CSA survivors would appear to be well justified (cf. Epstein & Bottoms, 1998, 2002).

As this chapter was being written, we learned of an as-yet unpublished research project by Ghetti et al. (in press) that sought answers to similar questions and from a forensic sample. The respondents (n = 138) in Ghetti et al.'s survey had all been victims of documented CSA some 13 years earlier and who had, as children, testified as to their abuse experiences, and had received psychological counseling in connection with the experience of investigation, prosecution, and beyond. Like Williams' (1994) seminal work, the Ghetti et al. study was prospective in kind because complete and accurate documents from the original investigations could be compared to the victims' current knowledge. Similarly, like the Williams study, the researchers' knowledge of the prior prosecution was not divulged to the respondents, not all of whom disclosed abuse when given the opportunity (also like members of Williams' sample). However, for those who did, the authors were interested to determine the frequency with which the members of the sample reported having forgotten the CSA experiences for some period of time and whether such forgetting might be predicted by a range of abuse and complainant characteristics. They also explored a range of individual difference variables, the subjective nature of the reports, and the match between documented and remembered abuse features. We focus here only on the claims of having forgotten the CSA experiences.

Several findings overlap with the data reported above. First, forgetting was infrequent with 21 of 138 (15%) who reported a prior period of no memory for the abuse. The percentage obtained in our Therapy group was 21%. Second, two of the variables that predicted repression in our Therapy sample also predicted forgetting in the Ghetti et al. sample. These were abuse severity (using a scale highly similar to that of intrusiveness) and complainant sex. Greater severity was predictive of more frequently reported forgetting. In contrast to our data and others (e.g., Epstein & Bottoms, 2002), males in the Ghetti et al. sample were more, not less, likely to claim forgetting than females. Finally, of interest is a significant positive correlation obtained between the reported number of days in therapy by Ghetti et al.'s participants and claimed forgetting with more forgetting with more therapeutic days. This latter finding adds some support to our suggestion that claimed repression may reflect discounted estimates of prior availability of CSA experiences to recall as a result of expectations about the benefits of memory-recovery activities in therapy.

LIMITATIONS

There are some important limitations of these data. First, there are at least two potentially important and related groups of CSA victims who are not included in the data: those who would have pursued a criminal charge but could not because the Crown declined to proceed to trial (i.e., exercised prosecutorial discretion to refuse to go to trial) and those complainants whose cases were heard in Provincial Courts where the decision was not forwarded to Quicklaw. Importantly, the majority of criminal cases are heard in provincial courts. It is not possible, from these data, to estimate the size of the absent groups or to determine if they are different, in predictable ways, from those complainants who are represented in these data. That is an empirical question that we believe is worth pursuing. We can say, however, that the cases included in these data comprise a reasonably comprehensive set of cases that is available to legal professionals and policy makers who will make decisions related to law, social policy, resource allocation, and research funding that affect HCSA survivors and HCSA researchers.

Second, the judge decides which facts will be recorded in the judgment and which facts will be omitted. We were only able to record information about a variable if relevant information was included in the decision. For the most part, this shortfall had its greatest impact on statistical power: If the judge did not provide relevant information, the cell was assigned a missing-data code and excluded from the analyses. There are a few notable exceptions: therapy, repression, and threats. It is unlikely that a judge would report the absence of these factors (i.e., "this complainant did not repress memory for the abuse" or "this complainant was not in therapy" or "this complainant did not report threats"). Thus, if the factor was not mentioned, it was coded as absent (e.g., no repression, no therapy, no threats, respectively) and included in the analyses. Of course, it is possible that the judge failed to mention the factor because it was deemed legally irrelevant. We submit that this is unlikely for the repress and threat variables, as they would be deemed legally relevant in most cases. However, it may be that some complainants who were recorded as not being in therapy were, in fact, receiving or had received some form of counseling and the judge simply failed to mention this fact in the decision.

Third, many of the offences included in this analysis occurred in the late 1970s and early 1980s. It is possible that factors articulated here are now less likely to discourage timely reporting of the offence. As imperfect as these data are, they are the best data we can obtain: There is no way to compare timely and delayed complaints in the year 2004 because there is no way to identify current CSA victims who will delay reporting for many years.

SUMMARY AND CONCLUSION

The delayed prosecution of CSA is a growing and important social and forensic phenomenon that has sparked debate, primarily in jurisdictions that do not have statutes of limitations on serious criminal offences. Explanations for delayed prosecution may be nonmemory based (i.e., characteristics of the offence) or memory based (i.e., reported repression). Our analyses of delayed and timely official complaints of CSA suggest that nonmemorial factors are important in understanding why some complainants wait a very long time before making an official complaint. In our analyses, being young and subjected to very intrusive abuse involving threats and alcohol by a person who is close to the child is associated with delayed reports of CSA. However, the correlations suggest that some abuse characteristics tend to co-occur and this greatly complicates the interpretation of predictors of delayed reporting of CSA. A small percentage of such complainants report having repressed and subsequently recovered memory for the offense. Not surprisingly, variables that predict repression are complex and moderated by other factors, most notably whether the complainant was reported to have been in therapy. This project represents a step toward understanding the complexities of HCSA prosecutions. These data can be used to stimulate continued research as well as to develop recommendations that will inform the ongoing discussion concerning criminal prosecution of HCSA.

ACKNOWLEDGMENTS

This research was supported by a Social Sciences and Humanities Research Council of Canada operating grant to the first author and an Alberta Law Foundation and Natural Sciences and Engineering Research Council of Canada grant to the second author. We thank Jennifer Lavoie and Pamela Van-Norden-Schaefer for invaluable assistance with data analyses.

REFERENCES

Alpert, J. L., Brown, L. S., Ceci, S. J., Courtois, C. A., Loftus, E. F., & Ornstein, P. A. (1998). Final conclusions of the American Psychological Association working group of investigation of memories of childhood abuse. *Psychology, Public Policy, and Law, 4,* 933–40.

Andrews, B. (2001). Recovered memories in therapy: Clinicians' beliefs and practices. In G. M. Davies & T. Dalgleish (Eds.), *Recovered memories: Seeking the middle ground* (pp.189–204). Chichester: Wiley.

Andrews, B., Brewin, C. R., Ochera, J., Morton, J., Bekerian, D. A., Davies, G. M., et al. (1999). Characteristics, context and consequences of memory recovery among adults in therapy. *British Journal of Psychiatry, 175,* 141–46.

Andrews, B., Brewin, C. R., Ochera, J., Morton, J., Bekerian, D. A., Davies, G. M., et al. (2000). The timing, triggers and qualities of recovered memories in therapy. *British Journal of Clinical Psychology, 39,* 11–26.

Arata, C. M. (1998). To tell or not to tell: Current functioning of child sexual abuse survivors who disclosed their victimization. *Child Maltreatment, 3,* 63–71.

Badgley Report. (1984). Report of the Committee on Sexual Offences Against Children and Youths. In Sexual Offences Against Children: Vol. 1. Ottawa: Ministry of Supply and Services Canada.

Beitchman, J. H., Zucker, K. J., Hood, J. E., DaCosta, G. A., Akman, D., & Cassavia, E. (1992). A review of the long-term effects of child sexual abuse. *Child Abuse & Neglect, 16,* 101–18.

Berliner, L., & Conte, J.R. (1990). The process of victimization: The victims' perspective. *Child Abuse & Neglect, 19,* 29–49.

Brewin, C. R., & Stokou, L. (2002). Validating reports of poor childhood memory. *Applied Cognitive Psychology, 16,* 509–14.

Briere, J., & Conte, J. (1993). Self-reported amnesia for abuse in adults molested as children. *Journal of Traumatic Stress, 6,* 21–31.

Briere, J., & Runtz, M. (1988). Symptomology associated with childhood sexual victimization in a nonclinical adult sample. *Child Abuse & Neglect, 12,* 51–59.

Brown, D., Scheflin, A. W., & Hammond, C. D. (1998). *Memory, trauma treatment, and the law.* New York: Norton.

Browne, A., & Finkelhor, D. (1986). Impact of child sexual abuse: A review of the research. *Psychological Bulletin, 99*, 66–77.

Connolly, D. A., & Read, J. D. (2003). Remembering historic child sexual abuse. *Criminal Law Quarterly, 47*, 438–80.

Conway, M. A. (Ed.) (1997). *Recovered memories and false memories.* Oxford: Oxford University Press.

Corwin, D. L., & Olafson, E. (1997). Videotaped discovery of a reportedly unreportable memory of child sexual abuse: Comparison with a childhood interview videotaped 11 years before. *Child Maltreatment, 2*, 91–112.

Davies, G. D., & Dalgleish, T. (Eds.) (2001). *Recovered memories: Seeking the middle ground.* Chichester: Wiley.

DeVoe, E. R., & Faller, K. C. (1999). The characteristics of disclosure among children who may have been sexually abused. *Child Maltreatment, 4*, 217–27.

Di Pietro, E. K., Runyan, D. K., & Fredrickson, D. D. (1997). Predictors of disclosure during medical evaluation for suspected sexual abuse. *Journal of Child Sexual Abuse, 6*, 133–42.

Ellenson, G. S. (1985). Detecting a history of incest: A predictive syndrome. *Social Casework: The Journal of Contemporary Social Work, 66*, 525–32.

Elliott, D., & Briere, J. (1995). Post-traumatic stress associated with delayed recall of sexual abuse: A general population study. *Journal of Traumatic Stress, 8*, 629–47.

Epstein, M. A., & Bottoms, B. L. (1998). Memories of childhood sexual abuse: A survey of young adults. *Child Abuse & Neglect, 22*, 1217–38.

Epstein, M. A., & Bottoms, B. L. (2002). Explaining the forgetting and recovery of abuse and trauma memories: Possible mechanisms. *Child Maltreatment, 7*, 210–25.

Finkelhor, D., Hotaling, G., Lewis, I. A., & Smith, C. (1990). Sexual abuse in a national survey of adult men and women: Prevalence, characteristics, and risk factors. *Child Abuse and Neglect, 14*, 19–28.

Gelinas, D. (1983). The persisting negative effects of incest. *Psychiatry, 46*, 313–32.

Ghetti, S., Edelstein, R. S., Goodman, G. S., Cordòn, I. M., Quas, J. A., Alexander, K. W., Redlich, A. D., & Jones, D. P. H. (in press). What can subjective forgetting tell us about memory for childhood trauma? Memory & Cognition.

Gomes-Schwartz, B., Horowitz, J. M., & Cardarelli, A. P. (1990). *Child sexual abuse: The initial effects.* Newbury Park, CA: Sage.

Goodman-Brown, T. B., Edelstein, R. S., Goodman, G. S., Jones, D. P. H., & Gordon, D. S. (2003). Why children tell: A model of children's disclosure of sexual abuse. *Child Abuse & Neglect, 27*, 525–40.

Gordon, J. D. (1998). Admissibility of repressed memory evidence by therapists in sexual abuse cases. *Psychology, Public Policy, and Law, 4*, 1198–1225.

Gries, L. T., Goh, D. S., Andrews, M. B., Gilbert, J., Praver, F., & Stelzer, D. N. (2000). Positive reaction to disclosure and recovery from child sexual abuse. *Journal of Child Sexual Abuse, 9*, 29–51.

Grunberg, F., & Ney, T. (1997). Professional guidelines on clinical practice for recovered memory: A comparative analysis. In J. D. Read & D. S. Lindsay (Eds.), *Recollections of trauma: Scientific evidence and clinical practice* (pp. 541–56). New York: Plenum.

Hazzard, A., Celano, M., Gould, J., Lawry, S., & Webb, C. (1995). Predicting symptomology and self-blame among child sexual abuse victims. *Child Abuse & Neglect, 19*, 707–14.

Herman, J., & Schatzow, E. (1987). Recovery and verification of memories of childhood sexual trauma. *Psychoanalytic Psychology, 4*, 1–14.

Home Affairs Committee (2002). The conduct of investigations into past cases of abuse in children's homes: Fourth report of session 2001–02. Retrieved January 15, 2004 from http://www.publications.parliament.uk/pa/cm200102/cmselect/cmhaff/cmhaff.htm

Lamb, S., & Edgar-Smith, S. (1994). Aspects of disclosure mediators of outcome of childhood sexual abuse. *Journal of Interpersonal Violence, 9,* 307–26.

Lindsay, D. S., & Briere, J. (1997). The controversy regarding recovered memories of childhood sexual abuse: Pitfalls, bridges, and future directions. *Journal of Interpersonal Violence, 12,* 631–47.

Lindsay, D. S., & Read, J. D. (1994). Psychotherapy and memories of childhood sexual abuse: A cognitive perspective. *Applied Cognitive Psychology, 8,* 281–338.

Lindsay, D. S., & Read, J. D. (1995). "Memory work" and recovered memories of childhood sexual abuse: Scientific evidence and public, professional, and personal issues. *Psychology, Public Policy, and Law, 1,* 846–908.

Lipton, A. (1999). Recovered memories in the courts. In S. Taub (Ed.), The legal treatment of recovered memories of child sexual abuse (pp.166–210). Springfield, IL: Charles C. Thomas.

Lipton, M. (1997). The effect of the primary caretaker's distress on the sexually abused child: A comparison of biological and foster parents. *Child and Adolescent Social Work Journal, 14,* 115–27.

Loftus, E. F. (1993). The reality of repressed memories. *American Psychologist, 48,* 518–37.

Loftus, E. F., & Guyer, M. J. (2002). Who abused Jane Doe?: The hazards of a single case history: Part 1. *Skeptical Inquirer, 26,* 24–32.

Lynn, S. J., & McConkey, K. M. (Eds.) (1998). *Truth in memory.* New York: Guilford.

McNally, R. (2004). The science and folklore of traumatic amnesia. *Clinical Psychology & Science and Practice, 11,* 29–33.

Melchert, T. P., & Parker, L. (1997). Different forms of childhood abuse and memory. *Child Abuse and Neglect, 21,* 125–35.

M.(K.) v. M.(H.), [1992] 3 S.C.R. 6.

National Center for Victims of Crime (1998). Extensions of the criminal & civil statutes of limitations in child sexual abuse cases. Retrieved January 15, 2004, from http://www.ndaa-apri.org/apri/programs/ncpca/ncpca_home.html.

Ney, P. G., Moore, C., McPhee, M., & Trought, P. (1986). Child abuse: A study of the child's perspective. *Child Abuse & Neglect, 10,* 511–18.

Paine, M. L., & Hansen, D. J. (2002). Factors influencing children to self-disclose sexual abuse. *Clinical Psychology Review, 22,* 271–95.

Polusny, M., & Follette, V. (1996). Remembering childhood sexual abuse: A national survey of psychologists' clinical practices, beliefs and personal experiences. *Professional Psychology: Research and Practice, 27,* 41–52.

Poole, D. A., Lindsay, D. S., Memon, A., & Bull, R. (1995). Psychotherapy and the recovery of memories of childhood sexual abuse: U.S. and British practitioners' opinions, practices, and experiences. *Journal of Consulting and Clinical Psychology, 63,* 426–37.

Quas, J. A., Goodman, G. S., & Jones, D. P. H. (2003). Predictors of attributions of self-blame and internalizing behavior problems in sexually abused children. *Journal of Child Psychology and Psychiatry, 44,* 723–26.

Read, J. D. (1999). The recovered/false memory debate: Three steps forward, two steps back? *Expert Evidence, 7,* 1–24.

Read, J. D., & Lindsay, D. S. (Eds.) (1997). *Recollections of trauma: Scientific evidence and clinical practice.* New York: Plenum.

Read, J. D., & Lindsay, D. S. (2000). "Amnesia" for summer camps and high school graduation: Memory work increases reports of prior periods of remembering less. *Journal of Traumatic Stress, 13*, 129–47.

Roesler, T. A. (1994). Reactions to disclosure of childhood sexual abuse. *The Journal of Nervous and Mental Disease, 182*, 618–24.

Ross, M. (1989). Relation of implicit theories to the construction of personal histories. *Psychological Review, 96*, 341–357.

Runyan, D. K. (1998). Prevalence, risk, sensitivity, and specificity: A commentary on the epidemiology of child sexual abuse and the development of a research agenda. *Child Abuse & Neglect, 22*, 493–98.

Sas L. D., & Cunningham A.H. (1995). *Tipping the balance to tell the secret: Public discovery of child sexual abuse.* London: London Family Court Clinic.

Sauzier, M. (1989). Disclosure of child sexual abuse: For better or worse. *Psychiatric Clinics of North America, 12*, 455–69.

Schooler, J. W., Bendiksen, M., & Ambadar, Z. (1997). Taking the middle line: Can we accommodate both fabricated and recovered memories of sexual abuse? In M. A. Conway (Ed.), *Recovered memories and false memories* (pp. 251–92). Oxford: Oxford University Press.

Shobe, K. K., & Schooler, J. W. (2001). Discovering fact and fiction: Case-based analyses of authentic and fabricated discovered memories of abuse. In G. W. Davies & T. Dalgleish (Eds.), *Recovered memories: Seeking the middle ground* (pp. 95–152). Chichester: Wiley.

Shuman, D. W., & Smith, A. M. (2000). *Justice and the prosecution of old crimes: Balancing legal, psychological, and moral concerns.* Washington: American Psychological Association.

Sjöberg, R. L., & Lindblad, F. (2002). Delayed disclosure and disrupted communication during forensic investigation. *Acta Paediatrica, 91*, 1391–96.

Sorenson, T., & Snow, B. (1991). How children tell: The process of disclosure in child sexual abuse. *Child Welfare, LXX*, 3–15.

Smith, D. W., Letourneau, E. J., Saunders, B. E., Kilpatrick, D. G., Resnick, H. S., & Best, C. L. (2000). Delay in disclosure of childhood rape: Results from a national survey. *Child Abuse & Neglect, 24*, 273–87.

Williams, L. R. (1994). Recall of childhood trauma: A prospective study of womens' memories of child sexual abuse. *Journal of Consulting and Clinical Psychology, 62*, 1167–72.

Williams, L. R. (1995). Recovered memories of abuse in women with documented sexual victimization histories. *Journal of Traumatic Stress, 8*, 649–73.

Yapko, M. (1995). *Suggestions of abuse: true and false memories of childhood sexual trauma.* New York: Simon & Schuster.

APPENDIX A
Definition of Categorical Variables

Variable Name	Coding
The Offence	*Abuse 1:* expose, fondle *Abuse 2:* masturbate, simulate intercourse, oral sex, digital penetration, attempt penile penetration *Abuse 3:* vaginal or anal penetration
Description of Frequency	A *pattern:* number of times per day/week/month/year, a pattern, regularly, every opportunity, a series, "would," different times, diverse dates A *lot:* hundreds, often, a lot, frequently, again and again, over and over, continuous, long-term, many, quite a few, substantial number, numerous, a number of times, an unspecified number, 21 or more instances were reported; A *few:* multiple, several, various, occasions, periodic, few, more than one, "offenses"
Relationship Between Complainant and Accused	*Parent:* mother or father (biological, common-law, step, or foster) *Other relative:* brother, sister, cousin, uncle, grandfather (biological, common-law, step, or foster) *Friend/Acquaintance:* boarder, mother's boyfriend, family friend, neighbor, parent of childhood friend, employer, babysitter *Community connection:* religious leader, mental health facilitator (e.g., psychiatrist, big brother) medical professional, educator

APPENDIX B
Recoding for Comparison with Badgley Data

Variable Name	Coding
Relationship Between Complainant and Accused	*Incest:* any blood relative other than those listed under "other blood relative" *Other blood relative:* aunt, uncle, cousin, niece, nephew *Guardianship position:* step-/foster father, male legal guardian, male employer/supervisor *Other family member:* adopted/foster/stepmother, adopted father, adopted/foster brother or sister, adopted grandparent, common-law mother, father, brother, sister, in-laws, step aunt or uncle. *Position of trust:* teacher, day care worker, doctor, dentist, babysitter, social worker, religious leader, big brother, big sister, school-bus driver, crossing guard, youth worker, counselor *Friend/Acquaintance:* a person known to the child who was a girlfriend or boyfriend, personal friends, family friends, acquaintances, neighbors *Other person:* other persons, not included in other categories, who was known to the child *Stranger:* person whose identify was unknown to the child

III

CLINICAL, LEGAL, AND POLICY IMPLICATIONS OF THE RESEARCH ON WHEN AND WHY CHILDREN DO AND DO NOT DISCLOSE ABUSE

12

A Holistic Approach to Interviewing and Treating Children in the Legal System

Karen J. Saywitz
University of California, Los Angeles

Phillip Esplin
Private Practice, Phoenix, Arizona

Sarah L. Romanoff
Los Angeles, California

In a safe and just society, children are protected from physical and emotional harm and adults are protected from unfair accusation and punishment. This is the overarching goal of contemporary social institutions that address the problem of child maltreatment. Reaching this goal requires balancing and prioritizing forensic and clinical objectives that are sometimes at odds with each other, and coordinating the efforts of social services, legal, and mental health systems that sometimes work at cross purposes. At present, however, there is insufficient knowledge on which to build a more integrated approach to practice and policy.

Over the years, three distinct subsystems have evolved to address both alleged and actual child maltreatment: the criminal justice system, the child protection system (CPS), and the mental health system. Although the structure in its entirety is fragmented, the interaction among subsystems is considerable and increasing (Finkelhor, Cross, & Cantor, 2005). In the case of sexual abuse, there is direct overlap because sexual abuse is considered a crime as well as an instance of maltreatment from which children are to be protected, and is a potentially traumatic event that may require mental health services for recovery. The child-witness is often involved in all three systems concurrently. When adults are falsely accused of child maltreatment, equally important challenges arise requiring comparable levels of cooperation among subsystems to resolve uncertainties. Hence, it has become increasingly clear that a more holistic approach is necessary. However, such an approach requires a knowledge base founded on greater mutual awareness of the respective research efforts and practice parameters of the forensic and clinical traditions. This chapter is one step towards that end.

First, we review the distinctions between the forensic and clinical approaches to gathering information from children that have emerged from previous research. Then we highlight areas of overlap that require researchers to change course and consider new opportunities for research that flow from a more holistic perspective. In this effort we discuss potential innovations derived from the clinical literature that could improve forensic interview techniques, especially when children offer vague or contradictory information, making it difficult to substantiate or reject unconfirmed suspicions of abuse. Likewise, we discuss solutions derived from the forensic field that could improve therapeutic interventions so that children's mental health needs are met without tainting their reports.

FORENSIC AND CLINICAL PERSPECTIVES: POINTS OF SEPARATION AND OVERLAP

Differences Between Forensic and Clinical Interviews

We start by clarifying key differences between forensic and clinical interviews, acknowledging that there is no single gold-standard protocol that defines either one. Forensic interviews are conducted for the purpose of determining whether legal action should be taken. Often the goal is to gather facts to support or dispute an allegation by providing an opportunity for children to report as much accurate information as they can, in their own words. The forensic interviewer is primarily a fact finder, objectively gathering details of legal relevance. Forensic interviewers typically remain supportive but refrain from developing a relationship that might unduly influence a child's report. A forensic interviewer might identify symptoms in need of treatment merely through observation. Or, important information may spontaneously arise related to safety through comments that reveal a child's propensity for running away, drug use, suicidal ideation or self-destructive behavior. However, if the interview is intended to serve a legal purpose, typically the forensic interviewer would not attempt to address or evaluate clinical symptoms in order to minimize the risk of distorting children's reports. Instead the child is often referred to a clinician for evaluation or monitoring.

The goals of the clinical interview are diagnosis, treatment planning, and symptom reduction; a basic aim of the therapeutic interview is to effect cognitive, behavioral, and emotional change. Hence, the clinician strives to build an alliance with the child through warmth and empathy. The child's behaviors and perceptions are central. There is great variability among therapists regarding detailed discussions of what actually occurred. There is no obligation when obtaining information relating to diagnosis or treatment to make a determination about how reliable the child may be as a historian; hence, there is less demand to pursue alternative hypotheses regarding children's statements or behaviors. For the forensic interviewer, objectivity is critical, remaining neutral to the veracity of the information provided. The therapist, however, might take on the role of advocate, educator, role model, or coach (Deblinger & Heflin, 1996).

With regards to documentation, forensic interviewers strive to document as much as possible, preferably via electronic recording, so that exact questions and verbatim responses are preserved. In contrast, therapeutic goals impose no such requirement. Hence, verbatim comments by children are rarely electronically preserved. Also, the parameters relating to confidentiality are not comparable. While forensic interviewers generally discuss with the child, in age-appropriate language, the absence of the confidential privilege and make it understood to legal guardians that the results may be used in litigation, confidentiality is a cornerstone of the therapeutic endeavor.

The value of maintaining such distinctions between forensic and clinical approaches is made clear in the following example: If in the course of treatment, a child reveals forensically relevant information and the therapist responds by interrogating the child in detail and is then called to testify, the therapist may be required to answer questions regarding the entire treatment (as well as the forensic event), revealing information provided in confidence. The child's trust in the therapist may be compromised and the therapeutic alliance undermined. Instead, if the child is referred to a forensic interviewer for detailed questioning, while continuing in therapy with the original therapist, the forensic interviewer could testify with little consequence to ongoing treatment.

For these and other reasons, scholars have highlighted the precariousness of dual roles (e.g., a mental health professional who treats and investigates either a victim or a perpetrator) (e.g., Melton, 1994; but see Sattler, 1998) and the dangers of blurring the distinctions between clinical and forensic efforts. Professional organizations recommend instead that forensic interviews of children suspected of victimization be conducted separately from therapeutic efforts, in separate sessions by different professionals, often with limited sharing of information between the two (e.g., American Academy of Child and Adolescent Psychiatry, 1998; American Professional Society on the Abuse of Children, 1997; American Psychological Association, 1998).

The blurring of these distinctions has caused serious harm to children, adults, and families while the growing tendency to respect these distinctions has enabled promising progress. Important strides have been made on the forensic side with the development of multidisciplinary child interview centers and research-based interview methods, and on the clinical side with regard to the development of efficacious therapies for treating posttraumatic symptoms of sexually abused children. However, now that visible boundaries and safeguards are being put into practice, researchers can undertake a more inclusive agenda that draws from the literatures of both fields. Greater cross-pollination may well produce research strategies that neither field could successfully develop alone.

Points of Overlap: The Need for a More Holistic Approach

At the interface of the clinical and forensic perspectives is a subset of complicated cases that exemplify the need for a more holistic approach to research. From the outset it is important to understand that many of these cases involve children who come to the attention of the CPS and police but who have not truly been abused. Out of the 2.6 million reports of child abuse each year in the United States, on average about 67% of reports are accepted by CPS for investigation or assessment; the rest are screened out quickly (Finkelhor et al., 2005). In the states where only serious allegations are formally investigated, a large majority of "screened-in"cases (approximately 70%) involve less serious allegations and lower levels of risk. These are not opened for investigation at all but are instead assessed by CPS only for the possibility of needed services (see Finkelhor et al., 2005, for further discussion of case flow).

The remainder of cases are formally investigated by CPS to determine whether suspicions of abuse are either substantiated or unfounded. In some states, there is third category, referred to as "inconclusive," denoting there is evidence consistent with abuse but not strong enough to substantiate or discredit the allegation. Only a few states track intentionally false cases. Where tracked, these tend to occur in less than 1% of all investigations (see Finkelhor, et al., 2005, for discussion). Referrals from CPS to police and prosecutors occur primarily at the stage of formal investigation. As part of the investigative process a majority of children undergo an interview. It is estimated that in over 90% of reports to police involve child interviews and that 46% to 60% of reports to CPS involve child interviews (see Finkelhor et al., 2005, for discussion).

To illustrate the need for a holistic approach, we turn our focus to the subgroup of these children who fail to provide unambiguous, straightforward information in these interviews, making it difficult to substantiate or reject unconfirmed suspicions of abuse. There are many reasons why children fail to provide clear, decisive information, including developmental limitations of memory or communication, coaching and external pressure from adults, and poor or suggestive interview techniques, to name a few well-researched topics from the existing literature. In this chapter, however, we focus on cases in which children experience motivational or emotional conflicts, and cognitive or behavioral impairments that complicate the information-gathering process —cases in which special methods may needed to elicit information sufficient to detect false denials and false allegations. It is likely that many of these children are not abused, but their statements are so contradictory, or difficult to interpret that some children create false allegations or at least fail to definitively dispel adult concerns. Likewise, a sizable cluster is children who have been abused but are afraid or unable to articulate their experiences clearly.

Some portion of these cases will fall into the inconclusive category. It is difficult to estimate the size of this population because most states and studies require evaluators to make a dichotomous decision—substantiated or unsubstantiated—and do not provide for an "inconclusive" category. Estimates of inconclusive results from national surveys of CPS evaluations vary from 23% to 4%, depending on the state (DHHS, 2004). Small studies of non-CPS evaluations estimate that in about 10% to 15% of cases children make no statement of abuse or discrepant statements, despite strong external evidence that abuse occurred (e.g., Keary & Fitzpatrick, 1994; Elliott & Briere, 1994). Herman (2005) proposes a scheme in which 10% to 20% of cases are classified as inconclusive. Without going into the details of these studies, suffice it to say that a group exists that cannot be ignored given the dire consequences of either false allegation or false denial. It is a group that may benefit greatly from a more integrated approach to research, one that ideally decreases the likelihood of both errors.

In some of these cases, there may be physical or medical evidence that causes professionals continuing concern, despite no disclosure of abuse. There may be age-inappropriate sexual knowledge or behavior (e.g., sexual overtures to other children, re-enactment of sex acts), high risk of imminent danger (e.g., child expresses fear of harm from care taker–suspect with continued access to child), or serious mental health problems, but no clear disclosure of abuse. Of course any of these behaviors or symptoms could be caused by other events (e.g., exposure to pornography), other motivations (e.g., fear of retaliation for misbehavior) or psychiatric disorders (e.g., Reactive Attachment Disorder) that have nothing to do with sexual abuse. Nonetheless, these children are often placed in treatment for monitoring of risk factors, suspicious behaviors (e.g., age-inconsistent sexual behavior), or psychiatric symptoms (e.g., nightmares, sleep disorders, anxiety attacks, flashbacks) forcing a mix of therapeutic and forensic goals.

When children are involved in multiple systems simultaneously, forensic interviews occur not in isolation but in the context of other interviews conducted for social service purposes (e.g., risk of danger if returned home, placement in foster care, custody arrangements, family reunification) as well as clinical purposes (e.g., diagnosis and treatment). There are myriad opportunities for disclosure of genuine abuse outside formal investigative interviews, as well as opportunities for suggestion or misinterpretation. The information-gathering phase becomes a prolonged process during which innocent adults incur multiple losses as legal cases drag on (e.g., loss of reputation, income, future employment opportunities, friendships, and contact with family and other support systems). Children become involved in greater levels of clinical intervention. While this may in turn increase the likelihood of additional forensically-relevant information emerging over time, it may also increase the potential for contamination, misunderstanding, or suggestion. Hence, this scenario calls for a broader conceptualization of the information-gathering process, the contexts in which it unfolds, and the circumstances under which forensic interview guidelines are called into play.

An array of therapeutic interventions are available in the community, but their effects on children's memories are relatively unknown—because they were not designed for the purpose of preserving and protecting the reliability of children's statements during this extended phase of information-gathering. Without the requisite research or guidelines, there is concern that if children are referred to therapists after formal forensic interviews are inconclusive, therapists will use questionable techniques with children who have no memories of abuse, thereby creating false allegations among nonabused children and ultimately compromising the credibility of those who have been abused.

For example, memory-recovery techniques like hypnosis have been used with adults, but in some states witnesses are prohibited from testifying if they have undergone hypnosis during therapy to refresh or generate memories, in part because of concerns that these techniques may increase false allegations (Lynn, Lock, Loftus, Krackow, & Lilienfeld, 2003). Similar concerns exist when children provide clear disclosures of abuse in formal forensic interviews and are then referred for treatment of posttraumatic symptoms while still involved in lengthy legal proceedings—that therapeutic techniques will alter testimony.

On the other hand, when children are not referred, their mental health needs remain unidentified and unmet. This is already a serious problem in the United States; it is estimated that only half the children with mental health problems actually receive mental health services (Burns et al., 1995; Shaffer et al., 1996). This is particularly alarming in situations in which children become seriously depressed and suicidal or they begin victimizing other children. When the legal case takes years, not weeks, to resolve and children with serious symptoms go untreated, symptoms can worsen or become chronic and resistant to treatment. As a result an ethical dilemma is created: Given that some suspicions of abuse will be unfounded, should we withhold treatment from such children to avoid the possibility of contamination, or given that we are dealing with a population at high risk for mental health problems, should we provide treatment, potentially raising the risk of false allegation? Unfortunately, there is little empirical evidence to guide this debate.

Even when therapies are limited to those interventions that are most efficacious and well accepted in the field, there remains a dilemma. In recent well-controlled treatment outcome studies with sexually abused children, trauma-focused cognitive-behavioral therapy (TF-CBT) outperformed the other therapies to which it was compared (See Saywitz, Mannarino, Berliner, & Cohen, 2000, for a review). This intervention employs techniques for reducing post-traumatic symptoms (e.g., graduated exposure and systematic desensitization) that involve discussion of the child's memories, attributions, and perceptions of the traumatic event. Although there is no evidence that such discussions must be conducted in a suggestive manner in order to be effective, the research needed to create guidelines for therapists is scant. In the only prospective, longitudinal investigation of the effects of therapy on memories of abuse, researchers followed a group of child witnesses (3 to 17 years old) who self-reported going to therapy immediately following prosecution. There was no evidence of negative or positive effects of therapy on memory of the original abuse when subjects were interviewed again 10 to 15 years later as teens and young adults (Goodman et al., 1992; Alexander et al., in press).

In this chapter, we propose that when confronted with reluctance, recantation, and confusion, forensic researchers mine the clinical literature for ideas about how to relate to and communicate with resistant or impaired children, then subject identified techniques to an empirical test of their effects on memory followed by modification as necessary. Another proposed course is to identify viable treatment strategies for children involved in both the mental health and legal systems simultaneously, and then establish efficacy for both therapeutic and forensic objectives. To facilitate this process, we call the reader's attention to three types of cases at the intersection of the forensic and clinical domains that illustrate of the need for a more holistic approach.

Complicated Cases: Reluctance, Disturbance, Disability

Motives of Fear and Reluctance. The first set of cases involves children who have been abused but have chosen not to disclose. For example, older children with experience in CPS may decide that disclosing abuse would subject them to worse consequences than denying its occurrence (i.e., being removed from family, friends, school, sports). Interviews of child witnesses in field studies suggest reasons that children are reluctant to talk are usually related to fear: fear of reprisal, of adult rejection and anger, and/or of punishment or separation/abandonment (e.g., Sas, 1993). Additional motives reported include self-blame, mixed loyalties, lack of parental support, family pressure, or the desire to protect vulnerable adults (e.g., mentally ill or alcoholic parents). In these cases, motivational factors rather than memory failure or distortion are at play, but there are few relevant studies. For example, cultural variables like immigrant status have rarely been examined, yet distrust of the system (i.e., government intervention) with which interviewers are typically associated (i.e., police) can raise both realistic and unrealistic motives to avoid disclosure (e.g., fear of parental deportation, or incarceration).

There is some evidence from field studies to suggest that motivational factors do delay or impede disclosure of abuse. In one study of 47 cases in which allegations of child sexual abuse were corroborated by a confession from the defendant, delayed disclosure was related to the child's kinship with the perpetrator (Sjöberg & Lindblad, 2002). In a field study of child witness interviews, children were more likely to remain silent, or say "I don't know" or "I don't remember," and to digress to avoid the topic when the suspect was a parent (Hershkowitz, Orbach, Lamb, Sternberg, Pipe, & Horowitz, chapter 6, this volume). Although laboratory research on the causes and cures of reluctance is scarce, these findings illustrate the need to develop methods that address motivational factors and test their effects on memory.

Psychiatric Symptoms and Behavior Problems. The second set of cases involves children with emotional or behavioral problems that interfere with functioning in ways that place children at greater risk for abuse and interfere with the process of assessing whether abuse occurred. These emotional and behavioral problems can predate the alleged abuse, be exacerbated by an abusive event, or be sequelae of an abusive event. It is estimated that 1 in 10 children or adolescents in the United States have a serious mental health problem; another 10% have mild to moderate problems (Burns et al., 1995; Shaffer et al., 1996) and children in clinical populations seem to be at greater risk for abuse than children in nonclinical samples (Sullivan & Knutson, 1998; 2000). For example, Sullivan and Knutson (2000) examined the records of 50,278 children. They found that the risk of sexual abuse in children with behavior disorders was five and a half times higher than for children without any disabilities. Behaviors associated with certain diagnoses might place children at greater risk for abuse, such as the inappropriate affection towards relative strangers displayed by children with Reactive Attachment Disorder (Diagnostic and Statistical Manual for Psychiatry-IV, 1994). And, symptoms may impair communicative, cognitive, or social processes that are necessary to clearly report abuse when it has occurred, or to reject adult concerns when it has not occurred. Further, the fact that these children may be involved in therapeutic interventions more often than other children raises concern about an increased risk of false alarms in this population, further complicating efforts to make sense of allegations.

Conversely, the proportion of child victims that exhibit psychiatric symptoms in need of treatment is not insignificant. The impact of child sexual abuse is highly variable. Some children show no detectable negative effects, others show highly adverse reactions with severe psychiatric symptomatology (e.g., Kendall-Tackett, Williams, & Finkelhor, 1993; Saywitz, et al., 2000). Studies estimate that as many as 50% of sexually abused children either meet full criteria for Post Traumatic Stress Disorder (PTSD) or display some symptoms of the disorder (e.g., McLeer, Deblinger, Atkins, Foa, & Ralphe, 1988; McLeer, Deblinger, Henry, & Orvashel, 1992).

Researchers find other symptoms as well among sexually abused children (McLeer et al., 1998): suicidal ideation (e.g., Wozencraft, Wagner, & Pellegrin, 1991), anxiety (e.g., Kolko, Moser, & Weldy, 1988), depression (e.g., Shapiro, Leifer, Marone,, & Kassem, 1990), substance abuse (e.g., Hibbard, Ingersoll, & Orr, 1990), aggressivity (e.g., Freidrich, Beilke, & Urquiza, 1987), and less severe posttraumatic stress symptoms (e.g., Conte & Schuerman, 1987; Wolfe, Gentile,, & Wolfe, 1999). While not proof of sexual abuse, such symptoms are frequently associated with it. Although two thirds to one half of sexually abused children improve over time, without treatment, many do not improve, and some deteriorate (Kendall-Tackett, et al., 1993; Oates, O'Toole, Lynch, Stern, & Cooney, 1994). Moreover, 30% of the children who are asymptomatic at the initial interview develop symptoms later (Kendall-Tackett et al., 1993). Researchers have found evidence of sleeper effects in severely abused children, with more serious symptoms not manifesting themselves until a year after discovery (Mannarino, Cohen, Smith, & Moore-Motily, 1991).

The U.S. Surgeon General's report on children's mental health highlights the fact that children involved in the legal system routinely fall through the cracks, their mental health needs remaining unmet (U.S. Public Health Service Report of the Surgeon General's Conference on Children's Mental Health, 2000). Professional organizations echo this concern (e.g., APA Resolution on Child Mental Health, 2004). Adding to the dilemma is a rich literature suggesting that child abuse is a major risk factor for adult psychiatric disorders and adolescent problems of substance abuse, promiscuity, depression, and delinquency (e.g., Berliner & Elliott, 1996; Fergusson, Horwood, & Lynskey, 1996; Mullen, Martin, Anderson, Romans, & Herbison, 1996; Putnam, 2003; Saunders, Kilpatrick, Hansen, Resnick, & Walker, 1999; Silverman, Reinherz, & Giaconia, 1996; Stevenson, 1999; Widom, 1999). Taken as a whole, these findings suggest that a substantial number of children in the legal system will need mental health services. They will benefit from a research agenda that lays the groundwork to address their mental health needs without contaminating their testimony.

Developmental Disabilities. A third group of children at the interface of the clinical and forensic domains are those with developmental disabilities. Persons with developmental disabilities are thought to make up 3% to 5% of the population (LaPlante & Carlson, 1996). While scientific evidence is limited, it is consistent in suggesting that children with developmental disabilities are at high risk for maltreatment (e.g., Vig & Kaminer, 2002; Sobsey & Doe, 1991). Sullivan and Knutson (2000) found that children who were mentally retarded had four times the risk of nondisabled peers for all types of maltreatment, including sexual abuse. It is also important to note that children with developmental disabilities (DD) and learning disabilities (LD) are not exempt from mental illness generally or from developing PTSD in the aftermath of abuse (e.g., Mansell, Sobsey, & Moskal, 1998).

In the Sullivan and Knutson (2000) study, children with speech and language difficulties had three times the risk for sexual abuse as nondisabled peers. Lyon and Saywitz (1999) found significant language delays in a population of 480 4- to 7-year-old alleged abuse and neglect victims who were awaiting a hearing at the Los Angeles Dependency Court. Difficulties communicating can clearly impede the information-gathering process. A holistic approach to research is exemplified by studies that adapt techniques from the field of communicative disorders to facilitate the communication competence of child witnesses. Saywitz, Snyder, and Nathanson (1999) demonstrated efficacy of a comprehension monitoring procedure for improving children's reports of past staged events. Subsequent studies of children with learning disabilities also show benefits to this population (Nathanson, Crank, Saywitz, & Ruegg, in press). These findings highlight the potential need for special interview methods with developmentally disabled children.

How Might Motives, Symptoms, or Delays Impede Information-Gathering?

The existing literature does not fully explain how motives, symptoms, or delays can complicate the information-gathering process. Hence, little has been done to develop and test new or old interview methods with these populations. The task may very well require a blending of the methods, paradigms, and theories from diverse literatures. Our aim is not to be comprehensive, but to highlight a few instructive examples.

Effects of Motive. Embarrassment is one motivational barrier to information-gathering that is beginning to be understood by a combination of field, analogue, and basic developmental studies. Sas and Cunningham (1995) found that of the 126 school-aged child witnesses interviewed, 20% of the nondisclosing group said that embarrassment was the reason they gave only incremental bits of information to police over multiple interviews. In an analogue study, Saywitz, Goodman, Moan, and Nicholas (1991) examined 5- and 7-year olds' reports of medical examinations involving genital and anal touch; older children failed to report genital touch in free recall more often that younger children. There was evidence to suggest this reverse developmental trend was due to embarrassment not lack of memory. Basic research on the development of embarrassment and self-consciousness (e.g., Tangney, 1999; Siedner, Stipek, & Feshbach, 1988) suggests that these traits emerge around 7 years of age. Hence, taken together, the results of these different paradigms provide greater insight into how embarrassment might impact the problem of nondisclosure among older but not younger children and the value of greater collaboration and integration of research efforts.

Effects of Emotional and Behavioral Symptoms. It is easy to speculate from the existing clinical and neuropsychological literature how untreated symptoms might affect interview performance. For example, the impulsivity and distractibility present in Attention Deficit Hyperactivity Disorder (DSM-IV, 1994) could interfere with listening carefully to questions or to retrieving memories in an organized, strategic, and systematic manner. A complete accounting of the potential interference of the various clinical syndromes would exceed our task, instead we focus on two syndromes, not uncommon among sexually abused children—depression and PTSD.

Hallmarks of depression include anhedonia (loss of interest in previously enjoyable activities), indifference towards life, profound feelings of hopelessness and worthlessness, social withdrawal, fatigue, difficulties in concentrating, and indecisiveness (DSM-IV, 1994). These difficulties can undermine children's beliefs in the ability of social service agencies to help them, can cause them to give up and feel impotent or not deserving of help, and can interfere with their interest in or ability to establish rapport or marshal the energy needed for demanding retrieval and communication efforts.

One possible framework for understanding the impact of depressive symptoms on memory is the theory of motivated remembering (e.g., Paris, 1988). This is the notion that expectations, incentives, and coping patterns are active determinants of memory performance for people of all ages. In this model, efforts to cope with anxiety or to protect self-image can alter the selection and employment of retrieval strategies. An individual might select an ineffective, but well-practiced, low-risk response strategy (e.g., avoidance, denial, acquiescence) instead of one that is more likely to result in detailed memories. This might occur because the more effective strategy requires higher levels of energy and motivation, and it carries greater risk of adverse consequences. Such a model explains how symptoms of depression might predispose an individual toward the selection of response strategies that require little energy, little motivation, with little risk of failure. The result can be an interview where little is revealed.

Perhaps the disorder whose impact on disclosure is best understood is Posttraumatic Stress Disorder. Learning theories of instrumental and respondent conditioning have been used to explain how victims become conditioned to avoid memories, conversations, activities, places, and people that remind them of original trauma (even though these stimuli are not dangerous in and of themselves) in order to evade the distress of re-experiencing the feelings associated with the event through flashbacks, intrusive thoughts, or nightmares. Successful avoidance reduces anxiety and makes the child feel safe and relaxed; it is positively reinforcing in and of itself. Unfortunately, the primary purpose of the forensic interview demands the child abandon the coping strategy of avoidance that has been repeatedly reinforced as instrumental to maintaining emotional stability. The interviewer and the child end up working at diametrically opposing goals. This brief discussion of depression and PTSD underscores the need for advances in theory, methodology, and practice that come from greater integration of forensic and clinical research.

Effects of Developmental Disability. There are unique factors that complicate the information-gathering process in children with developmental disabilities as well. Cognitive deficits increase the need for assistance with daily living skills and increase exposure to multiple caretakers. Desire for acceptance leads to acquiescence to behavior children do not want, for fear of losing social contact. Additionally, these children have unique difficulties communicating their concerns and needs to others. This can make determining whether caretakers are engaged in assistance or abuse an arduous task when relying on the verbal output of children with mental retardation. Such children tend to violate social boundaries, talk to strangers, and engage in inappropriate laughing, excessive hugging, and inappropriate sexual behavior. These characteristics make it difficult to determine if observed or described interactions are a function of the child's inappropriate behavior, or of abuse.

There is a small literature relevant to the witness capabilities of children with deficits in cognitive functioning (e.g., Agnew & Powell, 2004; Clare & Murphy, 2001; Michel, Gordon, Ornstein, & Simpson, 2000; Milne & Bull, 2001; Perlman, Ericson, Esses, & Isaacs, 1994; Wyatt & Conners, 1998). Studies from the educational literature often find the narration skills of children with learning disabilities to be deficient in comparison to same aged non-LD peers (Wiig, 1993; Lerner, 1997; Scott & Windsor, 2000). In studies of children with mental retardation, researchers tend to find quantitative differences in recall for staged events and videos. Disabled children report fewer, but not qualitatively different, kinds of information (e.g., Agnew & Powell, 2004). Michel et al., (2000) found that children with mild or moderate mental retardation accurately recalled a health check, provided detail, and resisted misleading questions about fictitious features when compared to children of comparable mental age. However, some researchers do find differences on responses to specific questions (e.g., poorer performance on closed yes–no misleading questions such as, "The lady jumped up and own a few times, didn't she?" and on questions about peripheral details) (e.g., Henry & Gudjusson, 1999; Gordon, Jens, Hollings, & Watson, 1994). Studies tend to find that children with mental retardation are more suggestible to certain types of questions than peers of similar chronological age but not those of an equivalent mental age. However, we do not know whether suggestibility of children with mental retardation increases with the stress of the situation, social pressure, or when questions are repeated. This could be the case because these children may exhibit a greater inability to disagree with adults or resist pressure to comply.

There is growing evidence to indicate that such children benefit from special interview techniques that provide them with memory enhancement strategies that they fail to generate and employ on their own. Two research-based interview procedures have been tested with learning disabled children: Narrative Elaboration Training and Cognitive Interviewing. In both instances, leaning disabled children provided more complete reports of past staged events, without increased errors, using the experimental techniques in comparison to standard procedures (Milne & Bull, 1996; Nathanson, Crank, Saywitz, & Ruegg, in press). These techniques were found to increase resistance to subsequent misleading and leading questions in children with learning disabilities. Although these experimental studies of recall for staged events are a good start, little attention has yet been paid to the many reasons why these children might fail to disclose (e.g., poor decision making abilities) or why they might be more susceptible to suggestion under certain circumstances (e.g., inability to read social cues or to anticipate consequences).

IMPROVING FORENSIC INTERVIEW TECHNIQUES FOR RELUCTANT, DISTURBED OR DELAYED CHILDREN: SUGGESTIONS FROM THE CLINICAL LITERATURE

Clinical Approaches to Enhance Trust and Build Rapport

Establishing a trusting relationship is pivotal to the goal of the forensic interview (Sattler, 1998), yet we know little about how children decide whom to trust and whom not to trust. Relevant research has been limited, despite the fact that clinical studies suggest that maltreated children are at higher risk for problematic interpersonal relationships (e.g., Cicchetti, 1987; Shirk, 1988) and have more difficulty establishing rapport with professionals than other children with mental health problems, even when severity of symptomatology is controlled across comparison groups (Eltz, Shirk, & Sarlin, 1995; Shirk, 1988). Moreover, researchers find sexually abused preschoolers to be more controlling and less responsive to the examiner than control groups (Toth, Cicchetti, Macfie, & Emde, 1997). However, efforts to develop rapport in child witness studies and forensic protocols are cursory interchanges that are not designed to overcome high levels of fear or inordinate concerns about safety, trust, embarrassment, or betrayal.

One exception is a series of studies on the effects of social support indicating that when it is not tied to specific content, but is provided independent of content, social support can help children overcome resistance and improve performance, without contaminating their accounts of nonabusive events, even after a one-year delay (Bottoms et al., this volume; Carter, Bottoms, & Levine, 1996; Davis & Bottoms, 2002; Goodman, Bottoms, Schwartz-Kenny, & Rudy, 1991). In these studies, social support usually consists of eye contact, smiling, warm intonation patterns, relaxed body posture, time spent developing rapport, and sometimes complimenting children on their effort without regard for accuracy.

In the clinical literature, a number of rapport-enhancing techniques are practiced, but the conditions under which they might have positive, negative, or no effects on memory remain unknown. Although space limitations prohibit a full listing of such clinical techniques, a few are provided below as examples.

Empathic Comments. One widespread clinical approach to facilitating communication and building rapport is the use of empathy (Matthews & Walker, 1997; Sattler, 1998; Saywitz & Lyon, 2002). Saywitz and Lyon (2002) suggest that empathic comments need not be suggestive. They can be comments that show understanding for the child's perception of the situation, without agreeing with or validating any specific content. For example, traditionally clinicians feel it is not helpful to downplay or devalue the significance of children's worries and fears with comments like "don't worry" or "don't feel nervous." In contrast, comments that acknowledge feeling states show understanding for the child's situation without endorsing the child's perception as reality. These comments can be phrased as open-ended nonleading questions (e.g., "What thoughts or feelings did you have about coming here today? What made you think that?"). In fact, open-ended questions that probe the reasons for the feelings open a channel of communication that can reveal whether a child has been coached or pressured to confabulate, exaggerate, or deny (e.g., "Sounds like you were worried about coming here. How come?" "I don't want to make a mistake." "Why not?" "My mom will be mad.").

Research testing the effects of such open-ended probes on memory for staged events in the lab (similar to studies of social support) in concert with applied studies of child witnesses in the field that measure children's perceptions of interviewer trustworthiness (and other attributions) could ultimately produce guidelines that identify conditions when greater rapport efforts are warranted. Such research could produce the kinds of precautions necessary to avoid suggestion and bias (e.g., focusing comments on topics that would be true, regardless of the accuracy of the allegations in the case).

Normalization. Typically clinicians do not assume that patients are eager to raise painful, embarrassing topics. Efforts to normalize feelings of ambivalence are common, but their effects on memory remain untested. Comments can be operationalized in a nonsuggestive or nonleading manner (e.g., "People often have mixed feelings. Part of the person wants to do something or say something, and another part does not want to do that."). Efforts to normalize feelings of resistance are common (e.g., "People often have good reasons for doing what they do. You said you don't want to talk. You probably have a good reason, too."). Normalizing comments, after open-ended questions fail, is one example of a clinical method that could be tested to determine whether it actually helps overcome resistance without distorting memory.

Saywitz and Moan-Hardie (1994) tested the effects of normalization on suggestibility in an experimental analogue study, as part of a larger intervention in preparing children for an interview. They tested 100 7-year olds' memories of a staged classroom event. Before the interview, half the children read a vignette about a child character who witnessed a fight on the playground. The character then acquiesced to the principal's misleading presumptions about who was at fault. Children proposed reasons why the story character would fail to openly disagree with the adult, or fail to resist his misleading suggestions (e.g., avoiding adult anger or disapproval) that were validated as reasonable and common. However, the interviewer also highlighted unanticipated consequences of acquiescence. Children who participated in the experimental condition made fewer errors in response to misleading questions than control subjects when subsequently interviewed about the classroom event. These results suggest that studies of comments that normalize fear and ambivalence might lead to guidelines for interviewing resistant and uncooperative children without increasing distortion.

Clinical Approaches to Managing Strong Emotion or Upset

When children become upset, frustrated, or sad, rapport and trust can turn on the interviewer's reaction. Clinical and forensic traditions diverge in how they seek to manage strong emotions that emerge during interviews. Typically, forensic interviewers do not intervene. Clinicians, however, employ anxiety reduction techniques, such as relaxation training and cognitive-behavioral self-statements, that are designed to teach children strategies for calming themselves down when upset (Meichenbaum, 1985). One avenue for future research would be to investigate the value of teaching vulnerable children strategies for coping with unwanted feelings at the beginning of the interview and then instructing them to use those same skills if they feel stressed during the interview. Below are two examples.

Relaxation Training. Typically, children are taught deep breathing and muscle relaxation techniques to reduce anxiety (e.g., Meichenbaum, 1985). Children are told that they will learn skills they can use any time they feel upset to calm themselves down and to feel in control of their feelings. For example, children are taught to identify the physiological correlates of tension and to collapse into their chair like a wet noodle when they feel tightness, increased heart rate, and so forth. Or, they are taught to progressively tighten and relax various muscle groups at the instruction of their therapist to demonstrate they have more control over states of tension than previously assumed (e.g., Kendall, Ashenbrand, & Hudson, 2003). These techniques have been used in court preparation programs to help children reduce stress because there is some evidence to suggest that children on the witness stand experience more variable heart rate patterns, indicative of a stress response, in concert with remembering difficulties on the stand (Goodman et al., 1992;

Nathanson & Saywitz, 2003). In at least one field study, this practice did not prevent children from testifying in court (Sas, 1993). Much could be learned from rigorous evaluation of court preparation programs and their effects on children's reports of abuse and legal case outcome.

Self-Statements. Many therapeutic interventions attempt to change the statements children say to themselves in their own minds (Meichenbaum, 1985; Kendall et al., 1992). Replacing negative, self-defeating cognitions with more positive self-statements is a mainstay of cognitive behavioral treatment (Seligman, 1991). Saywitz and Moan-Hardie (1994) examined the effects of cognitive-behavioral self-statements on the suggestibility of 100 7-year olds, as part of a larger intervention. Before the interview, half the children participated in a procedure designed to increase resistance to suggestive questions by teaching children self-statements that promote the ability to defy and contradict the questioner's suggestions and assert their own response instead (e.g., "I knew there would be questions like this. I can do it. I won't go along. I will tell her she's wrong.") as well as to inhibit inappropriate responses like guessing (e.g., "I won't hurry into a wrong answer."). Children who practiced self-statements before the interview showed better recall and greater resistance to suggestion than children in the control group. Similarly, court preparation programs teach children to use self-statements to cope with anxiety on the stand (e.g., "This is hard but that's okay, I knew some of the questions might be really hard. Nobody is expected to know all the answers. It's okay to say "I don't know.")" (Sas & Cunningham, 1995; Saywitz & Nathanson,1993; Saywitz, Nathanson, Snyder, & Lamphear, 1993). Investigation of the effects of self-statements on interview performance could be instrumental in overcoming resistance to disclosure in genuinely abused children and in minimizing suggestion when children have not been abused.

While clinically derived techniques may not be necessary in the majority of cases, the dire consequences of false allegation or false denial demand that our research trajectory not ignore the subgroup for whom such techniques could be necessary and beneficial.

DEVELOPING INTERVENTIONS THAT MEET MENTAL HEALTH NEEDS WITHOUT TAINTING CHILDREN'S REPORTS

In this final section of the chapter, we mine the clinical literature to examine the viability of various therapeutic techniques for use with children involved in the legal system in two circumstances: first, when forensic interviews are inconclusive and children are referred to therapists for monitoring of risk factors and symptoms, and second, when children make clear disclosures that are substantiated in some reliable manner. In the former case, we need to know what kinds of therapeutic interventions could be implemented during this extended phase of information gathering to provide an opportunity for clarity to emerge while meeting children's mental health needs. In the latter case, we need to know how to treat posttraumatic symptoms effectively, and in ways that preserve the reliability of children's evidence during protracted legal proceedings.

The questions at hand are: Which therapies are efficacious for reducing the types of symptoms sexually abused children exhibit? Can these therapies be unpackaged and the individual components examined for their effects on children's memory? Which techniques require discussion or remembering of the facts of the case to be effective? Is repeated discussion of memories in and of itself contaminating? Can such discussion be conducted in a way that is unbiased, nonleading and still effective?

A variety of treatments are available in the community, including psychotropic medication, cognitive–behavioral therapy, family therapy, play therapy, supportive psychodynamic therapy, crisis intervention, parental training in behavior management, and psychoeducation, to name a few. They vary dramatically in terms of the level of empirical support for their efficacy with regard to symptom reduction or recovery. They also vary widely in terms of how much treatment efficacy depends upon discussion of the facts of the case and thus how great or little the risk of contamination or false accusation. For example, psychopharmacological interventions for PTSD may involve no discussion of the facts of the case whatsoever; however, there is little empirical support from well-controlled studies for their efficacy at this time (e.g., see Cohen, Berliner, & Mannarino, 2003 for review). Additionally, there are psychosocial techniques of questionable efficacy, often referred to as "memory recovery techniques," that when employed with patients who present with no memories of abuse may be highly suggestive, for example, hypnosis, age regression, dream interpretation, and body memories (see Lynn et al., 2003, for review). A complete review of the extant therapies would be beyond the scope of this chapter; instead we review the therapies with the most empirical support and consider their viability as interventions with children in the legal system.

Which Interventions Are Effective With Sexually Abused Children?

There is a rapidly growing research base on the efficacy of child therapies that addresses many of the symptoms displayed by sexually abused children, namely, anxiety-related symptoms, depression, or behavioral problems. Several large meta-analytic examinations of hundreds of fairly well-controlled studies suggest that psychosocial therapies are effective with children and adolescents and are more effective than the passage of time alone (e.g., Kasdin & Weisz, 1998; Weisz, Weisz, Han, Granger, & Morton, 1995). Reviews of the empirical literature find the following interventions to be efficacious or probably efficacious for the kinds of symptoms sexually abused children exhibit: cognitive behavioral therapy for childhood anxiety, coping skills training for childhood depression, parent management training based on behavioral techniques, and cognitive problem-solving training for externalizing behavior problems. (e.g., aggression) (e.g., Kazdin & Weisz, 1998).[1]

Although the number of studies involving sexually abused children is relatively small in comparison, there is growing evidence from well-controlled treatment outcome studies using randomized controlled trials, at multiple sites, demonstrating support for trauma-focused cognitive-behavioral techniques (TF-CBT), in conjunction with psychoeducational interventions, coping skills training, and behavior management training for parents, with gains maintained up to a year later (e.g., Cohen, Deblinger, Mannarino, & Steer, 2004; Deblinger, Lippman, & Steer, 1996; Celano, Hazzard, Webb, & McCall, 1996; Cohen & Mannarino, 1996, 1998, 2000; Putnam, 2003; Saywitz et al., 2000). The fact that efficacious therapies exist makes it that much harder to justify withholding treatment from children who demonstrate serious symptoms when forensic and clinical goals conflict.

Trauma-focused cognitive-behavioral treatment (TF-CBT) has consistently outperformed the other treatments to which it has been compared, including nonspecific supportive psychotherapies that do not make the traumatic event a focus of treatment. TF-CBT was developed to resolve posttraumatic stress disorder, and depressive and anxiety symptoms, as well as to address underlying distortions about self-blame, safety, and the trustworthiness of others and the world. There are versions for preschoolers and for elementary school aged children. With 3-to 6-year olds, intervention focuses heavily on parents, since postevent adaptation is significantly affected by how parents interpret and respond to the abuse. With older children, there is greater focus on individual work with the child. Typically, therapy involves at least 12 sessions with children and non-offending parents seen individually, as well as joint parent–child sessions to enhance family communication. The treatment seeks to put sexual abuse into perspective and into the broader context of children's lives so that their primary identity is not that of a victim (Deblinger & Heflin, 1996). As an intervention package, it is intended for use in substantiated cases of sexual abuse.

---

[1] Although findings support behavioral therapy and CBT over nonbehavioral therapies, this does not mean that behavioral approaches are best for all types of children and all types of problems. These approaches may enjoy the greatest support, in part, because they are the most frequently studied. They are short-term and are among the easiest to manualize, standardize, and therefore utilize in well-controlled treatment trials. Other treatments may be equally or even more effective but have not been adequately studied. See Saywitz et al., (2000) for further discussion.

Which Components of TF-CBT Might Be Useful After Inconclusive Forensic Interviews?

When children fail to disclose abuse or fail to reject reasons for ongoing concern, there needs to be an avenue of agency response that (a) provides an opportunity for continued monitoring of suspicious behavior, symptoms, or risk factors, and (b) provides an opportunity for forensically relevant information to emerge, if it exists, without distorting children's statements. This includes the opportunity for information to emerge that determines a report to be false as well as true. Therapeutic techniques that teach children how to cope with negative affect might be one such approach that could be implemented in this context. Generally, children learn coping skills and practice them in regard to distressing situations they identify themselves, hence they need not necessarily be about abuse, although children may bring up the topic of abuse spontaneously or in response to open-ended probes about what makes them happy or sad. Therapists can explore what happened in a nonleading manner for therapeutic purposes and then refer to a forensic interviewer for further elicitation of forensic details.[2]

Emotional Expression Skills Training. With this technique children learn to label, communicate, and cope with their feelings rather than avoid them. Children learn to identify feeling states, in themselves and in others, sometimes in photographs, or pictures on a chart of facial expressions, sometimes in role play (e.g., Joseph & Strain, 2003). As children learn to identify their own feeling states, they are asked to discuss real and personal (although not necessarily abuse-related) situations that have led to a variety of emotions (e.g., "Tell me about a time when you felt excited/happy/mad/sad. What were you excited about? Could anyone else tell you were excited?" [Deblinger & Helfin, 1996, page 54]). Children learn to develop appropriate means of expressing emotions ("What do you do when you feel sad? When was the last time you felt sad? What did you do then?"). When children describe maladaptive ways of responding to different feelings ("I sit in my room alone. I keep it to myself."), therapists encourage children to consider alternative coping responses.(e.g., "Does that help you feel better? What would you do to make someone else feel better when they were sad? Let's think of some things you can try to feel better: What about talking with someone important to you about how you feel; drawing or painting a picture; writing a poem or story

---

[2] When deployed as a component of TF-CBT, coping skills training is employed in the beginning, before children are confronted with gradual exposure to anxiety provoking stimuli. This is done to ensure children possess the skills to cope with the negative affect that exposure will create. In fact exposing patients to anxiety provoking stimuli who do not possess sufficient coping skills may exacerbate their symptoms and interfere with complete and accurate recall of the relevant memories.

about your feelings or problems?"). In the context of an extended phase of information gathering, therapists could be instructed to use nonleading, open-ended questions when abuse-related information is raised.

Is there reason to believe that such discussion of abuse memories, if they arose, would necessarily damage the reliability of the information provided to law enforcement or to courts? Clearly, if conducted in a biased and suggestive manner it could (e.g., Leichtman & Ceci, 1995). However, recent reviews of the literature have concluded that simply asking children to recall an event again and again does not have a detrimental effect on their memory and may even help them consolidate the memory, facilitating greater recall over short delays (Fivush, Peterson, & Schwarzmueller, 2002; Poole & White, 1991, 1995; Fivush & Schwarzmueller, 1995). Studies do not find detrimental effects of repeated nonsuggestive interviews using open-ended questions; in fact, repetition may benefit long-term retention for children over 7 years of age (e.g., Flin, Boon, Knox, & Bull, 1992; Memon & Vartoukian, 1996). Moreover, when suspicions of abuse are unfounded, emotional expression skills training may enable a child to more definitively reject vague concerns by adults regarding the possibility that the child had been sexually abused, allowing the therapist to pursue the real causes of the child's symptoms. Certainly, studies are needed to examine the effects of questions and comments used in emotional expression skills training, but there is reason to believe that this approach might be an excellent choice with children in inconclusive cases.

Cognitive Coping Skills Training. This clinical technique is one step further along the continuum of interventions that involve remembering and discussing the traumatic event. In theory, traumatized children work hard to avoid thinking, talking, or being reminded of the trauma. This pattern prevents them from putting the experience in perspective or understanding and processing its impact, potentially leaving them with misperceptions and inaccurate cognitions. Through trauma-focused therapy children learn ways to communicate about and cope with maladaptive abuse-related thoughts, feelings, and reminders.

To treat anxiety and depression, therapists focus on the connections between thoughts, feelings, behaviors, and physiological states (e.g., Kendall et al., 2003; Weisz, Southam-Gerow, Gordis, & Connor-Smith, 2003). Children learn that thoughts can influence feelings, and that thoughts and feelings influence behavior. Vignettes are often used to help children understand how different thoughts about the same situation can result in different feelings. Children come to understand that we can think about a problem in ways that lead to more hopeful and optimistic feelings or to more negative and pessimistic feelings (Seligman, 1991). Then they learn to dispute negative thoughts, realizing they are not necessarily true or permanent no matter how much we believe them, and they practice changing them into more positive thoughts and emotions. The distorted cognitions to be disputed need not be related to abuse, but children may raise the topic when asked for examples. Research would be needed to assess whether these helpful clinical techniques harm, enhance, or are neutral to obtaining accurate information from children who have experienced abuse and whether they can be used to enhance the detection of false reports from children who have not been abused.

Which Treatment Components Might Be Useful to Treat Posttraumatic Symptoms in Substantiated Cases?

Cognitive Coping Skills. In substantiated cases, these same cognitive coping skills are used to address thoughts related to the abuse that are often intrusive and negative. Children role play what advice they would give friends to convince them that their negative thoughts are not true, or rehearse positive statements by pretending to be the host of a radio talk show. Deblinger and Heflin (1996) describe an array of maladaptive cognitions and abuse-related attributions to be addressed in therapy this way (e.g., confusion about causes of abuse, overpersonalized explanations for why it occurred and who is responsible, reactions of other people upon discovery, misperceptions about sexuality and body image). Perhaps analogue studies testing the effects of this approach on recall for a staged event (e.g., where children's attributions about a confusing event are challenged) could help create precautions and guidelines for therapists in substantiated cases to minimize influence on the memories of the event itself.

Gradual Exposure and Systematic Desensitization. These procedures enjoy high levels of empirical support for confronting anxiety and fear (e.g., Kendall et al., 1992). They are typically employed only in substantiated cases (Deblinger & Helfin, 1996). Children are given a rationale for therapy that directly connects to the problems they raised in their initial assessment. Children are reminded that they told the therapist they had thoughts about their abuse that bothered them (interrupted them during school or at nighttime, produced bad dreams, etc.). For example, children are asked if they want to learn ways to stop their thoughts and worries from bothering them so much. It is a way for children to become comfortable with painful memories.

Typically children prepare a list of anxiety-provoking stimuli (feared/upsetting), ordered from situations that would be relatively easy for the child to tolerate to more feared stimuli, such as their thoughts and memories of the abuse (e.g., Kendall et al., 2003). Children are asked to think about an item on the list. They are then asked to recall the scene as clearly as possible and to concentrate and describe details that they remember. The therapist asks the child what he or she was thinking and feeling and what happened next. The goal is to sit with the anxiety until it dissipates without resorting to avoidant or dissociative coping mechanisms. The therapist encourages the child to use the coping strategies taught earlier in the treatment to deal with the feared situations (e.g., relaxation skills). This gradual exposure aims to disrupt the maladaptive effects of the more extreme negative emotions that develop as a result of respondent conditioning (e.g., Deblinger & Helflin, 1996; Foa, Rothbaum, Riggs, & Murdock, 1991).

The exposure exercises do not require or encourage fantasy or speculation but the description of a real experience. Therapists gently redirect children back to the feared stimuli, perhaps by simply repeating the child's verbal description of sexual abuse and, if needed, using open-ended questions to elicit information about the sensations, emotions, and thoughts experienced by the child during the episode described. There is no effort to interrogate the child; the goal is to tolerate the anxiety associated with discussion until it dissipates, using the new coping strategies. However, details of the abuse are discussed, perceptions analyzed, and thoughts challenged. A more integrated approach to research is necessary to determine whether these clinical techniques can be employed in ways that both reduce posttraumatic symptoms and preserve the child's statements without distortion.

This might involve testing the effects of interview techniques developed for forensic purposes but applied in the service of therapeutic as well as forensic objectives. For example, one experimental technique for helping children describe and elaborate on events in their own words, Narrative Elaboration Training (NET), has now been tested in nine studies with over 660 children, aged 4 to 12, and an additional 115 children with learning disabilities, aged 7 to 12 (e.g., Brown & Pipe, 2003a, 2003b; Camparo, Wagner, & Saywitz, 2001; Dorado & Saywitz, 2001; Nathanson, Crank, Saywitz & Reugg, in press; Saywitz & Snyder, 1996; Saywitz, Snyder, & Lamphear, 1996). In the field, this technique has been applied in trauma-focused CBT to guide discussion during therapy, although this application of NET has yet to be tested experimentally. It is possible that forensic interview techniques might be implemented as part of a therapeutic intervention in a treatment outcome study to guide recall of abuse or of traumatic events other than abuse (e.g., graduated exposure to memories of earthquake, terrorist attack, car accident). Results demonstrating symptom reduction, despite introduction of forensic techniques, could then be complemented by results of analogue studies testing the effects of the combined approach on recall for a staged event (e.g., where children's misperceptions about an ambiguous event are challenged). In short, much could be accomplished by a research agenda that entails greater collaboration of clinical and forensic researchers, combined with greater integration of theories and research paradigms.

CONCLUSIONS

The social institutions that address alleged and actual child maltreatment have evolved, by and large, along separate paths, and in a fragmented manner, exacerbated by the adversarial nature of a legal system that tends to polarize both practitioners and researchers. In this chapter, we have tried to make the case for changing course toward a more integrated and holistic approach to research as regards (a) eliciting reliable and sufficient information from children to substantiate or reject suspicions of abuse, (b) meeting children's mental health needs without tainting their reports, and (c) prioritizing actions when forensic and clinical goals conflict.

Our focus on reluctant, emotionally impaired, and developmentally delayed children at the intersection of the forensic and clinical domains serves to illustrate a subgroup of cases, not insignificant in number, who require a new direction in research with greater collaboration between clinical and forensic researchers and practitioners. Our intent was to raise the level of mutual awareness, making clinical interventions more transparent to forensic researchers and the need for forensic safeguards more apparent to clinical researchers, at least for the subset of children involved in both the legal and mental health systems simultaneously. Our ultimate goal is a knowledge base sufficient to balance and prioritize legal and clinical objectives as the basis for policies and methods that protect both the children and the adults involved.

REFERENCES

Agnew, S. E., & Powell, M. B. (2004). The effect of intellectual disability on children's recall of an event across different questions types. *Law and Human Behavior, 28,* 3, 273–94.

Alexander, K. W., Quas, J. A., Goodman, G. S., Ghetti, S., Edelstein, R. S., Redlich, A. D., Cordon, M., & Jones, D. P. H. (in press). Traumatic impact predicts long-term memory for documented child sexual abuse. *Psychological Science.*

American Academy of Child and Adolescent Psychiatry. (1998). Practice parameters for the assessment and treatment of children and adolescents with posttraumatic stress disorder. *Journal of American Academy of Child and Adolescent Psychiatry. 37,* 4S–26S.

American Professional Society on the Abuse of Children. (1997). *Guidelines for psychosocial evaluation of suspected sexual abuse in young children.* Chicago: American Professional Societ on the Abuse of Children.

American Psychological Association. (1998). *Professional, ethical, and legal issues concerning interpersonal violence, maltreatment, and related trauma.* Report of the ad hoc committee on legal and ethical issues in the treatment of interpersonal violence. Washington, DC: American Psychological Association.

———. (February, 2004). *Resolution on Children's Mental Health.* Washington, DC: American Psychological Association.

American Psychiatric Association. (1994). *Diagnostic and Statistical Manual-IV.* Washington, DC: American Psychiatric Association.

Berliner L.,& Elliott, D.(1996). Sexual abuse of children. In J. Briere, L. Berliner, J. Bulkley, C. Jenny, and T. Reid (Eds.), *The APSAC handbook on child maltreatment* (pp. 51–71). Thousand Oaks, CA: Sage.

Brown, D.,& Pipe, M. E. (2003a). Variations on a technique: Enhancing children's recall using narrative elaboration Training. *Applied Cognitive Psychology, 17,* 377–99.

————. (2003b). Individual differences in children's event memory reports and the narrative elaboration technique. *Journal of Applied Psychology, 88,* 195–206.

Burns, B., Costello, E., Angold, A., Tweed, D., Stangl, D., Farmer, E., & Erkanli, A., (1995). Children's mental health services use across service sectors. *Health Affairs (Millwood), 14,* 147–59.

Camparo. L. B., Wagner, J. T., & Saywitz, K. J. (2001). Interviewing children about real and fictitious events: revisiting the narrative elaboration procedure. *Law and Human Behavior, 25(1).* 63–80.

Carter, C., Bottoms, B. L., & Levine, M. (1996). Linguistic and socio-emotional influences on the accuracy of children's reports. *Law and Human Behavior, 20(3),* 335–58.

Celano, M., Hazzard, A. Webb, C. and McCall, C. (1996). Treatment of traumagenic beliefs among sexually abused girls and their mothers: An evaluation study. *Journal of Abnormal Child Psychology, 24,* 1–16.

Cicchetti, D. (1987). Developmental psychopathology in infancy: Illustrations from the study of maltreated youngsters. *Journal of Consulting and Clinical Psychology, 55,* 837–45.

Clare, I., & Murphy, G. (2001). Witnesses with Learning Disabilities. *British Journal of Learning Disabilities, 29,* 79–80.

Cohen, J. A., Berliner, L., & Mannarino, A. P. (2003). Psychosocial and pharmacological interventions for child crime victims. *Journal of Traumatic Stress, 16(12),* 175–86.

Cohen, J. A., Deblinger, E., Mannarino, A., & Steer, R. (2004). A multisite, randomized controlled trial for children with sexual abuse-related PTSD symptoms. *Journal of Child and Adolescent Psychiatry, 43(4),* 393–402.

Cohen, J. A., & Mannarino, A. P. (1996). A treatment outcome study for sexually abused preschool: Outcome during a one year follow-up. *Journal of the American Academy of Child and Adolescent Psychiatry, 34,* 1402–10.

————. (1998). Interventions for sexually abused children: Initial treatment findings. *Child Maltreatment. 3,* 17–26.

————. (2000). Predictors of treatment outcome in sexually abused children. *Child Abuse and Neglect, 24,* 983–94.

Conte, J., & Schuerman, J. (1987). Factors associated with an increased impact of sexual abuse. *Child Abuse and Neglect, 11,* 201–11.

Davis, S. L., & Bottoms, B. L. (2002). The effects of social support on the accuracy of children's reports: Implications for the forensic Interview. In M. L. Eisen, J. A. Quas, & G. S. Goodman, (Eds.), *Memory and Suggestibility in the Forensic Interview.* (pp. 437–58). Mahwah, NJ: Lawrence Erlbaum Associates.

Deblinger, E., & Heflin, A. H. (1996). *Treating Sexually Abused Children and Their Nonoffending Parents.* Thousand Oaks, CA: Sage Publications.

Deblinger, E., Lippman, J., & Steer, R. (1996). Sexually abused children suffering post-traumatic stress symptoms: Initial treatment outcome findings. *Child Maltreatment, 1,* 310–21.

Department of Health and Human Services (DHHS). (2004). Child Maltreatment 2002. Washington, DC: DHHS. Retrieved from http://nccanch.acf.hhs.gov/general/stats/index.cfm.

Dorado, J., & Saywitz, K. (2001). Interviewing preschoolers from low and middle income communities: A test of the narrative elaboration recall improvement technique. *Journal of Clinical Child Psychology. 30(4),* 566–78.

Elliott D., & Briere, J. (1994). Forensic sexual abuse evaluations of older children: Disclosures and symptomotology. *Behavioral Sciences and the Law, 12,* 261–77.

Eltz, M. J., Shirk, S. R., & Sarlin, N. (1995). Alliance formation and treatment outcome among maltreated adolescents. *Child Abuse and Neglect, 19*(4), 419–31.

Fergusson, D., Horwood, L.J., & Lynskey, M.T. (1996). Childhood sexual abuse and psychiatric disorder in young adulthood: II. Psychiatric outcomes of child sexual abuse. *Journal of the American Academy of Child and Adolescent Psychiatry, 35,* 1365–74.

Finkelhor, D., Cross, T. P., & Cantor, E. N. (2005). The justice system for juvenile victims: A comprehensive model of case flow. *Trauma, Violence and Abuse, 6*(2), 1–20.

Fivush, R., Peterson, C., & Schwarzmueller, A. (2002). Questions and answers: The credibility to child witnesses in the context f specific questioning techniques. In M. Eisen, J. Quas, & G. Goodman (Eds.), Memory and suggestibility in the forensic interview. (pp. 331–54). Mahwah, NJ: Lawrence Erlbaum Associates.

Fivush, R., & Schwarzmueller, A. (1995). Say it once again: Effects of repeated questions on children's event recall. *Journal of Traumatic Stress, 8,* 555–80.

Flin, R., Boon, J., Knox, A., & Bull, R. (1992). The effects of a five month delay on children and adult's eyewitness testimony. *British Journal of Psychology, 83,* 323–36.

Foa, E. B., Rothbaum, B. O., Riggs, D. S., & Murdock, T. (1991). Treatment of PTSD in rape victims: A comparison between cognitive behavioral procedures and counseling. *Journal of Counseling and Consulting Psychology, 59,* 715–23.

Friedrich, W. N., Beilke, R. L., & Urquiza, A. (1987). Children from sexually abusive families: A behavioral comparison. *Journal of Interpersonal Violence, 2,* 391–402.

Goodman, G. S., Bottoms, B. L., Schwartz-Kenney, B. M., & Rudy, L.. (1991). Children's memory for a stressful event: Improving children's reports. *Journal of Narrative and Life History, 1,* 69–99.

Goodman, G., Pyle-Taub, E. P., Jones, D. P. H., England, P. Port, L. K., Rudy, L., and Prado, L. (1992). The effects of criminal court testimony on child assault victims. *Monographs of the Society for Research in Child Development, 57*(229), 127–34.

Gordon, B, Jens, K., Hollings, R., & Watson, T. (1994). Remembering activities performed versus those imagined: Implications for testimony of with mental retardation. *Journal of Clinical Child Psychology, 23,* 239–48.

Henry, L., & Gudjonsson, G. (1999). Eyewitness memory and suggestibility in children with mental retardation. *American Journal of Mental Retardation. 104*(6), 491–508.

Herman, (2005). Improving decision making in forensic child sexual abuse evaluations. *Law and Human Behavior 29*(1), 87–120.

Hibbard R. A., Ingersoll, G. M., & Orr, D. P. (1990). Behavior risk, emotional risk, and child abuse among adolescents in a nonclinical setting. *Pediatrics. 86,* 896–901.

Joseph, G. E., & Strain, P. S. (2003). *Enhancing emotional vocabulary in young children.* Urbana-Champaign, IL: University of Illinois at Urbana-Champaign.

Kazdin, A. E., & Weisz, J. R. (1998). Identifying and developing empirically supported child and adolescent treatments. *Journal of Consulting and Clinical Psychology, 66,* 19–36.

Keary , K., & Fitzpatrick, C. (1994). Children's disclosure of sexual abuse during formal investigation. *Child Abuse and Neglect. 18,* 543–48.

Kendall, P. C., Chansky, T. E., Kane, M. T., Kim, R. S., Kortlander, E., Ronan, K. R., Sessa, F. M., & Siqueland, L. (1992). Anxiety disorders in youth: Cognitive-behavioral interventions. Boston, MA: Allyn & Bacon.

Kendall, P. C., Aschenbrand, S. G., Hudson, J. L. (2003). Child-focused treatment of anxiety. In A. E. Kazdin, & J. R. Weisz (Eds.), Evidence-based psychotherapies for children and adolescents. (pp. 81–119). New York: Guilford Press.

Kendall-Tackett, K., & Williams, L., & Finkelhor, D. (1993). Impact of sexual abuse on children: A review and synthesis of recent empirical studies. Psychological Bulletin, 113(1), 164–80.

Kolko, D. J., Moser, J. T., & Weldy, S. R.(1988). Behavioral/emotional indicators of sexual abuse in psychiatric inpatients: A controlled comparison with physical agues. Child Abuse and Neglect, 12, 529–41.

LaPlante, M. M., & Carlson, D. (1996). Disability in the United States: Prevalence and Causes, 1992. Based on the National Health Interview Survey, Disabilities Statistical Report (7). Washington, D.C.: National Institute on Disability and Rehabilitation Research.

Leichtman, M. D., & Ceci, S. J. (1995). The effects of stereotypes and suggestions on preschoolers reports. Developmental Psychology, 31, 568–78.

Lerner, J. (1997). Learning Disabilities: Theories, Diagnosis and Teaching Strategies, 7th Ed. New York: Houghton Mifflin Company.

Lynn, S. J., Lock, T., Loftus, E. F., Krackow, E., & Lilienfeld, S. O. (2003). Remembrance of Things Past. In Lilienfeld, S. O., Lohr, J. M., & Lynn, S. J. (Eds.) Science and Pseudoscience in Clinical Psychology. (pp. 205–39). New York: Guilford Press.

Lyon , T. D., & Saywitz, K. J. (1999). Young maltreated children's competence to take the oath. Applied Developmental Science, 3, 16–27.

Mannarino, A. P., Cohen, J. A., Smith, J. A., & Moore-Motily, S. (1991). Six- and twelve month follow-up of sexually abused girls. Journal of Interpersonal Violence, 6, 494–511.

Mansell, S., Sobsey, D., & Moskal, R., (1998). Clinical findings among sexually abused childrenwith and without developmental disabilities. Mental Retardation, 36(1), 12–22.

Mathews, J. R., & Walker, E. C. (1997). Basic Skills and Professional Issues in Clinical Psychology. Boston: Allyn and Bacon.

McLeer, S. V., Deblinger, E., Atkins, M. S., Foa, E. B., & Ralphe, D. L. (1988). Post traumatic stress disorder in sexually abused children. Journal of the American Academy of Child and Adolescent Psychiatry, 27, 650–54.

McLeer, S., Deblinger, E., Henry, D., & Orvaschel, H. (1992). Sexually abused children at high risk for post-traumatic stress disorder. Journal of the American Academy of Child & Adolescent Psychiatry, 31(5), 875–79.

McLeer, S. V., Dixon, J. F., Henry, D., Ruggiero, K., Escovitz, K., Niedda, T., & Scholle, R. (1998). Psychopathology in non-clinically referred sexually abused children. Journal of the American Academy of Child and Adolescent Psychiatry, 37, 1326–33.

Meichenbaum, D. (1985). Stress Inoculation Training. New York: Pergamon Press.

Melton, G. (1994). Doing justice and doing good: Conflicts for mental health professionals. The Future of Children: Sexual Abuse of Children, 4, 102–18.

Memon, A.& Vartoukian, R. (1996). The Effects of Repeated Questioning on Young Children's Eyewitness Testimony British Journal of Psychology, 87, 403–15.

Michel, M. K., Gordon, B. N., Ornstein, P. A., & Simpson, M. A. (2000). The abilities of children with mental retardation to remember personal experiences: Implications for testimony. Journal of Clinical Child Psychology, 29(3), 453–63.

Milne, R., & Bull, R. (1996). Interviewing children with mild learning disability with the cognitive interview. Issues in Criminal and Legal Psychology, 26, 44–51

————. (2001). Interviewing witnesses with learning disability for legal purposes. *British Journal of Learning Disabilities, 29*, 93–97.

Mullen, P. E., Martin, J. L., Anderson, J. C., Romans, S. E., & Herbison, G. P. (1996). The long term impact of the physical, emotional, and sexual abuse of children: A community study. *Child Abuse and Neglect, 20*, 7–21.

Nathanson, R., Crank, J. N. Saywitz, K. J., & Ruegg, E. (in press). Enhancing the oral narratives of children with learning disabilities. Reading and Writing Quarterly.

Nathanson, R., & Saywitz, K. J., (2003). The effects of the courtroom context on children's memory and anxiety. *The Journal of Psychiatry and Law, 31*, 67–98.

Nathanson, R., Saywitz, K. J., & Ruegg, E. (1999). *Enhancing Communicative competence during the judicial process in children with learning disabilities.* Paper presented at the annual meeting of the American Educational Research Association. Montreal, Canada.

Oates, R. K., O'Toole, B. I., Lynch, D. L., Stern, A., & Cooney, G. (1994). Stability and change in outcomes for sexually abused children. *Journal of the American Academy of Child and Adolescent Psychiatry, 33*, 945–53.

Paris, S, (1988). Motivated Remembering. In F. Weinert & M. Perlmutter (Eds.), *Memory development: Universal changes and individual differences* (pp. 221–42). Hillsdale, NJ: Lawrence Erlbaum Associates.

Perlman, Ericson, Esses, & Isaacs, (1994). The developmentally handicapped witness: Competency as a function of question format. Law and Human Behavior, 18, 171–87.

Poole, D. A., & White, L. T. (1991). The effects of question repetition on the eyewitness testimony of children and adults. *Developmental Psychology, 27*, 975–86.

————. (1995). Tell me again and again: Stability and change in the repeated testimonies of children and adults. In M. S. Zaragoza, J .R. Graham, G. C. N. Hall, R. Hirschman, & Y. S. Ben-Porath (Eds.), *Memory and testimony in the child witness* (pp. 24–43). Thousand Oaks, CA: Sage.

Putnam, F. W. (2003). Ten year research update review: Child Sexual Abuse. *Journal of the American Academy of Child and Adolescent Psychiatry, 42*(3), 269–78.

Sas, L. D. (1993). *Three years after the verdict: A longitudinal study of the social and psychological adjustment of child witnesses referred to the child witness project.* London, Ontario: London Family Court Clinic, Inc.

Sas, L. D.& Cunningham, (1995). *Tipping the Balance to Tell the Secret: The public discovery of child sexual abuse.* (Available from the London Court Clinic, 254 Pall Mall St., London, N6A 5P6).

Sattler, J. M. (1998). Clinical and forensic interviewing of children and families. San Diego: Jerome Sattler, Publisher, Inc.

Saunders, B. E., Kilpatrick, D. G., Hansen, R. F., Resnick, H. S., & Walker, M. E. (1999). Prevalence, case characteristics, and long term psychological correlates of child rape among women: A national survey. *Child Maltreatment, 4*, 187–200.

Saywitz, K. J., Goodman, G. S., Nicholas, E., & Moan, S. (1991). Children's memories of a physical examination involving genital touch: Implications for reports of child sexual abuse. *Journal of Consulting and Clinical Psychology, 59*, 682–91.

Saywitz, K. J., & Lyon, T. D. (2002). Coming to grips with children's suggestibility. . In M. L Eisen, J. A. Quas, & G. S. Goodman (Eds.), *Memory and Suggestibility in the Forensic Interview* (pp. 85–114). Mahwah, NJ: Lawrence Erlbaum Associates.

Saywitz, K. J., Mannarino, A. P., Berliner, L., & Cohen, J. A. (2000). Treatment for Sexually Abused Children and Adolescents. *American Psychologist, 55*(9), 1040–49.

Saywitz, K., & Moan-Hardie, S. (1994). Reducing the potential for distortion of childhood memories. *Consciousness and Cognition, 3*, 257–93.

Saywitz, K. J., & Nathanson, R. (1993). Children's testimony and their perceptions of stress in and out of the courtroom. *International Journal of Child Abuse and Neglect, 17*, 613–22.

Saywitz, K., Nathanson, R., Snyder, L, & Lamphear, V. (1993). *Preparing children for the investigative and judicial process: Improving communication, memory, and emotional resilience* [Final Report to the National Center on Child Abuse and Neglect, Grant No 90-CA–1179].

Saywitz, K., & Snyder, L. (1996). Narrative Elaboration: Test of a new procedure for interviewing children. *Journal of Consulting and Clinical Psychology, 64*(6), 1347–57.

Saywitz, K., Snyder, L., & Lamphear, V. (1996). Helping children tell what happened: Follow up study of the narrative elaboration procedure. *Child Maltreatment, 1*(3), 200–212.

Saywitz, K., Snyder, L., & Nathanson, R. (1999). Facilitating the communicative competence of the child witness. *Applied Developmental Science, 3*(1), 58–68

Scott, C., & Windsor, J. (2000). General language performance measures in spoken and written discourse produced by school-aged children with and without language learning disabilities. *Journal of Speech, Language, and Hearing Research, 43*, 324–39.

Seligman, M. (1991). *Learned Optimism.* New York: Knopf.

Shaffer, D., Fisher, Dulcan, M., Davies, M., Piacentini, J., Schwabstone, M., Lahey, B., Blurdon, K., Jensen, P., Bird, H., Canino, G., & Regier, D., (1996). The NIMH Diagnostic Interview Schedule for Children Version 2.3: Description, acceptability, prevalence rates, and performance in the MECA Study. Methods for the Epidemiology of Child and Adolescent Mental Disorders Study. *Journal of the American Academy of Child and Adolescent Psychiatry, 35*, 8655–877.

Shapiro, J. P., Leifer, M., Martone, M. W., & Kassem, L., (1990) Multi-method assessment of depression in sexually abused girls. *Journal of Personality Assessment, 55*, 234–48.

Shirk, S. R. (1988). The interpersonal legacy of physical abuse in children. *Childhood and Adolescence*, 57–81.

Siedner, L. B., Stipek, D. J., & Feshbach, N. D. (1988). A developmental analysis of elementary school-aged children's concepts of pride and embarrassment. *Child Development, 59*, 367–77.

Silverman, A. B., Reinherz, H. Z., & Giaconia, R. M., (1996). The long term sequelae of child and adolescent abuse: A longitudinal community study. *Child Abuse and Neglect, 20*, 709–23.

Sjöberg , R. L., & Lindblad, F., (2002). Delayed disclosure and disrupted communication during forensic investigation of child sexual abuse: a study of 47 corroborated cases. *Acta Paediatr, 91*, 1391–96.

Sobsey, D., & Doe, T. (1991). Patterns of sexual abuse and assault. *Journal of Sexuality and Disability, 9*(3), 185–99.

Stevenson, J., (1999). The treatment of long term sequelae of child abuse. *Journal of Child Psychology and Psychiatry, 40*, 89–111.

Sullivan, P. M., & Knutson, J. F. (1998). The association between child maltreatment and disabilities in a hospital-based epidemiological study. *Child Abuse and Neglect, 22*, 271–88.

———. (2000). Maltreatment and disabilities: A population-based epidemiological study. *Child Abuse and Neglect, 24*, 1257–74.

Tangney, J. P. (1999). The self-conscious emotions: Shame, guilt, embarrassment and pride. In Dalgleish, T., & Power, M. J. (Ed). *Handbook of cognition and emotion.* (pp. 541–68). Chichester, England: John Wiley & Sons Ltd.

Toth, S. L., Cicchetti, D., Macfie, J., & Emde, R. (1997). Representations of the self and other in narratives of neglected, physically abused and sexually abused preschoolers. *Development and Psychopathology, 9,* 781–96.

U.S. Public Health Service. (2000). *Report of the Surgeon General's Conference on Children's Mental Health: A National Action Agenda.* Washington, D.C.

Vig, S., & Kaminer, R. (2002). Maltreatment and developmental disabilities in children. *Journal of Developmental and Physical Disabilities, 14*(4), 371–86.

Weisz, J. R., Southam-Gerow, M. A., Gordis, E. B., & Connor-Smith, J. (2003). Primary and secondary control enhancement training for youth depression. In A. E. Kazdin, & J. R. Weisz (Eds.), Evidence-based psychotherapies for children and adolescents. (pp. 165–83). New York: Guilford Press.

Weisz, J. R., Weisz, B., Han, S. S., Granger, D. A., & Morton, T, (1995). Effects of psychotherapy with children and adolescents revisited: A meta-analysis of treatment outcome studies. *Psychological Bulletin, 117,* 450–68.

Widom, C. S. (1999). Posttraumatic stress disorder in abused and neglected children grown up. *American Journal of Psychiatry, 56,* 1223–29.

Wiig, E. H. (1993). The role of language in learning disabilities. In *Spectrum of Developmental Disabilities XIV: ADD, ADHD and LD.* The Johns Hopkins School of Medicine. Parkton, MD: York Press. (pp.139–54).

Wolfe, V., Gentile, C., & Wolfe, D. (1989). The impact of sexual abuse on children: A PTSD formulation. *Behavior Therapy, 20*(2), 215–28.

Wozencraft, T., Wagner, W., & Pellegrin, A., (1991). Depression and suicidal ideation in sexually abused children. *Child Abuse and Neglect, 15,* 505–10.

Wyatt, B. S., & Conners, F. A., (1998). Implicit and explicit memory in individuals with mental retardation. *American Journal of Mental Retardation, 102*(5), 511–26.

13

Clinical and Organizational Perspectives on Denial and Delayed Disclosure

Clara H. Gumpert

Karolinska Institutet, Stockholm, Sweden

Assessing children suspected of being sexually maltreated is not easy, and over the years the issue of how sexual abuse should be assessed and diagnosed has evoked much debate. On one hand, professionals have been accused of "over-diagnosing" sexual abuse (Quinn, 1989), due to over reliance on vague data and lack of appropriate assessment techniques (Edvardson, 1996; Horner, Guyer, & Kalter, 1993). On the other hand, it has been claimed that the majority of instances of sexual abuse of children go undetected (Berliner, 1989). Several chapters in the current volume attest to the large number of children who remain silent about their abuse, at least during childhood (London et al., chapter 2, this volume). In part, the controversy about whether abuse is over- or underdiagnosed emanates from the different procedures and purposes of clinical and forensic assessment procedures, respectively. Numerous authors have emphasized the importance of recognizing a distinction between clinical and forensic assessment procedures (Borum & Grisso, 1996; Campbell, 1997; Heilbrun, Rosenfeld, Warren, & Collings, 1994; Skeem, Golding, Cohn, & Berge, 1998; Wiklund, 1999), and the importance of acknowledging the different responsibilities of a legal as opposed to a clinical decision-making process (Campbell, 1997; Horner, Guyer, & Kalter, 1993).

The purpose of this chapter is to explore some of the dilemmas and issues faced by clinicians who work with children who may have been abused, when the clinician must also consider the forensic implications of their work. In the first section, the reasons that clinicians are likely to encounter many children and adults who have, at some point, been abused but do not disclose the abuse are outlined, and the implications for clinical practice described. In the second section, the responsibilities of professional clinicians are described and potential conflicts with forensic practices considered. In the third section the question considered is whether disclosure of abuse that has occurred is of benefit, and therefore a therapeutic goal.

THE ROLE OF THE CLINICIAN

There is ample evidence that children who become victims of sexually abusive behavior risk developing both mental ill health and disturbed behaviors (Fergusson & Mullen, 1999; New & Berliner, 2000). Among the negative consequences are higher rates of adjustment problems such as mental health symptoms, low self-esteem, and behavioral disorders such as aggression, delinquency, and sexualized behaviors (Fergusson & Mullen, 1999, p. 54). Adult survivors of childhood sexual abuse also constitute a risk group with regard to mental disorder and psychological distress. Among the problems reported for adults are increased rates of depression, anxiety disorders, antisocial behaviors, eating disorders and substance abuse disorders, to mention a few (Fergusson & Mullen, 1999, p. 68). The severity of the abuse, whether or not force was involved, and the victim's relationship to the perpetrator seem to be of special importance with regard to social and emotional outcomes (Tyler, 2002).

Because abused children are more likely than others to develop psychological ill health or disturbed behaviors, they will be overrepresented in clinical populations. These children will often present for reasons other than the disclosure or identification of abuse. As a result, health care professionals as well as social workers, are likely to encounter a group of child clients whose problems can be fully or partially explained by the fact that they are currently being, or have been, abused, although the abuse has not yet been diagnosed. Professionals who are involved in the assessment of children displaying psychopathological or behavioral symptoms are well aware of this and are trained to look for different underlying explanations of the child's atypical behaviors. In seeking an explanation, clinicians typically explore a number of circumstances in the child's life including hereditary, social, familial and individual factors.

Assessing the psychological and physical health status of children constitutes a challenge, however, because there are seldom clear or simple reasons why an individual child has a particular problem or set of problems. Similar clinical profiles may be explained by different underlying factors and it is not always possible to determine the cause of a specific disturbance by mapping symptoms or deviant behaviors. Thus, the clinical approach needs to acknowledge that it is not always easy to identify a single target for intervention. On the contrary, interventions often need to be both broad and multifaceted and may involve such diverse measures as pharmacological treatment of the child, adjusting the school situation or securing financial support for the parents through contacts with social service agencies.

The complicated nature of evaluation procedures allows us to identify several potential pitfalls. One such pitfall is the conscious or unconscious search for monocausality. If, in any particular case, one clear problem is identified—let us say, for example, that a parent overconsumes alcohol—there is a risk that the identified factor may serve as the only explanation why a child has problems. Evaluation procedures may be finished halfway and interventions may be planned to do something about "the problem" (in this case, alcohol abuse) even though there may be several other problems—individual or familial—that are never identified. A second related concern is that some clinicians may be better equipped to diagnose certain conditions than other conditions because of area of interest and specialization. Similarly, some clinicians may be prone to explain phenomena less well understood as being caused by external factors rather than, for example, being signs of an underlying individual disorder or vice versa. The most complicated situation occurs when specific symptoms, for example sexual behaviors, may be explained *either* by individual or external factors or *both*. In practice, this may lead to a situation in which proponents of different explanatory models may each be partially "right." Such situations have the potential to create professional conflicts, either within an organization or between agencies with different theoretical emphases. The presence of different prevailing theoretical frameworks guiding the work with children and families may also serve as a possible complicating factor, particularly when children display symptoms that are difficult to interpret or when only scarce or vague information is available.

To conclude, a substantial number of children who come in contact with the health system may suffer from maltreatment, but the clinical picture alone may not give clear answers as to why an individual child displays symptoms. Clinicians need to be aware of the possible complex background of child problems and apply a holistic and flexible perspective on assessment and treatment.

CLINICAL AND FORENSIC APPROACHES TO INTERVIEWING CHILDREN

For child professionals within the health care system or the social services, it is important to recognize that there are different types of professional conversations between children and adults. The ways in which adults communicate with children for diagnostic or therapeutic purposes may be different from those appropriate for a forensic interview. Special caution needs to be taken when a child is interviewed for forensic purposes (Lamb, Sternberg, & Esplin, 1998), because an interviewer's questioning style may influence a child's account (Ceci & Bruck, 1995, Poole & Lamb, 1997). Moreover, it is possible that children's responses in a forensic interview may be influenced by interviews, whether formal or informal, that have taken place earlier in different contexts.

All interactions between children and adults, verbal as well as nonverbal, are surrounded by specific (often unexpressed) rules. Although developing communicative skills is an important part of any training for child professionals, there are nonetheless contexts in which clinicians may rely on everyday conversational techniques. In daily conversation, adults frequently interrupt children or have the authority to decide how much time may be spent discussing certain topics. They frequently provide feedback relating to what the child has said, for example, as in paraphrasing, when an adult repeats what the child has said but changes the original phrase so that it makes grammatical sense (Myklebust & Alison, 2000). As a consequence, children are accustomed to adults repeating and possibly correcting what they have said. Another common conversational technique is to summarize what a child has said in order to confirm whether the intention of an utterance or account has been correctly understood, or to help the child put together different pieces of information. In verbal interactions between children and adults, therefore, adults are typically not only the more active conversational partner, but they also take on a large responsibility for formulating and interpreting what is being said because of the uneven balance of power between children and adults.

In a regular clinical setting, such everyday conversational styles may not constitute any obvious problem. Indeed, to the contrary, the fact that both the child and the professional adult act in accordance with what is to be expected most certainly serves as a way of creating a sense of recognition and safety for both participants. During a diagnostic session, time is often scarce and there may be a need for quick gathering of specific information; focused interview techniques may thus seem necessary. Moreover, in a therapeutic session, the therapist may deliberately use a more interpretative conversational style as a therapeutic tool.

During such clinical sessions, there is always the possibility that a clinician may come across information that will raise suspicions of maltreatment. The information may be in the form of a verbal statement, although in many cases a combination of different pieces of information together provides an impression that something is wrong. Suspicions of abuse may arise both in situations in which the child and the professional have developed a mutual trust, for example during therapy, and also during the first encounter between the child and the professional, for example during a physical examination or when a sibling has been identified as a victim of abuse. In either case, health care professionals need to be prepared for the unforeseen and to take appropriate action when needed.

How, in such situations, does the professional balance the competing demands of the clinical and legal processes? Over the years, various initiatives have been taken in order to protect children at risk. In Sweden, as in many other countries, the first line of action usually involves contacting the child protective services (CPS), a practice that is strongly encouraged by mandatory reporting. The formulation of this rule has changed over the years since first introduced in Sweden in 1924 (Socialstyrelsen, 2004). Today a wide group of professionals are obliged to adhere to this principle. The current legal statute requires staff in all agencies working with children, as well as in all agencies in the fields of health and social services, to notify the child protection services of every child whom they suspect to have been abused or neglected. The suspicions need not be confirmed, which means that cases with no verbal disclosure or only minimal information may be reported. The responsibility for investigating and acting on the reports rests with the community social service agencies.

Despite the obligation to contact the child protective services, far from all professionals comply with the requirement to report suspected cases (Lagerberg, 2000). There may be many reasons for this, including the fact that the suspicions are vague and difficult to put in words. The professional may be afraid of losing contact with the family once a report is made, and may worry that things will become worse for the child (Socialstyrelsen, 2004). To the individual professional, the decision to involve the legal authorities may become a dilemma. Good support may be offered through organizational measures such as supervision and clearly expressed routines for documentation and reporting. Such actions may serve as tools to protect all those involved: the patient, the professional, and the therapeutic relationship.

When abuse is suspected, child protective services—at least initially— often have to rely on information retrieved through the health care (or other professional) contacts. What, then, should a clinician do when a child provides information indicative of ongoing abuse? The health care professional must recognize the need to function as a professional whose primary focus is the health needs of the child patient. It would be unethical to suddenly change this focus or role. To do so may even jeopardize the mutual trust of the relationship, which may be the reason the child disclosed the abuse or otherwise raised the suspicion in the first place. However, clinicians also have a responsibility—a facilitory role—in relation to the legal process. Specifically, without losing sight of the therapeutic process, or without changing the style of interaction with the child, the clinician must also take steps to "protect" the information in at least two ways: first by ensuring that it is well documented, and second, by ensuring that the information provided by the child is not contaminated by the professional.

Clinicians need to have good routines for documenting what has been said and under which circumstances. Documentation is always part of clinical practice but is even more vital when abuse is suspected but not disclosed or even denied because any utterance from a child (or adults familiar with the child) will inevitably be scrutinized when the suspicions are later being re-evaluated. Documentation is, in fact, the only way to protect both the clinician and the child from errors or misinterpretations of what actually took place during a conversation. Usually, children have talked to other adults before coming in for formal forensic interviews. The mere fact that such conversations have occurred may raise concern and questions about the reliability of the child's statement (Gumpert & Lindblad, 1999). That is, if it is known that a child has talked to others before a formal interview, this may be considered a complicating factor during a legal process. As an illustration, some examples from written expert testimony that have previously been used in Swedish court proceedings are included (Gumpert & Lindblad, 1999, p.294):

> Influence from the discussion with the mother, the lawyer, and later during the police interview, has filled a proposed abusive event with content despite that it never occurred.

> [The girl's] expanding statement concerning [description of abuse] have primarily been judged as a product of "talk" between the girls and their parents . . . .

If previous clinical contacts need to be discussed during a legal procedure, documentation may help to assist in a correct evaluation of the quality of the child's statement. Suspicions of abuse without disclosures pose particular challenges for professional systems because the level of anxiety tends to rise when there is concern but no clear information to rely on. In such cases, documentation may protect whatever information there is by clearly describing how the suspicions have arisen and what has been said on both sides. Thorough documentation may also facilitate communication between agencies and reduce the risk of conflict among professionals.

Clinicians must also have a basic understanding of what is considered important when a child's statement is to be used for forensic purposes. Awareness of how questioning style may influence the children's accounts is essential to help clinicians avoid the most common pitfalls. For example, best practice techniques from a forensic perspective emphasize the importance of obtaining open-ended narratives from the child with minimal input from the professional. Although summarizing children's statements may be useful for clarification, as described above, reformulating the child's statements and introducing new information, particularly in a coercive interviewing style, may contaminate the child's account. This does not mean that the clinician should suddenly change conversational style and start performing forensic interviews. Instead, professionals who are aware of different professional roles and tasks may assist both the therapeutic and forensic purpose by letting the child decide what to say, how to say it and when.

Basic knowledge of the legal process and the demands it poses on children's testimony will assist the clinician to facilitate a potential disclosure. Such knowledge includes being aware of differences in conversational style and applying good documentation routines.

IS DISCLOSURE THERAPEUTIC?

The decision to disclose sexual abuse may be difficult and related to serious consequences, such as decreased well being and separation from caretakers. Ligezinska and colleagues found increased levels of emotional and behavioral difficulties following disclosure among children who had been subject to extra familial sexual abuse (Ligezinska, et al., 1996). Still, there may also be possible gains. Berliner and Conte (1993) found that only 1 out of 82 children regretted telling about abuse, even though the period following disclosure was a troublesome time for many of them (Quas et al., 2005).

It is important to keep in mind, however, that we only study or come in contact with that proportion of abuse victims who actually disclose abuse. The degree to which this group of individuals is representative of all children who are subject to sexual abuse is unknown. Thus, there is a systematic bias that may influence clinicians as well as researchers in the way we draw conclusions. The fact that many sexual crimes against children are not formally reported could indicate that there may be other ways of handling complicated life situations. For example, informal networks have been identified as ways of getting support, "although help from family and friends does not necessarily bring about justice-based solutions to criminal victimization" (Kaukinen, 2002, p. 451).

Should a clinician encourage a child to disclose abuse once the suspicion has occurred? Unfortunately, there is no simple answer to that question. On the one hand, the answer should definitely be "yes." As long as ongoing abuse is kept secret, there is little chance that a child will get assistance from the outside. And as noted above, the majority of informants in the study performed by Berliner and colleagues did not regret coming forward. On the other hand, some caution is warranted. If "encouraging" is translated into "pursuing," a child may feel pressured, which in turn might harm a developing but vulnerable trust between the child and an outside professional, and hamper the communication between the two. Legal procedures are dependent on cooperation from the child, and children need to be given the best possible conditions should they decide to disclose that they have been or are being maltreated.

Some results from a study recently undertaken at the Division of Forensic Psychiatry at Karolinska Institutet in Stockholm might serve as illustrations of the complicated nature of the disclosure process. The informants were children and young adults who had been involved in legal processes concerning sexual abuse. The study focused on disclosure processes (what made these children tell anyone about the abuse?) and their experiences from the legal investigation. Many of these children were positive about disclosing abuse, but some of their comments demonstrate the difficulties the children had to face.

Anna is 19 years old and was abused for many years by her foster father. She disclosed the abuse several years after she had left the foster home. Looking back, she feels that she tried to tell people around her of what was going on.

> Interviewer: "Can you give an example of what you did?"
> Informant: "I had this friend. His mother, well I felt I could talk to her. [—] Yes, and I tried. I only told that he had been touching me. I thought

"I will start like this." But, well. . . .

Interviewer: "Do you remember what she said? How she reacted?"

Informant: "Well, she didn't seem upset. I felt as if I didn't get any response."

Interviewer: "Did you tell her anything more then?"

Informant: "No. You know, at that point, you give up. And I had tried to tell before, not that I was being used, but there were lots of problems at home and that I had been beaten. And that I had been treated unfairly. But that was part of bringing up children, I was told."

Eventually, Anna disclosed the abuse during a police interview.

Interviewer: " . . . what can you teach us . . . what would you like to tell us if you look back?"

Informant: "Well . . ."

Interviewer: "I meet police every day who speak to children who do not say anything."

Informant:"Yes. Right . . . what can I say? First of all, it takes time. A lot of time. And that you don't give up, but handle things in a psychological way. [. . .] They did it well. They took their time, and I could be with [the same female police], and they supported me all the time. Because if someone just sits there and pushes you to give information, well you give up. You can't stand it. But if you are supported . . . "

Interviewer: "And support, was that the information you got?" [author's note: the police had informed Anna that other children in the same family were safe and her the man had been arrested]

Informant: "Yes! That is rather important."

Lena is 12 years old. A few years ago, she was abused by a man who lived close to the playground where she and her friends used to play. She told her mother of the event immediately after it happened.

Interviewer: " . . .if a friend came up to you and told you that some adult person had done anything like this—what would you tell her or him?"

Informant: "That they should tell. Talk to someone they know."

Interviewer: "Even if it was difficult?"

Informant: "Yes."

Interviewer: "Did you ever regret that you told your mother or the police?"

Informant: "No."

Hanna is 9 years old and was abused by an acquaintance of the family. She did not say anything until several weeks after the event.

Interviewer: "If you met, if you had a friend who told you that someone had behaved this way toward them, what would you tell them?"

Informant: "I would say that if they hadn't told their mother, I would tell them that it happened to me, too. And that I had told my sister and so on. Then I would say that if you have a sister you can tell her."

Interviewer: "You think one should tell."

Informant: "Yes. And that they shall call the police."

Interviewer: "Do you think there are children who do not tell anyone at all?"

Informant: "Yes."

Interviewer: "Why do you think it may be that way?"

Informant: "I don't know. I just think so."

However, there was also information pointing in other directions. If questioning was perceived as premature it could prevent the child from disclosing. For example, Susanne was 20 years old and had been abused by her father for years. When suspicions arose in relation to another child in the family, Susanne was taken to the police station for an interview. She was shocked and did not say anything.

Informant: "I only remember that I was really scared and there were a lot of questions and they asked all the time if I understood . . . 'Do you understand? Do you understand?'"

Interviewer: "Do you remember what you thought at that time?"

Informant: "That they were stupid! [—] And then, I don't know, I forgot about everything or what should I say, I became so stressed, it was as if the door just closed . . . [—] . . . then I didn't remember anything for several years! [—] . . . they told me: 'Can you tell us?' and I just said 'No, I don't know' and 'I don't know anything' and 'I don't understand' You know, it was as if I became stupid instead."

Susanne did not disclose the abuse until several years later. She displayed psychological symptoms and had frequent contacts with the local child and adolescent psychiatric clinic.

Interviewer: "Did you think about the abuse at all during those years?"

Informant: "No."

Interviewer: "If I had been working in that psychiatric clinic, let's say when you were 13, and I would have asked you 'did anyone ever use you for sexual purposes' . . .

Informant: "I would have denied it, straight away. That I would have done."

As child professionals, we may expect that a child understands that disclosing abuse will create an opportunity to mobilize help from the outside. However, such a way of thinking requires that a child also perceives the abuse as abnormal. What may appear as logical reasoning to an adult does not always make sense to a child.

> Interviewer: "Before that, didn't you realize something was wrong? Didn't the fact that your father told you not to talk to anyone about it make you suspicious?"
>
> Informant: "I think I was too young to understand that this was wrong. It was more like, you know, you never talk to anyone about the fact that you go to the bathroom several times a day . . . it was a thing like that." (Susanne, 20).
>
> Interviewer: "when it happened, did you understand that it was wrong?"
>
> Informant: "No."
>
> Interviewer: "How long did it take before . . . or what was it that made you understand?"
>
> Informant: "Several years passed. When you're around 11 or 12, then you understand that things are not what they should be."
>
> Interviewer: "What was it that made you understand?"
>
> Informant: "Well, I saw what it was like in other families. That's when you can compare, you know, you realize that this isn't sound. But . . . at that time, that was all I knew. I didn't know anything else, he kept telling . . . you know, it is still someone you look up to, and you expect them to do the right things with someone who is little . . ." (Anna, 20)

When a child displays symptoms, adults know that this may be caused by external factors such as maltreatment. Children may not make that connection. Carl, a boy of 15, was abused by a relative between 11 and 13 years of age. During that time he was having problems at school and there were many conflicts at home. His parents were concerned about his acting out behavior and contacted different professionals in order to get help. But Carl did not believe he had any particular problem; nor did he connect the ongoing abuse to the way he was behaving.

> Interviewer: "If I put it like this: Did you think—before you told anyone—that you had any problems?"
>
> Informant: "No."
>
> Interviewer: "You didn't think you were different in any way?"
>
> Informant: "No!"
>
> Interviewer: "The fact that your parents brought you to the psychologist or the hospital . . ."

Informant: "That only made me more pissed off!"

Interviewer: [—] . . . so you didn't connect your way of being with what was going on with this man?"

Informant: "No."

Pushing for information at a time when a child is unprepared, or assuming that a child understands that telling might help, or that symptoms may be related to abuse, are all preconceptions that may add to communicative difficulties between children and adults. With the best interests of the child in mind, clinicians may be blinded by their own perspectives and pursue disclosing, even though this might jeopardize the legal as well as the therapeutic process. A hampered legal evaluation may influence the well-being and level of emotional stress in the child. Thus, we need to recognize that the therapeutic and the legal process are dependent on each other, and that we need to protect both of these processes to the best of our ability. Disclosure is unpredictable and in the individual case, we do not always know what motivates a child to talk. Rather than pursuing disclosure, we need to learn more about how to optimize the conditions, so that we can create an arena in which we are prepared to listen and children are allowed to bring up what matters to them at a time of their own choosing.

To summarize, despite the different professional goals of the legal and the therapeutic systems, they do not work independently of each other. Children are likely to at times disclose abuse during encounters with the health care system, and when they do, the legal system is dependent on a reasonable level of forensic knowledge among health professionals in order to protect the criminal investigation procedure as much as possible. The legal process may also require active support from competent health professionals, as witnesses or expert witnesses, to present important information before the court. A child or family who is under the pressure of a legal investigation may be in need of therapeutic support from clinicians. Regardless, if such interventions are provided before or during legal proceedings, they must be delivered with thoughtful consideration.

The caring systems, be they child protection or health care, do not supply their services isolated from the legal process. The presence of a criminal conviction may enhance the rehabilitation process through the provision of the possibility of protecting a child from further abuse. That being said, it is obvious that clinicians may face dilemmas if there is concern for a child who does not disclose. Being a child health professional implies encountering legal as well as moral and ethical issues in relation to patients. In order to optimize responsiveness for children and families at risk, clinical organizations are obliged to support their employees through adopting a proactive approach. At a minimum, this should include case supervision, education on legal matters and the establishment of good routines for documentation and reporting.

REFERENCES

Berliner, L. & Conte, J. (1995). The effects of disclosure and intervention on sexually abused children. *Child Abuse & Neglect, 19,* 371–84.

Berliner, L. (1989). Resolved: child sexual abuse is over diagnosed. *Journal of the American Academy of Child and Adolescent Psychiatry, 28,* 789–97.

Borum, R., & Grisso, T. (1996). Establishing standards for criminal forensic reports: An empirical analysis. *Bulletin of American Academy of Psychology & the Law, 24,* 297–317.

Campbell, T. W. (1997). *Indicators of child sexual abuse and their unreliability. American Journal of Forensic Psychology, 15,* 5–17.

Ceci, S. J. & Bruck, M. (1993). Suggestibility of the child witness: a historical review and synthesis. *Psychological Bulletin, 113,* 403–39.

Cederborg, A.-C., Orbach, Y., Sternberg, K. J., & Lamb, M. (2000). Investigative interviews of child witnesses in Sweden. *Child Abuse & Neglect, 24,* 1355–61.

Davey, R. I. & Hill, J. (1999). The variability of practice in interviews used by professionals to investigate child sexual abuse. *Child Abuse & Neglect, 23,* 571–78.

Edvardson, B. (1996). *Kritisk utredningsmetodik [Critical Assessment Methodology].* Stockholm: Liber Utbildning.

Fergusson, D. M., & Mullen, P. E. (1999). *Childhood sexual abuse. An evidence based perspective.* Thousand Oaks, CA: Sage Publications.

Gumpert, C. H. & Lindblad, F. (1999). Statement analysis in Sweden: A review of expert testimony regarding alleged child sexual abuse. *Expert Evidence, 7,* 279–314.

Heilbrun, K., Rosenfeld, B., Warren, J., & Collins, S. (1994). The use of third-party information in forensic assessments: A two-state comparison. *Bulletin of American Academy of Psychiatry and Law, 22,* 399–406.

Horner, T. M., Guyer, M. J., & Kalter, N. M. (1993). The biases of child sexual abuse experts: Believing is seeing. *Bulletin of the American Academy of Psychiatry and the Law, 21,* 281–92.

Kaukinen, C. (2002). The help-seeking decisions of violent crime victims. An examination och the direct and conditional effects of gender on the victim-gender relationship. *Journal of Interpersonal Violence, 17*(4), 432–56.

Lagerberg, D. (2001). A descriptive survey of Swedish child health nurses' awareness of abuse and neglect. *Child Abuse & Neglect, Vol. 25,* 1583–1601.

Lamb, M. E., Sternberg, K. J., & Esplin, P. W. (1998). Conducting investigative interviews of alleged sexual abuse victims. *Child Abuse & Neglect, 22,* 813–23.

Ligezinska, M., Firestone, P., Manion, I. G., McIntyre, J., Ensom, R., & Wells, G. (1996). Children's emotional and behavioral reactions following the disclosure of extrafamilial sexual abuse: Initial effects. *Child Abuse & Neglect, 1996, 20,* 111–25.

Myklebust, T. & Alison, L. (2000). The current state of police interviews with children in Norway: How discrepant are they from models based on current issues in memory and communication? *Psychology, Crime & Law, 6,* 331–51.

New, M. & Berliner, L. (2000). Mental health service utilization by victims of crime. *Journal of Traumatic Stress, 13*(4), 693–707.

Quinn, K. M. (1989). Resolved: child sexual abuse is overdiagnosed. *Journal of the American Academy of Child and Adolescent Psychiatry, 22,* 789–97.

Skeem, J. L., Golding, S. L., Cohn, N. B., & Berge, G. (1998). Logic and reliability of evaluations of competence to stand trial. *Law and Human Behavior, 22,* 519–47.

Socialstyrelsen (2004) [National Board on Health and Welfare]. *Anmälningsskyldighet om missförhållanden som rör barn [Mandatory reporting of maltreatment related to children].* Stockholm: Socialstyrelsen.

Sternberg, K .J., Lamb, M. E., Davies, G. M., & Westcott, H. L. (2001). The Memorandum of Good Practice: theory versus application. *Child Abuse & Neglect, 25,* 669–81.

Tyler, K. A., Hoyt, D. R., & Whitbeck, L. B. (2000). The effects of early childhood sexual abuse on later sexual victimization among female homeless and runaway adolescents. *Journal of Interpersonal Violence, 15,* 235–50.

Wiklund, N. (1999). Oskyldigt dömda: erfarenheter och lärdomar [Innocent and convicted: experiences and lessons.] *Svensk Juristtidning [Swedish Law Review],* 562–67.

14

Forensic Interviewing in New Zealand

Karen Wilson
Department of Child, Youth and Family, New Zealand

In 1989 New Zealand introduced legislation to enable children's evidence-in-chief to be prerecorded on videotape. Since then a national forensic interviewing infrastructure has developed, resulting in the specialization of forensic interviewers, a single national training program, and national peer review processes. Referring children for forensic interviews has become an integral part of the New Zealand social work care and protection and investigation process. Approximately 2,000 videotaped interviews are conducted annually, with statistical data from these interviews having been collated into national reports since 1998 (Basher, 1999, 2001, 2003, 2004).

This chapter will outline the forensic interviewing infrastructure in New Zealand and provide statistical data for three fiscal years (2000 to 2002). Issues of relevance to disclosure and nondisclosure are highlighted and discussed.

THE NEW ZEALAND CONTEXT

New Zealand is a small country with a population of approximately four million people. The ethnicity figures from the last census showed that 80% of the population identified as European, 14.7% as Maori (the indigenous population), 6.5% as Pacific Peoples, 6.6% as Asian, and 0.7% as Other (Statistics New Zealand, 2001). Some people identified with more than one ethnic group.

The statutory agency charged with ensuring the care and protection of children under 17 is the Department of Child, Youth, and Family. This agency has a national, regional, and local structure, and its statutory powers and obligations are contained in the Children, Young Persons, and Their Families Act (1989). National interagency protocols exist between Child, Youth, and Family and the police to ensure a joint agency approach to the care and protection of children (New Zealand Children, Young Persons, and Their Families Service and the New Zealand Police, 2001 & 2003). This joint focus is designed to ensure that the protection of the child and the investigation of a crime are both properly considered.

New Zealand introduced changes to child witness legislation in 1989 through two Acts: the Evidence Amendment Act and the Summary Proceedings Act. Prior to 1989 child witnesses in sexual abuse cases were required to give evidence in open court in the presence of the alleged perpetrator. Corroboration was required for a conviction and judges had a duty to warn juries to scrutinize the evidence of young children with special care.

The 1989 legislation aimed to better facilitate children's access to legal processes. For sexual abuse complainants this meant the need for corroborative evidence was abandoned, children under 17 at trial were able to give their evidence-in-chief via a prerecorded videotaped interview, and the duty to warn juries about children's evidence was removed. Although the complainant is still required at the trial for cross-examination, alternate modes of evidence can be requested (such as closed circuit television outside the courtroom, or screens in court to prevent the child from seeing the accused). The use of intermediaries does not appear to be prohibited by the legislation but as yet this remains untested in the legal arena.

Through common law precedents and the "inherent jurisdiction" of the court, the child witness provisions have now been extended to crimes other than sexual abuse and to children who are not themselves complainants. Videotaped forensic interviews are now routinely conducted for sexual abuse allegations, serious physical abuse allegations, and in cases in which children have been witnesses to violent crime, such as domestic violence and murder. Referral criteria for interview include a clear allegation from the child, or in the absence of an allegation a high threshold of concern that abuse has occurred. If a child repeats or makes an allegation at interview, an *evidential* format is followed. If a child does not repeat or make an allegation during an interview, a *diagnostic* (exploratory) format is followed. Processes exist within the broader sexual abuse investigation system that provide a continuum of default options for nondisclosing children where there are serious concerns.

The Forensic Interviewing Infrastructure

Child, Youth, and Family and the police are jointly responsible for ensuring that at-risk children have access to a forensic video interviewing service. The Evidence (Videotaping of Child Complainants) Regulations (1990) and Joint Police and Child, Youth, and Family Operating Guidelines for videotaped interviews (1996) set out the legal standards that forensic (both evidential and diagnostic) interviews have to meet to be accepted as evidence-in-chief in court. For example the videotape must be continuous, must include names, times, date, and location, and an analogue clock with a sweeping hand must be in view throughout the interview. The interviewer is required to establish the child's competency through a child-friendly version of the oath, covering the child's understanding of truth, lies, and promises and obtaining a promise to tell the truth when these concepts appear to have been understood.

There has been a growing acknowledgement in New Zealand that the role of forensic interviewing is complex and is best provided by full-time specialist staff rather than by staff working generically as social workers or police officers (Dawson, 1995; Dawson, Morgan & Rugg, 1996; Eichelbaum, 2001; Hamlin & Nation, 1997; Wilson, 1993,1995, 2002). Although there are still parts of the country utilizing generic staff in dual roles, many police and Child, Youth, and Family districts now provide full-time staff working out of a Video Unit location. Coupled with the small size of the country, this has allowed a national forensic interviewing infrastructure to develop. A joint Police/Child, Youth, and Family national training system, regular regional and national peer review processes, and clinical supervision are all factors that have enhanced consistency in forensic interviewing practice.

Prior to conducting a forensic interview, all interviewers (whether police or social workers) must have completed the national evidential interviewing training course held annually at the Royal New Zealand Police College. This course is jointly funded and coordinated by the police and Child, Youth, and Family. Ten social workers and 10 police officers are selected each year with selection based on individual suitability criteria and geographical need.

The training course is a two-week residential program that combines theory and practice. Workshops are run on the child witness legislation, sexual crimes, sexual abuse dynamics, child development, international forensic research, video unit processes, caregiver preinterview, court precedents, expert testimony, sexual offender behaviour, bicultural practice and stress management. In the practical component of the course, practitioners are taught a structured interview method through demonstration and practice. On the last two days trainees conduct live videotaped interviews with actors and are assessed by experienced practitioners regarding their level of competence and suitability to continue in the role.

After the course, trainees are expected to continue training at Video Units, with strong emphasis being placed on the importance of continued monitoring, role-play practice, and supervision to increase competency. Initial interviews are expected to be carefully selected, for example, with an articulate child who is alleging a single incident of abuse and is ready to talk about what has happened. In addition to regular clinical supervision, interviewers are expected to attend regular regional Peer Tape Review workshops and annual National Peer Tape Review meetings. The latter provide interviewers from all over the country with a forum to hear relevant speakers, discuss practice issues, critique tapes, and work towards practice standardization. A new week-long advanced national training course for experienced practitioners was implemented in 2002 and is likely to continue biannually.

Evidential (Forensic) Videotaped Interview Format

The early New Zealand evidential interviewing model was adapted from the American models of the late 1980s. Since then the international field of forensic interviewing research has greatly influenced practice and the New Zealand model has evolved accordingly. The national model is reviewed and updated by the national trainer every year, and the revised training manual is sent to all existing practitioners with changes being discussed at national peer review meetings (Wilson, 2003).

The first stage of the interview is designed to meet the legal requirements of the act and the regulations and to facilitate free narrative practice on neutral topics. Ground rules are covered and younger children are asked questions about colors, counting, and prepositions. The child-friendly oath is a compulsory requirement for all age groups.

The question "Why have you come here today?" is used as the transition question to the second stage of the interview. Free narrative techniques and open questions are taught as the favored means for gathering details of the allegations. Interviewers are advised not to introduce prior knowledge, and are made aware of issues to do with source monitoring. Recent complaint evidence (the first person the child told) is covered, as the recipient of that initial disclosure is exempted from the hearsay rule and permitted to give evidence at court. Nonanatomical body outlines are sometimes used as a clarifying tool following verbal allegations where names used for body parts might be ambiguous. Anatomically correct dolls are not used, but clothed dolls are permitted to clarify body positioning when the child's verbal account is unclear. Timelines and floor plans are other tools sometimes used to assist children to describe their experiences.

The closure stage of the interview begins with the interviewer consulting briefly with the monitor (either the investigating police officer or another forensic interviewer) who has been observing the interview on closed circuit television and keeping notes. Clarifying questions are then asked and the interview is closed. Depending on the complexity of the case, interview length varies from 30 minutes to an hour and a half, with the majority being less than one hour long. It is very rare for children to undergo a second evidential interview regarding the same allegation (Basher, 1999, 2001, 2003).

Diagnostic (Exploratory) Videotaped Interview Format

Videotaped diagnostic interviews are conducted with nondisclosing children (usually aged between 3 and 10) when there is a high level of risk that they are being abused. The threshold for entry to this process is high and includes children who have sexually transmitted diseases or other medical concerns, children who have made partial unclear allegations, children who have had contact with known offenders, children displaying unusual and persistent sexualized behaviors, and situations where the abuse has been witnessed but not disclosed, or there have been offender admissions. There is no national standardized training for diagnostic interviewing, although practice guidelines are contained in the joint operating guidelines for evidential and diagnostic interviewing on videotape (New Zealand Children, Young Persons and Their Families Service and the New Zealand Police, 1996).

Diagnostic interviews are predominantly undertaken by Child, Youth, and Family forensic interviewers who have completed evidential interviewing training. The interview process is designed as an exploratory, nonleading process of up to three interviews and has a more flexible structure than an evidential interview. However, a diagnostic interview on videotape must be conducted in accordance with the Evidential Regulations, which means that the first stage of the interview is the same as that used for evidential interviews. This is considered important given that a diagnostic interview may continue as an evidential if a child does disclose, and conversely an evidential interview may default to a diagnostic interview if the child is reluctant or nondisclosing. This reduces the potential for multiple interviews as both types of interview become admissible in the criminal court system.

Topics covered in a videotaped diagnostic interview format may include family members, people of concern, feelings, likes and dislikes, routines, secrets, hurts, worries, adult allies, and personal safety strategies. Free narrative is encouraged and the subject of body parts and touching is not introduced unless raised by the child. Most children are interviewed once, with referrals being made to other assessment services if strong concerns remain.

NATIONAL DATA FROM NEW ZEALAND FORENSIC VIDEO UNITS

In 1997 Forensic Interviewers decided to collect standardized statistics about every videotaped diagnostic and evidential interview conducted in New Zealand. This practitioner-driven initiative has resulted in close to total national data capture since 1998 with all statistics being collated manually on an Excel spreadsheet program at Manuwai Specialist Services, Child, Youth and Family, in Hamilton. The information has been summarized in annual reports by Basher (1999, 2001, 2003, 2004) and used to answer government and media questions, as well as to highlight the importance of the interviewing function in care and protection processes. Although at this time the analysis is limited by Excel capabilities, there is potential to transfer the existent data to a more robust program in the future. There is no current ability to separate substantiated cases from unsubstantiated cases; therefore the data collected relates to alleged abuse rather than abuse that has been corroborated.

The national data presented here combines raw Excel data collected from the fiscal years 2000 to 2002, inclusive.[1] For this three-year period the statistical capture form was altered to better separate sexual abuse interviews from physical abuse ones. Combined physical and sexual abuse figures are presented first and interview outcomes are compared. The following sections focus specifically on sexual abuse data, particularly in relation to interview outcomes and disclosure (termed *allegations*). There is no capability within the current system to extract details about the time delay between the alleged abuse and a child's disclosure.

General Features: Sexual Abuse and Physical Abuse Combined

Approximately 2,000 videotaped interviews are conducted annually in New Zealand. Figure 14.1 shows that a total of 5,652 videotaped interviews with 5,384 children were conducted in the three-year period, with 96% of the children having a single interview.

In total, 69% ($n = 3,714$) of the 5,384 children were referred for evidential interviews following a prior disclosure to somebody about sexual abuse or serious physical abuse (figure 14.2). Approximately 3% of these children were eye witnesses to abuse rather than victims themselves. The majority of the

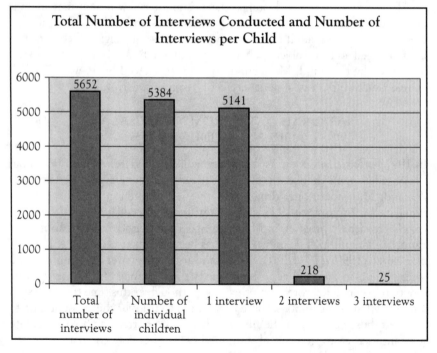

Figure 14.1 Total number of interviews conducted and number of interviews per child.

---

[1] Some of the same raw data has been produced and discussed by Basher (2004) in *Social Work Now*, vol 27, and is reprinted here with permission.

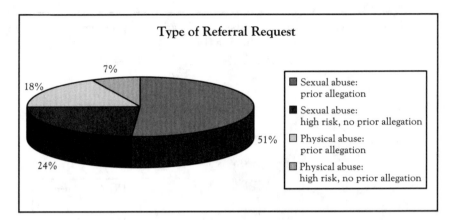

Figure 14.2 Type of referral request.

5,384 children were referred for concerns about sexual abuse ($n = 4,060$) with 68% of this group having made a prior allegation to somebody ($n = 2,756$). Only 31% of those interviewed had made no previous allegation with a total of 1,304 diagnostic interviews conducted for sexual abuse concerns and 372 for serious physical abuse concerns.

Of the 5,384 children interviewed 73% ($n = 3,905$) made an allegation of sexual abuse or serious physical abuse at interview. Not all of the 3,708 children who were referred following a prior allegation repeated the allegation in their evidential interview, and in some cases the interview clarified that no actual abuse had occurred (for example if an adult had misunderstood a child's initial remarks and the child provided a credible explanation at interview).

Sixty-five percent of all referrals were for girls ($n = 3,503$) with 82% of these being for sexual abuse concerns. The gender differences for sexual abuse allegations will be discussed in a later section. Slightly more boys than girls were referred for physical abuse (691:633) with 90% of girls and 86% of boys making allegations in these interviews.

Figure 14.3 provides an age breakdown for the children interviewed and the numbers of allegations made by each age group at interview. Fifty-six percent of children interviewed were aged between 5 and 10 ($n = 2,998$). Sixty percent of the 5- to 7-year old group made allegations at interview as compared to 76% for the 8- to 10-year olds. Only 9% ($n = 528$) of those interviewed were of preschool age (under 5) and this group had the lowest rate of allegations at 42%. The 11 to 13-age group comprised 25% of the total ($n = 1,370$) with 88% of the 11 to 16-year olds ($n = 1803$) making an allegation at interview. This age group was more likely to have been referred for evidential interviews after prior disclosure, so a higher allegation rate would be expected. The over 16 category is small and consists predominantly of intellectually delayed adults being interviewed for sexual abuse concerns.

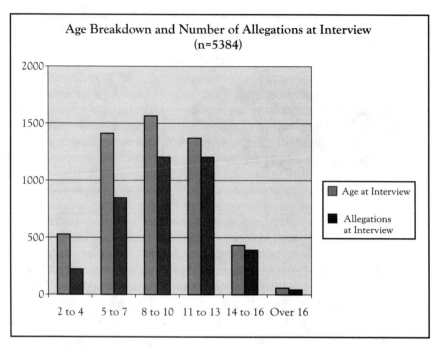

Figure 14.3 Age breakdown and number of allegations at interview (n = 5,384).

Outcome Data for Interviews for Sexual Abuse Concerns

Over the three-year period a total of 4,060 children were referred for interviews about sexual abuse concerns (2,870 girls and 1,190 boys). Fifty-five percent were European, 33% Maori, 7% Pacific Island nations, and 3% from other ethnicities. The majority (68%) had made a prior allegation to somebody and most of these children were interviewed in an evidential format. The interview defaulted to a diagnostic format for those children who were reluctant or unable to repeat the allegation at the interview. The majority of the children (95%) were interviewed once, with only 201 children returning to a video unit for further interviews related to the same concern.

Of the 4,060 children interviewed, 2,744 (68%) made allegations at interview (figure 14.4). This included 117 children who had witnessed sexual offenses against other children or were assessed as having been engaged in noncoercive sex-related activities. Of the children referred following a prior allegation, 12% (n = 341) either did not repeat the allegation at interview or were able to clarify the referral concerns. The diagnostic interview format produced a 25% allegation rate (n = 329) for children who had not previously alleged abuse.

Of the 2,870 girls interviewed for sexual abuse concerns, 79% made an allegation at interview compared to only 57% of the 1,190 boys. This gender dif-

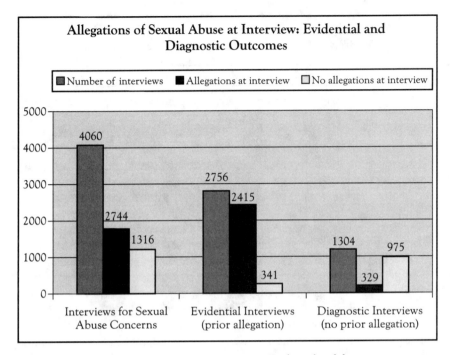

Figure 14.4 Allegations of sexual abuse at interview: Evidential and diagnotic outcomes.

ference is of concern given that the referral criteria and thresholds for entry to the interviewing process is the same for both sexes. The system used for data capture does not allow a further breakdown of this difference, for example linking gender with age for the boys that did not make allegations.

The percentage of children making allegations at interview increased with age (figure 14.5). Preschoolers had the lowest rate at 40%, and the 14- to 16-year olds, the highest rate at 88%. The allegation rate for those aged under 8 was 47% as compared to 79% for those aged 8 and over. One explanation for this may be that the older children were more likely to have been referred following a prior allegation. It may also indicate that the interviewing processes are better suited to older children.

Forensic interviewers are asked to record their level of ongoing concern for children who made no allegation at interview. This is a subjective measurement based on the referral information, the information provided by the caregiver, and the child's presentation at interview.

For the three-year period reported here, there were 1,316 children referred for sexual abuse concerns who made no allegation at interview. Interviewers classified their level of ongoing concern into four broad categories. The majority (52%) were considered to be at no risk of ongoing abuse, often because the referral concern was clarified at interview. A further 24% were ei-

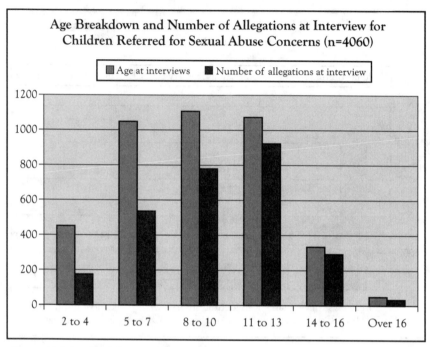

Figure 14.5 Age breakdown and number of allegations at interview for children referred for sexual abuse concerns ($n = 4,060$).

ther considered too young developmentally to complete the interview process, or provided information that was too confused to make an assessment. The remaining 24% of cases were assessed as having a continued level of concern. Of these, 153 children were considered to be at some risk that sexual abuse had either occurred or was ongoing, and 160 children were considered to be at high risk. Unfortunately an age and gender breakdown is not available for this group.

Given that concerns remained, or were unable to be clarified, for 626 of 1,316 the children who made no allegation at interview, it is surprising that only 201 of all the 4,060 children referred for sexual abuse concerns had returned for a second or third interview. It is likely that a high percentage of these second and third interviews were with the children considered at the highest risk, but there is no way of confirming this through the data. Other children were referred to external psychological or counseling services for further assessment of their safety, and may have returned to a Video Unit at a later date to document any allegations made in that external setting.

Figure 14.4 shows that of the 1,304 nondisclosing children referred for diagnostic interviews, 25% made an allegation at interview. Of these 13,04 children, a subgroup of 584 were referred for having had contact with an alleged sexual offender, often because a sibling or family member had made an allegation against that person. Of this group, 190 (33%) made an allegation at interview. This suggests that there may be efficacy in routinely interviewing all children who have been in contact with named perpetrators.

Ninety-three percent of the allegations made were about perpetrators known to the child, with 53% being intrafamilial prior relationships and 40% extrafamilial acquaintances. Strangers continue to account for very few of the overall allegations (7%). The gender of the children making the allegations could not be identified from the prior relationship data.

Alleged perpetrators were predominantly males (96%) with adult males accounting for 74% of the total. Males between 12 and 16 years old were named by 17% of the children, which is consistent with international findings and previous New Zealand reports (Basher, 1999, 2001, 2003, 2004). The 35 adult females named represent 1% of the total, which is also consistent with previous figures. *Indecent assault* and *sexual violation* were the most common types of abuse alleged by the children, with sexual violation (vaginal, anal, or oral penetration) being a feature of 35% of the allegations.

Overall the data indicates that the evidential and diagnostic interviewing process appears to help facilitate disclosure for many children. However, there is some evidence that postinterview processes are inadequate with only 40% of children having been referred on for individual counseling. Although this may represent a recording problem, it is of concern that many children may not be receiving appropriate follow up services. This is suggested by the fact that of the 2,744 children who made sexual abuse allegations at interview, 545 (20%) had been diagnostically or evidentially interviewed previously at a Video Unit. Some of these children may not have been ready to disclose at a previous interview and others had previously reported abuse by a different perpetrator.

IMPLICATIONS FOR DELAY, RELUCTANCE AND NONDISCLOSURE

Although there are limitations for how the data can be analysed, many of the figures presented here have relevance to the current debate on delayed, reluctant, and nondisclosure of child abuse.

Disclosure of sexual abuse is acknowledged as a complex process for children. Factors such as age, cognitive ability, gender, level of familial support, loyalty to the perpetrator, and fear of consequences all impact on a child's ability or willingness to disclose. The New Zealand forensic interviewing process does not offer a magical formula for overcoming reluctance. It does, however, provide a carefully structured interviewing process through which children can repeat previous allegations or choose to raise allegations that were previously undisclosed. The fact that 88% of those interviewed following a prior allegation repeated the allegation at interview, and that 25% of those interviewed for high risk made allegations at interview for the first time, indicates that the New Zealand system is achieving this broad purpose.

However, the current forensic interviewing system relies on children having the cognition to understand the interview process and the willingness and ability to make clear verbal allegations. This has particular implications for very young children (especially those under 5 years old) and does not cater adequately for preverbal, reluctant, or inarticulate children. The compulsory aspect of the child-friendly oath further limits children's ability to complete the process to legal requirements. The process appears more suited to girls (79% of whom made sexual abuse allegations at interview as compared to 57% of the boys), and appears effective with nondisclosing children who are referred for contact with an alleged sexual abuser.

The New Zealand data relates to unsubstantiated allegations of sexual abuse, and it is not possible to estimate to what extent there are false positives included in the figures. It is likely, however, that there are false negative outcomes amongst the 1,316 children who did not make allegations at interview, especially for the 313 children assessed by the interviewer as being at continued risk. While the evidential requirement for free narrative techniques, nondirective questioning, and neutrality around prior knowledge are accepted by interviewers, other focused questioning techniques may be necessary for this high risk group.

The New Zealand evidential and diagnostic data provides no information on the time delay between the last incident of alleged abuse and disclosure. It is not possible to gather this information retrospectively from the data forms, but a section on time delays could be included in the future. Similarly the data form does not ask interviewers to comment on children's perceived barriers to disclosure, such as fear of consequences and embarrassment. Many children do raise these issues in response to interviewer questions about who they told and what made them decide to tell at that time (recent complaint evidence). Qualitative recording of these responses is a future option, but consistent capture across all the children interviewed would be unlikely. Other research options, based on substantiated cases, would be more appropriate for attaining this information.

Nondisclosing children do pose a challenge to the care and protection system. Entry to the forensic interviewing process for these children requires a high threshold of concern. In this sense diagnostic interviewing offers an additional assessment tool to social workers who are investigating care and protection notifications that indicate abuse is likely to have occurred. Despite the high threshold level, the Video Unit data reported here shows that of the 4,060 children referred for sexual abuse concerns, 690 (17%) were assessed by forensic interviewers as likely to be currently "safe." Even though abuse cannot be ruled out for this group, the data does suggest that forensic interviewing provides a screening service for risk. This assists social workers and the police to direct investigation and therapy resources into children who have either disclosed abuse, or are assessed as being at a high risk of abuse.

One potential negative outcome when abused children do not disclose at forensic interview is parental disbelief that the child is at risk. However, forensic interviewing is just one option on a continuum for nondisclosing children and is not always appropriate. Child Focused Interviewing courses are available to generic social workers, and this has resulted in a preforensic screening process in some regions. A range of services, from standardized school self-protection programs, to counseling and extended forensic evaluation assessments, are available, with the Family Court as a further option for making decisions about likely risk. Children can enter the assessment process at different points along this continuum, and referrals for a forensic interview can occur at any stage. Although regional variances exist, the New Zealand system could potentially provide an integrated statutory and nonstatutory evaluation service for abused children.

Unfortunately little impact evaluation on the forensic interviewing legislation has been conducted, and it is difficult to ascertain whether more child complainants are appearing in court cases. This is complicated by the fact that the Ministry of Justice sexual abuse conviction figures combine child witnesses with adults who have laid retrospective complaints. Anecdotally, it would appear that alternative modes of evidence (in particular the videotape combined with closed-circuit television) are being used fairly routinely for younger child witnesses, and on a case by case basis for older children.

The evidential and diagnostic data reported here does suggest that children's allegations are being taken seriously. Of the 4,060 children interviewed for sexual abuse concerns, 2,797 cases were referred to the police for further investigation. This represents a higher number of children than those who made allegations at interview (n = 2,744). Again, limitations in cross-agency recording systems mean that there is no way of knowing how many of these resulted in guilty pleas, prosecutions, or convictions. It could be argued that fewer court cases for children and more guilty pleas by defendants would be the best measures of success.

The New Zealand child witness reforms may have unintentionally raised the standard of proof required to keep children safe. The New Zealand care and protection system places the onus on the statutory agency to prove that abuse has "probably occurred" or is likely to occur on a "balance of probabilities." This means that disclosures at forensic interviews assist social workers to show the Family Court that a child is in need of care and protection. Similarly, the criminal justice system requires proof "beyond reasonable doubt," and police are unlikely to pursue charges without clear verbal evidence from a child complainant. There is a risk that children who are experiencing abuse, but have made no allegations during a forensic interview, may not receive the same level of ongoing investigation, or referrals to support services, as a disclosing child. Nondisclosure may also contribute to system denial that abuse has occurred, which may reduce the likelihood that the child is kept safe in the future.

International analogue and field research about the danger of repeat interviewing and the risk of contamination are taken seriously in New Zealand, with 96% of children having a single forensic interview. It can be argued that the forensic interview setting is not intended to be therapeutic and is not the appropriate forum for evaluating possible false negative outcomes. However, the presumption that more than one forensic interview might reduce evidential validity needs to be weighed against care and protection concerns, and should not result in premature case closure. The perceived level of risk, the fact that disclosure is not a discrete event, and the potential positive effect of increased rapport, all need to be considered when making decisions about whether children should return for further interviews.

Fear of suggestibility and contamination may also have resulted in fewer social work assessment interviews with disclosing or at risk children, with direct referrals being made to forensic Video Units instead. While this is sometimes appropriate, there is a risk that as the forensic interviewing field becomes more research-based, generic social workers may feel less competent in talking to children. Clear interfaces are required between the interviewer role and the role of the social worker to ensure that social work practice remains child centered. The forensic interview must not be seen as the only way a child's allegation can be validated, and the quality of the social work investigation should not be compromised.

Similarly, New Zealand parents are often told by police or social work professionals not to question their children about alleged abuse because it may contaminate the forensic interview or the court process (Davies, 1999; McKenzie, 1999). Parental influence is frequently used as a defence argument to accuse parents of deliberately coaching or misleading their children (Davies, Henderson & Seymour, 1997; Davies, Seymour & Read, 2000). However, given that parental support has been shown as positive for the disclosing child (McKenzie, 1999), it is important that a distinction is made between *talking* to children in a supportive way and *questioning* them inappropriately. There are ways that parents can communicate with a disclosing child that are noncontaminating, and more thought needs to be given to assisting parents to do this well. Contamination is also often used as a reason to defer counselling (Davies, 1999) which suggests that evidential matters are being given more weight than the child's therapeutic needs and well-being.

What becomes most important in this context is the *quality* of the statutory and nonstatutory services that are available to both disclosing and nondisclosing children. All practitioners who are involved in the evaluation of abused children, or with their therapy and counseling, need to ensure they are familiar with the latest research on questioning techniques, suggestibility, memory, and recall. Best practice should minimize the risks of contamination while maximising an abused child's opportunity to disclose.

CONCLUSION

In New Zealand, forensic interviewing is recognized as an integral part of the overall care and protection system. This is supported by the fact that approximately 8.5% of all statutory care and protection cases that require further action are referred for a videotaped diagnostic or evidential interview as part of the investigation. The small size of the country, the specialization of interviewers, and posttraining tape review processes have all contributed to improved practice standardization for interviews. The interviewing process, regardless of whether children repeat or make allegations, can provide crucial information about potential risk and can inform interagency casework decisions.

The New Zealand statistical data reported here indicates that the forensic interview is a supportive process that does facilitate disclosures for many children. However, continued research on how to facilitate disclosure with reluctant children will further inform practice. This has the potential to reduce the false negative outcomes that may be occurring with high risk children in the current child protection system.

REFERENCES

Basher, G. (1999). Children who talk on tape: The facts behind the pictures. *Social Work Now, 12,* 4–12

Basher, G. (2001). *Videotaped interviewing in New Zealand: National data on videotaped interviews comparing Fiscal 1998 with Fiscal 1999.* Manuwai Specialist Services. Inpublished manuscript.

Basher, G. (2003). *Videotaped interviewing in New Zealand: A three year analysis of national data.* Manuwai Specialist Services. Unpublished manuscript.

Basher, G. (2004). Videotaped interviewing in New Zealand: A three year analysis. *Social Work Now, 27,* 11–18.

Davies, E. (1999). *Sexual abuse investigation and criminal court processes: Doing justice to the child?* Unpublished doctoral dissertation: University of Auckland.

Davies, E., Henderson, E., & Seymour, F. W. (1997). In the interests of justice? The cross-examination of child complainants in criminal proceedings. *Psychology, Psychiatry and Law, 2,* 1–13.

Davies, E., Seymour, F. W. & Read, J. (2000). Children's and primary caretaker's perceptions of the sexual abuse investigation process: A New Zealand example. *Journal of Child Sexual Abuse, 9*(2), 41–56.

Dawson, M. (1995). Evidencing care and protection needs. *Social Work Now, 2,* 27–30.

Dawson, M., Morgan, L. & Rugg, S. J. (1996). Specialist interviewing of children: Its role and value in the care and protection of children: The South Auckland (New Zealand) model. Paper presented at the 11th International Conference for the Prevention of Child Abuse and Neglect, Dublin.

Eichelbaum, T. (2001). *The Peter Ellis case: Report of the Ministerial inquiry.* Report for the Honourable Phil Goff, New Zealand Government.

Hamlin, P. & Nation, G. (1997). *Expert evidence in sexual abuse cases.* New Zealand Law Society seminar booklet.

McKenzie, K. (1999). Parents and disclosure. What to say to children who disclose sexual abuse. *Social Work Now, 14*, 4–12.

New Zealand Children, Young Persons and Their Families Service and the New Zealand Police. (1996). *Evidential and Diagnostic Interviewing on Video under the Evidence Amendment Act 1989: Joint CYPFS and Police operating guidelines.* Wellington: Department of Social Welfare.

New Zealand Children, Young Persons and Their Families Service and the New Zealand Police. (2001). *Memorandum of understanding between Department of Child, Youth and Family Services and New Zealand Police.* Wellington: Department of Child, Youth and Family.

New Zealand Department of Child, Youth and Family and the New Zealand Police. (2003). *Joint Child, Youth and Family/Police Child Abuse Team protocol: Interagency protocol for the reporting and investigation of child sexual abuse and serious physical abuse.* Wellington: Department of Child, Youth and Family Services.

Statistics New Zealand (2001). New Zealand census of population and dwelling. Wellington: Government Printer.

Wilson, K. J. (1993). *Proposals for a minimum practice standard for diagnostic and evidential interviewing within New Zealand Children and Young Persons' Service.* Unpublished manuscript.

———. (1995). Getting it taped: Implementing video legislation for child witnesses in New Zealand, England and Wales. *Social Work Now, 1*, 11–16

———. (2002). New Zealand evidential interviewing within an international context. *Social Work Now, 23*, 9–14.

———. (2003). *Evidential interviewing structure for child complainants.* National training manual for New Zealand Police and Child Youth and Family. Unpublished manuscript.

15

The Silence of Abused Children: Policy Implications

Dvora Horowitz
Israeli Ministry of Social Affairs, Jerusalem, Israel

The sexual and physical abuse of minors has recently gained a great deal of public attention in Israel, as in other countries of the world. In Israel this is evident in the development of both legislation and services for the investigation and treatment of allegedly abused children. Youth investigators, who are social workers employed by the Ministry of Social Affairs, are the only officials authorized to interview children under the age of 14, and authorized to decide on children's competency to testify in court. In collaboration with researchers at the National Institute of Child Health and Human Development (NICHD), the children's and youth investigating unit in Israel has trained youth investigators to interview child witnesses using the NICHD protocol in all interviews of children (Lamb, Sternberg, Orbach, Hershkowitz, Horowitz, & Esplin, 2002).

The NICHD protocol operationalizes research-based recommendations into specific and concrete guidelines for interviewers, introducing interviewing strategies that are likely to elicit accurate and complete information and protect children's testimonies from potentially contaminating input (Hershkowitz, Orbach, Lamb, Sternberg, & Horowitz, 2002; Orbach, Hershkowitz, Lamb, Sternberg, Esplin, & Horowitz, 2000).

Researchers and field experts have devoted a lot of effort to determining how to evaluate the credibility of testimonies given by abused children (Lamb, Sternberg, & Esplin, 1995; Undeutch, 1982) and how to identify children who make false allegations of abuse (Hershkowitz, Lamb, Sternberg, & Esplin, 1997). Although these are very important questions to anyone involved with investigating abused children, it seems that the number of false allegation made by children is much smaller then the number of complete or partial nondisclosures of abuse. To date, the problem of helping reluctant children talk about their abuse while protecting them from further exposure to risks has not been solved. Therefore, efforts should be invested in exploring this problem, especially in cases for which we have strong reason to believe that the children have been abused.

This paper will refer to Israeli laws concerning the protection of abused children (see Sternberg, Lamb, & Hershkowitz, 1996, for further details), discuss ways used by youth investigators in Israel to deal with reluctant children, and introduce a case to demonstrate interviewing strategies and characteristics of reports made by reluctant children during the presubstantive (introduction and rapport building) and postdisclosure phases of forensic interviews.

THE LAW IN ISRAEL

Law of Evidence, Revision: Protection of Children Law (1955)

In 1955, when the country of Israel was only 7 years old, the "Law of Evidence, Revision Protection of Children Law" was introduced. The law then related to sexual abuse and was later extended to include physical and emotional abuse, as well as neglect of children by their guardians. This law enabled the protection of abused children during the legal process in several important ways:

Victims or witnesses under the age of 14 who were sexually, physically, or emotionally abused, or suffered neglect by parents or guardians, are interviewed by youth investigators, who are social workers employed by the Ministry of Social Affairs, and not by the police. The law made sure that the interviewers of children would be held under conditions different from those used by the police, and that the children's needs would have priority over the needs of the investigation.

Youth investigators have the authority to prevent children from testifying in court. In such cases the investigator will testify instead of the child. Although such testimony is considered to be hearsay, it is admissible in court along with corroborative evidence. Youth investigators also evaluate the reliability of the children's testimony.

The law raised public discussion and objection, mostly by legal experts, to the alleged violation of defendants' rights (Straschnov, 1996, 2000) because it precludes the court from obtaining direct impressions of and conducting cross-examination of child-witnesses. Child advocates worried that, if the law changed, some or all of the protection given to abused children would be removed. In reality, the law was extended to apply to a wider range of offense types (e.g., severe violent offences within or outside the family), and to a wider population (e.g., abuse by guardians, not only by parents). Several bills are now under consideration reflecting a move to extend this law even further.

Youth Law: Care and Supervision Law (1960)

This law regulates the treatment of children who are abused by parents or guardians. Child protection officers are obliged to assess children's needs and, if necessary, refer children for treatment even before court orders are issued. Child protection officers can take any measure to protect allegedly abused children, including placing children in protective shelters. A court order has to be obtained to continue treatment if needed.

Amendment (no. 1338) to the Penal Code (1989)—Mandatory Reporting

This law requires that any person who suspects that a child was abused by his or her parents or guardians report it as soon as possible to a child protection officer or to the police, who must inform and consult with each other. By law, not reporting such suspicions carries a penalty of up to several months of imprisonment.

DEALING WITH RELUCTANT CHILDREN

According to our data (Horowitz, Hershkowitz, & Lamb, chapter 4, this volume; Horowitz & Livneh, 2002) between 20 and 30 percent of the children interviewed by youth investigators in Israel did not make allegations, despite evidence that they had been abused. Most of these children were believed not to disclose their abuse experiences because they were afraid, ashamed, or threatened. It is important to remember, however, that some of them may not have disclosed because they did not understand that they had been abused. Some children disclosed prior to the investigation but, as they were not believed or listened to at that time, they did not repeat the allegations during forensic interviews. Some of those who disclosed prior to forensic investigation may also have been threatened to avoid further discussion of their experiences.

What do youth investigators do when children do not talk, give irrelevant information, or provide partial information, hiding the main part of the abuse, when there are strong reasons to believe that the children had actually been abused? The issue of getting reluctant children to talk can be risky so investigators have to avoid, by all means, putting words into children's mouths in their efforts to reveal the truth. Since 1995, the NICHD investigative protocol has been in use by all youth investigators in Israel when interviewing suspected victims of abuse. Following the presubstantive rapport building and preparatory phase, The NICHD protocol introduces a sequence of prompts—"getting the allegation" prompts—designed to elicit allegations in a non-suggestive way. The first step youth investigators take after interviewing children who seem to be withholding information is to collect information about the investigated cases from every other possible source (Breitman, 2003). A second interview with the same child is then considered for understanding possible inconsistencies between the child's first account and information gathered from other sources or details reported in the child's later interviews. At the beginning of the second interview, the interviewer tells the child that she or he has doubts about the accuracy of the child's first account and asks the child to describe the event again. In some cases, children choose to change their version at this stage by adding information, changing details, or confessing that they lied in the first interview. If there are still doubts about some details or about the truthfulness of the child's testimony, or if the child still does not disclose at this stage, the investigator confronts the child in a noncoercive manner about the inconsistencies in the accounts. In some cases, children have simple explanations for such inconsistencies, but in others cases, children maintain their original versions.

In addition, when the investigator still has some doubts, they may take one or more of the following steps:

- Referring the child to a child-protection-officer to consider onset of treatment even before the end of the investigation. Sometimes, taking children away from the offender gives them the courage to talk.

- Advising the police investigator to place the suspect in custody. Sometimes when the child feels that the offender is not capable of hurting him or her, they are better able to disclose, although an arrest of the suspect may also frighten the child and delay disclosure by increasing feelings of guilt.

- Asking a significant other to give the child permission to talk. Many times, this is all the child needs to talk.

- Conducting a repeated interview. In most cases, the youth investigators conduct a single interview. When children do not make allegations, however, it is recommended that they are interviewed more than one time. A 10-year-old girl who did not disclose abuse, despite being pregnant, for example, was interviewed seven times before disclosing. Another girl who was photographed performing oral sex in a park denied the event in several interviews until she finally disclosed. Repeated interviews are usually conducted if the investigator has solid evidence of the offense but lacks information about the suspect.

- Referring children to psychological or psychiatric treatment in order to assess their likelihood of disclosure at some point in the treatment. This option is used only when there are no other options available, in order to minimize the risks of suggestibility.

- Referring children for medical examinations, even when they do not make allegations, in order to assess the presence of physical symptoms likely to be caused by abuse.

- Interviewing children at the scene of the crime. In general, visits to the scene of the crime add information to that reported in the first interview at the investigator's office (Hershkowitz, Orbach, Lamb, & Horowitz, 1998; Hershkowitz, Orbach, Lamb, Sternberg, & Horowitz, 2001; Orbach, Hershkowitz, Lamb, Sternberg, Esplin, & Horowitz, 2000; Orbach, Hershkowitz, Pipe, Lamb, & Sternberg, 2004). Visits to the scenes of the abuse are also helpful for understanding what really happened and for confirming or contradicting the children's versions. In some cases, a visit to the scene of the crime helps the child to open up and report the details about the event. In a recently investigated kidnap and rape case, a 9-year-old girl from a conservative family refused in the course of a long interview to tell the investigator what happened to her at the rapist's home, but described the event in detail once she was brought there.

- Calling the police officer's attention to the required interrogation directions in order to obtain case information from any possible source. This information is likely to help the youth investigators conduct follow-up interviews with reluctant children. When children understand that investigators know what happened, they are likely to fill in the missing information without feeling responsible for disclosing the event.

- Asking children what would happen if they disclosed. Surprisingly, many children who have not disclosed details of the abuse were ready to tell exactly what happened to them and by whom after explaining why they cannot tell. Often children's response to this question would be enough to start the interrogations of the offenders, for example, after the investigator asked about what might happen if the child described what had happened, the child told the investigator that his father would lock him in the toilet and make him kneel on salt for a few hours if he disclosed.

- Offering children alternatives to verbalization, such as drawing or writing their answers, and then asking them to talk about that. Often, children who were embarrassed to talk about sexual abuse were able to start talking after drawing or describing the event in writing while the investigator was out of the room.

- Trying to understand and discuss the motives for children's nondisclosure (e.g., shame, fear).

CASE DEMONSTRATION

The case described below was recently exposed in Israel. It demonstrates the extent to which some children may avoid disclosure while illustrating some of the practices used by youth investigators when dealing with reluctant children.

The case involves a family comprising a mother, stepfather, and four sons (aged 10, 11, 12, and 16).

The schoolteacher of the three younger brothers noticed that the three children had difficulties sitting. She asked the children what was wrong but failed to receive a plausible answer. She suspected that the children were abused and reported it, as required, to the child protective-services, who reported the case to the police. The police referred the children to the youth investigation unit. The children were interviewed by different youth investigators but did not make any allegations. Although they insisted that nothing had happened and that they have "caring and loving parents," they were given medical examinations during which massive burning and blue bruises marks on their genitals, testicles, and anuses were documented. It was clear that somebody was cruelly abusing them.

Following these medical examinations, the children were reinterviewed and again did not make any allegations. They were then referred to the child protective services for treatment. The child protective officer placed the children in a protective shelter. The stepfather and the 16-year-old brother disappeared. The mother was interviewed but gave no information, and so she was arrested as a suspect. Shortly after the mother's arrest, the 16-year-old brother appeared in a police station, asking to "tell everything." He testified that the stepfather used to return home drunk every night, wake the children up, order them to kneel on all fours, stick toilet paper in their anus and light it. The brother also told the police officers that the stepfather used to abuse the children's genitals, using pliers. Following her 16-year-old son's testimony, the mother was interviewed again, and she gave an identical account. The mother was asked by the police to call her sons and permit them to disclose the abuse details, and she did.

While staying in the protective shelter, the children were interviewed for the third time. This time, all three children made allegations, including details identical to those reported by the mother and older brother, even though they did not have the opportunity to speak to the mother or brother before being interviewed. The stepfather was caught by the police, convicted, and sentenced to 22 years imprisonment.

Characteristics of Accounts by Reluctant Disclosers

Investigators describe some common characteristics of interviews with reluctant children:

- *Short reports:* All the interviews are surprisingly short, lasting between 18 and 21 minutes (including the presubstantive phase), even when the cases involve ongoing abuse, including multiple incidents of varying severity, and the children being interviewed are not very young.

- *Lack of free narrative:* Reluctant children do not give free narratives even in the episodic memory training phase. Their answers are short and skeletal. When asked to describe a birthday party, for example, they respond with only one sentence, whereas most of the children interviewed provide much longer descriptions.

- *Digressions:* Reluctant children keep digressing from the subjects posed by the investigators. When an interviewer asked S. if somebody hurt him, for example, the child started talking about songs he used to sing the previous year. When another suspected victim was asked if somebody did something wrong to his body, he answered, "I fell," and in the same breath, "Is it true that Sally put a record in the tape recorder?"

- *"I don't know" answers:* More "don't know," "don't remember," and "don't want to tell" statements characterize reports by nondisclosers.

- *"I don't understand the question":* During the interviews of reluctant children, such answers are given repeatedly.

- *Lying:* Trying to deflect the suspicions (e.g., "my parents are loving and caring, and they are good providers") or by denying ("nothing happened").

- *Providing irrelevant accusations:* "My brother hit me."

- *Giving irrational explanation:* When a child was asked why he asked the teacher not to send a letter telling his parents that he was missing school, he answered, "I was afraid that my brother would be mad at me."

- *Giving irrational explanation to body injuries:* "I couldn't walk or sit. I dropped some water on the floor and I fell," answered S. when he was asked to explain why he missed several days of school.

- *Trying to leave the interview room:* In his second interview, S. asked to go out and eat a few minutes after the interview had started.

THE DISCLOSURE

Accounts by children who disclose abuse after first denying also appear to have unique characteristics:

- The testimony remains skeletal. Testimony is provided unwillingly. Details are not described but merely hinted. Thus, when the 12-year-old was asked about being burned by his stepfather ("Tell me everything that happened from the minute it started till it was over"), he replied, "when we were sitting . . . and then . . . he burned us; and then he told us. . . . 'That's it. I'm done. That's it. I won't do it anymore to you.' And he was going on . . . that's all."

- Talking with a very low voice.
- Minimizing the abuse. The children do not describe the full abuse, even when they are asked to do so.
- Not volunteering information. When they are willing to disclose, children provide incomplete information. Investigators have to prompt specifically and directly about each kind of abuse that he may have heard described by other witnesses.
- Not remembering. "I don't remember/ know" responses continue even after disclosure, even when the children are interviewed following a very short delay.
- Lack of contextual embedding. Minimal contextual information is reported by reluctant disclosers.
- Using scripted language. Reluctant children do not specifically describe any single episode, even when the investigators repeatedly ask them to do so. Rather, these children provide generic responses, like "He used to burn us."
- Attempting to explain and justify the abuser's behavior. Children adopt the abusers' explanations for their behavior (e.g., in the case of the stepfather who burned the children's anus and genitals, "Because he used to help us clean it. Because it has to be clean."
- Refusing to describe what the abuser did to other victims. "No. Let him tell you. I do not want to tell."
- Trying to protect family members. When one of the victims was asked where the mother was when it all happened, he answered, "She used to protect us," when it was completely obvious that she didn't.

In sum, testimonies of reluctant children bear some of the characteristics of fabricated accounts. In the case mentioned above, for example, one might have had difficulty believing the children's disclosure if there had not been so much corroborative evidence. The children did not volunteer information and the investigator had to elicit the information, based on what he knew from the testimonies of the mother and the 16-year-old brother. Had the abusive stepfather not been brought to trial and convicted, the children would have continued to suffer the terrible abuse and would likely have been punished cruelly for revealing information.

CONCLUSION

Many children who experience physical or sexual abuse do not disclose the abuse for many possible reasons (e.g., shame, fear for themselves, fear that somebody close to them may get hurt, fear that they would not be believed, or guilt). The challenge for professional case workers who deal with these most vulnerable children is to determine how to help reluctant children disclose abuse without being suggestive. These children are abused repeatedly, and they continue to feel helpless and unable to break the circle because those who abuse them are often the very same people who are supposed to protect them. Research is needed to develop a special protocol to guide investigators to conduct interviews with children who appear to have been abused but are not willing to disclose.

REFERENCES

Breitman, M. (2003). Coping with doubtful testimonies in children's investigations. In D. Horowitz (Ed.), *Through the lens: Investigating Abused Children.* Tel-Aviv, Israel: Cherikover. (Hebrew).

Hershkowitz, I., Lamb, M. E., Sternberg, K. J., & Esplin, P. W. (1997). The relationships among interviewer utterance type, CBCA scores, and the richness of children's responses. *Legal and Criminological Psychology, 2,* 169–76.

Hershkowitz, I., Orbach, Y., Lamb, M. E., & Horowitz, D. (1998). Visiting the scene of the crime: Effects on children's recall of alleged abuse. *Legal and Criminological Psychology, 3,* 195–207.

Hershkowitz, I., Orbach, Y., Lamb, M. E., Sternberg, J. K., & Horowitz, D. (2001). The effects of mental context reinstatement of children's account of sexual abuse. *Applied Cognitive Psychology, 15,* 235–48.

Hershkowitz, I., Orbach, Y., Lamb, M. E., Sternberg, J. K., & Horowitz, D. (2002). A comparison of mental and physical context reinstatement in forensic interviews with alleged victims of sexual abuse. *Applied Cognitive Psychology, 16,* 429–41.

Horowitz, I., & Livneh, C. D. (2002). *Investigation of children involved in sexual abuse and in caregivers' abuse of minors: A Report for the years 2001–2002.* Jerusalem, Israel: Ministry of Social Affairs. (Hebrew).

Lamb, M. E, Sternberg, K. J., & Esplin, P. W. (1995). Factors influencing the reliability and validity of statements made by young victims of sexual maltreatment, *Journal of Applied Developmental Psychology, 15,* 255–80.

Lamb, M. E., Sternberg, J. K., Orbach, Y., Hershkowitz, I., Horowitz, D., & Esplin, P. W. (2002). The effects of intensive training and ongoing supervision on the quality of investigative interviews with alleged sex abuse victims. *Applied Developmental Science, 6,* 114–25.

Law of Evidence, Revision: *Protection of Children* (1955). Israeli Statutes, 184, 96. (Hebrew).

Orbach, Y., Hershkowitz, I., Lamb, M. E., Sternberg, K. J., Esplin, P. W., & Horowitz, D. (2000). Assessing the value of structured protocols for forensic interviews of alleged child abuse victims. *Child Abuse and Neglect, 24,* 733–52.

Orbach, Y., Hershkowitz, I., Lamb, M. E., Sternberg, J. K., & Horowitz, D. (2000). Interviewing at the scene of the crime: Effects on children's recall of alleged abuse. *Legal and Criminological Psychology, 5,* 135–47.

Orbach, Y., Hershkowitz, I., Pipe, M., Lamb, M. E., & Sternberg, K. J. (2004, March). *Effects of repeated interviews on the information retrieved by child-witnesses in forensic interviews.* A paper presented in a symposium at the Annual Conference of the American Psychology and Law Society (AP-LS), Scottsdale, AZ.

Penal Code—1977, Amendment no. 1338 (1989). *Abuse of minors and helpless victims.* Israeli Statutes, 54, 6/1. (Hebrew).

Sternberg, K. J., Lamb, M. E., & Hershkowitz, I. (1996). Child sexual abuse investigations in Israel. *Criminal Justice and Behavior, 23,* 322–38.

Straschnov, A. (1996). Sexual abused children testifying in court: A different approach. *Hapraklit, 43,* 2.

———. (2000). *Children and youth in a legal perspective.* Israeli Bar Association, Tel-Aviv, Israel.

Undeutch, U. (1982). Statement reality analysis. In Trankell (Ed.), *Reconstructing the past: The role of psychologists in criminal trials* (pp. 27–56). Stockholm: Norstedt & Sons.

Youth Law: *Care and Supervision* (1960). Israeli Statutes, 311, 52. (Hebrew).

16

Reflections on the Concept of Disclosure

Frank Lindblad
Karolinska Institutet, Sweden

The terms "disclosure" and "nondisclosure" are central to any discussion of theory and practice in relation to child sexual abuse. Like the related concepts of "delayed disclosure" and "disclosure process," they appear to have clear and consistent meanings. In reality, however, they may be used and interpreted in very different ways in different contexts. Such ambiguity may create misinterpretations and obstruct collaborative research as well as communication between professionals. For example, the very term disclosure seems to imply that something has happened that could be disclosed (but may or may not be disclosed) whereas the term "allegation" implicitly questions whether something happened (in the face of a verbal statement that it has). These terms (disclosure, nondisclosure, disclosure process, and delayed disclosure) are conceptually intertwined. Although this chapter focuses on one of these terms, disclosure, the discussion is relevant to the other concepts also.

The ambiguity of disclosure may be handled in different ways. One way is to refrain from using the word in scientific and clinical texts (Jones, 2000). Although such an approach would have obvious advantages, the concept of disclosure is too strongly established scientifically and clinically to make such a solution possible. Another approach, advocated in this chapter, is to try to be explicit about the meaning of the concept whenever the term is used in clinical, legal, or scientific settings. Such an approach necessitates a thorough analysis of the word. The aim of this chapter is to offer tools for such an analysis. I begin with a discussion of the contributions of the two main actors—the discloser and the receiver of the disclosure—and then proceed to analyze the interaction between the discloser and the receiver as well as the social context in which their interaction is embedded. Subsequently, three different aspects of disclosure—time, structure, and credibility—are described. Case vignettes are used to illustrate the theoretical discussions. Minor details have been changed in some of these vignettes to avoid identification of the individuals involved.

THE DISCLOSER, THE RECEIVER, AND THE INTERACTION

The Discloser

The main subject of the disclosure procedure is the person who tells, the discloser. It seems reasonable to reserve this concept for a person who tells about his or her own experiences, whereas a person who brings forward information from another should be called something else, such as messenger or informant. As shown in an example below, however, this distinction may be difficult. It should also be recognized that the messenger is an important person in the disclosure process.

Some developmental achievements turn out to be important prerequisites for the ability to disclose because the individual must have attained the cognitive capacity necessary to make a disclosure. This means that the individual must have adequate memory and communicative skills. Very young children and individuals with cognitive dysfunctions of various kinds may not be able to disclose in a way that can be recognized by others as a disclosure. This means that we also need to define the minimum structural contents of a disclosure.

> **Case Vignette.** A male perpetrator, working at a day care center, has confirmed abuse of six children in day care. Fifteen of 30 children verbally describe incidents that might have involved sexual abuse. For the youngest children, the details are scarce or absent (Lindblad & Kaldal, 2000). A boy, 2 years of age, is interviewed by a police investigator. The only comment with a possible relation to abuse is something like "The willie hurts." Directly afterwards he departs with his mother and, outside the police officer's earshot, he repeats "The willie hurts" and then adds "Bill bit" (Bill was the name of the perpetrator).
>
> These comments may be related to abuse experiences, but they may also be interpreted differently. They need to be supplemented by other information in order to be understood. The question is whether such verbal comments should be categorized as a disclosure. The example also illustrates differences between telling parents and telling a police investigator during a formal interview. This theme will be discussed in greater detail below.
>
> Psychiatric conditions may influence an individual's capacity to make a convincing disclosure. For example, autism may complicate disclosure, mainly because the inability to speak or the limited ability to communicate verbally may make disclosure difficult. Since autistic individuals, by definition, also lack the ability to correctly understand

and take an active part in interpersonal interactions, responses to questions may actually be unresponsive to the questions asked. Thus, autistic individuals who have been abused and whose verbal capacity is restricted to, at best, a few words like "yes" or "no" have limited capacities to disclose convincingly.

Disclosure is often regarded as an act of volition but "unintentional disclosures" and "accidental disclosures" have a tenuous link to the concept of volition. Thus, a disclosure may follow a conscious decision by the discloser, but it may also reflect the unexpected intervention by someone else, thereby illustrating the interactive character of disclosures. Even if the decision to disclose is unintentional, the term disclosure seems to imply consciousness about the sexual events.

In quite a few cases, the discloser seems to struggle with ambivalence about telling. This ambivalence may also color the verbal communication. For instance, a disclosure may have the shape of a hint, which also often necessitates either a continuation of the dialogue or others' interpretations of the hint.

Case Vignette. A 14-year-old girl contacted the school health service to get help for a sexual medical problem (Lindblad, 1989, p.25). The school doctor found it noteworthy that the girl´s sexual debut had occurred so early, and she wanted to ask some screening questions about the girl´s psychosocial situation. When they talked about the girl´s home life she said that she had a stepfather who was very firm with her. The school doctor then asked, "Does he beat you?" The girl answered, "No, he does not BEAT me," putting the stress on "beat." The school doctor decided to continue by asking more questions about the relation to the stepfather. When she asked the girl if she had been treated badly in some other way by the stepfather, the girl told that they were involved in a sexual relation. The stepfather subsequently confirmed what the girl had described.

The formulation "No, he does not BEAT me" could hardly be regarded as a disclosure although it may certainly invite a dialogue that leads to a disclosure. It seems to express ambivalence about disclosing. Furthermore, the vignette illustrates the importance of the receiver's response . In this case, another reaction to "No, he does not BEAT me" might have obstructed the disclosure.

The ambivalence of the discloser may also yield unconvincing disclosures, as when a disclosure based on self-experienced events is retracted, and raises questions about whether the first "disclosure" should still be categorized as a disclosure after it has been retracted?

Case Vignette. An adolescent girl had given hints to the school nurse about abuse by her stepfather. When she met a child psychiatrist for an interview, she told how her stepfather had forced her to have intercourse several times. When the child psychiatrist explained the need to contact social authorities, the girl hesitated. She wanted a break in the interview. When the dialogue was resumed, the girl changed her story. She said that her intention had been to examine what would have happened if one told the school nurse about sexual abuse experiences. The reason for this was that she had a friend who was continuously abused by her father and this girl wanted to know what would happen if she disclosed to the school nurse. The teenager maintained this second version, even after social authorities were involved. It was never elucidated which version was the correct one— or if both were either correct or false.

This case illustrates that the concepts of disclosure and credibility are highly intertwined. The narratives may be understood either as a disclosure followed by a retraction or as a false disclosure, in which a message about another girl´s exposure to abuse is hidden and subsequently brought forward. The case also illustrates that a disclosure may not be a stable phenomenon. Furthermore, the case demonstrates the importance of a respectful approach by the professional, adapted to the emotional situation of the child. However, even when such an approach is adopted, a teenager may react impulsively and unexpectedly and the disclosure process may be very complicated, from both psychotherapeutic and forensic perspectives.

THE RECEIVER

The receiver is a person who is presented with information about the events in question by the discloser. As discussed above, consideration of the receiver is important for understanding disclosures. The receiver may or may not have been informed about the events by other sources. Further, conceptualizing disclosure as a process, a discloser may tell several receivers both around the time of the first disclosure and also later in life. Moreover, a child may want to disclose but the receiver may respond in a variety of ways to the child´s attempts at communication. He or she may not perceive the child's statements or understand that the child is referring to the abuse. Frequently the receiver simply does not want to know and may have a strong personal interest in what will happen if the disclosure is recognized as such. The most obvious example is a parent who wants to protect the other allegedly perpetrating parent.

Is it reasonable to designate a nonrecognized disclosure as a disclosure? The concept of "unsuccessful disclosure" may be one reasonable term for such a process.

Also relevant is whether the receiver takes action, perhaps involving other people. If he or she does not, the disclosure will remain a secret between the discloser and the receiver. Some categories of receivers will be expected to take action, others not. For instance, disclosure to a 12-year-old friend who will listen and possibly talk to an adult is different from a disclosure to an adult who will probably intervene. Thus, the discloser´s selection of a specific receiver may reveal the intentions of the discloser.

The degree of personal involvement by both formal and informal receivers may affect their interpretation of the reality underlying the disclosure. For instance, information given to parents may imply more reliability problems, but the information may on the other hand be richer.

> *Case Vignette.* In the case involving abuse at a day care center, the information given by the children to the police investigators was less extensive than the information given by the children to their parents. The example of the 2 year old illustrates this phenomenon. What might be considered crucial information was given when the child had left the police interview. There were also children who did not disclose when formally interviewed but who told their parents about abuse, and vice versa. Six children reported to the parents only, three to the police only, and six to both parents and police (Lindblad & Kaldal, 2000).

> When parents are receivers of disclosures by their children about abuse at the day care center, they may be highly emotionally involved. For the investigator, it is important to distinguish the impact of the disclosure from the receiver's strong personal involvement. Behind the façade of false allegations, there may be a receiver who is dedicated to the idea that the child has been abused.

Disclosure Interaction

The importance of the interaction between the discloser and the receiver has already been emphasized and illustrated with a case. Such interactions may be constructive in eliciting correct information about the abuse events, but they may also constitute an important bias from the forensic perspective. The concepts of "spontaneous disclosure" and "induced disclosure" are often used to describe two extremes of the degree of influence from the receiver. At minimum, a spontaneous disclosure necessitates an emotionally and cognitively attentive partner. An induced disclosure may be well justified by the circumstances; occasionally, however, the person trying to provoke a disclosure may have other—conscious or unconscious—motives for doing so.

> *Case Vignette.* An adult woman consults a psychiatrist by telephone to discuss her psychiatric symptoms. She also tells about a psychotherapeutic contact with a male therapist. The woman says, "My therapist keeps telling me that I have been sexually abused as an infant although I have forgotten it. He says that this is the reason why I have these symptoms. I think that I am beginning to be able to grasp my memories by now."

Even acknowledging the memorial abilities of infants, we would not expect an adult woman to put such memories from the first months of life into words. Most probably, this woman was developing false memories, induced by her therapist. When she made the phone call, she had not developed any coherent story about abuse, but obviously she was on her way. One may question, therefore, whether any future verbal communications about abuse should be viewed as disclosures.

Case Vignette. A 13-year-old girl was caught several times stealing from shops. Somewhat strangely and to the surprise of people close to her, she stole only baby equipment. When confronted with her behavior, she finally said that she had been raped by a neighbor. She was convinced that she had become pregnant and that she was going to have a baby. For a number of reasons she had not wanted to tell anyone about her abuse experiences, including that she did not expect any help or support. It was not possible to find any other explanation for her changed behavior (Lindblad, 1995).

In this case it seemed reasonable to confront the girl with her strange behavior. Those who did confront her did not, apparently, suspect that the girl had been abused. Even if they had such suspicions, the confrontation would have been justified. The girl´s narrative is well described as a disclosure.

"Disclosure work" is sometimes used to refer to a professional intervention aimed at facilitating disclosure, based on the presumption that a child has been abused but is unable to talk about it. A clinician may conclude that a child's behavior most likely reflects resistance to disclosure and, being familiar with how to work with resistance in a psychotherapeutic setting, may choose to be active in helping the child to overcome inner obstacles to disclosure. Although such an approach may seem well justified from a protection perspective, it may also involve the risk of unconsciously eliciting a false disclosure from the child, or of eliciting false details in an otherwise accurate report about the abuse. Another consequence may be a retraction of what has initially been reported. Even if the child is not influenced in any of these ways, a professional approach involving a high degree of active intervention designed to decrease resistance may complicate the understanding and evaluation of the child´s narratives in the legal context. Disclosure work may still be justified in a medical or psychological setting if a disclosure is supposed to be of major importance for the child´s mental health, for instance, as a necessary step to prevent suicidal actions. Professionals should, however, be aware of the legal drawbacks of this approach. In most cases it is possible to find a way of avoiding suggestive prompts while facilitating disclosure. Nonetheless, in a clinical setting, the theme of possible victimization must often be introduced by the clinician. My impression is that such focusing interventions may be performed without necessarily compromising credibility significantly. Possibly the most important aspect of constructive disclosure work is the professional attitude, conveying a message that "I will listen if you want to tell me."

Social Context

On the social and interpersonal level, factors other than the discloser–receiver relation may be important in interpreting a statement or series of statements as a disclosure. The relation between the victim and the perpetrator, the formal character of the disclosure setting—that is, investigative or noninvestigative—and the social context including social-cultural norms, may all influence the disclosure process.

As described in several chapters in this volume, the relationship between the victim and the perpetrator affects the delay to disclosure. Closer familial relationships complicate disclosure and increase the risk for very delayed disclosures. Questions about secrecy and loyalty turn out to be crucial.

Case Vignette. In the day care center case described earlier, a 3-year-old boy had a special relation to the perpetrator. The boy adored the man and was sad when he was discharged. The affection appeared to have been mutual. It also seemed as if this boy had experienced the sexual acts as something mainly positive, at least at his present age. He gradually and somewhat reluctantly made statements about abuse, although characteristically these were intertwined with denials of some details. When adults talked to him about the abuse, they often implied that the man had done "naughty things." The boy's statement "naughty is fun" seems likely to reflect his personal dilemma.

This boy did not have an obvious wish to talk about the sexual contact, although he admitted the events. Indeed, "admit" seems to be a more appropriate word than "disclose" to describe his verbal communications. It is important that professionals recognize personal dilemmas of this kind and, further, that mental health professionals recognize that an investigation such as this one may provoke guilt, for example, because it redefines what the boy has experienced. For the legal professional, the boy's dilemma is an important piece of information in interpreting his verbal communications, which were colored by minimizations and denials of some parts and confirmations of others.

A major distinction is between a disclosure given to a person who is a representative of the authorities (formal receivers) or to a layman, usually someone close (informal receivers). A disclosure to a formal receiver is given either in an investigative or a noninvestigative setting. Investigative settings are primarily the legal, social welfare, and medical systems. Noninvestigative disclosures include statements made in those same settings, when the contact is initiated for reasons other than those related to the abuse. Non-investigative disclosures also occur when children tell teachers, day care center staff or other professionals. To a young child, the distinction between a formal or informal receiver may be inappropriate. Indeed, this distinction may not be clear cut even for older children and adolescents.

Social norms also influence when disclosure is considered an appropriate term. Implicit in the concept of disclosure is the implication that something forbidden or unwanted is revealed (if the actions revealed have another character, it is doubtful if disclosure is a suitable categorization) and rules about what is forbidden or unwanted vary across contexts. Laws constitute the most distinct regulations, but norms from other sources may also be relevant. Thus, norms may influence how a certain behavior is labeled, for instance as "abuse" or "sexual activity." Such labeling, in turn, determines whether disclosure is an appropriate designation.

Case Vignette. A 14-year-old girl had an established sexual relationship with an 18-year-old boy. The girl was below the age of consent according to Swedish law. However, the sexual relationship seemed to be accepted within the couple´s network . For instance, the girl's mother, who had been informed by her daughter about the sexual relationship, gave the boy condoms as a Christmas present. When a conflict arose between the boy and the girl's mother, however, she reported him to the police for child sexual abuse, that is, his sexual contact with the 14 year old.

It would be strange to call the girl's discussion of the sexual relationship with her mother a disclosure although from a strictly formal perspective, one might argue that this would be a correct designation. For clinical and scientific purposes, however, it is not in the same category as when a child reluctantly tells a trusted person about having been sexually abused by somebody close. This illustrates the importance of being clear about the definition of disclosure.

DISCLOSURE: SOME BASIC CHARACTERISTICS

An Event or Process? Temporal Considerations

At one extreme, one could regard disclosure as a distinct step, when the discloser suddenly moves from secrecy to openness. In this respect, a disclosure is something very rapid, even if it is certainly followed by a dialogue with a presentation of further details. At the other extreme, disclosure could be seen as a lengthy—even almost lifelong—process. Temporal variables are intertwined with other variables in determining how the concept of disclosure is defined. If disclosure refers to what is revealed during a formal investigation, the duration of the investigation defines the temporal dimension of the concept of disclosure. Consideration of the timing of statements is therefore necessary for understanding different meanings of disclosure.

What does it mean to regard disclosure as a process over time? One approach is to understand disclosure as a process through which the description of the sexual abuse develops and reaches its seemingly "final" formation (which nevertheless does not mean that new "final" versions may develop or even that retractions may occur). Another approach implies that disclosure is best regarded as a procedure that can be repeated—or be performed differently—under different psychological circumstances. A constructed example illustrates this point: First, the child may disclose to her mother. Two months later she may disclose to a police investigator during a forensic interview. Two years later she may disclose to her boyfriend. Later on in life she may choose to disclose to her husband, to her employer, and to a general practitioner. At the end of life, she may disclose to a nurse who takes care of her. All these situations may have been preceded by an inner—possibly not uncomplicated—choice between openness and secrecy. However, to justify the designation of a disclosure, the receiver should not have heard the discloser tell him/her about this before.

The Structure of Disclosure

In this context, the structure of the disclosure relates to its factual contents. A minimum level of information turns out as necessary for defining a statement or a series of statements as a disclosure. Furthermore, information can be obtained from a supposed victim verbally (usually orally) or behaviorally—or both.

For a verbal communication to be designated a disclosure the narrative must include a certain amount of detail. If, for instance, a 5-year-old girl says, "He touched my private parts," but cannot clarify further or indicate what parts of her body were touched, it is doubtful that the statement should be called a disclosure. The structural components are strongly related to the capacity of the discloser to produce rich statements about abuse and, consequently, also to age. When details are sparse, more interpretation by the receiver is required and issues relating to credibility also arise. The case vignettes from the day care center are illustrative. There is no general agreement about the minimum components of a disclosure. Generally speaking, it would be reasonable to require some information about the identity of the perpetrator (who may, however, also be anonymous) and some descriptive information about the sexual act. Information about when, where, how often, and for how long, as well as information about emotional experiences may not be necessary for designation of a verbal statement as a disclosure although, of course, such details may be crucial in other contexts, most notably the legal arena.

One further consideration regarding structure is whether the verbal communication needs to be oral or if a written statement may also be designated as a disclosure. It is probably more common for verbal descriptions to be considered as disclosures, but there are no obvious arguments for excluding written disclosures, even if the discloser does not intentionally tell. It would be natural to describe a written statement by a child who does not speak as a disclosure, just as it may also be justified to designate a discovered diary as an accidental written disclosure.

Young children may appear to disclose abuse through behavioral changes. They may not be consciously aware of what they are enacting, and even if they experience inner images from an abuse event, they may not be fully aware of the context and the course of events (Terr, 1988). It seems reasonable to limit the designation of a disclosure to verbal communications, however, and to label behavioral manifestations of this type differently. Nevertheless, to the extent that telling necessitates a degree of interpretation by the recipients of the communication, behavioral changes may offer a psychological background for such interpretations.

Credibility

Concerns about credibility are built into the concept of disclosure. The very decision to use the concept of disclosure actually implies that the narratives are related to self-experienced events of the kind described. However, in scientific discussions terms like disclosure are often used as a more neutral term, without any presuppositions about credibility. An implicit definition in such cases might be described as communications about events that the receiver understands as self-experienced child sexual abuse. At the very least, the receiver does not register any obvious signs indicating false statements. The receiver may be doubtful about the credibility but still designate the narratives as a disclosure, even if the concept "false disclosure" may ultimately prove to be more appropriate in such a situation.

In another wrinkle, disclosers may be aware of a lack of accuracy and not regard the statements as a disclosure themselves, even though receivers consider it a disclosure. It is also possible that a discloser may be falsely convinced that an event has occurred although it has not. The case vignette of the adult woman, described earlier, provides an example. Her psychotherapist had persuaded her that she had been abused. From the perspective of the discloser, it may be justified to define the concept of disclosure as the revelation of an inner image, perceived as real. A further complication is that whereas some details of a statement about abuse may be self-experienced, thus constituting a disclosure, others may be the result of memory errors or contamination by others. One example of this is when a victim first—and accurately—recounts abuse by her father and then—inaccurately—describes abuse by other people also.

Case Vignette. A mother strongly suspected that her 6-year-old child had been abused by the girl's stepfather. The girl underwent a child psychiatric evaluation but made no statements about abuse. It was noted that the girl was very observant of her mother's state of mind. The mother had been hospitalized once due to a paranoid psychosis. She now felt that she was treated differently than other parents by the child psychiatric investigators. When the girl did not tell, and no support for the allegations emerged, the mother was upset. She started to have interviews with her daughter every day, putting much emphasis on the need to talk about abuse. After a few weeks, the girl finally made statements about abuse of the same type that her mother had expected. The statements were also given in the presence of a formal investigator.

Since doubts about credibility commonly arise when a person recounts sexual abuse, the easiest solution may be to exclude credibility from the definition of disclosure.

CONCLUSIONS

Disclosure is a multifaceted concept with both intra- and interpersonal dimensions. Several people and groups can influence the disclosure process. To facilitate clinical communication and the interpretation of scientific results, it is necessary to clarify the different meanings of the term "disclosure" in different contexts. The context of disclosure is a key consideration and it is, for example, necessary to specify whether the disclosure occurred in a formal or nonformal setting. Relatedly, the interactive aspects of disclosure should be specified because they affect the child's credibility. Timing issues must also be considered, and it is important to specify whether the word describes a single event or a process. Using an analytic approach like that presented here, disclosure emerges as a central concept in the development of theory about child sexual abuse.

REFERENCES

Jones, D. P. H. (2000). Editorial: Disclosure of child sexual abuse. *Child Abuse & Neglect,* *24,* 269–71.

Lindblad, F. (1989). Child sexual abuse. Evaluation of allegations—a hermeneutical approach. *Acta Paediatrica,* Suppl. 358.

———. (1995). Evaluation of child sexual abuse—what should be evaluated? *Scandinavian Journal of Social Welfare, 4,* 55–58.

Lindblad, F., & Kaldal, A. (2000). Sexual abuse at a Swedish day-care centre—allegations, confessions and evaluations. *Acta Paediatrica,* 89, 1001–9.

Terr, L. (1988). What happens to early memories of trauma? A study of twenty children under age five at the time of documented traumatic events. *Journal of the American Academy of Child and Adolescent Psychiatry, 27,* 96–104.

Author Index

Subject Index